International African Library 25
General Editors: J. D. Y. Peel, Colin Murray and Suzette Heald

ASANTE IDENTITIES

D1615177

The *International African Library* is a major monograph series from the International African Institute and complements its quarterly periodical *Africa*, the premier journal in the field of African studies. Theoretically informed ethnographies, studies of social relations 'on the ground' which are sensitive to local cultural forms, have long been central to the Institute's publications programme. The *IAL* maintains this strength but extends it into new areas of contemporary concern, both practical and intellectual. It includes works focused on problems of development, especially on the linkages between the local and national levels of society; studies along the interface between the social and environmental sciences; and historical studies, especially those of a social, cultural or interdisciplinary character.

International African Library

General Editors

J. D. Y. Peel, Colin Murray *and* Suzette Heald

ASANTE IDENTITIES

HISTORY AND MODERNITY
IN AN AFRICAN VILLAGE
1850–1950

T. C. McCASKIE

EDINBURGH UNIVERSITY PRESS
for the International African Institute, London

INDIANA UNIVERSITY PRESS
Bloomington and Indianapolis

This book is for
Ivor Wilks

ɔprɛm nfwere nnam

© T. C. McCaskie, 2000

Transferred to digital print 2009

Edinburgh University Press Ltd
22 George Square, Edinburgh

Typeset in Plantin
by Koinonia, Bury, and
Printed and bound in Great Britain by
CPI Antony Rowe, Chippenham and Eastbourne

A CIP record for this book is available
from the British Library

ISBN 0 7486 1510 5

For other publications of the International
African Institute, London, please visit their
web site at www.oneworld.org/iai

Published in the United States and Canada
by Indiana University Press,
601 North Morton Street, Bloomington,
Indiana 47404

A catalog record for this book is available from
the Library of Congress

ISBN 0-253-34030-6 (Indiana cloth)
    0-253-21496-3 (Indiana paper)

CONTENTS

LIST OF MAPS AND FIGURES

PREFACE

Thirty years ago I was researching a Ph.D. on Asante in Cambridge. I shuttled daily between the reading and tea rooms of the University Library. I was in danger of becoming what the French call *un rat de bibliothèque*. I needed a break. I was given one by Isaiah Berlin. He asked me to look at French accounts of the 1812 invasion of Russia to see if they mentioned his – and my then father-in-law Tosco Fyvel's – matrilineal antecedents. These were the family of the celebrated Rabbi and *zaddik* ('saint') Schneur Zalman Schneerson who founded the Lubavicher sect of the Hassidim in the Smolensk district of imperial Russia in the 1780s. I became fascinated as I trawled through diaries and letters. I also became frustrated. When I called a halt, I had a mass of information but an even greater mass of loose ends.

I reported my findings with an apologetic emphasis on their inconclusiveness. This diffidence was misplaced. Berlin was enthralled by the textural details and above all by the circumstantial possibilities of what I had put together. Napoleon himself might have encountered the Schneersons. What did they make of one another? Cued by this speculation Berlin launched into an extemporisation on the nature of history (and all the memoirs are right; he really was a brilliant talker). What I drew from his torrent of words was affirmation of ideas I had about the sort of history I might some day try to write. He ranged over many things but talked mainly about the ways in which the historian should explore the vividness (*Anschaulichkeit*) of human lives as these were revealed in but also concealed by the incomplete record of the past. The goal was always and endlessly to embrace complicating possibility in people's lives while remaining duly sceptical about the sorts of understandings offered up by the literal content of the sources. Historical texts should be read between the lines and against the grain for the meanings secreted in their silences and absences. The historian did not possess licence but – Berlin concluded with his characteristically rapid intensity – he ought to ask himself and his source materials the novelist's questions about human motive and behaviour.

Thirty years on I have written what follows with Berlin's remarks in mind. This is a book about the lives of West African men and women in the Asante forest village of Adeɛbeba between the mid-nineteenth and mid-twentieth centuries. As such, it builds upon my own work and that of others in Asante

historiography. But it also departs from that work in its concentration upon
the daily lives of ordinary people, recalled and retold as far as possible in
their own words. Throughout the book the worlds of Asante and beyond are
seen from the perspective of Adeɛbeba villagers. The approach is microhistorical. Hence the book is detailed, but not I hope narrow or in any other
way circumscribed by that fact. What I have tried to do is to write something
that pays the closest attention to motive and behaviour in individual Asante
lives, but that simultaneously looks outward to broader issues of historical
and cultural analysis. My aim has been to marry together some of the novelist's questions (in Berlin's sense) with the 'thick description' of ethnographic
reporting and the dense empiricism of the historical record in order to
portray Asante lives in and of themselves but also in relation to the local
reception and understanding of those global phenomena conventionally
attached to the concept of modernity. This, then, is a study in continuity and
change and of the relationship between the precolonial era and its colonial
successor in the lives and times of Asante villagers. My watchword has been
multum in parvo and my hope is for more such localised historical studies of
African societies.

There are providential conditions that played an indispensable role in the
writing of this book. First, the Ashanti Social Survey (1945–6) furnished an
outstandingly detailed testimonial record to ponder over, work with and
enlarge upon. Second, already existing Asante historiography – arguably the
most developed body of work concerning any sub-Saharan African society –
provided the contextual background that allowed me to foreground a single
village and its people as a field of study. In both cases I have stood with
gratitude upon the shoulders of others. Without Meyer Fortes (1906–83),
Robert Steel (1915–97) and the ASS's marvellous team of Asante researchers literally none of what I have tried to write here would have been possible.
Equally, without the diligent labours of that cohort of scholars who have
done so much to illuminate Asantesɛm (Asante matters) I would not have
had the guidelines within which to frame this book. Above and beyond this
I owe an unrepayable debt to the Asante people. In over three decades of
working with and among them I have been the beneficiary of their legendary
talent for hospitality and the pupil of their formidable sense of their own
history. In looking back I know I have been fortunate indeed to meet and
learn from them.

I have specific obligations. Meyer Fortes and Robert Steel I recall with
much more than scholarly gratitude. In a like manner I remember the late
Asantehene Otumfuo Opoku Ware II (1970–99), who aided my endeavours
with what I can only think of as kingly grace. Kwame Arhin (Nana Arhin
Brempong) has taught me a great deal over endless cups of tea in Ghana and
the UK, and I feel privileged to count him as a friend. Emmanuel Akyeampong

and Richard Rathbone are also valued friends and demonstrated this by taking the trouble to comment in writing and at length on successive versions of this book. Karin Barber is a colleague as well as a friend, and her input nourished this book and its author alike. Gareth Austin sustained me more than he will ever know in the course of marathon telephone conversations. At the last here I want to place on record my continuing gratitude to John Peel, a scholar and a friend alike of the rarest quality.

I would also like to thank those who came to my aid on particular occasions with information, insight, support or opportunities to take stock by inviting me to speak or write. Accordingly I am grateful to Jean Allman, Thomas Aning, Karel Arnaut, Sara Berry, David William Cohen, Wilhelmina Donkoh, the late Jane Drew, Paul Jenkins, Ray Kea, Nancy Lawler Wilks, John Lonsdale, Ato Quayson, Terence Ranger, Jeff Rice, Greg Spencer, Emmanuel Terray, Pierluigi Valsecchi, Fabio Viti, Larry Yarak and Werner Zips. I thank them all, but of course exonerate them from responsibility for whatever uses I have made of their help. I have two final debts. One is to Lynne and Anna. The other is expressed in the dedication to this book.

1

INTRODUCTION

TEXTS: SURVEYING ASANTE

On 20 January 1947 in London the Royal Geographical Society played host to the Royal Anthropological Institute. The purpose of this joint meeting was to present and discuss the findings of the Ashanti Social Survey (ASS) carried out in 1945–6. The three principal ASS researchers all read papers. The anthropologist M. Fortes, leader of the project, spoke first about the 'origin and organisation' of the ASS and then later about its 'anthropological aspect'. The geographer R. Steel discussed the project's 'geographical aspect'. Finally the economist and statistician P. Ady talked about the 'economic aspect' of the team's research. The presentations were fairly long and there was little discussion afterwards. The largest contribution from the floor came from the anthropologist R. Firth, who had paid a site visit to the ASS in the field at the end of 1945. He praised the ASS's interdisciplinary approach to the problems of colonial 'development and welfare'. The Chairman then concluded the meeting with a vote of thanks and said that all attending looked 'forward to the publication of the results' of the ASS in full in due course. In the interim the Royal Geographical Society published the verbatim proceedings of this joint meeting under the title 'Ashanti Survey, 1945–6: An Experiment in Social Research' in late 1947.[1]

Fortes told his listeners that the reasoning behind the ASS was his desire 'to study a people who have been caught up in the full tide of social and cultural change due to western influence'. The Asante were ideal, for their complex culture retained a robust historical 'vitality' in its encounter with change. The terms of this encounter were 'a mystery that was irresistible to an anthropologist', and especially so since the Asante had kept their 'way of life' while exhibiting 'avidity' in the pursuit of 'everything European civilization had to offer'. From the outset Fortes envisaged a wide-ranging project that would gather survey data useful 'from a comparative point of view'. But he recognised too that the issues he intended to work on were 'fluid', 'complex' and 'heterogeneous'. They would not yield to understanding 'in terms of one social science only'. Accordingly, he recruited a geographer and an economist to his team. In the geographer Steel, seconded from war work on the Admiralty Handbooks, he had someone with prior field experience of surveying and mapping land use systems in the forests of Sierra Leone. In the economist Ady, already seconded from Oxford University to a National Income Study for the Gold Coast government, he had a collaborator with expertise in designing surveys and analysing their statistical results.

The particular skills of his colleagues dovetailed with Fortes' plan 'to get a broad, general picture of the social and political structure of Ashanti today'. Hence, 'much use was made of questionnaires and other prepared enquiry forms' by the ASS during its eighteen months of fieldwork. Fortes justified this methodology as 'the quickest and most reliable means of gathering the quantitative data we needed' in 'the circumstances that now exist in Ashanti'. But he acknowledged that survey questionnaires were 'rightly regarded with suspicion by anthropologists', and went on to reassure his audience that a battery of other fieldwork methods was also used by the ASS. It 'sifted' a 'large quantity of official papers, court record books, and other documentary material'. More to the point, it made full use of all of the 'customary procedures' of British structural-functionalist ethnographic inquiry. The ASS kept fieldwork notebooks and diaries; observed, participated in and recorded 'group activities'; interviewed 'selected informants', repeatedly and at length; and set out to accumulate detailed 'case histories' of individual lives.

All of these approaches were employed by the ASS. The result was a mass of raw quantitative and qualitative data generated in research conditions that combined ready access with ample funding. If the ASS was planned by Fortes, then it was made possible by colonial government. In broad terms, British policy makers saw the ASS as a means to an end. Its research would supply information of the kind needed to give substance to the proposals for ameliorating and improving the lot of West African subjects as set out in the Colonial Development and Welfare Act of 1940. British policy is not of concern here, except inasmuch as to note that the ASS would not have come into being without the shifts in colonial thinking that took place during the Second World War.[2]

Thus, Fortes' modest scheme for an Institute of West African Culture in the Gold Coast secured no government support in the later 1930s. But his much expanded plan of 1943 for a West African Institute of Arts, Industries and Social Sciences attracted official interest and backing in the changed climate of the war years. As Head of the Sociological Department of this Institute, Fortes was able to set up, fund and implement the ASS with the blessings of the Colonial Office, its Colonial Research Council, and the government of the Gold Coast and Asante. After the event, he was generous in his praise for the 'support' and 'backing' given him and his team by these bodies and their personnel. Now, much ink has been spilled on the question of whether or not Fortes and his fellow anthropologists were witting servants of British imperialism. This debate has its interest. But it has produced more heat than light, and on the whole it has been conducted in terms that fail to address the historically obvious. Granted that Asante was a British Crown Colony, the plain and simple fact is that without government approval the ASS would not have taken place. That said, it should be added that both a close reading of the records concerning the ASS and lengthy discussion with Fortes and Steel show that there were in fact areas of mutual suspicion between the researchers and their official sponsors. But both parties had an overriding interest in negotiating their differences in order to get the job done. In practical terms the ASS was generally answerable to its patrons, but it enjoyed considerable latitude and freedom of action in the field.[3]

Be all that as it may, how and where did the ASS work? From discussion with R. S. Rattray and intensive reading in that pioneer's ethnographies of the 1920s, Fortes formed the opinion – congenial to his own training and experience – that 'the village is the key unit of social life and political structure' in Asante. But for the purposes of survey research, as Ady pointed out, villages had to be 'large enough' to permit statistically meaningful quantitative research as well as its qualitative counterpart. The Chief Commissioner of Asante, E. G. Hawkesworth, helped Fortes to decide on the neighbouring settlements of Asokore and Effiduase, some twenty miles north-east of Kumase, as sites for preliminary survey research. 'The two places are easy to reach from Kumasi', the CCA minuted, and 'are peaceful and long established. Asokori contains eight hundred people while Effiduasi is about twice that size.'[4] The ASS went to work. Survey lessons learned in these two settlements were later applied elsewhere, and most intensively to Agogo twenty miles further to the east. But by the time that the ASS was launched fully into its quantitative survey work at Agogo, a plurality of other research initiatives was in train. This was a conscious decision. Beyond its survey work on living conditions the ASS had 'no such thing as a master plan'. However, Fortes did want to maximise opportunistic information gathering for comparative purposes by as many different methods and in as many different places as possible. To this end he imposed minimal 'direction' and instead encouraged 'complementary' work wherever and whenever this seemed feasible. The result was that 'members of the team worked intensively in more than a dozen places in different parts of Ashanti', while 'enquiries were made in many other villages by ourselves and our field staff'.[5]

The key to all of this busy diversity of effort by the ASS was its Asante field staff, variously seconded from schools (older pupils as well as teachers) and government service, or recruited individually on an *ad hoc* basis through personal contact with the British researchers. Fortes estimated that during 'one period we had over forty African field staff at work'. But a register from January 1946 gave a figure of fifty-three employees, and Steel remembered the grand total as being 'close to sixty-five'.[6] Three reasons accounted for these discrepancies. First, numbers fluctuated. People were taken on in the short term to administer questionnaires, after which some were set to additional tasks while others left the project's employ. Second, ample funds exempted a grateful Fortes from the onerous business of maintaining precise employment records. Responsibility for paying the majority of field staff devolved upon the ASS itself, but an unquantifiably high percentage of employees (those working on Ady's surveys or Steel's maps) were remunerated from monies already allocated to the National Income Study or from other government budgets. Third, like research itself, the hiring of staff was decentralised. Once investigations were up and running in various parts of Asante, Fortes, Steel and Ady all took on local staff on their own recognisance and paid them from budget without recording either names or numbers. The number of ASS field staff, then, varied greatly over the duration of the project. The figure fluctuated in complex ways, and no one had any pressing incentive to keep a meticulous record of its size or composition. But whatever the actual number involved, it represented a lot of researchers.

Many of the Asante field staff are known to us by name for the simple reason that their autographed notebooks, reports and interviews composed a large part of the ASS data base. Much anonymous work is attributable too because of handwriting, stylistic flourishes and presentational tics recognisable from signed documents. Some among the Asante field staff – like T. E. Kyei (in Agogo), J. C. Frimpong, I. A. Amankwah, S. Adjaye and Emily Aboagye (in south Kumase and Amansie), or the Dentu brothers (in Sekyere and Ahafo) – were remarkable researchers in their own right. They worked for the project, but also shaped it in creative and important ways (as both Fortes and Steel gratefully acknowledged).[7] Others deserve to be remembered for first-rate contributions on particular topics. Thus for example, the 25-year-old trainee teacher Emily Selanor and her classmates from Wesley College carried out intensive research in Kumase central market; the government Land Registry clerk Kwasi (Ezekiel) Antwi-Barimah from Sɔkɔban recorded detailed life histories in the villages just south of Kumase; the teacher and catechist Kwame (Amos) Mensah worked for Steel but proved so acute that he was 'set at liberty' to observe and record on his own account in Amansie and Sekyere; and yet others too numerous to list collected invaluable testimonies about farming methods, local politics, family dynamics, urban living, history, customs, folklore, education, belief, money, morals, aspirations, and all the rest of the preoccupations that animated people in colonial Asante.[8]

The Asante field staff of the ASS worked alongside the British investigators in Asokore, Effiduase, Agogo, Hwidiem, Kasei, Nkawie Kumaa, Kotei and Patasi. But they also worked independently in Kumase, Obogu, Bonwire, Konongo, Bompata, Ofinso, Obuase and the Mponoa and Lake Bosomtwe villages. Importantly for this present study, numbers of the Asante field staff came from the peri-urban villages to the immediate south of Kumase. These carried out a deal of research among kin, neighbours and contacts in the crowded settlement belt along or adjacent to the Kumase–Bekwai road. This was survey and census work on a small scale. But it was accompanied by intensive interviewing that was wide ranging and commonly repeated several times with the same respondents. It is known from traces in the texts produced from such encounters – the forms of address, the naming of mutual acquaintances, the sharing of familiar knowledge of locale, the joint presumptions about things understood by one another – that the interlocutors were often at ease in their talking. The result was conversation rather than interrogation, a confiding disclosure rather than a submitting of evidence. This was close fieldwork carried out in colloquial exchanges. The flow of talk occurred in Twi, but the ASS required that it be set down on paper in English for use as data. Hence, interviewers often rendered their material into English on the spot to save themselves the effort of writing it up twice. But commonly too they recorded hybrid Twi and English texts and sometimes, for whatever reason, they wrote in untranslated Twi. The result of all their efforts was an immensely rich archive of everyday life, difficult to use because of its disordered complexity but rewarding in its close-grained revelations of detail and nuance. Fortes, Steel and Ady were gratified by the production of all this qualitative information, but they regarded it as being of secondary importance by comparison with the quantitative work carried out at Agogo and other chosen sites. Steel recollected that 'one-to-one interviewing was mostly in the hands of Africans'. He acknowledged that it amassed 'much helpful information' but – telling phrase – 'in support of the main effort of census and survey taking'.[9]

In 1946 the work of the ASS was wound up and its data was crated and shipped to the School of Geography at Oxford University, the British base of the West African Institute. Fortes and Steel took up posts at Oxford, the first as Reader in Social Anthropology (until 1950, when he moved to Cambridge), the second as Lecturer (then Senior Lecturer) in Colonial Geography (until 1957, when he moved to Liverpool). Ady too returned to Oxford's Institute of Statistics, where she had worked before the war. Until 1950 a stream of letters and documents arrived from officials and former field staff in Asante and were added to the ASS holdings. But the real task now was data analysis. This was a formidable undertaking. Looking back

over forty years, Steel recalled that ASS materials were 'stacked up in boxes
in Mansfield Road [the School of Geography], in my [Jesus] college, and in
M.F.'s rooms and my own'. The problem was that the ASS's success in
accumulating information created a paper juggernaut that overwhelmed all
attempts to order and classify it in the field. Then at the end of the project
broad categories by place or subject were improvised so that the material
might be divided up for shipment. This was unsatisfactory. It meant
imposing arbitrary filing decisions on a mass of disparate and still largely
undigested or even unread material. The result was that when the crates
were opened up in Oxford, 'we did not really know the extent or content of
what we had'. Another sorting out now took place. Quantitative data were
extracted for immediate review and analysis. Qualitative data were returned
to boxes and stored.[10]

A year after the joint presentation of 1947, Fortes published the first
results of his team's analyses of the quantitative data amassed by the ASS.
As its title implied, 'The Ashanti Social Survey: A Preliminary Report' was
an interim accounting of the broad trends in Asante life as revealed by ASS
censuses, surveys and statistics. This approach was later refined and
elaborated by Fortes in a very detailed study of demographic patterns in
Agogo commissioned by UNESCO and published by that organisation in
1954.[11] Thereafter, however, little was done that publicised the constituent
detail of the quantitative data, while the empirical wealth contained in the
qualitative material continued to languish in boxes. No blame attaches to
this neglect. Both Fortes and Steel were social scientists. Their intellectual
project was functional-structural in method and comparative by inclination.
Their interests lay in identifying principles and trends and in the generali-
sations that might be derived from them. Thus, after the initial flurries of
situating and describing the ASS data in a specifically Asante context, both
tended to deploy the material to illustrate and footnote generic problems.
Deep meditation on the ASS findings informed Fortes' extensive later
writings on kinship and descent, affect and amity, groups and individuals,
and all the rest of his many anthropological concerns. Steel made less use of
the ASS data, but when he did so it was in exemplification of arguments
about African forestry, land use, demography and urbanisation. After about
1950 the ASS material clearly fed into and shaped the work of Fortes and
Steel, but at a distancing remove from its actual empirical Asante content.
Abstracted and used to explore a social scientific anthropology and
geography, it remained unanalysed on its own terms even as the passing
years conferred upon it the status of a unique historical archive of Asante
life.[12]

It is well and good to talk of the separately grounded and differently
evolving aims of the anthropologist, geographer and historian. But research
careers are as much (or even more) about messy practicalities as they are

about detached intellection. When Fortes removed from Oxford to Cambridge in 1950, the practical matter of disposing of the ASS data was renewed. By this time both Fortes and Steel were involved in other concerns, while Ady's links with the project were attenuated. What to do with all the boxes in Mansfield Road and elsewhere? An agreement was made to divide them up. Fortes and Steel retained their own personal diaries and notebooks. Fortes then made a claim on the quantitative material from Agogo, Asokore and Effiduase on which he was still working. But after these dispositions were made the mass of material remaining, so Steel recalled, 'was split up on a pretty *ad hoc* basis. Most of the boxes, I'm afraid to say, we allocated to the one or the other of us without reopening. It was all done quickly and in good humour. Meyer [Fortes] took about half and this went off to Cambridge. The rest remained with me in Oxford.'[13] As time elapsed after 1950, Fortes used the Cambridge data in the manner (but with the limitations) already described. Steel by contrast 'rarely looked into' the Oxford boxes after he went to Liverpool in 1957. When Fortes retired from the William Wyse professorship at Cambridge in 1973 he still retained his ASS data privately at his Grantchester house. When Steel became Principal of the then University College of Swansea in 1974 (and later Vice-Chancellor of the University of Wales) he too still retained his ASS material privately, albeit in sealed boxes piled up against the rear wall of the garage at his Langland residence.[14]

CONTEXTS: ENVISAGING KUMASE

It is early afternoon, August, 1997, and hot. I am standing outside a supermarket (air-conditioned, imported goods at expatriate prices) by the side of the recently resurfaced Kumase–Bekwai road. The supermarket is new, or at least it wasn't here in 1995. The glut of stalled traffic is new as well, vehicles crawling south to Senfi junction and Bekwai, vehicles stuttering north into the congested heart of Kumase. In both directions it is bumper to bumper, a shimmer of gasoline fumes rising over the throb of idling engines. Heat, noise, smell, drive me away from the road. I walk south by the ribbon of open storm drain along the roadside. In ten minutes I reach a large building, squat, foursquare, concrete slabbed. Its blank north wall supports a boxy green neon cross winking on and off. Its facade is pierced by tiny balconies girded by ochre railings streaked with rust. Above is a sign that looks down on the traffic. It reads 'Adiebeba Hospital'. I walk past it and turn left off the main road.

I wander among the houses off the highway. Here there are no tarred roads. Phone and power lines, water and sewage pipes, street lights and junction boxes are all sketched not realised presences. The vivid rawness of new metal and plastic draws the eye, but only to underline its rarity. The whole is implicit, incomplete, a sense reinforced by the amount of construction

going on. This area is a building site. It is busy even now in the heat of the
day, for this is the season when people return from abroad to inspect
progress on the houses they are putting up with remitted cash. Cars are
parked all about (Japanese, German, an elderly Dodge Charger – a rusted
behemoth with raised suspension and fat squashy tyres). There is a buzz of
talk and argument is audible above the din made by gangs of labourers.
Clients and contractors are locking horns over the universal vexations of
building work, all of which boil down to spiralling costs and receding
completion dates.

I walk on through ziggurats of cement bags, concrete blocks and roof
tiles, past a maternity clinic ('Mother and Baby Heaven'), a blindingly white
row of occupied houses (Italianate arches, wide patios, lawns, sprinklers,
shade trees, all glimpsed behind smugly high walls with sheet-iron gates
concealing barking guard dogs), a battleship-grey, three-storey apartment
block crowned with a huge satellite TV dish (Zenith in jaggedly bold red
cursive, lightning flash logo inside the bowl, other information age
numerological heraldry visible but coated with laterite dust and too high to
read anyway), a spattering of stalls and sheds (few sellers and even fewer
buyers around at this stifling time of day) offering cooked snacks and drinks,
shirts and trousers ('High Class Men's Tailoring'), electrical goods and
services ('Expert Repair On The Spot, All Make [sic] Refrigerators, Photo-
copying'), hair styling and care ('Miss Louisa, Afro and French Roll, Cut
and Curl, Braiding, Weaving'), and arrive at last at the end of a short rutted
street. Here the buildings are old, stained, dilapidated, narrow fronted,
close packed. Some are compound houses with mud-brick walls, some are
bungalows with drooping eaves and corrugated-iron roofs. One has a
portico (a brace of peeling stuccoed columns, British imperial hybridised
Doric–Ionic, but not Corinthian, the detail too convoluted to achieve),
another has a weathered stone lion guarding its entrance. No one is about.
It is now unbearably hot (stagnant air metallic to mouth and nostrils, a
storm is coming), and those few people who are not away about their
business have sought the shade. It is hushed to the stillness of a tableau, the
distant noise of traffic from the main road muted to a bass hum just below
the level of consciousness.

I walk up the street. Near its end the old buildings are demolished and the
ground where they stood is levelled and scored with trenches. Pegs strung
with yellow twine trace the floor plans of new dwellings that will rise here. I
am greeted by and pause to talk with a man in a polo shirt, slacks and
sandals who is leaning against the bonnet of a tan Peugeot hatchback
(Belgian plates) with an unwieldy blue and white architectural drawing in
his hands. He is wiry, bearded, jovial, originally from Edweso, now working
as a surveyor in Willesden (London). He indicates the plot where his house
will stand. He folds the drawing (which he made himself) and uses it to give

me some idea of how things will look. I wish him luck and we shake hands. I walk on to where the street ends at a 'T' junction. Here to right and left are more construction sites. Part finished dwellings rear out of the scrubby grass, cloaked in wood scaffolding and blue polythene sheets. People are working here too and the air tastes of gritty dust. I turn left, walk ahead and then cut to the left again to circle back.

Twenty minutes later I am once more at the supermarket by the main road. Afrane and the Mitsubishi 4x4 are waiting. I clamber into the air conditioning and with the horn braying we join the northbound traffic into Kumase. At the ring road we turn left, go north to Kwadaso junction, and then west out along the Sunyani road past Asuyeboa to where I am staying at Tanoso. The journey is less than ten miles but takes ninety minutes (the rush hour is starting). In the big yellow house at Tanoso I retreat to the upstairs balcony. I drink tea and write up my diary for the day. My host joins me and we talk about mutual acquaintances until the conversation turns to my afternoon in south Kumase. Quickly this becomes generalised to a topic we discuss often. This is the inexorable growth of Kumase and the changes that have resulted since I first came here in the 1960s. The city has expanded steadily and since the 1980s explosively. All around its edges it has reached out, annexed and remade satellite villages that lay beyond its grasp less than thirty years ago. Until very recently Tanoso itself, where we are talking, was a rural settlement separated from Kumase by open bush. But today it is engulfed by the onward march of the city's ribbon development along the Sunyani road.

The same is true of south Kumase where I spent this afternoon walking around an urbanised landscape of choking traffic and relentless building. But until fifteen or even ten years ago this area was peri-urban countryside. Sawmills, timber yards, railway sidings, artisanal workshops, cocoa sheds, barns and gardens were dotted about in a setting of long grass, scrub timber and marshy streams. Taxis used to bring me out here from Kumase to talk with people who worked farms around their villages. This is gone now. The grass, trees, streams and farms are under concrete and the villages survive only in the names of city wards, sub-divisions or housing estates. Of course the process of change is incomplete. Despite submergence and erasure the past does persist, but in ever diminishing traces that need the nudging work of memory to retrieve them. Today I walked up an anomalous street – a few elderly houses marooned in and soon to be overwhelmed by an encroaching sea of new buildings. I came here many times in the past, and perhaps that is why it is an effort to reconcile the sight before me to an understanding that this doomed enclave is all that remains of the village of Adeɛbeba.[15]

The precolonial Asante capital of Kumase was controlled, regulated and given over to government business and ritual performance. Its resident

population – peaking at about twenty-five thousand in the nineteenth
century – was dominated by a self-conscious elite of office holders, palace
officials, functionaries and their servants that revolved around the royal
personage of the *Asantehene*. To be 'a Kumase person' (*kumaseni*) was to
identify oneself and to be identified by others with the power and prestige of
the state, however humble or tenuous the affiliation. The residents of
Kumase distinguished themselves from villagers (*nkuraasefoɔ*), and imposed
upon and condescended to them. However, the capital depended on the
countryside and on the labour of its population. A ring of satellite villages
encircled Kumase and fed and otherwise serviced its inhabitants. These
settlements were peopled by free and slave subjects (*nkoa*) of the *Asantehene*
and his Kumase office holders. They worked the land to support their
political masters and themselves. Apart from their labour value, these subjects were mobilised as and when needed to travel into Kumase to compose
the entourages of office holders on great public occasions. On the festival
days of the Asante ritual calendar (*adaduanan*), the flood of participants
coming into the capital from surrounding villages contributed mightily to
the temporary quadrupling of the population.[16]

In the later nineteenth century Kumase declined in power and
population because of the cumulative effects of civil wars and British
interventions that culminated in the deportation (1896) of the *Asantehene*
Agyeman Prempe, his close kin and key members of his government. When
the Asante capital was formally annexed to the British Crown (1901), it was
only a shadow of its former self. Ruined buildings and overgrown streets
housed a rump population of less than four thousand, many of them once
prohibited Akan or other immigrant foreigners (*ahɔhoɔ*). But if Kumase
itself was a diminished place overtaken and disoriented by sudden political
events, then the topographical landscape in which it was sited remained
much the same as it had been throughout the nineteenth century. A Basel
Mission map of Asante composed in 1907 (pioneering cartography in the
sheer wealth of detail provided by people who had to walk everywhere and
did so to carry the Christian message) shows Kumase enmeshed in its
precolonial web of villages. In its reduced state the Asante capital (and now
infant colonial town) still appears as a hub. Its nineteenth-century 'suburbs'
of Bantama, Asafo and Dadeɛsoaba are marked, and through and beyond
these a tangle of roads and paths radiate outward from Kumase into the
girdle of settlements around it.[17]

On the 1907 map the villages of Patasi, Kwadaso, Apire, Fankyenebra,
Santaase, Atasomaaso, Atasomaaso Kumaa, Adeɛmmra, Toase, Adeɛbeba,
Asokwa and Kaase are shown distributed around a shallow arc running
from west to east to the immediate south of Kumase. Each is clearly
separate from the capital, but none lies more than five miles from it. In the
nineteenth century all these villages contained subjects of the Kumase office

holders and servants of the *Asantehene* (and the *Asantehemaa*). The impress of government meant that historic patterns of authority and rights in land here very close to Kumase were immensely convoluted, even by Asante standards. Thus – but in brief, and by no means comprehensively – the land at Patasi belonged to the *Anyinase* stool, but it supported subjects of the Kumase *Gyaasehene* and *Atipinhene* together with royal heralds, fanbearers and gold weighers; other treasury officials lived at Kwadaso alongside royal mausoleum attendants and maidservants of the Asante queen mother; subjects of the Kumase *Mamesenehene* and *Manwerehene* shared the land at Apire; *Gyaase* and other Kumase subjects resided at Fankyenebra on land belonging to the *Baworohene*; royal gun bearers from the Ankobia farmed at Santaase; at Atasomaaso and Atasomaaso Kumaa *Atasomaaso* stool subjects lived with royal traders and sandal bearers; Kumase *Ankobia, Atipin, Ananta* and *Kronko* incomers shared Adeɛmmra with subjects who served the historic military office of *Asafohene/Akwamuhene*; more royal gun bearers and servants of the *Gyaasehene* lived at Toase; *Manwere* stool subjects resided at Adeɛbeba; royal hornblowers and traders under the Kumase *Asokwahene* shared Asokwa with servants charged with the upkeep of the palace in Kumase; and the people of Kaase, a pre-Asante foundation, served the *Asantehene* via the *Kaasehene* in the *Ananta* section of the Kumase *Gyaase*, and shared their land with craftsmen who made pottery and metal utensils for the royal household. These and many other villages existed because of and in relation to the centripetal force exercised by eighteenth- and nineteenth-century Kumase. As will be seen in due course, the roles, functions and much else in the lives of the people of these villages changed with the coming of the colonial order. But whatever else transpired, these settlements remained oriented to twentieth-century Kumase for reasons of geography, history and the continuing centrality of the city within the colonial dispensation. 'Kumasi was the King's town in the past', observed Kwadwo Toase of Adeɛbeba in 1945, 'and it is still today the heart and soul of Ashanti. It is big now as in former days of glory. People here [in Adeɛbeba] and in the places all around are thinking of Kumasi as a second home.'[18]

Colonial officials envisaged building a new Kumase to the west of the old town on both slopes of the SW–NE ridge that ran parallel to the Nsuben river valley. In 1910 a comprehensive planning document to this effect was drawn up, but uncontrolled growth rapidly outstripped it and all of its piecemeal successors. Outside of the British administrative cantonment and commercial area, colonial Kumase developed relentlessly but haphazardly. Given these complex conditions the British resigned themselves to monitoring and supervising growth as and when it happened, rather than authorising and implementing it in relation to a sequenced master plan. It was only when congestion levels finally threatened to choke Kumase in the

1940s that government reasserted itself to produce an overall development programme for the rationalisation and expansion of the Asante capital. With hindsight, it can be seen that the problems that reached critical mass during the Second World War originated in and evolved from the terms under which the colonial city was created.

In 1901 the British variously estimated the population of Kumase as 3–4,000. The decennial censuses of 1911, 1921 and 1931 returned figures of 18,853, 23,694 and 35,829. War ruled out the census of 1945, but an informed assessment made in that year gave a figure of 45,133.[19] As the British acknowledged, all of these arithmetical numbers were unreliable. But considered as a gross scale of magnitude, they described the ever steepening curve of demographic increase. Natural growth played a part in this but the main cause was immigration, Asante and otherwise. Be that as it may, the rate of housebuilding could not keep pace. British statistics tell some of this story. In 1921 there were 1,575 registered dwellings in Kumase; by 1945 this number had risen to 5,420. But while average density per house was 15.2 persons in 1921, it was up to 17.5 by 1945. Colonial officials knew that this was only part of the problem. Kumase had a large, shifting number of unregistered dwellings ranging from permanent buildings to temporary shacks.[20] Congestion on this scale was produced by two factors that interacted with population growth. One was the small size but magnetic attraction of the city centre. Residents and immigrants alike gravitated to the heart of Kumase, where most jobs and amenities were concentrated. The other was the obstructive difficulty of building in Kumase, a situation produced by the nature and conditions of urban landholding under the British.

Under the terms of the instrument of annexation in 1901, dispositionary rights over all Kumase lands were vested in the British Crown and its representatives and agents. Worried about provoking a hostile reaction in Kumase, and hence uncertain as to what policy to pursue, the British contented themselves with a token use of their prerogative. They claimed for the Crown no more than the land within one mile around the fort in Kumase (and subsequently all land for 100 yards on either side of public highways outside the town). All of the rest they left under customary jurisdiction and tenure. Not only that, but large blocks of the Crown land itself were leased back to Kumase office holders in 1905 for development as the residential kernel of the new colonial town. These were emollient concessions, intended to reconcile Kumase people to the loss of the *Asantehene* and the coming of British rule. But what they in fact did was to reinforce the hold of stools over Kumase land, and in the process mortgage the development of the colonial town to the will – good or otherwise – of office holders and their associates.

The history of housebuilding in colonial Kumase remains to be written, but there is abundant and dauntingly complex evidence concerning it. In some central areas – first Adum and Kagyatia, and then later Ashanti and Fanti New Towns, Mbrom and Manhyia – office holders themselves, together with rich residents and immigrants who contrived to sub-lease multiple plots from them, scrambled to put up modern, prestigious multi-storey houses. These pioneers inspired innumerable aspirants to pursue the same goal. Many Asante, it was noted in 1945, 'desire to build a house at Kumasi, pass their last days in the town and play the Ashanti gentleman', for the 'mere possession of a house at Kumasi increases the Ashanti man's rank and prestige'.[21] This tendency, in conjunction with the more modest housing demands of an ever growing urban population, meant that chiefs and their business partners were in a position to earn substantial income from building and renting in their own right or, as was more often the case, from sub-leasing plots to wealthy people who wanted to do the same thing. A moneyed individual from outside the town often built a house in Kumase 'before thinking of erecting one in his village, because at Kumasi higher rents are charged and this means a constant flow of money to the pocket of the landlord'.[22]

As central Kumase became congested, chiefs moved to exploit their leaseholdings of stool land all around the perimeter of the town. Typical and instructive in this regard was the urban development of Amakom village in the early 1930s. Amakom lay just east of the overcrowded Muslim Zongo extension, and in 1932 the CCA informed the *Amakomhene* that an unspeci-fied part of his leaseholding was needed by government to relieve the pressure. The *Amakomhene* Kwaku Ata agreed, but on condition that he be permitted to keep no less than seventy plots in the area earmarked for development. The CCA refused and reminded Kwaku Ata that he was a tenant at the discretion of the Crown. The *Amakomhene* responded by claiming that the seventy plots at issue were for the use of his stool subjects. The British knew what was going on. 'The large blocks of Stool Plots already leased to Kumasi Chiefs have already caused Government a great deal of trouble' because tenants 'sub-let them off' privately for unreported rents. The British confessed they had 'very little control' over such arrange-ments. Keeping track of them depended entirely upon the honesty of the contracting parties. But people needed houses and leaseholders wanted to maximise revenue. The result was that everyone involved had a vested interest in avoiding scrutiny and regulation, and so did 'very little to assist' authority. Simply, Kwaku Ata wanted to keep control of as much Amakom land as possible for sub-leasing and renting to housebuilders. He was aware that the British needed to resolve the matter, so his tactics – throughout a protracted and meandering correspondence – were to obfuscate, complicate and delay in the hope of gaining concessions. This worked, for the British allowed him his seventy plots with the feeble proviso that Amakom subjects should register occupancy so as to pay ground rent. Government rationalised its submission by pleading haste. But it knew that imposing its will would antagonise the chiefship structure. It knew too that its mandated local government administration was a blunt instrument. In matters of land, successive metropolitan authorities were given few teeth by the British for fear of alienating customary authority. In a sense this was a superfluous precaution since local government in colonial Kumase was influenced by chiefship because it was staffed and infiltrated by stool holders and their clients.[23]

In the precolonial era the *Asantehene*-in-council functioned in a local as well as a national capacity. He adjudicated cases from first instance to final appeal in all matters of jural custom (*aman bre*) affecting Kumase, including rights in land. Thus when the British overthrew the Asante government by exiling the *Asantehene* and his councillors, they also decapitated the local customary authority in Kumase. The British solution to this problem was to constitute a Kumase Council of Chiefs in 1905, with its appointed members presided over by the Chief Commissioner. The simple intention – borne out by the legitimising efforts made by British officials to identify and replicate the office-holding membership of the precolonial council of Kumase – was that the CCA and his nominated advisers were to assume the role of the missing *Asantehene*-in-council in governing Kumase. This arrangement – the Chief Commissioner-in-council – endured until 1926. In so doing, it gave decisive shape to the history of colonial Kumase. It was direct government by office holders who had unique advisory access to the CCA, and so were ideally placed to urge and defend their own interests and those of chiefship in general. Furthermore, and in the manner of a young or inexperienced *Asantehene*, the CCA depended on his councillors for informed advice on custom. The two parties relied upon one another to govern Kumase, and records show that the CCA rarely found for outsiders who litigated with his councillors.[24]

In 1924 a serious outbreak of plague in the Zongo finally persuaded the British that Kumase needed a local executive to deal with the practical problems of urbanism. A Kumase Public Health Board (KPHB) was created in 1925. Its remit included the planning of new residential layouts, but excluded rights of acquisition over the land needed to build them. The Kumase Council of Chiefs retained its powers to advise and consent regarding land policy, and its members were well represented on the KPHB. More significantly, the *Asantehene* Agyeman Prempe – repatriated in 1924 as a private citizen after nearly thirty years in exile – was nominated to the KPHB by the British. Then in 1926 he was granted the colonial title of *Kumasihene* and leadership of a divisional organisation that replaced the Kumase Council of Chiefs but incorporated its members. Agyeman Prempe died in 1931, but in 1935 the title and privileges of the *Asantehene*-in-council were restored to his successor, Osei Agyeman Prempeh II. At last, in

1943 – fourteen years before the end of colonial rule – customary rights over the Kumase lands were reinvested in the *Asantehene*-in-council 'in trust for the Golden Stool'.[25] The gradualist British policy that led to these rehabilitations is not germane here, except to note one significant fact. The restoration of the Kumase lands in 1943 occurred in tandem with the abolition of the KPHB and its replacement by a Kumase Town Council (KTC). Both events were influenced by British recognition that radical measures were urgently needed to bring order and planning to Kumase. It was hoped that the *Asantehene*-in-council would impose his authority in the matter of land required for urban expansion. It was hoped too that the KTC – which for the first time included elected members from the six wards into which the town was now split – would provide executive efficiency in implementing urban policy. But things turned out differently.

After 1945, planning recommendations finally led to a long overdue expansion of the Kumase town limits. Peri-urban areas and satellite villages were incorporated to provide new land for housing and other developments. Further enlargements followed – piecemeal but wholesale, especially in the 1960s and 1980s–1990s – until by 1997 the city boundaries enclosed nearly sixty square miles, of which twenty were classified as 'built-up' while the rest was 'in process of urban improvement'. Accelerated population growth, to an estimated 800,000 today, necessitated and justified successive waves of expansion.[26] This process has continued for over half a century now, but it is still transacted in ways and by means first established in its beginnings. Instead of creating the rational urbanism hoped for by the British, post-1945 expansion initiated a scramble for land rights in newly incorporated areas. The profits to be made from controlling acreage for building for sale or rent around the ever spreading periphery of Kumase, together with British and Ghanaian government tax breaks and soft loans for undertaking house construction, drew the *Asantehene*-in-council, the KTC, and armies of businessmen, entrepreneurs, speculators, fraudsters and dreamers into struggles of an unprecedentedly intense kind over rights in land.

It would be otiose here to do anything other than list the major players who joined in this battle as the years passed: the Asante National Liberation Movement (NLM), Nkrumah's CPP and successive Ghana governments since the 1950s; the local authority bodies that followed on from the KTC after it was wound up in 1954 – the Municipal Council (until 1962), the City Council (until 1974), the District Council (until 1989), and the quondam Metropolitan Assembly now District Council (current); Lebanese residents, Asante expatriates in Europe and the USA, foreign investors, established denominational churches and a rising proliferation of independent ones, local development banks and financial syndicates, and an uncountable army of others. It might be argued that the evolution of British colonial Kumase through the Second World War was ineptly or at least

minimally planned outside of the 'Garden City' centred on the European
administrative and commercial districts. But its development was carried
out by a small group of people working in a small area, and the levels of
patronage, fixing and profit-taking pale beside what has happened since
1945.

Post-war Kumase – a restless, continuously expanding urban agglomer-
ation with an ever rising and today a surging population – was (and is still
being) built in and by a maelstrom of competitive interests. It is important
to understand that this was and is a discontinuous process in geographical
terms. Changing political priorities and shifting economic imperatives have
colluded together in the manufacture of a patchwork landscape of completed, unfinished and abandoned projects. The signature of the whole is a
ceaseless building in response to an insatiable appetite for housing. Thus, in
the past fifty years Kumase has been subject to a perpetual but uneven
remaking around its fluid, restless and dynamic outskirts. The quiddity, feel
and atmosphere of the place have been transformed out of all recognition,
and this continues apace. This is not simply the view of an outsider – myself
– walking disorientedly around south Kumase in 1997. Longstanding Asante
residents sense the same thing, and now often comment on how the town is
mutating away from their familiar understanding. 'When I travel down to
Sɔkɔban now', an old friend complains of south Kumase, 'I hardly recognise
anything anymore. I used to get palm oil from some women in the village
there, you know. But the village is now just a part of Kumase. All swallowed
up, Tom [laughs].'[27]

TEXTS AND CONTEXTS: APPROACHING ADEƐBEBA

The regime that overthrew Nkrumah in 1966 set up commissions of inquiry
to look into government malfeasance during Ghana's First Republic. One
such body was empowered to investigate the affairs of the Kumase City
Council. It 'sat 181 times, examined 1,423 witnesses' and admitted 'four
hundred and nine (409) exhibits' before submitting its 277-page report in
1968. Among many matters it considered was the failure of the KCC to
provide amenities to the irate ratepayers of south Kumase. Giving evidence,
the City Engineer blamed the Omnibus Services Department and the
Electricity Corporation for the lack of public transport and power in the
area. Adeɛbeba and Atasomaaso in south Kumase had no mains water
supply, he continued, because the KCC Water Supply Division was 'short
of pipes'. But pipes or no pipes, he concluded, no more of south Kumase
could be connected because the city had an 'acute' shortage of potable
water, and so the unannounced decision had been taken 'to suspend all
extensions'.[28] This vignette is just one circumstantial episode from an
ongoing saga of overwhelming demand and overwhelmed provision in the
building of modern Kumase. But it has a particular resonance for me. I first

visited south Kumase in 1968, and my diary from that time records that many people complained about the derelictions of the metropolitan authority.

In 1968 I was lecturing and working on an M.A. in Asante history at the University of Ghana at Legon. I was twenty-two years old, on a three-year contract, and had every intention of returning home to work at something else. But in the end I chose differently, and have been involved with Asante ever since. Throughout the 1970s I went back to south Kumase for a number of reasons. One of them was to carry out fieldwork on the Kumase *Manwere* stool, an important but little studied office created in the mid-nineteenth century. Archival work in Kumase (by Ivor Wilks as well as myself) revealed an important historical link between *Manwere* and a village named Adeɛbeba. People in Kumase confirmed this, and arranged for me to talk with other people at Adeɛbeba. The place turned out to be – and I cannot think of a better term – *rus in urbe*, a peripheral part of the developing city of Kumase that still retained much of the look and feel of a village. At any rate, I enjoyed my visits there, published some of the findings, and moved on to other topics.[29]

In 1978 the Asante Collective Biography Project, of which I was co-director, held a workshop in Chicago on the Asante and the other Twi-speaking Akan peoples. The keynote speaker was Meyer Fortes, by then retired from his Cambridge chair. In conversation he talked animatedly about the Ashanti Social Survey and of plans to reclassify and catalogue his materials from it. The following year I returned to Cambridge to live. I went to see Fortes and was told that he had secured funds for a study of kinship and cocoa production in Asante to be based on his ASS survey findings. This project was completed in 1980. In the process, both the fieldwork data used and many additional ASS materials were reorganised under a series of broad categorical headings and placed on public deposit in Cambridge.[30] I met with Fortes regularly at this time. We talked much about his memories of living and working in Asante and of my own research. These were congenial and stimulating encounters. On one such occasion – a dinner at the Fortes house – Isaac Schapera was present. The two distinguished anthropologists reminisced their way through the history of their discipline. Talk about the sad decline of intensive and sustained fieldwork in Africa led to discussion of comparative method and of quantitative and qualitative approaches to research. I spoke of the historian's qualitative concerns, and specifically about the explanatory horizons opened up by fine-grained empirical detail. The evening ended and we dispersed. However, the next time I saw Fortes he produced a box of papers – 'odds and ends of the sort that interest you' – and invited me to inspect and make use of them. They were files (many untitled) taken by Fortes when he divided up the ASS data with Steel in Oxford in 1950, and they contained a mass of qualitative empirical documentation. None had been classified for the project completed in 1980, because they were 'superfluous' (the term used by Fortes) to its quantitative approach and sociological purposes. To subsequent meetings Fortes brought more documents of the same provenance and kind. Then I left Cambridge and Fortes fell ill and died in 1983.

The papers I was given access to were disorganised and concerned an assortment of subjects. They ranged from half-page accounts of happenings and personalities to lengthy participant-observation pieces and verbatim records of interviews and conversations. Some were in Fortes' handwriting, but most were produced by the ASS's Asante research assistants. Some were in Twi, but most were written down in English (albeit with many untranslated passages and interpolations). As I worked through them I saw that most concerned southern Asante, running from Atwoma to the southwest of Kumase eastward through Amansie, Mponoa and the lake Bosomtwe district into Asante Akyem. I saw too that they were incomplete. The items to hand were cross-referenced to other materials that were missing. Taking only the case in point, there was much about Adeɛbeba and its neighbours. But reading this made it frustratingly plain that there was even more on Adeɛbeba that I did not have. For example, there was no trace of a much mentioned 'Adeɛbeba Household Survey'. However, what I did have was diverse and complex evidence in and of itself. Among many other things, it renewed my interest in Adeɛbeba.

Lightning can and does strike twice in the same place. In 1987 I was introduced to Robert Steel when he was on a visit to Birmingham. I explained my interests and talk turned to Asante, to the ASS and to Fortes. Steel acknowledged that it had been some years since he had thought about his Asante materials and confessed that he was no longer even sure where he had stored them. His wife rescued him by asking if what we were discussing might be in the boxes that took up so much space in the garage of their Swansea home. Steel promised to check, and a letter duly arrived confirming that his ASS files were indeed where his wife thought they were – 'piled up in the garage against the back wall'.[31] In 1988 the first instalment of Steel's ASS papers arrived in Birmingham. There was a covering letter with the box: 'I am really pleased at the thought that some of this material might be useful to someone after forty years', he wrote, adding that he planned to bring 'the bulk of the stuff up to Birmingham the next time I come by car'.[32] This he did, but our meeting on that occasion had an added bonus. Steel had emptied his garage, but at the prompting of his wife he had looked for and located further ASS files in their house and was convinced that still more remained to be found. Over the next two years further materials arrived in the post until Steel was satisfied that there was nothing left to send.

To cut a long story short, I found that Steel had furnished the materials mentioned in the Fortes papers but missing from them. And not only that, for it was now also clear that when the ASS files were split in 1950 a disproportionately large amount of the qualitative material had remained in Oxford with Steel. It was Steel himself who told me how this had come about because of Fortes' immediate concern to collate, analyse and write up the survey data. Be all that as it may, Steel's holdings comprised a hetero-geneous mass of empirical information obtained from people in many different parts of Asante. Like the Fortes material, it was mostly generated by the ASS's Asante researchers. It contained a deal of evidence about Adeɛbeba and its neighbours, including the elusive and – as it now turned out – misleadingly named 'Adeɛbeba Household Survey'. This file certainly included questionnaires and statistical returns of the kind suggested by its title, but also deposited in it (and in supplementary folders) were Adeɛbeba life histories, personal testimonies and accounts of interviews and conversations. Revived interest in Adeɛbeba now began to move towards the forefront of my concerns, and this book is the result.

Adeɛbeba was never a large or important village and today it is only a small part of Kumase. So, why a book about it and its people? What is being attempted here? By way of preliminary explanation, let us consider some of the historiographical precedents that have informed and influenced the thinking behind this study. Three linked approaches have played important roles in shaping the analysis offered here. These are Italian microhistory (*microstoria*), French responses to that body of work and the distinctively German 'history of everyday life' (*Alltagsgeschichte*). I have learned from all of them in ways that are set out below and afterwards related to the matters of Adeɛbeba and Asante history and the project of recuperating the African past.

Italian *microstoria* is not a school but an ongoing accumulation of studies that have been appearing since the mid-1970s. What links together the influential works of Ginzburg, Levi, Grendi, Poni, Cerutti, Gribaudi and others is 'a new approach based on intensive but limited samples of social reality: communities, social networks, individual careers, and so on'.[33] Such analyses commonly combine the episodic with the systemic. Thus Levi's seminal and much cited study of the seventeenth-century Piedmontese community of Santena – 'I have chosen a banal place and an undistin-guished story' – portrays the richly episodic life and times of the exorcist priest Giovan Battista Chiesa in tandem with a painstaking systemic recon-struction of the village milieu inhabited by the man and his parishioners.[34] The now widely acknowledged significance of such studies is that micro-historical observation is not simply social history miniaturised and writ small. Rather, by shifting the scale of observation *microstoria* reveals novel configurations of the social and in so doing it permits a critical reconsideration of the paradigms and objects of social history itself. The

standpoint of the village, so to speak, is not a view from below but a revelation of protocols that embody and express a (sometimes radically)
different perspective on the ordering of the social. Now, ethnographers have
long known this to be the case (and Levi and his colleagues have borrowed
from Barth, Geertz and others), but the signal contribution of *microstoria*
has been to historicise the anthropological at hitherto unprecedented levels.
The result is an exposition of agency, alterity and possibility in the
understanding of the social that is innovative in its (non-anthropological)
grounding in a documented chronology.[35]

   The French contribution to *microstoria* has been to refine its conceptu-
alisation of the spatial unit of analysis and to explore further its relationship
to other scales of observation. Fundamental to both enterprises is the
deployment and development (by Lepetit, Revel and others) of the carto-
graphic understanding of *l'échelle* – a term resistant to economic translation,
but used by map makers to describe ideas of appropriateness in selecting
variable observational scales to furnish answers to particular questions.[36]
Cartographers have long employed combinatory scales (and iconographies)
to illustrate detail and complexity. The lesson for historians is that the
microhistorical *échelle* resonates most resoundingly in combinatory play
with other observational scales. The microhistorical unit of analysis is enriched by a porosity that opens into and reciprocates with other geographical spaces, and this in turn conduces a persuasion towards polythetic rather
than rigid categories of interrogation. Understandings derived from the
centripetal aggregation described by *microstoria* benefit from strategic
dialogue with the centrifugal disaggregation (alas, one can no longer say
deconstruction without fear of being misunderstood) proposed by alternative observational scales. The key to such comparisons is that they reverse
the conventional procedures of social history. The macrohistorical is read
for clues to the microhistorical and higher order abstraction is disprivileged
in favour of open-ended exploration of the richness of being.[37] This approach
is necessarily aporetic, provisional and messily resistant to closure, but its
focus on individual agents within localised fields of action can – and does –
supply a nuance and texture otherwise inaccessible to analysis. There are
caveats. The pursuit of the microhistorical presupposes bodies of evidence
amenable to investigation at this level. Furthermore, the dialogic procedure
in which the microhistorical is used to interrogate the macrohistorical to
generate new understandings presumes that 'the enfolding society' (*la
société enveloppante*) is itself adequately documented and explored.[38] I will
return to these matters in due course.

   Microhistory in both its Italian and French incarnations focuses on
agents and the relationships between them. German *Alltagsgeschichte*
combines historical analysis with elements of the national tradition in
anthropology ('the politics of recognition' in Hegel, Mead and Schutz) to

concentrate on the lived experiences of men and women in the past.[39]
Alltagsgeschichte is simultaneously more programmatic and more self-
consciously 'political' in its interventions than are its Italian and French
counterparts. It sets out to explore 'social history in its experiential or
subjective dimensions' so as to transcend received 'distinctions between the
"public" and the "private"' in the cause of establishing 'a more effective way
of making the elusive connections between the political and cultural
realms'.[40] In practice this has meant a concentration on the *menu peuple* and
a 'political' investigation of their 'housing and homelessness, clothing and
nakedness, eating and hunger, love and hate'.[41] Like Italo-French microhistory, German *Alltagsgeschichte* dates from pioneering work done in the
mid-1970s. Today the two projects are in close dialogue but they remain
quite distinct.[42] The contribution of 'the history of everyday life' has been
twofold. First, by examining lived experiences it has opened many windows
on to the discontinuous processes of *bricolage* involved in the construction of
historical 'lifeworlds' (thereby grounding the Habermasian concept in
concrete situations and specific temporal conjunctures). Second, by
anatomising the unstable constituents of historically rooted selfhoods it has
explored the reciprocities of absorption and transformation (*Verwandlung*)
between interiority and intersubjectivity.[43]

Microhistory and 'the history of everyday life' interest themselves in
examining a historicised point of view rather than questing after the exemplary or typical case. Both enterprises are valid, and in a mature historiography the interpenetrations of the empirical with the comparative are
conducted as a dialogue between partners. However, no such dynamic
symmetry exists in African historiography – construed here as a practice that
accords primacy to recuperating the empirical experience of Africans in the
past. The dearth of African microhistories might be explained in a variety of
ways: fragmentary, diverse or otherwise recalcitrant sources, practical problems of funding, fieldwork and language, or the investment of time needed
to make sense of detail and complexity.[44] Be all that as it may, the consequences are evident and dire. First, the ground of comparativism has
shifted from the empirical to a derivative theorising. This front-loading
generates texts that address each other instead of the historical evidence
(which is knowingly 'problematised', a sleight of hand that describes
difficulty but evades the labour of tackling it). Surely I cannot be alone in
finding emperors with no clothes in works that purport history but situate a
malnourished historical empiricism in the overwhelming shadow of
interpretative superstructures.[45] Second, African history is now broken
backed with the fracture line separating the twentieth century from all of its
predecessors. The persuasion to twentieth-century history may answer to a
widely felt need for contemporary relevance, but all too frequently it is
conducted as an autonomous practice in which the matters at issue are

hermetically sealed off from their own past. In simple terms, much twentieth-century African history has no adequately documented antecedents.[46]

In case these strictures jar with current sensibilities, let me end by returning to first principles. Fortes was a structural-functionalist. The anthropologist Radcliffe-Brown famously described the project of structural-functionalism as follows: 'the actual relations of Tom, Dick and Harry may go down in our field notebooks and may provide illustrations for a general description. But what we need for scientific purposes is an account of the form of the structure.'[47] These have never been the priorities of historians, and I can only record my gratitude that Fortes (and Steel) preserved the testimonies of many an Asante 'Tom, Dick and Harry'. But of course these priorities no longer obtain among anthropologists and other social scientists either. As part of a generalised repudiation of the 'scientific purposes' of the social sciences, it was noted that structural-functionalism and its peers had marginalised and neglected 'historical contingencies and political action'.[48] True, and all well and good to draw attention to the matter. But the consequence for social studies has been the foregrounding of contingency (articulated as 'theory') and political action (framed as hand-wringing about the authorial 'I') at the expense of history. In African studies as elsewhere there is a willed or negligent somnambulance about trying to find out what might have happened to people in the past. In the extreme case, suspicion about facts can produce a scholarly indulgence towards amnesia. Africa is ill served. The historiography of its peoples lacks empirical density and resonant depth.

In this book I have tried to unite together insights from other historical fields with the findings of Asante historiography and to bring this to bear upon the question of the historical experience of Adeɛbeba people between the mid-nineteenth and mid-twentieth centuries. The justification for this enterprise lies in its – I think still rare – attempt to portray African lives in detail, over an extended historical period, on their own terms, and in their own words. I have tried to convey something of the *Alltagsgeschichte* of Adeɛbeba people and their neighbours. Equally, I have followed the precepts of *microstoria* (and *microhistoire*) in seeking to evaluate the macro-historical environment – Asante and British colonial states, westernisation, modernisation – from the point of view of Adeɛbeba witnesses. I intend no firm or fast conclusions (the *échelle* has many variations), but I make a consistent effort throughout to document historical complexity in the fashioning of Adeɛbeba lives. Two codas: if the book has an epistemology it is ambient rather than prescriptive and akin to the radically discontinuous texts celebrated by de Certeau as a source of pleasure in historical discovery; if the book has a figural metaphor for the sort of history it embodies then it is not the helpless stare of Benjamin's *Angelus Novus* but rather something akin to the revelatory gaze in Brodsky's meditative catechism as he stood before the sculptural busts in the Hermitage.

One day, staring at the little white face of some early Roman *fanciulla*, I lifted my hand, presumably to smooth my hair, and thus obstructed the single source of light coming to her from the ceiling. At once her facial expression changed. I moved my hand a bit to the side: it changed again. I began moving both my hands rather frantically, casting each time a different shadow upon her features: the face came to life.[49]

A poeticised vision, certainly, but also a description of the kaleidoscope of shifting angles of vision and changing grounds of disclosure that animate – in every sense, I hope – my discussion of the lives of the Adeɛbeba people.

2

ADEƐBEBA LIVES: THE NINETEENTH CENTURY

BEGINNERS: FOUNDING *MANWERE* AND ADEƐBEBA, 1790s–1840s

The Congreve rocket was refined from Indian prototypes and entered service with the British artillery in 1806. Its hollow iron head carried a bursting charge of up to sixty pounds weight of shot, shell or canister wrapped in an incendiary composite. Its launch mechanism (external paper fuse, propellant flash ignition) was unreliable. Its guidance system (directional cradle rest, eight- to twelve-foot stabilising stick) was inaccurate. But when discharged on a flat trajectory in battery salvoes at a rate of up to ten a minute, it was fearsomely destructive of massed infantry at any range below 1500 yards.

On 7 August 1826 Congreve rockets launched by the British struck and ignited the Asante ammunition train at the battle of Katamanso on the tinder dry plains north of Accra. In the explosive conflagration that followed, the grass, scrub bush and trees caught fire and the battlefield was enveloped in a pall of thick smoke. Further rockets and artillery rounds combined with the prevailing winds to wreak havoc in and disorient the Asante order of battle. In this carnage and confusion the Asante centre led by the Kumase *Gyaasewahene* Opoku Frɛfrɛ and the *Asantehene* Osei Yaw's bodyguard inadvertently engaged each other in crossfire. The Asante line buckled, broke and disengaged. Savage firefights ensued as disorganised parties of Asante troops battled their way out towards the north-west and home. Opoku Frɛfrɛ, shamed and badly wounded, committed suicide on the Atwea scarp near Akuropon; Osei Yaw, defeated and slightly injured, halted finally at Saawua south of Kumase, where his army had mustered before the campaign.

Authoritative tradition recounts that at the height of the fighting the *Asantehene* 'ordered that the Golden Stool [*sika dwa*] should be separated from him' and kept in a place of safety by its custodians [*nkonnwasoafoɔ*] 'to avoid its falling into the hands of the enemy'. The disastrous consequence of this tactic was that Osei Yaw neither had the Golden Stool in his possession nor even knew where it was when he quit the field in disordered haste. Failure to safeguard the *sika dwa* at any time was shameful behaviour (*nea ɛyɛ aniwu*) in an *Asantehene*; but to abandon it in the face of an enemy was an abomination (*akyiwadeɛ*), for its loss in war was held to presage national catastrophe.

The rumour that the Golden Stool had fallen into British hands panicked Asante rearguard troops still fighting at Katamanso. By report the situation was saved by the heroic decisiveness of the *Abakomdwahene* Kwaku Dua, the heir-apparent to the *sika dwa*.

> Barima Kwaku Dua, who afterwards became King Kwaku Dua I, and his men then came to the place of disaster, and very angrily he inquired after the King and the Golden Stool. He was told that the King had been wounded and gone ahead of them; but they did not know where the Golden Stool was. He then exclaimed and said that without the Golden Stool he could not possibly go back to Asante. He therefore ordered his followers to beat their drums and blow their horns. This attracted the attention of those men who were in charge of the Golden Stool and Yaw Dabanka, the King's Head Stool-Carrier came to the spot with it. Some time afterwards Boatin Akuamoa, Dwabenhene and Kontanasehene Antwi also came to the spot, and on seeing the Golden Stool, Boatin asked Barima Kwaku Dua to let him take charge of it to Kumase. Barima refused the request and said both of them would bring it to Kumase, and therefore both of them escorted the Golden Stool to Saawua where they overtook the King and handed it to him.[1]

According to a British officer who was at Katamanso the use of Congreve rockets

> thrown among the Ashantees occasioned the most dreadful havoc and confusion: the hissing sound when thrown, the train of fire, the explosion and frightful wounds they inflicted, caused them to suppose that they were thunder and lightning, called *snow-man* in Fantee, by which name they are now known among the natives.[2]

The '*snow-man*' of British transliteration was *ɔsraman* (lightning) in Twi. In the repertoire of horn calls of the Kumase *Manwere* stool the first incumbent Kwasi Brantuo was memorialised as *ɔsraman apae ase no so ne ho ayɛ fɔ paa* ('though the lightning has struck him he is still very handsome') to signify his bravery under rocket fire at Katamanso. Indeed, Kwasi Brantuo was credited with saving Kwaku Dua on the battlefield when he heard the latter's horn calling in distress *woagyaw me nku to kore* ['I am left here quite alone'].

> At Akantamasu [*sic*] the Akwamuhene fired at us from behind, and we lost and had to retire; there the Ashanti army lost thirty Safohenfo [*Asafohene*]. In this battle the Asantehene's nephew Kwaku Dua was cut off on the battlefield, and was rescued by one Obrantu [Kwasi Brantuo] an *ahinkoa* [*ahenkwaa*] of the Asantehene. So when Kwaku Dua came to the Stool he made this man Sanahene [*Sanaahene*] or

Fotuohene [*Fotɔɔhene*]. After that war Kwaku Dua said he would never fight again, and later he did £1,000 worth of trade with the Europeans for guns, powder, cloth and rum.[3]

Battles are intense human experiences. In Asante understanding they were *ntam* (lit. 'betwixt and between'), a liminal rupturing of life by chaos and death and the uncontrolled emotional states attendant upon these extremes. As such they called forth retrospective narratives to domesticate and try to make sense of tumultuous memories. The truth sought was not literal but emblematic. Thus, the intertwining of the valorous tales of Kwaku Dua and Kwasi Brantuo at Katamanso *may* recount what actually took place (*wie es eigentlich gewesen ist*), but the persuasive power of the story resided in firmer understandings. Kwaku Dua became *Asantehene* and Kwasi Brantuo rose to be one of the richest stool holders in all Asante history. The two were intimately associated with one another, quite literally from birth to death. By achieved status, therefore, and hence in remembrance such men were heroes (*akofonfoɔ*), and their acknowledged closeness in life undergirded and guaranteed a narrative recall that bound them together on the battlefield at Katamanso and set them in the amber of great deeds jointly performed. The pairing of Kwaku Dua and Kwasi Brantuo manifested an Asante ideal of trust and understanding between two people of like mind (*nnipa baanu*). It was said of such relations that if either one of the two said *medaase pii* ('thank you very much indeed') then the other always responded *yɛ nni aseda* ('you don't owe me any thanks').

Kwasi Brantuo was born about 1790 at Heman Ampatua in the Atwoma district about six miles south-west of Kumase.[4] His mother belonged to a lineage from Asoromaso. Her maternal kin were subjects (*nkoa*; sing. *akoa*) of the *Nkwantanan* stool of Heman, but her father was a servant (*ahenkwaa*; pl. *nhenkwaa*) of the *sika dwa* in the capacity of gunbearer (*atumtuni*). Kwasi Brantuo's own father was also a royal *ahenkwaa* in service to the *Asantehene* Osei Kwame. With this background the boy was clearly destined to be trained up to follow in his father's and maternal grandfather's footsteps.

Two circumstances intervened to determine the precise nature of Kwasi Brantuo's apprenticeship as an *ahenkwaa* and so define the trajectory of his life. First, in or about 1790 his mother's overlord the *Nkwantananhene* Boakye Yam Kumaa married the widowed Amma Sewaa, a Kumase royal and the only surviving full sister of the reigning *Asantehene* Osei Kwame. This was an unorthodox match. There was a considerable status gap between husband and wife, but presumably Amma Sewaa talked her brother into allowing her to marry the man of her choice (*ɔdɔfo*). Be that as it may, Amma Sewaa already had two sons and a daughter named Afua Sapon by her first marriage. Her union with Boakye Yam Kumaa produced three more boys.

The youngest of these was Kwaku Dua who was born about 1797. Second, Boakye Yam Kumaa and Kwasi Brantuo's father were close companions (*ahokafoɔ*). So, after Kwaku Dua was named, his father asked his friend to give up his own small son Kwasi Brantuo to look after and attend upon the royal infant. This was a conventional enough arrangement, but it requires some explanation.

It was an Asante axiom that 'a royal child does not carry its own sleeping mat' (*ɔdehyeɛ abofra nansoa akɛtɛ*). From infancy onwards a royal was attended by a designated personal servant. The person chosen for this task was *ɔbagyegyeni* (pl. *mmagyegyefoɔ*), usually and not inaccurately translated as 'nanny' or 'nurse'. The etymology of the term combined together the senses of supporting (*gye*) and sustaining (*gyina*) a child (*ɔba*). The corps of *mmagyegyefoɔ* was a small body of specialist *nhenkwaa*. Its recruits were schooled in truthfulness (*nokwaredi*) and good conduct (*afɛfesɛmdi*) so as to furnish a role model for emulation. The job was gendered: males served boys and females served girls. It was also qualified by age: usually the *ɔbagyegyeni* was no more than a few years older than the royal child, the object being to induce socialisation through play (*agoro*) as well as by example (*nhwɛso*) because 'everything depends on learning' (*nneɛ ma nhina dan sua*). As is the way of such things, some children detested their 'nannies' and suffered and endured until adulthood allowed them to sever relations. By contrast, other children forged unshakable bonds with their *mmagyegyefoɔ* that lasted as long as both were alive.

Whatever the nature of the earliest encounters between the boy Kwasi Brantuo and the infant Kwaku Dua, their relationship was soon marked by unexpected and dramatic events. At the close of the eighteenth century dynastic conflict between the *Asantehemaa* Kwaadu Yaadom and the *Asantehene* Osei Kwame reached crisis point and threatened civil war. As the two antagonists manoeuvred for advantage, Boakye Yam Kumaa died in unclear circumstances. At the same time his two eldest sons by Amma Sewaa were killed by Kwaadu Yaadom's agents, as were his wife's boys by her first marriage. With his brother-in-law and nephews dead Osei Kwame removed his court to Dwaben about 1800, taking with him to safety his bereaved and newly widowed sister Amma Sewaa, her adolescent daughter Afua Sapon, her sole surviving infant son Kwaku Dua, and that child's ten-year-old *ɔbagyegyeni* Kwasi Brantuo. In the event the Kumase office holders rallied to Kwaadu Yaadom and Osei Kwame's cause was lost. In 1803–4 he abdicated and committed suicide. This cleared the way for the ruthlessly ambitious *Asantehemaa*. Over the following thirty years (1804–34) three of her sons in succession – Opoku Fofie, Osei Tutu Kwame and Osei Yaw – occupied the *sika dwa*.

So complete was Kwaadu Yaadom's victory that Osei Kwame's surviving kin were simply left to cope as frightened, humiliated and impoverished refugees in Dwaben. This was the context of Kwaku Dua's childhood and the reason why his stock phrase as a boy is said to have been the lamentation 'when am I going to become a real person?' (*se me bie ye onipa yi?*), a despairing interrogation of hopeless conditions. The suspicion he manifested in later life surely arose during this fraught time in exile. It was encouraged into being as he came to understand the fate that had befallen his father, brothers and maternal uncle. Then again Kwaku Dua must have become painfully conscious of his mother's distress and recurring terror. On more than one occasion, Kwaadu Yaadom sent executioners (*adumfoɔ*) to Dwaben with cloth to cover the indigent Amma Sewaa; but this was a poisoned gift, for the pattern of the cloth was *nkum me fie nko su me abo nten* ('don't kill me in private and then mourn me in public'), a deliberately threatening reminder to Amma Sewaa that the *Asantehemaa* thought of her as an irreconcilable foe who yet might suffer the death penalty. At other times Kwaadu Yaadom sent eggshells (*nkesuahono*) as token of her mocking opinion that the refugees were ingrates (*abonniayɛfɔ*); after all, whatever the emptiness of their lives they still had their skins. Living this narrow and hazardous existence, the exiles were forced into dependence upon one another. Kwaku Dua drew close to his half-sister Afua Sapon and looked to Kwasi Brantuo for levels of comradely reassurance beyond the remit of an *ɔbagyegyeni*. The older boy's ready response to the needs of the younger was the foundation of the lifelong bond between the two of them; kindnesses shown in childhood meant that 'Nana Adjiman [Kwaku Dua] raised up Brentuo [Kwasi Brantuo] in later life' because 'every good turn deserves another'.[5]

In a condescending gesture arising from conviction of her dynastic impregnability, Kwaadu Yaadom at last ordered the Dwaben refugees to be repatriated to Kumase shortly before her own death in 1809. Kwaku Dua, now aged about twelve, was marginalised and his royal status was discounted. This became evident over the next few years and was confirmed about 1815 when the *Asantehene* Osei Tutu Kwame instructed him to occupy his father's office as *Nkwantananhene*. A minor stool, *Nkwantanan* was created about 1775 by the *Asantehene* Osei Kwadwo and awarded thereafter to a series of diligent *nhenkwaa* like Boakye Yam Kumaa, who served as government tax gatherers, traders or diplomats. Its subaltern status meant correspondingly meagre resources. The Heman land grant that supported the stool holder belonged originally to the Kumase *Akwamuhene/Asafohene* and it was by no means large. Kwaku Dua needed, begged for and was given some more uncleared bush at Heman to maintain himself and his dependants. He sent Kwasi Brantuo, now in his twenties, to supervise the production of food from this land.

A number of factors – the genealogical narrowness of the Kumase royal family, unexpected deaths within it and considerations of age and experience among its diminished cohort of surviving adult members – led to the rehabilitation of Kwaku Dua and his kin out of simple dynastic necessity. Valorous conduct in the Gyaman war of 1818–19 reinforced Kwaku Dua's resurgent importance, as did his mother's brief incumbency as *Asantehemaa* prior to her death about 1820. The *Asantehene* Osei Tutu Kwame died in 1823. His successor was his uterine brother Osei Yaw, the heir-apparent and the last born of Kwaadu Yaadom's six sons. Kwaku Dua was the best qualified and indeed the only plausible candidate to occupy the *abakom dwa* as heir to Osei Yaw, and he was duly appointed to that office.

Kwaku Dua soon discovered that his elevation was not the end of his difficulties. The *Asantehene* Osei Yaw cast him as a rival and seized every opportunity to insult him. The weapon used was *mpoatwa*, a way of talking that asserted superiority by listing the shortcomings of another so as to 'inflate oneself' by comparison (*huw mframa hyɛ ade*). Kwaku Dua was impugned on the grounds that his father was only an *ahenkwaa*, and so his male line of descent boasted no ancestral 'great names' (*aboadenfoɔ*). It was even suggested that Amma Sewaa was promiscuous so as to encourage scurrilous gossip about the identity of Kwaku Dua's father. All this was symptomatic of the barbed relationship between the *Asantehene* and his once exiled and discounted successor-in-waiting. So too was the matter of Kwaku Dua's restoration of the Golden Stool to Osei Yaw at Saawua after the battle of Katamanso.

> Before his Elders and Chiefs the King heartily thanked Barima Kwaku Dua and the Dwabenhene for having brought the [Golden] Stool to him safely. In order to avoid any shade of suspicion, Barima Kwaku Dua stood up and swore to the Great Oath [*ntamkesɛɛ*] that he was entirely the servant of the King, and that anything that he did in connection with the Golden Stool was done in the King's service, and that it was not at all necessary that the King thanked him highly.[6]

In the years after the military disaster at Katamanso Osei Yaw became capricious, tyrannical and unpopular. As he did so, support for Kwaku Dua increased. In 1834 Osei Yaw died and the heir-apparent Kwaku Dua was enstooled as *Asantehene*.

When Kwaku Dua became *Asantehene* he summoned Kwasi Brantuo from Heman to Kumase to serve him. He raised him to a senior position in the corps of elephant tail bearers (*ahoprafoɔ*; sing. *ɔhoprafo*) and gave him important responsibilities for fiscal affairs. In confirmation of this favour and regard Kwaku Dua charged Kwasi Brantuo with the ritual safekeeping of *nana katakyie mmra*, the golden elephant tail made by the second *Asantehene* Opoku Ware (c. 1720–50) in token of his success in amassing wealth. Gratitude for this signal honour was commemorated in Kwasi Brantuo's horn call *me tiri ne me kɔn wura Asantehene* ('the *Asantehene* owns

both my head and my neck'). To support his enhanced dignity Kwasi
Brantuo was given a part of the Heman lands in his own right; Kwaku Dua
also awarded him a servant named Sebe to take over the duties of farm
overseer.

> When the time came when he Nana Agyeman [Kwaku Dua] was to
> ascend the Golden Stool he said to my grandfather my predecessor
> [Kwasi Brantuo], 'When I go upon the Throne I will always like to
> have foodstuffs, fish, palmwine [and] water sent me from Hinman
> [Heman].' 'I am taking you to Kumasi, but who will send me all the
> above', he said again to my uncle [again, Kwasi Brantuo]. My uncle
> said that his brother Adutwim [ɔheneba Adu Twum, son of Kwasi
> Brantuo's mother Akuntunku's second marriage to the Asantehene
> Opoku Fofie (c. 1803–4)] would do that. But Nana Agyeman said
> Adutwim was the son of one of the Asantehene Kings [sic], and so he
> would not like him to do the work of a domestic. Before Nana
> Agyeman became Asantehene he was succeeding his father, Boakye
> Yam [Kumaa]. Nana Agyeman presented to my grandfather Brentuo
> [Kwasi Brantuo] one Serbeh [Sebe] Nana Agyeman's father's servant,
> to take care of the land ... Nana Agyeman said to my grandfather, 'I
> will make a present of the land to you. Apportion part of it to Serbeh to
> make farms thereon that he may send me foodstuffs through you [to
> Kumase].'[7]

As will become apparent, these events launched Kwasi Brantuo on a
career that brought high office and great wealth in Kwaku Dua's service.
The relationship that made this possible was rooted in the bond forged
between the royal child and the ɔbagyegyeni during a time of shared
adversity, despondency and fear. The effects of these traumas on Kwaku
Dua were evident to contemporaries. As an adult and as an Asantehene he
was wary, aloof, prickly, capricious, autocratic and, above all else, trusting
of very few people. An estimate of his character supplied by Asante
witnesses shows us the ruler and is richly suggestive in relation to the
background that formed the man. It was reported that

> [T]he circumstances of his father belonging to the humbler classes is
> said to have been not without its effects on King Quaku Duah's
> conduct both as a sovereign and as the Head of the Royal Family of
> Ashantee. Princesses of the blood are usually bestowed upon men of
> power and rank in the kingdom, and Quaku Duah, though the law of
> the country secured him the throne by right of his mother, no matter
> who or what his father might be, felt all through life that his birth was
> the subject of uncomplimentary remark.
> [The Asantehene] Osai Qwaku Duah was a sagacious and politic
> prince, reserved in manner, dignified and courteous, not fond of war,

shrewd and sensible in administering justice, patient to hear, somewhat severe towards the more powerful of the nobility; withal, jealous
and suspicious of those whose wealth and influence gave them much
weight in the state, if they seemed disposed to display too great a
degree of independence. In the selection of his ministers and agents,
political and commercial, he showed much wisdom ... King Quaku
Duah countenanced no fools, employed no men of half measures, nor
gave ear to the counsels of those who leaned to the side of mercy.[8]

Kwasi Brantuo and Kwaku Dua were boyhood comrades (*mfɛfoɔ*). But as
they grew up the nature of their relationship was qualified by differences in
ascriptive rank and status. They were never friends (*ayɔnkoɔ*), for in Asante
understanding friendship presumed an intimacy of sharing between persons
of equivalent social standing. Instead, they were *nnamfoɔ* (sing. *adamfo*),
associates of unequal rank who enjoyed close familiarity and mutual trust in
the context of relations between patron (*nipa a ɔgyina ana ɔtaa kuw bi akyi*)
and client (*nea ɔdan obi*). Clientship (*adan*) was structurally implicit in dealings between any commoner and a Kumase royal, and it furnished forth the
norms and vocabulary of all transactions with an *Asantehene*. Kwasi Brantuo
was Kwaku Dua's lifelong confidant (*nipa a wɔ tumi ka kokomusɛm ana
tirimusɛm ana ahiasɛm kyerɛ no*), but this was a one-way street. Whatever
dynamic existed between the two, Kwaku Dua controlled the conditions of
its expression. By corollary, Kwasi Brantuo knew his place and comported
himself accordingly. He looked to Kwaku Dua as an indispensable prop and
support (*tetantwere*) because everything flowed from his patronage; and
once the patron became *Asantehene* this understanding was fixed forever,
because now Kwaku Dua was clothed in the nimbus of exalted power that
surrounded the *sika dwa*. Whenever Kwasi Brantuo addressed the *Asantehene*
Kwaku Dua he lauded him as 'the only giver of things' (*ɔmafo*). Then he
acknowledged a lifetime of dependence, now suitably formulated as the
anxious pleading of the courtier: *Nana ɔboafo yɛ na* ('Nana, it is a hard thing
to get a good helper'). Finally he calmed his own fears, reaching the rhetorical point of the exercise by asserting continuing confidence in his patron's
largess: *Nana Otumfuo n'adaworoma* ('Nana, when I come to lean on you for
help, you always give'). Once these preliminaries had reaffirmed the basis of
relations, Kwasi Brantuo turned to whatever business needed to be talked
over with the ruler he had watched over when both of them were children.

Becoming *Asantehene* was an act of ritual enstoolment, a momentary
entitlement in history. Being *Asantehene* was a process of lived involvement,
an unfolding engagement with history. Each and every *Asantehene* in turn
came to inhabit his role differently and to master it with varying degrees of
authority. Success in this enterprise was achieved as a form of imprimatur,
a stamping of existential selfhood upon public persona that proclaimed the

seamless indivisibility of the man and the role. In the transit from a becoming (*wayɛ*; 'he becomes') to a being (*oyɛ*; 'he is') an Asante ruler experienced a maturation (*nyin*) conferred upon him by the *sika dwa*. In the eyes of others this took the form of shedding the wilfulness (*asowui*) and accompanying tribulations (*kotroka*) of irresponsible youth and assuming the identity of 'the one who exercises power' (*otumfuo*) and 'the one who possesses wisdom' (*onyansafo*). When he was judged to have achieved this separation from an earlier persona, his office holders and *nhenkwaa* acknowledged that 'he has cut off the hind part' (*twa to*). He was understood to have entered into his own and was entitled to say 'I have made a cap for myself now' (*ma ye kyew ma fa*) in affirmation of that fact. Reign and rule were now synchronised and the new *Asantehene* was seen to be acting in a dispensation of his own making that set him apart and distinguished him from his predecessor(s).

The *Asantehene* Kwaku Dua took a decade over this process. Enstooled in 1834, he spent the first ten years of his incumbency asserting his legitimate right to rule in the face of scurrilities concerning his descent; during this time he confronted his critics and suppressed his foes, real or imagined. By the early 1840s Kwaku Dua had reached a plateau of confident self-realisation in his being as *Asantehene*. The following sequence of events then occurred.

> The King of Yebo [Daboya] tried to expand his power by conquering the smaller states in the Ntaman [Gonja], to enable him to rise against the *Asantehene*. This scheme was revealed to the *Asantehene* by the Yaanehene [the Dagomba *ya na*]. Without the least hesitation the King sent an army under the command of Asamoa Nkwanta, Anantahene, whose army was augmented by the army of the Yaanehene. When they met together, a bloody battle was fought in which the King of Yebo was captured and beheaded, and very many prisoners were brought to Kumase.
>
> Shortly after this battle, the King created a Fekuo [*fekuo*; an administrative group of offices] which he named 'Manwere', and captained it with Akwasi Brantuo. The King then created another Fekuo which he named 'Asabi' and captained it by Boakye, and placed it under 'Manwere'. He also raised many of his sons to be sub-chiefs and placed them all under 'Manwere'.[9]

In the early 1840s unrest in Daboya and other component divisions of the Gonja state led Kwaku Dua to dispatch an army to reimpose Asante tributary control over the northern savanna. Troops under the Kumase *Anantahene* Asamoa Nkwanta left Kumase during the dry season of 1841. The campaigning was arduous and slow. It took three years and many casualties before Asamoa Nkwanta completed his task and returned home.

He and his men were accorded a formal reception into Kumase on *monodwo* (Monday) 3 June 1844. For eight hours on that day the *Asantehene* Kwaku Dua presided over a public review of Asamoa Nkwanta, his staff and some thirty to forty thousand returning infantry. The achieved synergy between man and role is apparent in an eyewitness report of Kwaku Dua's strikingly assured conduct on this occasion. He took his seat at Kumase Dwaberem ('the place of assembly') around 12.30p.m. before one of the largest assemblies in all of nineteenth-century Asante history. Then, just before the army processed and the formal review began, the *Asantehene* Kwaku Dua suddenly

> left his stool and advanced to a considerable distance among the delighted crowd. His rising was the signal for a general shout ... The King, with about six thousand attendants, walked near a hundred yards, and then seating himself in his palanquin, he looked round upon the vast assembly, and spreading abroad his hands, appeared, as if welcoming their return, and giving them his blessing. While being carried to his throne amidst the acclamations of his people, he seemed rapt in the most profound delight, and as he gazed upon the throng, evidently felt, that no nation could compare with Ashanti, and no Kingdom cope with his powerful Kingdom.[10]

Shortly after this triumphalist display the *Asantehene* Kwaku Dua again exercised his sovereign will and demonstrated his personal authority. Beginning in July 1844 he set in train the formation of the Kumase *Manwere fekuo* – the tenth and the last created such administrative grouping, and the only one founded in the nineteenth century – and he appointed Kwasi Brantuo to its headship as the first incumbent of the *Manwere* stool. The very name of this office – *ɔman* ('nation': embracing concepts of people, place and polity) + *were* ('just vindication': implying a body of men who punished wrongdoing on behalf of the *Asantehene*) – conveyed Kwaku Dua's sense of inhabiting and incarnating the justified power of prerogative. The *manwerefoɔ* (those assigned to serve the *fekuo* stools) were nicknamed 'ears' (*aso*), because they acted to spy out (*sra*) and deter (*tu obi aba mu*) enemies of the *Asantehene*. It was (and to this day is) said that because of his experiences Kwaku Dua lived in fear of plots (*adwemmbɔne nhyehyɛ*). Hence *Manwere* was given to Kwasi Brantuo, a servant of proven devotion and a lifelong executor of Kwaku Dua's orders.

As noted, Asamoa Nkwanta's troops were received into Kumase on *monodwo*, the most auspicious of all days in the recurring forty-two-day calendrical cycle of the Asante *adaduanan*. The very next *monodwo* was Monday, 15 July 1844. On that propitious day Kwasi Brantuo ('Brentu') performed a public ritual in Kumase that was both crucial to and symbolic of his aggrandisement.

Two of the principal Chiefs have, at the King's command, been 'showing themselves, and their Gold' today. One of them (Brentu) is a treasurer of the King's. The other (Afarqua) [presently unidentified, at least in as much as a number of possible identifications exist] is reckoned to be among the most wealthy among his aristocratical compeers. All their people were in attendance, as well as their numerous wives. The King and all the Principal Chiefs were seated in the Market [Dwaberem]. These two 'Gentlemen', whose turn it is to be thus honoured, appear to feel their vast importance. Nor are they at all insensible to the fulsome praises, bellowed forth by their equally vain attendants. At the close of the ceremony a variety of presents were made by each of the two, to His Majesty. It is expected that these will be returned tomorrow, with interest.[11]

This public display of wealth was one in a prescribed series of rituals undertaken by an aspirant to the supreme rank and title of ɔbirɛmpɔn (pl. abirɛmpɔn; lit. 'big man') and to the possession of the mena (syn. mmra: elephant tail), the coveted heraldic insignia of that exalted status. It was in fact one of the culminating acts in a mandatory sequence of events that extended over one entire adaduanan cycle. The whole was a ritualised mnemonic of crucial passages from Asante history. The candidate ɔbirɛmpɔn

- must exhibit his wealth publicly by presenting £9-6/- to all the Abrempons in Kumasi; and 10 pereguans (£80) to the King.
- He would then go to Tafo [a pre-Asante polity in the Kumase area] and pay £1-6/- to the chief there [Tafohene] who would give him an egg to throw against a silk cotton tree.
- He would then return to Kumase.
- He would then go to Essumja Santimanso [Asumagya Asantemanso south of Kumase, the place of origin of the Asante according to tradition] and buy a carpet (nsa) for £24 from the subjects of the chief [Asumagyahene] there. He must only dance on it and leave it after presenting the Essumjahene with another £24. Your going and coming expenses (including the £48) will cost you some 20 pereguans [£160].
- He would buy an elephant tail [mena] from the Assinhene (son of Essumjahene) [Asen Dominasehene] for £9-6/-.
- He would tie the elephant tail around the waist of one of his slaves and he must then past [sic] around the outskirts of the town [Kumase] lying on the leaves of a palm tree which have been strewn around the town, firing at his slave with blank fire from time to time. The slave falls down eventually and he then cuts the string to which the tail is fastened and takes the tail – then the ceremonies are completed and his people applaud him.

- Next morning he would get mashed yam mixed with 30 pereguans [of gold dust: £240] and be carried on a litter round the town of Kumasi scattering largesse of the yam mixture.
- On the following morning he would be carried in a litter with all his regalia, his skin plastered with white clay [*hyire*: a token of joy]. Then he would fix a spear [*pɛmɛ*: the weapon of the earliest Asante 'big men'] at Dwabirim (the market place) [Dwaberem] and challenge those of the same rank to remove it.
- After this he is called Brempon.[12]

Shortly before publicly displaying his wealth the aspirant *ɔbirɛmpɔn* performed the ritual of 'hunting the elephant.' In this mime (described above) a slave or subject was dressed as an elephant [*ɛsono*]. He was 'besmeared all over with chalk, holding in his hand a small tusk, which he occasionally applied to his mouth, and having an elephant's tail tied by a piece of string behind'. The hunter enacted stalking and shooting this 'elephant' and then took possession of the symbolically charged tail. The hunt took place 'according to usage' over a piece of land 'not far from Kumasi' that had been donated for the purpose by an individual who was himself of *ɔbirɛmpɔn* status. Afterwards, the recipient exercised tenurial rights over this tract and settled subjects on it. In so doing he became someone 'who lives on his own land with his own subjects', and by that token was 'known by the King as an Abrempon'. It was most probably at some point around the close of the first week of July 1844 – the likeliest date being the auspicious *kwadwo* (Monday, 8th) – that Kwasi Brantuo performed the ritual of 'hunting the elephant' prior to exhibiting his wealth in Kumase. The hunt took place over a piece of land that became thereafter 'Kwasi Brantuo's village' (*brantuokrom*) or Adeɛbeba.[13]

Adeɛbeba and the area around it just south of Kumase were a part of the Kaase chiefdom that was conquered and incorporated into the nascent Asante state in the 1680s by the first *Asantehene*-to-be Osei Tutu. Then, from the start of the eighteenth century land in this vicinity conveniently close to the Asante capital was used – and often parcellised and severally re-used – for the mime of 'hunting the elephant'. The historical complexities involved can be approached by looking at Adeɛbeba in conjunction with some other lands and villages within a three- or four-mile radius of it.

Fankyenebra (impl. 'a settling down on better land') was less than two miles west of Adeɛbeba. The site was a 'crossroads' (*nkwantanan*), a node of supernatural power that protected Kumase against surprise attack. In consequence, the forest surrounding Fankyenebra was called *ebia* (impl. 'maybe there is something there'). The whole area belonged originally to the *Baworo* stool, but during the eighteenth century parts of it were allocated to various *abirɛmpɔn* to 'hunt the elephant'. In the 1730s, during the reign of the *Asantehene* Opoku Ware, the *Baworohene* Poku Anakutini donated a tract of Fankyenebra *ebia* so that the *Antoahene* Opoku Agyeman might 'hunt the elephant' there and become an *ɔbirɛmpɔn*. A later *Baworohene* granted another tract to the *ɔheneba ɔbirɛmpɔn* Owusu Ba Dankyi, a son of the *Asantehene* Osei Kwadwo (1764–77); this particular donation was on the southern edge of Fankyenebra and abutted on the Santaase lands belonging to the *Atasomaasohene*. Like Fankyenebra, Ahodwo to the immediate south of the Adeɛbeba land was a place where *abirɛmpɔn* went to 'hunt the elephant'. The Ahodwo land belonged to the Kumase *Gyaasehene*, head of the *fekuo* of that name and occupant of the *Saaman* stool of Saawua. At least two incumbents of Kumase *Adum* – Agyei Kɛsɛɛ in the 1740s and (probably) his son Adum Ata in the early 1800s – 'hunted the elephant' over Ahodwo land grants.

Adeɛbeba (impl. 'a property where nature (lit. palm trees?) rewards effort') and Adeɛmmra ('a property where riches (cf. *mmra*) are to be obtained'), a scant mile to the west, were taken from the defeated *Kaasehene* and given by Osei Tutu to the Kumase *Akwamuhene/Asafohene ɔbirɛmpɔn* Awere. Shortly thereafter, in the early years of the eighteenth century, the *Denyasehene* Kwasi Aduonin displayed his wealth in Kumase before Osei Tutu in order to be recognised as *ɔbirɛmpɔn*. He 'hunted the elephant' over a section of the Adeɛmmra land awarded to him by Awere. He went on to found Adeɛmmra village on this donation and gave it into the care of one of his daughters so that he might be supplied with food in Kumase when he visited from Denyase in Amansie. A century later, in the reign of the *Asantehene* Osei Tutu Kwame, the *Akwamuhene/Asafohene ɔbirɛmpɔn* Kwaakye Kofi granted a part of the Adeɛmmra/Adeɛbeba lands at 'Darkwadwam' (later Dakodwom village) to the *Gyaasewahene* Opoku Frɛfrɛ when the latter performed the rites to secure the *mena*. Then at mid-century, during the tenure of the *Asantehene* Kwaku Dua, at least two historically identifiable office holders 'hunted the elephant' over land at Adeɛmmra/Adeɛbeba allocated to them for this purpose by the then incumbent *Akwamuhene/Asafohene ɔbirɛmpɔn* Akwawua Dente. One was the Kumase *Ankobiahene* Kwaku Tawia, who founded Akroasi village on his donation. The other was the newly promoted *Manwerehene* Kwasi Brantuo, who founded Adeɛbeba village on the land where he had 'hunted the elephant'.[14]

The larger purpose of personal wealth was communal wellbeing. Those honoured with the *mena* were enjoined and expected to 'put something back in' (*de sika yɛ nea ɔde mfaso bɛba*) for the benefit of others as well as themselves. Villages (*nkuraa*; sing. *akuraa*) founded on land donations (*adekyɛde*) given to 'hunt the elephant' rewarded and memorialised individual achievement but also substantiated and advertised social commitment. In Asante the creation of settlements signalled a virtuous dedication to increasing the stock of material and cultural capital on behalf of one's contemporaries and posterity. By the nature of things, however, some of these villages flourished

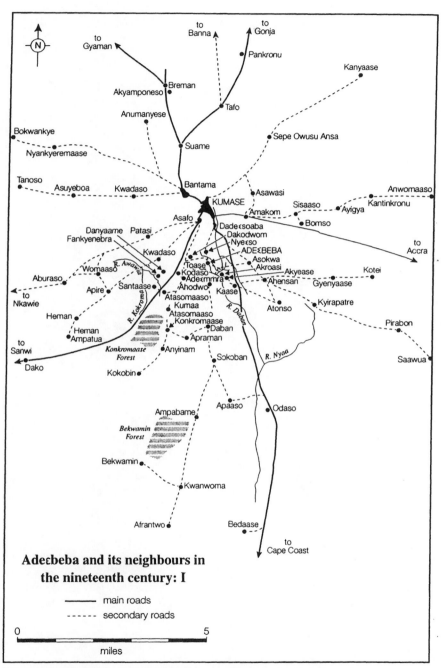

**Adeɛbeba and its neighbours in
the nineteenth century: I**

——— main roads
- - - - - secondary roads

0   5

miles

Map 2.1 Adeɛbeba and its neighbours in the nineteenth century: I

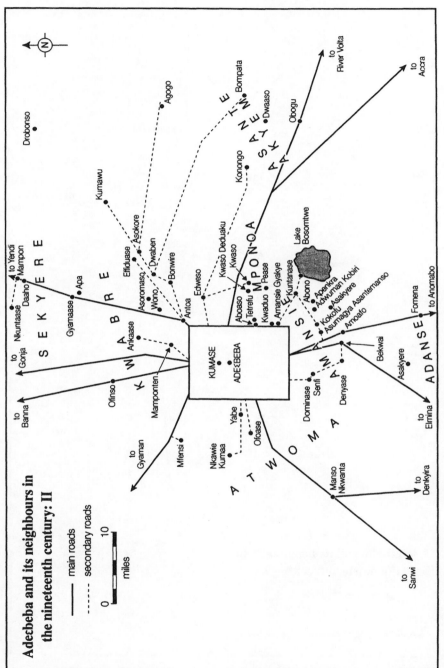

Map 2.2 Adeebeba and its neighbours in the nineteenth century: II

and grew while others stagnated and vanished. The village of Adeɛbeba was one of those that endured in an area that was a complex historical palimpsest of failed, erased and supplanted foundations. Even today *Manwere* tradition avows that *brantuokrom* was built over an earlier, long-vanished settlement; this is variously given as *oseikrom* (Osei's village) or the punningly similar *ɔseekrom* (*ɔsee*: 'ruins, to be in a state of ruin'), but without any further elaboration.

From 1844 until his death aged about seventy-five on 17 October 1865 Kwasi Brantuo paid frequent visits to Adeɛbeba. By report he used to ride there in his palanquin, surrounded by subjects and slaves chanting his praise names and playing his horn calls. In the mind's eye we can see Kwasi Brantuo on the path from Kumase via Kaase to Adeɛbeba, borne aloft amidst ten, twenty or perhaps more of his *nkoa*. He is being acclaimed *Nana Brantuo a otuo sika peɛ*, to signify a man of huge wealth; his horns are calling out in celebration of his good fortune *Akyampon Kwasi i, yɛsere wɔ twetwe, yɛsere wɔ twetwe twetwe* ('Akyampon Kwasi, you are the subject of mockery, indeed you are the subject of mockery'; that is to say, 'Once upon a time I was mocked because I was poor, but not now when I am wallowing in wealth'). He is accompanied perhaps by his favourite granddaughters', for it is his pleasure and conceit to watch these small girls playing amidst his accumulated gold dust at Adeɛbeba. Upon arrival in the fledgling village Kwasi Brantuo is helped down from his palanquin. He might eat there and go back to Kumase before dark; he might stay a number of nights (as he does increasingly in later life); he might inspect his farms and inquire after his crops; he might weigh his gold dust (*sika futuru*), give orders for the making of new regalia or ornaments, and pause to watch forge and bellows at work; he might call for and examine the *mena* he keeps in the village as mark and mnemonic of his achievement; he might take inventory of the valuables that he stores in trust at Adeɛbeba on behalf of the *Asantehene* Kwaku Dua, all the while reflecting on how, with the passage of the years, the royal infant that he once watched over as a 'baby nurse' has become the indispensable author and patron of his own good fortune. 'The King', it was recalled, 'promoted him Berantuo over all his other dignitaries, and consequently he became very rich. Only the King himself surpassed him in elegance.'[15]

Kwasi Brantuo might do any, all or none of the things listed above. But before any consideration of such pursuits there is the preliminary, as he dismounts from his palanquin, of being greeted by and reciprocally greeting the assembled people of Adeɛbeba. There is a salute of welcome: *dweaa Kumasekwaa a* ('here comes the handsome nobleman from Kumase'). Kwasi Brantuo's entourage responds: *me ne adehyeɛ na goro* ('my childhood playmates were royals'). An exchange such as this is mandatory, a matter of etiquette and social positioning, but it is also about virtue, reward and satisfaction. These are *his* subjects, the *nkoa* of *his* village, the people that he has resettled on *his* land to found Adeɛbeba and to make it prosper and grow for the good of all. In that same mind's eye, then, we can imagine Kwasi Brantuo looking them over – births and deaths, gains and losses – every time he comes to the village and gets down from his palanquin. To create a village takes people – *akoa te sɛ twɛrebo enni otuo ano a nyɛ ye* ('a subject is like a gun flint, for if it is absent the gun itself is useless'). Let us look now to the matter of the peopling of Adeɛbeba.[16]

There are clear and obvious lacunae in our evidence concerning the peopling of a small mid-nineteenth-century Asante village. That said, however, it is known that five identifiable groups of subjects were resettled at Adeɛbeba by Kwasi Brantuo. Possibly there were others, but these five endured and formed a demographic core and a nucleus for future population increase. At least two and perhaps three of them included kin of the *Manwerehene*.

Mention has been made of Kwasi Brantuo's Asoromaso and Heman connections. His matrilineal antecedents were members of an *asenɛɛ* lineage originally resident as subjects at Asoromaso in Kwabre, about fifteen miles north-east of Kumase. The *Asoromaso* stool itself was vested in an *atena* lineage. About 1740 a Mampon *atena* wife of the *Asantehene* Opoku Ware grossly abused and assaulted him. She and her kin were executed. The incensed husband then abolished her clan (*atena gu mbra*) throughout Asante and ordered all its component lineages to assume a *bretuo* identity. The *Asoromasohene* Kwaa Asare demurred and was heavily fined. To meet this obligation he sold most of his *asenɛɛ* subjects to the *Dadeɛsoaba* stool of Kumase, which in its turn disposed of half (*ɔfa*) to settle a debt to the *Nkwantanan* stool of Heman. Among those sold on was Kwasi Brantuo's maternal grandmother Afua Sie. She was living at Heman in the 1750s when she was given in marriage to the royal gun bearer Kwame Nkyera. Their daughter Akuntunku reinforced the Heman link when she married an *ahenkwaa* who was on close terms with the *Nkwantananhene* Boakye Yam Kumaa. Then, as we have seen, in or shortly after 1834 the *Asantehene* Kwaku Dua awarded Akuntunku's son Kwasi Brantuo a part of the Heman lands together with the servant Sebe. Following these gifts, Kwasi Brantuo petitioned to have his lineage kin at Heman transferred to his own jurisdiction from that of *Nkwantanan*. Kwaku Dua consented, and in or soon after 1844 Kwasi Brantuo removed a number of these Heman subjects to his new village of Adeɛbeba. By report the *Manwerehene* then said to his royal patron 'the half is not the whole' (*wo mfa ade ɔfa to mu ho*), an allusion to the retention of part of the Asoromaso people by *Dadeɛsoaba*. Again Kwaku Dua responded and Kwasi Brantuo was allowed to purchase descendants of the Asoromaso *nkoa* (including his own distant relatives) kept back by *Dadeɛsoaba* when the rest were transferred to *Nkwantanan* about a century before. Some of these people were then reunited with their remote lineage kin at Adeɛbeba.

The transplantation of these two groups involved a modest number of people. The evidence for this is fragmentary, but it does allow some cautious estimation. In 1945–6 a household survey was conducted in Adeɛbeba. In the course of this one Kwasi Dabo, an aged royal hornblower (*asokwani*) and elder paternal brother of the then incumbent Adeɛbeba village head (*odekuro*), testified that his maternal great-grandmother Afua Nimaako, her daughter Amma Donko, and ten others composed the entire Heman contingent relocated by Kwasi Brantuo. The Adeɛbeba resident Yaw Antwi Abayie confirmed this in 1951, declaring that his village was founded by less than a dozen people from Heman. But if the Heman immigrants were few, then their Asoromaso/*Dadeɛsoaba* counterparts were fewer still. Kwasi Yentumi, his wife and their four children formed the entire pioneering group. These people brought with them a shrine of the 'god' *atwere* ('the one who strikes'), which was connected with the celebrated manifestation of the same entity at Dwaben, four miles to the east of their own ancestral home at Asoromaso. In Adeɛbeba *atwere* lacked followers, and when Kwasi Yentumi tried to lord it over the people from Heman he was reminded that his family was outnumbered and so constituted the *benkum* (lit. 'the left hand') or inferior element in the population. The settlers from Heman saw themselves as the superior *nifa* (lit. 'the right hand'), by dint of their majority and because they claimed to have arrived first. This status was confirmed by Kwasi Brantuo when he invested them with the village headship. The making of any Asante village (*akuraa hyɛ ase*) was attended by arguments of the sort described, and these were revived whenever conflicts arose over precedence (*nea ɔdi biribi kan*). This was the norm, even in relations between the two immigrant kin groups of less than twenty people that established Adeɛbeba.[17]

In addition to pioneers from Heman and Asoromaso/*Dadeɛsoaba*, a third group of subjects from Wono was afterwards settled at Adeɛbeba. From the mid-eighteenth century onwards the majority of *nkoa* at Wono served the *Asantehemaa*. These included the *ama abaawa abusua*, an *asenee* lineage of Denkyira origin that supplied female fanbearers (*nkotimsifoɔ*; and note *abaawa*, 'maidservant') to the *Asantehemaa* and that appears to have been related to Kwasi Brantuo's antecedents at Asoromaso, barely two miles north of Wono. Whatever the precise nature of this connection, Kwasi Brantuo certainly acquired some of these Wono people – most probably after the disgrace and death of the *Asantehemaa* Afua Sapon in 1858–9 – and resettled a part of them at Adeɛbeba. By 1945–6 there were thirty-one self-identified adult descendants of this group living in Adeɛbeba. Their head (*abusua panin*) Kwadwo Konkoma stated that his lineage derived from only two families of original settlers. The link with Wono was still recalled, but it had become attenuated because 'the families there disintegrated and (were)

given to Ejisuhene Afrani'; that is, by the terms of the settlement that
concluded the civil wars of the 1880s the *nkoa* at Wono passed under the
control of the *Edwesohene* Kwasi Afrane Kɛsɛɛ.[18]

The Heman, Asoromaso/*Dadeesoaba* and Wono pioneers were few –
apparently no more than thirty in all – but they formed the overwhelming
majority among the earliest inhabitants of Adeɛbeba. A fourth group of
subjects transplanted to the village comprised only three adults. Yaa Atiwaa
and her two brothers had neither an actual nor a putative kinship
connection with Kwasi Brantuo. They belonged to an *asona* lineage that
originally served the *Saawua* stool. But this kin group was confiscated by the
Asantehene Osei Yaw and then awarded to the twins Ata Panin and Ata
Kumaa of Kwaso Deduaku. In 1844 these famously wealthy individuals
(*asikafoɔ*) were tried for murder and compounded their offence by angering
the *Asantehene* Kwaku Dua. He executed them, seized their property, and
thereafter allotted Yaa Atiwaa and her brothers to Kwasi Brantuo. They
served the *Manwere* stool in Kumase until Kwasi Brantuo sent them to farm
his land at Adeɛbeba.[19]

The fifth and final group of people who established Adeɛbeba were also
nkoa, but in the category of slaves rather than subjects. Numbers are
impossible to establish and identities are elusive. It is known that some of
the early settlers themselves acquired individual slaves, but the details are
sparse. The best-documented case involved two sons of the pioneer Kwasi
Yentumi, the custodian of the *atwere* shrine. These two were sent by Kwasi
Brantuo (or perhaps his successor in office) to trade kola for shea butter in
the northern savanna. At Yendi in Dagomba they acquired two slaves, a
man and a girl, and brought them back to Adeɛbeba. It was the girl's
reputation that lodged in collective memory. She was recalled as being
insolent and promiscuous. Her sexuality – she was said to have been highly
active and accomplished (*tumi to ni pa yi ye*) – provoked the young men of
the village and occasioned quarrels between them. Beatings failed to make
her docile and in the end she was sold on to one of her besotted lovers from
Kumase. Scandalised testimonies concerning this case are revealing in
general terms. It is evident that the girl was viewed as being somehow
ungrateful, with the implied corollary that slaves were treated well. This is a
moot point and one beyond the scope of the available evidence to resolve.
On the one hand, slaves were property and so were subject to slight, abuse
and exploitation. On the other hand, slaves possessed some minimal
purchase on jural rights and, more directly, worked alongside and lived
cheek by jowl with their owners. Social distance and personal intimacy were
both characteristics of the master–slave relationship.

A little more can be said about one type of slave in Adeɛbeba. In 1945–
6 it was severally claimed that war captives (*sa nneduafoɔ*) were added to the
village by its founder. If this was indeed the case, then the people in question

may have been northern slaves (*nnɔnkɔfoɔ*) allocated to Kwasi Brantuo's lot from the spoils of Asamoa Nkwanta's campaigning in Gonja. Be that as it may, the earliest body of enslaved prisoners of war at Adeɛbeba that can be identified with confidence was captured in the trans-Volta campaigns (1867–71). There were five of them and they came from Matse near Ho. One was a child who was given the Asante name Yafowa (cf. *ayimafowa*, 'a person of no importance'). He grew up to court and eventually to marry Afua Amoakwaa, a granddaughter of that Amma Donko who was among the Heman pioneers at Adeɛbeba. Their son Yaw Ankama, a well-to-do Kumase property owner and trader in dry goods (*nniema*) during the colonial period, supplied intriguing insights into his father's marriage to his mother. 'My father was not an Ashanti born,' stated Yaw Ankama, but he overcame prejudice and opposition to his suit 'as he was known to one and all as industrious.' More precisely, 'there was no supply of ready husbands at hand' and so the Adeɛbeba *odekuro* encouraged and sanctioned the match. Asante political authority had its own agenda, and this sometimes dictated a blurring of certain distinctions between slave and free subjects in the interests of social engineering. Subjects in the end were all producers, whether slave or free, and pragmatic forms of integration between the two groups within a village (*yɛ ɔkuw anaa akuraa bi fa*) forged interdependence and cooperation and hence increased work efficiency.

This last point raises a further one. Of the five identifiable groups of people that pioneered Kwasi Brantuo's village none was composed of *awowanifoɔ*, those put into mortgage (*awowa*) as security on a loan or surety on a debt. Pawnage was an endemic feature of Asante life, and pledged subjects were commonly a part – and sometimes a significant part – of many village populations. The presence of *awowanifoɔ* in settlements reflected politico-economic market realities. But though the practice of acquiring and resettling such people was widespread, it was still regarded with some scepticism by office holders in that it fell short of an ideal. Pawns were known collectively by the dismissive name *yɛmpɔw* ('we do not want you'), and a punning contrast was made between their status as people made to do all kinds of work (*nkwagyaafoɔ*) in one village while longing for redemption and restoration to their kin in another (*nkwagyefoɔ*). In short, *awowanifoɔ* were held to be difficult to integrate and commonly disruptive; communal harmony – *wo tiri ne wo ɔhonam ɛnyɛ wo ya bio* ('head or body won't pain you any more') – was easier to achieve when they went back where they came from. An office holder who created a village preferred to have only his own subjects and slaves working his own land. In practice this was a remote ideal for all but the wealthiest and most influential. Kwasi Brantuo was one such person because of his access to the favour and patronage of the *Asantehene* Kwaku Dua. As a result the people and land at Adeɛbeba were his alone (*ɔdede*), in that both were free and clear of any encumbrance (*nea gye asabawmu*). The peopling of Adeɛbeba village achieved a desirable but elusive goal – *manya ɔde na manya aburo* ('I have got yam (*nkoa*), but no corn (*awowanifoɔ*)').[20]

PIONEERS: MAKING A SETTLEMENT AT ADEɛBEBA,
1840s–1880s

What was life like for these pioneering settlers and their children? This question can be answered in some historical detail – in part at least, and for certain spheres of daily activity – without a constant recourse to ethnographic generalisation. The portrait that follows hews closely to the lines taken by the available evidence. It aims at salience and texture rather than comprehensiveness. Not the least part of any attempt to breathe a controlled imagining into the surviving record must be the frank acknowledgement that many gaps that exist are unlikely now to be filled.[21]

That duly noted, let us look first of all to the shaping imprint of that larger world of power and ultimate disposition that was centred around the *Asantehene* and his office holders in Kumase. It was this world that decreed Adeɛbeba and enfolded its inhabitants. In its foundation the village was first and foremost a political creation. It was intended, indeed designed, as locus and emblem of the soaring dignity of Kwasi Brantuo as *ɔbirɛmpɔn* and *Manwerehene*. However (and for reasons explored in due course), the political destiny set out for Adeɛbeba failed to translate from the proleptic to the actual. Unlike its near neighbour Saawua, for example, Adeɛbeba never fully realised itself as an *ɔbirɛmpɔn* town. Its status as mnemonic site of Kwasi Brantuo's achievement was fragmented and for a long time dissolved in the vicissitudes that overtook the *Manwere* stool and then Asante itself in the later nineteenth century. Dissonant consciousness of this blighting, of an exalted future lost somewhere in a stricken past, runs like a thread through many of the testimonies collected in Adeɛbeba in the twentieth century.

Something of this can be seen in accounts of the endemic rivalry of Adeɛbeba with Atasomaaso (Atasomanso), a scant mile to the south-west. Atasomaaso was an old village, settled by *bretuo* immigrants from Adanse. Its rulers fought with distinction in the wars that created and enlarged Asante, and were rewarded with the titles of *abirɛmpɔn* and the dignity of 'soul washers' (*nkradwarefoɔ*) to the *Asantehene*. But nineteenth-century Atasomaaso was something of a backwater that traded on past glories, and particularly so after the *Atasomaasohene* Daabra Kwakwa was executed for peculation by the *Asantehene* Kwaku Dua and the stool lost its land along the Daban river as a result. Certainly, no nineteenth-century *Atasomaasohene* enjoyed the wealth or prestige of Kwasi Brantuo; and unlike the *Manwerehene*, as Adeɛbeba folk liked to recall, the *Atasomaaso* stool was not a *fekuo* head but instead 'followed' the *Adumhene* in the Kumase *Akwamu fekuo*. But Atasomaaso was home to numbers of royal *nhenkwaa*, and this and its history lent it an air of consequence that was resented by its Adeɛbeba neighbours. Indeed, Adeɛbeba touchiness about what was construed as the presumptuous vainglory (*ahuhude*) of Atasomaaso became sedimented into platitude, to be dragged out and repeated on the many occasions when the two villages quarrelled over farm boundaries or marriage payments. Akosua Ababio, a trader from the Heman group at Adeɛbeba, gave voice to this litany of stereotype and complaint.

> I married from Atasomanso because of my mother's brother. My husband's people did not want my marriage. Atasomanso people are too proud and bite others like the tsetse fly. They think they are ruling the roost and put on airs. This Atasomanso was very full of Prempeh's people [royal *nhenkwaa*] who liked to lord it and swagger [their] conceit. But the town is only very little. It is underneath Adum [the Kumase *Adumhene*] but Adiebeba is big man [i.e. *ɔbirɛmpɔn*] town. No love is lost with this Atasomanso. The inhabitants there are seeing themselves better than anybody. Though the place is not a big one it is lordly to look down on us and none (of us) enjoys our fufu [food] there. None knows why they go on singing this song at us. Our ears never hear it because this Adiebeba of ours is better in all regard and attention can never be given to boasters with airs and graces.[22]

Views of a comparably sour kind informed comments on Asokwa and Kaase to the east, settlements that had the great good fortune to be on the Cape Coast–Kumase main railway line after 1903. Unlike Adeɛbeba, so the villagers there felt, such places had only prospered by ceasing to be truly Asante. In terms of this ideology of defensive insecurity, authenticity and stagnation went hand in hand, for the enviably 'monied people' in Asokwa and Kaase were immigrant parvenus, and it was these and not 'true natives of the soil' who were busily putting up modern dwellings to proclaim their success. Adeɛbeba countered its long-term failure and marginalisation by making strident appeals to history. By the mid-twentieth century it was asserting a spurious connection with Komfo Anokye, retrojecting itself ever further into a sanctified past that long preceded its own existence in an anxious attempt to shut out a clamorous present that was passing it by.

> A tree stands at the outskirts or boundary of this village of Adiebeba. It is an old tree worn down with age and decay. When the tree falls down tender green shoots of the same tree sprout back up as bigger trees. The tree has lived for centuries since Ashanti began and it lives still. A white cloth is tied to this tree to show reverence and respect to the planter. Every year the tree is given a sheep and food. The tree is adored. Okomfo Anokye planted the tree to make Adiebeba. It is said in fact that he did not plant the tree but made a bonfire to show a place

where he performed a miracle for Osei Tutu. He placed a stick on the
bonfire. The stick grew and grew into this present great tree. The miracle
was done and Adiebeba was brought into its existence by Anokye.[23]

'K.B.'[24] who supplied this story later admitted that it might not be true, but
clearly implied that it ought to be. Adeɛbeba, he declared, was 'a historic
place' and 'a part of the greatness of the Ashanti past in the times of Osei
Tutu and Okomfo Anokye'. Its relative decline in the nineteenth century
and underdevelopment in the twentieth, it was suggested, were attributable
to its adherence to a self-conscious understanding of the value of custom,
tradition and history. The past might have become another country
elsewhere in mid-twentieth-century Asante, but not in Adeɛbeba. But we
are getting ahead of ourselves. None of these thoughts were in the minds of
the pioneers of the 1840s as they set about making *brantuokrom*, at once a
fitting memorial to the attainments of the *Manwerehene ɔbirɛmpɔn* Kwasi
Brantuo and a viable home for themselves and their posterity.

Adeɛbeba village was established at the northern edge of the land grant
made to Kwasi Brantuo. Proximity and access to Kumase determined the
location. Thus, the land that supported Adeɛbeba lay to its south, in a fan
shape depending from the apical point formed by the settlement. The soil
was a rich, sandy loam, shallow and light rather than deep and heavy, and
quite well drained except along the runs of the lush, swampy valley bottoms
formed by the Ataso, Daban, Sasa, Nswatem and Woahyae rivers. Once
cleared, this was good, reliably watered farmland, but its soil and drainage
encouraged some crops rather than others. Thus by the later nineteenth century Adeɛbeba was a specialist grower of shallots (*gyeene*; *Allium ascalonicum*)
for the Kumase market; but in the twentieth century cocoa initiatives failed,
excluding the village from the benefits (and setbacks) of this sovereign
colonial cash crop, and driving local people stubbornly interested in its
profitability to emigrate to Ahafo. Another feature of Adeɛbeba was its lack
of big trees and their timber. Twentieth-century residents blamed the
firewood needs of precolonial Kumase, but in more sanguine moments
admitted that the problem lay in the sandy soil with its overlay of rotted
vegetation. This was ideal for ground, bush and stunted shrub cover as well
as rapidly growing sapling trees, but it inhibited any proliferation of true
forest giants. In the folk memory of its farmers Adeɛbeba was 'all bush and
weeds and streams and barely any trees of good size'.[25]

The Adeɛbeba land grant was sub-divided into five areas by Kwasi
Brantuo. As the villagers cleared and planted they gave each of these a
name. By common consent the most fertile area was *dodow* (lit. 'eat it until
you are sick'), an elongated north–south depression centred between the
shallow valleys of the Daban and Woahyae rivers. The oldest food farms at
Adeɛbeba, notably including those earmarked for the support of Kwasi

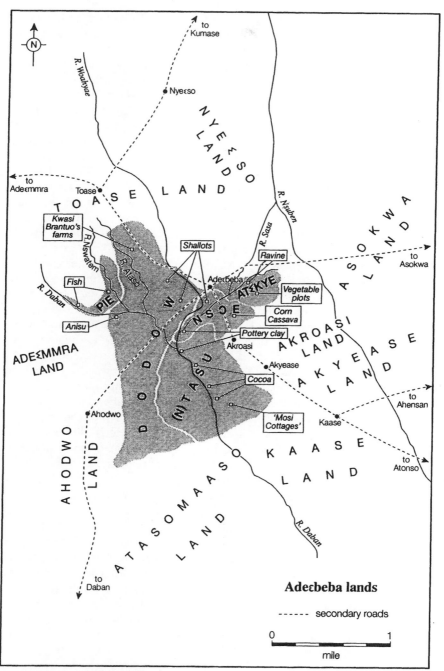

to
Kumase

R. Woahyae

Nyeɛso

N Y E Ɛ S O
L A N D

T O A S E   L A N D

to
Adeɛmmra

Toase

R. Nsuben

R. Sasa

A S O K W A
L A N D

to
Asokwa

Kwasi
Brantuo's
farms

R. Nswatem

R. Alaso

Shallots

Ravine

Adeɛbeba

ATƐKYE

Fish

PIE

NSOE

Vegetable
plots

AKROASI
LAND

R. Daban

Anisu

Corn
Cassava

D O D O W

Pottery clay

Akroasi

Akyease

A K Y E A S E
L A N D

ADEƐMMRA
LAND

(N)TASU

Cocoa

 Ahodwo

'Mosi
Cottages'

Kaase

to
Ahensan

A H O D W O
L A N D

K A A S E

L A N D

to
Atonso

A T A S O M A A S O
L A N D

R. Daban

to
Daban

Adeɛbeba lands

- - - - - secondary roads

0   1

mile

Map 2.3 Adeɛbeba lands

Brantuo's Kumase household, were established in *dodow* at its northern-most point along the run of the Ataso stream towards Toase. Most of the land and then the farms here belonged to the Heman settlers. Clearing *dodow* was backbreaking work, and it was still going on into the 1880s when Kwabena Donko's uncle sent 'two slaves, a man and boy, to clear roots and pick rocks out of the ground'.[26] In fact, *dodow* was never fully brought under cultivation. The parts of it closest to the rivers were frequented by lovers, even though the shady declivities there were said to be the home of 'little people' (*mmoatia*). They were also a childhood playground, and fondly remembered as such by old men and women in the mid-twentieth century.

Some of the Heman people, including the male (*odekuro*) and female (*obaapanin*) village heads of Adeɛbeba, and those from Asoromaso/ *Dadeɛsoaba* cleared and planted at *(n)tasu*. Two stories attached to this name. For some it meant 'a place to watch for game' (*tasu*), because of the dense thicket that originally covered the land. For others it denoted 'spittle' (*ntasu*), because it was recalled that when Kwasi Brantuo was marking out boundary trees (*ntɔmme*) there he drank a lot to combat the heat and con-stantly spat on the ground.[27] Be that as it may, *(n)tasu* was the southernmost part of the Adeɛbeba land. As such, it shared a boundary with Ahodwo to the immediate south-west and with Atasomaaso still further to the south. Dispute was a notable feature of the history of *(n)tasu*. Atasomaaso farmers encroached on it, and in the twentieth century it was prey to the attentions of migrant intruders from Saawua, Aboaso and Pirabon to the east. It was desirable to outsiders in its own right, but also because it was the gateway to the rich land at *dodow* with its easy access to Kumase and its markets.

Heman and Asoromaso/*Dadeɛsoaba* subjects at Adeɛbeba were allocated the most promising lands at *dodow* and *(n)tasu*. Other pioneers and later immigrants farmed the three less rewarding sub-divisions. The largest of these lay in the middle of the land grant. It was named *nsɔe* ('thorns'), because when people first came to clear it they were daunted by its densely entangled ground cover and observed: *se ye pɛ se yekotua sa asare no so a yɛ bɛyɛ den no ya tumi nsɔe nsɛ e no?* ('If we want to occupy this land, then how are we going to remove the thorns?'). In due course the thorns were removed, but this was never a very fertile area. Its food farms were relatively unproductive by Adeɛbeba standards. Corn was extensively intercropped here (because it gave two harvests in a growing year), and in the early twen-tieth century cassava came to predominate. This was indicative, for Asante consumers disliked cassava and tended to cultivate it on marginal land. A century after Adeɛbeba was founded its poorest inhabitants farmed *nsɔe*.

The other two areas marked out by Kwasi Brantuo were smaller than either *dodow*, *(n)tasu* or *nsɔe*. On the western side of Adeɛbeba where it abutted Adeɛmmra lay *pie* (lit. 'bulwark'), named not for its frontier position but for a particular method of trapping fish in stockades sunk into the beds of the Daban and Nswatem rivers. This area was indifferent farmland but rich in fish, and Wono subjects specialised in taking and trading the catch. Childhood reminiscences going back before the civil wars of the 1880s were detailed on the subject of fishing in *pie*. Thus, apart from stockades (used whenever rains flooded the rivers), nets, hooks, poisons and 'carrying off' (*ahweε*: draining to leave fish stranded) were employed at different seasons. Some seventeen types of fish were recalled by name, including *apatre, apasa, mmadeε* and *nkaayaa*, which were much sought after by the office holders and people of Kumase. Thus, Adeεbeba fishing families were able to barter for goods like cloth, salt and gunpowder and were well supplied with protein besides. Like other communities of this sort, *pie* folk were somewhat detached from their fellow villagers and followed a way of life that threw up its own traditions and heroes. Kwabena Domfe, a Wono settler, was a famously skilled fisherman who became part of Adeεbeba folklore. About 1870 the *Asantehene* Kofi Kakari's wife Sakyiamaa consulted the shrine of the *nyiaa ɔbosom* at Kyirapatre. A crocodile emerged from the Nyiaa river and attacked her. Kofi Kakari was perturbed by this inauspicious happening and ordered that the crocodile be caught. Several failed attempts were made until the second *Manwerehene* Kwasi Brantuo Kyei Kumaa suggested Kwabena Domfe. The *pie* fisherman travelled east to Kyirapatre and killed the crocodile with a mouse baited with poisonous seeds and 'medicine' (*hwe dufa*). The *Asantehene* rewarded Kwabena Domfe with gold and a slave girl, and the fisherman went home to *pie* and into legend.[28]

The last, smallest and least regarded of the five areas of land marked out by Kwasi Brantuo was *atεkye* ('swamp'). This was situated close to Adeεbeba village in the direction of Atonso and Ahensan to the east. Vegetable plots rather than farms predominated here, for apart from being waterlogged *atεkye* was little more than an unworkable ravine (*obon ketewa a mu dε yie*). The section nearest Adeεbeba was used as a village midden (*sumina*). Further south, it was recalled, slave labour was employed in the later nineteenth century to dig ditches (*nsuka*) in a forlorn attempt at drainage. This failed, and the slaves were sent to cut and gather sapling wood that grew in the shelter of the ravine slopes. This must have been exacting work – hot, wet, muddy and with the air full of biting insects – and it led to a tragedy. A slave boy called Aketekete (cf. *ketekete*: 'small, trivial') slipped on the incline and broke his neck. He belonged to the Heman pioneer Amma Donko, but died while working on loan to Wono people. Compensation was not forthcoming. Amma Donko prepared to go to law. But the case was never heard because the deposition of the *Asantehene* Mensa Bonsu (1883) threw Kumase into confusion. Without resolution there could be no reconciliation, and the matter of Aketekete was aired as late as 1932 in a land dispute between Amma Donko's daughter and the

Wono lineage elders. There is a suggestion in the evidence submitted then that a second boy was killed while working at *atɛkye*.[29]

Tales of the sort just recounted became embedded (and no doubt embellished) in the memories of Adeɛbeba villagers, in part because they stood out in a seasonal farming cycle of endless recurrences and repetitions. Clearing land for growing the staple crop association was undramatic work, but it was also protracted, arduous and labour intensive. Throughout the middle years of the nineteenth century, the limited (but steadily increasing) human resources of Adeɛbeba were fully engaged in establishing self-sustaining subsistence agriculture. Kofi Boaten of the Heman group created his first farm at *dodow* in the 1860s. Eighty years on his son Kwaku Adade reminisced about the travails experienced by his father.

> The cultivation of food farms was the only aspect of agriculture that engaged the attention of almost the whole of the Adiebeba people when my father when a young man made his first farm. The principal food crops were yams, cocoa yams, plantain, garden eggs, pepper and onions. My father stuck for ten years and more in making his farm. His land was all Kwaye [*kwae*: forest, wilderness] when he started. Roots and big stones were taken away. This was hard, hard work. Parts of the farm too were soaked with water. The water came back and the yams spoiled over again [*sic*]. My father persevered as what else could he do. But life was to be endured in those days as a farmer. My father never heeded any council of despair even when things mounted all the time against him. He took sustenance from all around him and everyone was in the same boat.[30]

Kofi Boaten and his farming neighbours finally produced surpluses that were part surrendered to the *Manwerehene* to support his Kumase retinue. Anything that then remained – what was termed 'over and above' (*nea ɛboro so*) – was used for bartering. Thus, for example, sheep were always scarce in Adeɛbeba. They were indispensable sacrificial animals, so villagers sometimes traded for one with nearby Adeɛmmra. This caused ill feeling. The vendors asked too much for sub-standard beasts, or so it was believed in Adeɛbeba, and Adeɛmmra became a byword for greed (*adifudepɛ*).

Adeɛbeba was not famed as a craft village, but it did acquire a modest reputation for one artifact that was bartered to obtain necessities and small luxuries from neighbouring settlements and itinerant pedlars. Pottery making was started, so it was said, by a daughter of the pioneer settler Yaa Atiwaa. Abena Takyiwaa began making pots in the 1860s using a shiny, mica-rich clay dug from the banks of the Daban river. Red clay (*ntwoma*) to polish the pots before firing was obtained from a site near the Heman lineage cemetery at Adeɛbeba. Abena Takyiwaa and the women she trained to work with her specialised in three sorts of pot: these were *apotoyowa* (for grinding vegetables), *ahina* (for carrying water or palm wine) and – most in demand – *aketekyiwamma* (for fumigating by burning herbs). None of these pots was blackened, for Adeɛbeba lacked sufficient wood carvers to provide ready supplies of dried chips (*nsensene*) to burn for smoking. The women potters traded their wares for cloth, shea butter and firewood in the nearby villages and as far away as Gyakye, Kwanwoma and Saawua. Once on her travels Abena Takyiwaa acquired a looking glass (*ahwehwɛ*) from a wandering Fante trader. This mirror caused a sensation in Adeɛbeba, and it became its owner's prized possession. Abena Takyiwaa passed it on to her elder daughter, and her daughter in turn still treasured it in the 1940s. By then Adeɛbeba pots had for long been an even more specialised business. In the early colonial period the women turned to the making of *nyankosoroma* ('God does not choose between people'), a complicated pot with a lid and apertures cut into it. This was in demand in Kumase, where it was seen as a decorative object by wealthy house owners. Latterly, it came to be used as an ornamental flowerpot by European and elite Asante wives.[31]

Nineteenth-century rural Asante was a localised society. Political structures and economic necessities bound people to the land and inhibited geographical mobility. Hence, as Adeɛbeba settlers laboured to make a community, their ties to the places they came from weakened over time and became exiguous. The practical realities of their lives were now centred in the new village and in sociabilities forged with the people of nearby settlements. Marriage patterns confirm this, and the volume of testimony about them underlines the significances attaching to local alliance and association in the context of procreation.

Adeɛbeba people followed custom in seeking to contract matrilineally exogamous marriages within their own settlement or among the kinship groups of neighbouring towns and villages. The Asante ideal was to marry within one's own village – *obi nware ne kuraamannii nnu ne no* ('nobody ever married a fellow villager and lived to regret it'). But this was not always possible, and particularly so in recently founded and sparsely populated places like Adeɛbeba. Acceptable compromise was sought in geographical proximity, for parents of marriageable children wanted to know as much as possible about putative partners and their kin, and in effect this meant alliances between settlements within convenient travelling distance of one another. By corollary, the Asante disliked 'stranger marriage' (*ahɔhɔ aware*) because it was difficult to gain information about and become familiar with the kin of an intended spouse who lived any distance away. Much evidence shows that Adeɛbeba folk shared in these general preferences and prejudices.

Once established, marital links with other villages tended to settle to an informal pattern of repetition that offered the reassurance of ever deepening knowledge and ever widening sociability. A tradition of marriages between Adeɛbeba villagers and those of neighbouring Ahodwo, Atasomaaso, Santaase and Toase was established early, amicably conducted (on the whole) and certainly valued by all participants. Stereotypes emerged from experience to guide Adeɛbeba families and their eligible children. Toase *nhenkwaa* (all royal gun bearers) made satisfactory husbands, but Ahodwo men tended to like girls more than marriage. Santaase women were said to be modest and obedient, but their Atasomaaso counterparts inclined to haughty or shrewish behaviour. The Adeɛbeba perception overall was that Santaase was the most reliable source of marriage partners and, for better or worse, this link was esteemed above any other. It was also said in Adeɛbeba that Santaase returned the compliment, but in the absence of evidence this remains unsubstantiated.

Santaase was nearly three miles south-west of Adeɛbeba. It was an eighteenth-century foundation with complicated allegiances. It was created by the *Asantehene* Osei Kwadwo (1764–77) for royal *nhenkwaa* who had resided first in the Kumase ward of Akyeremade, then on land allocated to them by the *Atasomaasohene* at Atasomaaso Kumaa and last at Santaase itself. Part of the Santaase land belonged to the Kumase *Ankobiahene*, and his subjects farmed there alongside tenants (*nea ɔte afuo mu anaa asaase so tua ka*) who served the *Oyoko Bremanhene*. But the Santaase *odekuro* himself and the *nhenkwaa* on the land served the *Asantehene* as members of the Kumase *Gyaase fekuo*. These royal servants were caretakers – builders and renovators of the Kumase palace, and it was with them and their female kin that the Adeɛbeba villagers entered into a succession of marriages.

Adeɛbeba families still valued the link with Santaase in the 1940s, and by then it was a historic one. The following case – one of a number – illustrates the matters at issue. The Santaase *ahenkwaa* Yaw Gyimaakye served the *Asantehene* Mensa Bonsu (1874–83) in the intimate role of doorkeeper of the bedchamber (*dabini*). In later life he married Abena Agyeman, a granddaughter of that Amma Donko who was among the pioneering Heman *nkoa* at Adeɛbeba. The marriage produced five children. Two were girls and both grew up to marry at Santaase. Then a daughter of Yaa Akumaa, the younger of these sisters, was herself courted unsuccessfully by a succession of Santaase suitors in the 1930s. Afua Tweneduaase, the girl in question, was accounted a great beauty (*ɔhoɔfɛfo*). Eventually she married a rich trader from Apa in Mampon and went to live with him in Kumase. This union was contracted against the wishes of her Adeɛbeba kin despite her husband's money. Family and lineage pressured Afua Tweneduaase to marry at Santaase 'for the keeping up of relations' with the people there. She flatly and repeatedly refused. When she married she was accused of eloping (*guan kɔware baabi*) out of greed and selfishness. In her turn she countered that in 'this modern age' she could and would marry whom she liked. Her mother and others deplored the morality of the young, but Afua Tweneduaase never came back to Adeɛbeba.[32]

Testimonies make it plain that the upkeep of marriage ties between Adeɛbeba and other villages was important to people. Such links helped to define the identity of *brantuokrom* by enmeshing it in localised networks of belonging. At the personal level, the generalised social fact of marriage provided an arena in and through which individual men and women expressed emotion and negotiated the affective dramas of daily life. There was an autonomy of self-representation within marriage that was not available to individuals to anything like the same extent when they negotiated their position within the densely populated field of kinship with its prescriptive determinations and ascriptive roles. In marriage the enjoined axioms of amity that arbitrated primary, enduring, often stifling relations with kin were exposed to a freer interrogation by feelings of personal like and dislike, love, hate or indifference. Such areas of human life are elusive of detailed historical recovery, and indeed the Adeɛbeba evidence only rarely yields up insights at this level. But when it does it casts a searchlight over the existential fragments of individual lives. Two narratives of Adeɛbeba married life are cases in point.[33]

During the civil wars of the 1880s a young woman named Akyaa fled Adeɛbeba for Gyenyaase, about four miles away to the east. Most Gyenyaase people were subjects of the *Saaman* stool and as such had strong links with Saawua. Whatever precipitated Akyaa's flight, it is reasonable to infer that she was connected to the Saawua element in Adeɛbeba's population and that she was looking for help from kinfolk at Gyenyaase. In the event she stayed in Gyenyaase and married there. By this union she had two daughters, one of whom died in infancy in spite of Akyaa's anguished supplications to the shrine of *asianka* ('make me stay') at neighbouring Kotei. Then about 1890 one Kwaku Ntoba of Adeɛbeba petitioned his overlord the *Manwerehene* Kwaku Kra to take steps to restore to him his betrothed Akyaa or otherwise to secure for him some compensation for his loss. Kwaku Ntoba went so far as to suggest that Akyaa was a victim of wartime kidnapping who was being held against her will. He swore an oath to this effect. The matter now came before the *Asantehene* Agyeman Prempe, who summoned the principals and other interested parties to appear before him. A hearing took place, but no account of it has survived. However, the upshot was that Akyaa was ordered to return to her Adeɛbeba home but refused to comply. Instead she fled eastward once more, taking her surviving child Yaa Afeni with her into Asante Akyem. Mother and daughter settled in Bompata. Akyaa worked there first as a hawker and then as a seamstress. Yaa Afeni grew up, married a Konongo cocoa buyer and had four children by him. When he died in 1918, she returned to her mother. Then Akyaa herself died in the 1920s. Yaa Afeni relocated to Kumase and

established links with her maternal kin at Adeɛbeba. Looking back, she said
that her mother had run away from home 'because of her bad treatment by
being force [*sic*] to marry against her will to someone (presumably Kwaku
Ntoba) she did not like'. She continued that her mother had been happily
married to her father at Gyenyaase and had 'felt it keenly to the last of her
days' when she was panicked into quitting that place (and her husband?)
from fear of being restored to Adeɛbeba. In Asante Akyem, Akyaa 'told to
me she would like to end her days alone better than to go to Adiebeba'.[34]

Unlike his younger contemporary Akyaa, Kofi Yankyira spent much of
his life in his natal village of Adeɛbeba. Both of his parents were pioneer
settlers. His mother was from the Wono group while his father was one of
Yaa Atiwaa's brothers from its Saawua counterpart. When Kofi Yankyira
reached adulthood in the 1860s, he asked his fellow 'youngmen' (*nkwankwaa*; sing. *akwankwaa*) to help him build a house on the *dodow* side of
Adeɛbeba. When the time came to thatch this house, people gathered to
offer aid and advice. Among them was Kwame Amofa, a son of the
Asoromaso/*Dadeɛsoaba* settler Kwasi Yentumi. He had with him a slave girl
acquired from a trader returned from the north. She was called Asemnyinaa
('every thing (on earth comes from god)') and Kofi Yankyira was immediately smitten. But Kwame Amofa refused to sell the girl. Kofi Yankyira
pleaded to the point of making a fool of himself (*gyimi*). His embarrassed
father now set about trying to find his lovelorn son a suitable wife, but all his
suggestions, cajolings and threats fell on deaf ears. Kofi Yankyira flatly
refused to marry and nursed his infatuation. Then Asemnyinaa died. Talk
about Kofi Yankyira faded away but he remained unwed. It was years later
in the 1880s that he shocked his fellow villagers by suddenly marrying
Abena Boatemaa, a young 'priestess' (*ɔkɔmfɔ ba*) who tended the shrine of
the *boa ɔbosom* at Konkromaase just south of Atasomaaso. It was reported
that Kofi Yankyira believed that the long-dead slave girl spoke to him
through his wife; when Abena Boatemaa was 'mounted' (*akɔm*) by her
ɔbosom, she addressed her husband with Asemnyinaa's voice and he 'babbled'
(*kasa kurokuro*) his responses. Whatever the dynamic involved, the marriage
was a happy one and produced three children. One of these named Kofi
Manu recalled that in old age his father used to sit in the evening in front of
the Konkromaase 'shrine house' (*ɔbosom fie*) waiting for Asemnyinaa to visit
him in spirit form (*anisoade*).[35]

The fundamental purpose of marriage was children, the comfort and
support of aged parents and the future of lineage and community. But the
evidence is scant concerning the specifics of childhood in precolonial
Adeɛbeba. Much of what there is commends the virtues of mothers and
grandmothers, a conventional piety but also heartfelt testimony to the very
real significance of such women in children's lives. 'My own maternal
grandmother Efua Kwakyiwa', said Kwame Amoa, 'took the best care of us

children and grandchildren and was ready at hand when illness struck';
Abena Sapon's grandmother was 'a very good story teller and singer' and a
paragon that 'we all of us when children liked for her kind attention to us';
the mother of Amma Ago (in her Christian daughter's remembrance) was 'a
heathen all her days but patient to hear and sympathetic'. But as was the
contrasting case generally throughout Asante, Adeɛbeba fathers and other
men were somewhat remote figures to children. The tenor and substance of
recollections concerning them differ from accounts of their female counterparts. Fathers and grandfathers offered affection, but this often came as a
part of the distancing framework of imparted pedagogies. In sum, adult
males taught and judged. 'Grandfather even when very old', said that same
Kwame Amoa just cited, 'was impatient with us as children if we were
heedless of his instructions and disrespectful in any way'; Kwasi Amponsa's
father came to visit his children in his wife's quarters and there 'told us what
was good for living in this world' and administered 'punishments as required'; this man's friend was Yaw Antwi whose own son remembered
being 'summoned to give accounts of all my doings when father called me'.[36]

Playing, exploring, learning, and helping in the house or on the farm were
staples of an Asante childhood in Adeɛbeba as elsewhere. There are
recollections of all these activities in general, but also sometimes in
particular. Thus, a favourite game of precolonial Adeɛbeba children was
ahenahene ('who is the king?'). This pastime mirrored the larger worlds of
adult power and behaviour and it worked to socialise through play.
Everyone took part and the experience was widely remembered.

> All the time we played at 'Ahenahene'. Everyone in the village took a
> part. Some were chiefs, linguists and 'Asafohene' whilst others were
> servants and stool carriers. I once 'married' a young girl to whom I
> gave crabs and meat and in return I was given dishes of Fufu in the
> evenings. It was the common practice of village children to organize
> miniature courts for the trial of cases and the punishment of offenders.
> Sometimes we chose an elderly man who was made the Chief and to
> him we brought our cases for settlement. The children met and all the
> complaints were gone into. The guilty were fined – sometimes they
> had to go to tap a pot of palm wine. This was a useful training and
> most children desired to have their cases tried instead of fighting or
> taking vengeance on their enemies. We played at this from morning to
> night or at any time when we were able. It was a thing children liked to
> do.[37]

At the other extreme from childhood and play was old age and death.
The degree to which death is present in memories of Adeɛbeba childhoods
is striking. Beyond accounts of commonplace imaginings – *sasabonsam*,
mmoatia and other monsters – there survived vividly detailed recollections

of what might be termed the social facts of death. Funerals, mourning, cemeteries and all the rest were remembered with a startling exactitude. Here is an account from 1945 of a funeral attended by the speaker in 1883 when he was a boy in Adeɛbeba.

> The funeral of my grand aunt Yaa Bɔm happened at Adiebeba when the Kumasi people were overthrowing King Bonsu [i.e. deposing the *Asantehene* Mensa Bonsu in 1883]. On the night of the previous day there was fasting by the relatives of the deceased. My father himself was wearing a dyed cloth so as to make 'Yerberu ayi' [*yerebru ayi*: 'preparing' the funeral]. Next day I saw my mother and the rest of the village women rending the air with lamentations. This was a moving rhapsody repeating with beautiful words the character of Yaa Bɔm so that everyone wept to see her depart. I was frightened and stood behind my older brother. The lamentation ended after fifteen minutes. Then there was a procession. The bereaved were covered with red clay. They walked not in an ordinary way but their hands were moving to and fro at their sides. They were singing 'Due asenee ɔba due' [*due asene ɔba due*: 'regrets, child of the *aseneɛ*']. During the day the youngmen [*nkwankwaa*] were drinking and calling out 'Ne mebo se asomorodwe' [*nne me bo asɔmorɔdwe*: 'I will drink all today as much as a thirsty beetle']. It came on to rain and the mourners became soaked to the skin. I fell down in the mud and wept for fright. Later on when the corpse was buried the rain was on again. The grave was already dug up and was filling all the time with water. I was not allowed to go to the cemetery for which I was grateful being frightened of the place as were all us children. Even now when I go and attend a funeral I think of Yaa Bɔm.[38]

It is time to pause and take stock. Recollections going back to the 1860s show that by then Adeɛbeba was an established village community. A clear proof of this status in Asante customary law can be dated to the tenures in office of the second *Manwerehene* Kwasi Brantuo Kyei Kumaa (1865–72) and of the third Adeɛbeba *odekuro* Akora Agyei. These two presided over what is said to have been the first transfer to outsiders of usufructuary rights in an area of uncultivated Adeɛbeba land. The land in question was a dried-up channel (*otugya*) of the Daban river in *dodow* with the unpromising name of *anisu* (lit. 'tears'). It was given over to *Saaman* subjects from nearby Toase who worked it on a tenancy basis in exchange for palm wine and firewood. The terms of the agreement between *Manwere* and *Saaman* were validated (*ɛyɛsaa*) in Kumase by the *Asantehene* Kofi Kakari. This could not have taken place unless Adeɛbeba was recognised as a village in law, with a devolved political authority exercising rights on behalf of the inhabitants over a demarcated area of land.[39]

In custom, membership in a village community as arbitrated by duly constituted authority was described by the term *kwannma ne (a)dwuma* (lit. 'permissions and injunctions': now often rendered by the Rawlsian 'rights and obligations'). These features were all at once *aman mmu* (immemorial custom), in that they described ethical norms of belonging, and *aman brɛ* (jural custom), in that they legislated actual rules of conduct. Inhabitants of an *akuraa* such as Adeɛbeba were expected to conform to both. But breaches occurred. Thus, soon before his death Kwasi Brantuo transferred a further group of subjects from Heman to Adeɛbeba. These people were originally resident at Apaaso, but were confiscated by Kwaku Dua and awarded to Kwasi Brantuo, who appointed them his stool drummers (*Manwere akyeremadefoɔ*). Trouble soon developed. It would seem that the drummers flatly refused to farm at Adeɛbeba and expected to be supported by others. They were thoroughly disliked but also feared because it was said that they had buried a dangerous charm (*bɔw*) in the village. Matters continued in this unsatisfactory way until the early 1880s when the then incumbent *Manwerehene* Kwaku Kra became persuaded that the Adeɛbeba *akyeremadefoɔ* were plotting to kill him. The alleged ringleaders were tried and executed. The *Asantehene* Mensa Bonsu impounded the remaining adults, mutilated them and exiled them to Ahafo. Kwaku Kra removed the surviving boys to Kumase to the relief and satisfaction of the other Adeɛbeba villagers. The episode became known as *adeɛbeba nkwankwaa nya asɛm oo! nya asɛm oo! oo!* ('young men of Adeɛbeba, you are really in big trouble') and passed into collective memory as a signal instance of anti-social behaviour. In short, it flouted the covenant of community.[40]

Little more can be added to what has been said about the peopling of Adeɛbeba. There were fewer than thirty pioneering settlers, inclusive of children but exclusive of slaves. In the early years these were joined by others such as the drummers and an unquantifiable but small number of individual slaves, pawns and runaways. In the early 1870s, a generation after its foundation, Adeɛbeba probably contained between fifty and one hundred inhabitants. By that time the landscape in which Adeɛbeba people lived and worked was explored, named and understood, if not wholly domesticated to use. By then too the fundamentals of custom and law that made Adeɛbeba viable as an *akuraa* – allocated, cleared and farmed land, localised political and lineage authority, established and expanding ties to neighbours, and the rest – were all matters of historical fact. Around this same date, as we shall see, an important 'god' (*ɔbosom*) manifested itself to the people of Adeɛbeba, setting a seal of a distinct kind on the status of the village.

Adeɛbeba was a small world of a kind replicated all over precolonial Asante. It was an endogenous community, busy over its square mile of territory with the cycles of its own agricultural and ritual affairs and preoccupied with parochial matters of birth, marriage and death. But settlements like Adeɛbeba were also the essential building blocks of Asante power and polity. Adeɛbeba after all was a small world commanded into being by a great world of affairs that lay only a few miles away in Kumase. During the lifetimes of the *Manwerehene ɔbirɛmpɔn* Kwasi Brantuo and the *Asantehene* Kwaku Dua, that great world looked upon Adeɛbeba with the interested oversight of proprietorship and patronage. But Kwasi Brantuo (1865) and then Kwaku Dua (1867) both died, and the great world changed, and the small world of Adeɛbeba and its people changed with it.

SUBJECTS: *MANWERE* AND ADEɛBEBA IN A TIME OF TRIAL, 1860s–1900s

On 17 October 1865 an eyewitness reported, 'the great-ensign Kwassie Brantuo died at Coomassee'. Between that date and 7 December some two hundred people were immolated in the funeral rites, the great number bearing testimony to Kwasi Brantuo's status and Kwaku Dua's regard. On 7 September 1866, a year later by the Asante *adaduanan* calendar, the final obsequies were performed for 'the great standard-bearer Akwasie Baantuo'. His stool was ritually blackened and kept at Adeɛbeba with other items of his personal regalia. Among these pieces was that known as *brantuo mpokyerɛ ne apa*, solid gold ankle and wrist fetters that Kwasi Brantuo ordered cast to symbolise the ties that bound him to Kwaku Dua. On his instructions, his remains were interred at *brantuokrom*. By report the mausoleum (*baamu*) was sited near 'the head of the village' (*tikuraa*) on the Kumase path because Kwasi Brantuo once pointed to a spot there and declared 'that is what I like' (*saa ne mepɛ*). The scene at Adeɛbeba can well be imagined, with the entire village turned out in mourning cloth as the remains were borne to their final resting place. At the last, emissaries were sent to Heman Ampatua to tell Kwasi Brantuo's ancestors that he had left to join them in 'the land of ghosts' (*asamandoɔ*).[41]

Kwasi Brantuo's successor in office was a son (actual or classificatory) of Amma Twumasi, the younger of his two full sisters. According to *Manwere* stool tradition, Kwaku Dua took an unusually close interest in the appointment and fully approved the choice. This was because the man selected was a nephew (and perhaps the only uterine one) of Kwaku Dua's childhood *ɔbagyegyeni* and lifelong associate. But an additional act of commemoration may also have been intended by the *Asantehene*. The man chosen to succeed was also a sister's son of the long-dead Amma Sewaa, Kwasi Brantuo's other full sister and a favourite wife of Kwaku Dua. She bore two children by him, but both died in infancy, and when she too then died (possibly in a third childbirth), her husband was grief stricken. Be all that as it may, the new *Manwerehene* assumed the stool name Kwasi Brantuo Kyei Kumaa (*kumaa*: 'younger, lesser'), most probably at Kwaku Dua's request and certainly to honour the memory of his great predecessor. This custom was institutionalised and later occupants of *Manwere* followed suit and commonly assumed 'the name Brantuo in honour of the first *Manwerehene*'.[42]

Soon after Kwasi Brantuo Kyei Kumaa was enstooled the *Asantehene* Kwaku Dua himself died on 27 April 1867. The royal funeral rites that followed were among the bloodiest in all Asante history. The huge number of victims (well in excess of a thousand) killed to honour Kwaku Dua *agyeman* ('defender of the nation') commemorated his longevity and authority, but the relentlessness, duration and savagery of the licensed violence that took place also vented underlying antagonisms. Virulent disputes surrounded the issue of the succession. But a semblance of consensus was finally arrived at and on 28 May:

> the Asante people made the appointment of a new King named Koffee Karkarie [Kofi Kakari] and he sat with the court and was carried by two slaves on their heads, and with all the gold emblems surrounding him ... and all the Captains of Asante in two parties, before him and behind him, went with him, walking around all the streets, and playing, to give thanks to all the people.[43]

Following this election, Kofi Kakari was enstooled as *Asantehene* on *monodwo* 26 August 1867. Reflecting afterwards on the conflicted circumstances that led to this happening, the *Asantehene* Kofi Kakari (1867–74) 'sometimes said that his ascendancy to the throne of Ashantee was like a dream to him'.[44]

Esteemed for his fiscal probity and good sense, the *Manwerehene* Kwasi Brantuo Kyei Kumaa was much troubled by the spendthrift ways of Kofi Kakari, nicknamed *akyempɔ* ('giver of largess, benefactor', but with the sense of buying popularity) and *ɔsape* ('prodigal', but with the sense of duplicity). The *Manwerehene* was by no means alone in thinking this, but he was the one who was finally galvanised to act when he became exasperated beyond endurance. His intervention proved fatal to himself, for interest and fear prevented anyone from supporting him. A very full and authoritative tradition recounts that 'one day' in 1872:

> Kyei, Manwerehene, who succeeded Brantuo, one of the King's Treasury keepers, and one of his principal advisers, found how the King [Kofi Kakari] was spending the money, and considering how his predecessor Brantuo himself and Nana Agyeman [Kwaku Dua], the late King, did wisely and vigilantly take time to accumulate the money in the Treasury, he humbly approached the King, to advise him. This is what he said: 'Nana, the Asante nation is very large, and it requires much money to manage her affairs, that is why there is a saying that the Asante nation is like a torn cloth, and it is sewn with gold. In time of peace or war, money is indispensable. This is the reason why your predecessors did accumulate so much wealth. But since your accession, no revenue comes to the Treasury; but money is withdrawn

almost daily in heavy drafts. Because of this, at the time of your election, many of your Elders opposed your election. Permit me, therefore, Nana, to advise you to check the spending of money in the Treasury.' The King, on hearing this, became very angry, and said: 'Why dare you come and tell me this? Why do you tell me not to spend the money which I have inherited from my predecessors? If you have any share in it, come and take your portion.' There and then the King sent for all the Elders, and told them that Kyei had come to tell him that at the time of his election, some of them opposed his election on the ground that he was spendthrift, and inquired whether this information was correct? The Elders swore in denial of any knowledge of what Kyei had told him. Kyei was therefore put in log [chained up], and was afterwards executed.[45]

The sub-text encoded within this retelling explains much. In effect, Kwasi Brantuo Kyei Kumaa publicly upbraided Kofi Kakari for being a feckless, inadequate and unworthy successor to Kwaku Dua. He criticised his defects as a ruler and as a man. He suggested there were widespread doubts about his suitability to occupy the Golden Stool. All this incensed Kofi Kakari. It challenged him as *Asantehene*, and was unpardonable for that reason alone. But it also humiliated him personally, for it struck home. In truth Kofi Kakari was insecure about his authority, and not least because the Kumase office holders all knew he had endured marginalisation, disrespect and even insult under Kwaku Dua. Thus Kwasi Brantuo Kyei Kumaa was certainly executed for offending the ruler, but he was also killed for disconcerting the man and embarrassing him before others.

These events were a disaster for the *Manwere* stool. Since it had been created and signally favoured by Kwaku Dua, the execution of its second incumbent served as a pretext for Kofi Kakari to wreak posthumous revenge upon his predecessor by dismantling its powers and prerogatives. The new *Manwerehene* installed by Kofi Kakari was Kwasi Kyei (Brantuo), nephew of his similarly named predecessor. He was the youngest child of his mother Abena Ako, herself the youngest sister of Kwasi Brantuo Kyei Kumaa, and he may well have been chosen because he was still a minor. In any event he was enstooled only to be immediately disempowered and sidelined. Kofi Kakari next turned his attention to the stools composing the *Manwere fekuo*. These were created by Kwaku Dua 'for his sons because there were many who did not like him at all', and in addition to forming a loyal cadre they constituted a following that bespoke the status of the *Manwerehene*. They were now disaggregated by design and default. In a mix of vengeful power and calculated insult, Kofi Kakari awarded two of these stools to his favourites and then further privileged his appointees. The 'soul washers' (*nkradwarefoɔ*) Yaw Bosommuru Tia and Kwaku Bosommuru Dwira were promoted to the offices of *Manwere Mmagyegyefoɔhene* and *Akomfodehene/ Nyameanihene* respectively, and then became the only *Manwere* representatives retained on the council of Kumase. The other stools composing the *fekuo* – *Asabi, Somi* and *Ayebiakyere* – became semi-detached as their holders took the hint and prudently elected to pursue autonomous careers in government.

Not content with having destroyed the institutional integrity of *Manwere*, Kofi Kakari also stripped out the bases of its material power. Kwaku Dua's transfer of treasury responsibilities from the *Gyaasewa* stool to *Manwere* was reversed. Most damaging of all in the longer run was the termination of that privileged access to wealth, land and subjects that Kwasi Brantuo had enjoyed under the patronage of Kwaku Dua. The *Asantehene* Kofi Kakari did not abolish *Manwere* (and perhaps felt that he lacked the support for such an extreme measure), but he left it hollowed out and crippled. In consequence its subjects and land were at increased risk of predation, for the *Manwerehene* no longer possessed the influence or resources to resist more. powerful office holders. This episode – the death of Kwasi Brantuo Kyei Kumaa and the behaviour of Kofi Kakari – is still counted as a catastrophe (*amane*) in *Manwere* tradition. In spite of the respect due to him as *Asantehene*, Kofi Kakari is privately given the character of death – *abɔ yen ti kwa twere kwa sen* ('he is the one who shaved our heads bare (leaving us nothing)'); and in a like manner he is alluded to in the *Manwere* horn call *ye waye n'anim osekyere wo* ('he is the one who is determined to ruin us (leaving us nothing)').[46]

The diminishment of *Manwere* was abrupt (and it was to last until the 1940s). The symptoms and effects of decline were apparent during the tenure in office of the fourth *Manwerehene* Kwaku Kra, a survivor of the civil wars of the 1880s, who was listed by the British as being no more than a 'Subchief of Gaasi (*Gyaase*)' when they imprisoned him for his part in the Anglo-Asante conflict of 1900–1.[47] Kwaku Kra was nicknamed *Kwaku Brantuo asae* ('Kwaku Brantuo the hammer'), and he was clearly a tough and resourceful man. He was among those office holders who carried Agyeman Prempe to military triumph and then enstoolment as *Asantehene* in the endgame of the civil wars. Afterwards, like many others and perhaps more than most, he hoped to be rewarded by the victor. But Agyeman Prempe was obliged to satisfy the demand for subjects and land from his powerful provincial supporters, and he did so at the expense of the Kumase office holders. In this bargaining process Kwaku Kra failed to redeem the position of his stool or *fekuo* and was humiliated in the attempt.

In 1888 a number of people fled to Kaase on the south side of Kumase to escape the fighting at the close of the civil wars. From there they sought refuge three miles to the east in the afforested Nyaa river valley near Kyirapatre. There they remained in hiding until the end of hostilities. Once peace was established, Kwaku Kra claimed five of this group as his subjects. He stated that all these people were kin to one another and farmed *Manwere* land at Heman. He further said that one of them named Kwadwo Bi was widely known to be his own personal messenger (*ɔbɔfo*). This was a strong case, for several witnesses recollected that during the recent military operations Kwadwo Bi had carried messages between Kwaku Kra and senior commanders. But the *Kumawuhene* Kwasi Krapa, one such general and an influential provincial backer of Agyeman Prempe, intervened to claim that Kwadwo Bi and his four relatives had been surrendered to himself by Kwaku Kra. The reason, it was said, was that the *Manwerehene* failed to reinforce Kumawu troops during the battle of Aboaso (1888), and finding himself unable to pay the fine imposed on the spot by an incensed Kwasi Krapa instead begged for mercy and gave up the subjects in dispute as compensation (*akatua*). But, Kwasi Krapa concluded, Kwadwo Bi and his kin had taken fright and fled. Against the burden of evidence, Agyeman Prempe gave these people to Kumawu after a hearing in which Kwasi Krapa reportedly insulted Kwaku Kra and the office he held. 'This Maweri [*sic*] is nothing', said the *Kumawuhene*, for 'the airs and graces taken up by this Chief of Maweri shows he is living in the past times. He is a small Chief now and could not pay me his debt.'[48]

No record has surfaced thus far of any immediate practical impact upon Adeɛbeba of the disgrace and death of the *Manwerehene* Kwasi Brantuo Kyei Kumaa. There must have been talk, speculation and even fear, but the small world of the village was ignored and left to its own devices by the great world of Kumase. This is not to say that the calamitous events of 1872 had no consequence in the longer term. In retrospect it can be seen that they ended any aspiration Adeɛbeba may have had that it would fulfil its destiny and become a large and prestigious town. Kofi Kakari simply abandoned it to the now crippled patronage of the *Manwerehene*, an overlordship that was to become attenuated to the point of virtual absence over the troubled years that lay ahead. But if villagers brooded on these matters at the time, then their attention – and that of the *Asantehene* – was swiftly redirected to more urgent concerns.

In 1873–4 the problems of the *Manwere* stool and the people of Adeɛbeba were engulfed in the national trauma of war and foreign invasion. On 31 January 1874 British forces, advancing northward from the Bosompra river along the main Cape Coast–Kumase road, defeated the Asante army at Amoafo, eighteen miles south of Kumase. Then on 4 February concerted Asante military resistance was broken at Odaso, seven miles south of the capital. British troops then advanced via Kaase to occupy Kumase from 4 to 6 February before commencing their withdrawal towards the Gold Coast. These days from 31 January to 6 February delivered a series of seismic shocks to the *Asanteman*. The *Asantehene* Kofi Kakari himself managed to elude capture, but over the course of a single week Asante troops suffered unprecedented military reverses on their own territory. These defeats culminated in the unthinkable – the seizure, looting and burning of Kumase by a foreign power.

The impact of these tumultuous days was felt across Asante, but most palpably along and nearby the line of the British advance via Amoafo, Odaso and Kaase to Kumase. Villages in this circumscribed area immediately south of the capital were in a war zone. They served as depots and assembly areas for Asante troops. They were sometimes the sites of skirmish and destruction. Above all, they were electric with the alarming reports and rumours of war. All this is sketched as background to military operations in the British sources. But it is the detailed foreground of Asante recollection. Thus the historic settlement of Ampabame, seat of a senior office holder in the Kumase *Kyidom fekuo* and a bare mile west of Odaso, was left abandoned as its people fled to seek refuge with their kin in afforested Bekwamin to the south-west. In like manner, the small village of Daban south of Atasomaaso was evacuated as its people vanished into the surrounding bush. Toase, very close to Adeɛbeba, was left empty after the *Toasehene* Ampofo was killed in battle.

Adeɛbeba itself is unmentioned in the British accounts, for it lay to the west of the line of advance. The path that linked it to Kaase still cut through sparsely farmed secondary forest in the early twentieth century. But if Adeɛbeba escaped actual fighting, it still suffered the shocks of being located within the intensely disordered area that was the cockpit of the war. The little evidence there is suggests great anxiety but no outright panic in Adeɛbeba. Some inhabitants temporarily withdrew to Apire, a village three miles to the west that contained *Manwere* subjects. Others removed to their farms and hunting camps. But the majority simply stayed put. Two things in particular about these fraught days lodged in the collective memory of Adeɛbeba. First, it was said that the 'god' *atwere* – brought from Asoromaso/Dadeɛsoaba to Adeɛbeba in the 1840s – had predicted that Kumase would fall to the British. It instructed its custodians to 'take it home', presumably to Asoromaso (or even Dwaben). In the event this injunction was not acted upon and *atwere* remained with its custodians in Adeɛbeba. But after this *atwere* was seen to 'weaken', becoming uncommunicative and finally 'dumb' (*mfum*). It only resumed its cooperative intercourse with the villagers several years after the war when the *Asantehene* Mensa Bonsu sent it a gift of sheep from Kumase. Second, at some point in the fighting a story circulated that the *Manwerehene* and a number of his men had been killed. This proved false, and in Adeɛbeba people rejoiced at the safe return of those believed dead.[49]

Information about Adeɛbeba in the 1873–4 war is scarce, but a story that became firmly rooted in village lore attaches to its aftermath. Adwowaa

Bemba was one of the Wono subjects at Adeɛbeba. She had a daughter named Yaa Kuruboaa. The girl was of marriageable age and comely. It was said that she was told by so many suitors that she looked pretty (*wo ho ayɛ fɛɛ paa*) that she was nicknamed Yaa Fɛfɛ (*fefɛ*: 'beautiful'). Just after the 1873–4 war a party of royal *nhenkwaa* from Kwaduo near Amansie Gyakye passed via Adeɛbeba on its way up to Kumase. The men were joiners and carpenters (*duadwumfoɔ*), summoned perhaps to repair war damage to the royal palace. Yaw Ahenkora was their leader and he had with him his young nephew Kwadwo Anin. This boy and Yaa Kuruboaa fell in love. Yaw Ahenkora was furious because he had already selected a Kwaduo bride for his nephew. Hot words were exchanged, and Yaw Ahenkora forcibly took his nephew away with him to Kumase. As a parting shot he cursed Yaa Kuruboaa and called down evil upon her.

It was during the *asafo agyei kɔ* (the Kumase–Dwaben war of 1875) that Yaa Kuruboaa fell dangerously ill. Her alarmed mother and kin were convinced that the girl was wasting away because of the evil curse (*nnome*) laid upon her by Yaw Ahenkora. Doubly worrying was the knowledge that Kwaduo was home to the potent *abatena ɔbosom* (cf. *aba a tena ase*: 'now that you have come you really must stay'), a 'god' with a wide reputation and a notoriously malevolent streak. It used a key (*safe*) to open people to its influence and then a padlock (*kradua*) to seal itself within them. Its speciality when offended was *kwaterekwa* (lit. 'stark naked'), a stripping away from a person of health, money or anything else of any value. Consulted by the *Asantehene* Kofi Kakari, Kwaduo *abatena* was much more extensively employed by his brother and successor Mensa Bonsu to search out the gold of rich men (*asikafoɔ*). In sum this was a frightening adversary and Adwowaa Bemba was determined to plead with it to relinquish its grasp on her daughter.

Accompanied by relatives, Adwowaa Bemba travelled the eight miles south-east from Adeɛbeba to Kwaduo. There she discovered that Yaw Ahenkora belonged to the lineage that supplied 'priests' (*akɔmfoɔ*) to *abatena*. This must have come as a shock, but the Adeɛbeba delegation pressed ahead with its mission.

> My mother came before the Fetish Abotena to pacify it. He spoke that he would kill Ya Kruboa [Yaa Kuruboaa] as she is bewitching his beloved child [Kwadwo Anin]. Mother cried out weeping to say she will give the Fetish any amount of things to stop from its killing. Abotena fetish linguist [*ɔkyeame*] spoke that 'The Fetish will kill your daughter unless you are paying 12/6d as sheep so she will be soon cleansed.' It was a lot but mother promised to go back to get it if it (*abatena*) will stop from its killing her daughter. It was agreed by all parties that mother was to bring the pacification and drinks to seal it all in a few days. At that she bade farewell to Akwaduo and took the road to home.[50]

We can well imagine that Adwowaa Bemba returned to Adeɛbeba as quickly as she could. We can equally well imagine her feelings when she reached home only to discover that Yaa Kuruboaa had died while she was in Kwaduo. But there was no time for grief and mourning. Everyone in Adeɛbeba believed that the girl had been killed by Kwaduo *abatena*, and custom in such a case ordained that the body should be 'thrown away somewhere' (*too gu*) without any funeral rites being performed. Adwowaa Bemba pleaded for Yaa Kuruboaa to be buried properly, but the community had already disposed of the corpse so as to protect the village.

This harrowing episode became part of Adeɛbeba's oral history, as widely recalled as it was richly detailed in the retelling. Some testimonies suggest that an attempt was made to seek compensation from the Kumase *Dadeɛsoabahene*, the overlord of Kwaduo, but if this did happen then it would seem that it came to nothing. Yaa Kuruboaa's melancholy fate became the subject of a song (*nnwonkorɔ*) that was still sung by Adeɛbeba women in the mid-twentieth century. Adwowaa Bemba's appalling experience led her to question and then abandon the Asante *abosom*. She was one of the earliest Wesleyan-Methodist converts in Adeɛbeba and was baptised Martha. She remained staunch in her Christian faith until her death at an advanced age during the First World War.[51]

British penetration of the Asante heartland in 1873–4 was traumatic but of short duration. Recovery in the Kumase area was correspondingly swift. The rhythm of daily life in villages like Adeɛbeba was quickly restored. But peace and normality did not last. Within ten years royals and stool holders plunged Asante into civil wars (1883–8) that opened the way to and facilitated British colonial intervention (1896) and annexation (1901). The evolution of high politics during this period was immensely complex but it has been severally construed and is understood in detail. Less studied is the impact of this time of unparalleled trial upon ordinary Asante lives. In popular memory the whole period is known by the allusive terms *basabasa* ('confusion') or – more pointedly – *ehiameɛ* (lit. 'something that distressed me').

The civil wars were prolonged, violently destructive and deeply corrosive of social norms and values. In their ebb and flow much of Asante became a battlefield. Daily life was hugely disrupted and often reduced to atomised incoherence. Dynasts, politicians and warlords all pressed villagers into taking part in seemingly endless, inconclusive and pointless cycles of fighting. Commoners were killed in battle, murdered, mutilated, kidnapped, displaced, enslaved and offered up as sacrificial victims (*akyere*) while their homes were destroyed, their families broken up and their farms ruined. As the fighting raged on, becoming ever more savage and desperate, thousands of people were reduced to immiseration. The leitmotif of the period was surely the sorry figure of the starving and terrified refugee. Chaos within Asante and flight from it took place on such a scale that the human and political consequences were still being untangled far into the twentieth century.

From the perspective of Adeɛbeba (or indeed any other village) the civil wars must be disassembled into and understood as microhistories of localised conflicts. The fighting was geographically mobile and therefore variable in its impact on different parts of Asante at different times. Thus in the opening phase, from the deposition of the *Asantehene* Mensa Bonsu (March 1883) to the execution of the former ruler Kofi Kakari (June 1884), the worst violence occurred north of Kumase. At this time settlements in an arc from Nyankyeremaase running east through Akyamponeso, Breman and Anumanyese to Kanyaase and Antoa, and south to Tafo and into the northern outskirts of Kumase were the crucible of intense fighting and devastation. In late 1884 however the area south of Kumase was drawn into the war zone, in its turn becoming a landscape scarred by violence, disruption and disorder. At first this phase of the conflict barely touched Adeɛbeba, being centred over fifteen miles away to the south-west among the Atwoma villages and beyond towards Manso Nkwanta, Dominase and Denyase. But then throughout 1885 the southern territorial divisions (*aman*) of Bekwai and Kokofu assumed an increasingly active military role in the struggle, while at the same time the *Saamanhene/Gyaasehene* Akyampon Panin of Saawua emerged as a political warlord of the first rank. It was this combination of locational factors, the spread of fighting across south Asante and the central role taken in it by nearby Saawua, that brought the war home to Adeɛbeba.[52]

The civil wars impacted directly on Adeɛbeba just as they approached their savage and inchoate climax. By this time reserves of fighting manpower and all other resources were in dwindling supply. Thus, in 1885–6 Akyampon Panin ordered a series of sweeps to round up recruits and seize provisions. In one of these he sent troops under one of his sons – possibly Owusu Kɔkɔ Kumaa – to the cluster of still largely undamaged settlements that extended north from Anyinam and Apraman through Atasomaaso and Santaase to Adeɛmmra and Adeɛbeba. This was little more than a spoiling expedition and it behaved as such. At Anyinam 'the Sewuah people robbed and took everything as they wished'; at Apraman the inhabitants fled the village, except for a contrary old man named Ofiri who was summarily put to death by stoning and then beheaded; at Atasomaaso some girls were seized and carried off; at Santaase the village was deserted and in a ruined condition; and at Adeɛmmra boys were rounded up to carry off the village stores of corn. This force with its human and other pillage then took the path east to Adeɛbeba.

No advance warning seems to have reached Adeɛbeba. Indeed, when the Saawua troops entered the village a funeral was in progress. There must have been a brief moment of mutual surprise as mourners and soldiers saw one another, and then

> a quarrel started. Kwabena Ntuoase who was mourning his sister and who was in a high excitement began arguing with those boys (i.e. the Saawua troops). They requested for some water to drink and he told them 'Enoo nie' (*ɛno ni*: 'here it is') and pointed to 'Amfoo' (*mfɔ*: a type of animal trap). This was too much and they began then to beat him 'Poro poro, poro poro' (cf. *porow*: 'to thrash') and [he] cried out for pity but they did not stop it for a moment. When the people round about saw this they ran off. Chase was given and aforementioned Ntuoase and two others more were caught and taken away. Houses were spoiled with broken cooking pots all lying round in the street. All were sore afraid and took their sleep under the stars.[53]

The fate of Kwabena Ntuoase and his fellow captives is unrecorded. After this 'no one thought good of the Sewuah King', and more especially since the implication of the evidence is that other visits of a like kind were made to Adeɛbeba.

This rift between Adeɛbeba and Saawua was reflected in and deepened by shifting political circumstances. In 1886 the *Manwerehene* Kwaku Kra took the side of Agyeman Prempe in his struggle for the Golden Stool with Yaw Twereboanna, one of whose principal supporters was Akyampon Panin. Evidently Kwaku Kra made some attempt to mobilise his Adeɛbeba subjects for this round of the fighting. In any event Agyeman Prempe's forces took Saawua in February 1887. Akyampon Panin was captured less than a mile away at Aboaso. He was taken three miles south to Amansie Gyakye and beheaded. His remains were divided and taken as war trophies by the victors; Kwaku Kra was allotted a jawbone and this was hung on the *Manwere* drums.[54] Afterwards mopping up operations around Saawua were conducted with the rapacity of exhaustion. Villages were fired and people seized. Just west of Saawua the small town of Pirabon (Apirabo) was sacked. Its enslaved inhabitants were apportioned among Agyeman Prempe's generals. Three girls who fell to the lot of Kwaku Kra were sent to Adeɛbeba. But it was discovered there that these were 'maidservants of Yah Achia who besought their return'. That is to say they were subjects of the *Asantehemaa* Yaa Kyaa, Agyeman Prempe's mother. In effect Kwaku Kra had seized his own allies and the presumption must be that they were set free.[55]

The bloody struggles just described brought no end to the conflict. But through mid-1887 the theatre of military operations in south Asante moved once more, this time away from the Kumase (and Adeɛbeba) area eastward beyond Saawua to the Mponoa towns north of lake Bosomtwe. In July a truce was patched up between the warring parties at Odaso (the site of the 1874 battle). No one expected this ceasefire to last and it did not. The civil wars now entered their terminal phase. By this time central Asante was devastated, its villages ruined and farms abandoned. Starving refugees and predatory warbands roamed through the countryside. The effects of this near total collapse of political, civil and material order were felt in Adeɛbeba.

Recollected testimony concerning all this is general rather than precise, but its tone speaks unmistakably of fearful despair. In old age those who had been children or adolescents in Adeɛbeba throughout the duration of the civil wars summarised the balance sheet of horror. Thus 'we had nothing to eat and with which to sustain us,' stated Afua Agyampomaa; 'I lived with my mother in Konkromasi forest [i.e. the forestlands south-west of Atasomaaso]. We were hungry. My brother died,' stated Abena Akwaduo; 'We ate roots and grass to keep from starving out. Kuntumi the Ashantihene's messenger [i.e. a swordbearer: *afenasoani*] came here to Adiebeba and despaired and shot himself,' stated Yaw Daanani; 'One of my uncles was killed and others from here also when Assibey revolutionised,' stated Adolphus Kwaku Boateng. This last statement makes reference to the final passages of the conflict in which the *Kokofuhene* Osei Asibe and others failed in their efforts to substitute Yaw Twereboanna for the elected *Asantehene* Agyeman Prempe.[56] This military endgame was played out across the southern front with a desperate ferocity; it extended from Manso Nkwanta and Atwoma in the west through south Kumase, Bekwai and Kokofu and on north-east to Mponoa and then further north still to Edweso east of the Asante capital. In this last act neutrality of any sort was no longer an option. In the interests of survival villagers switched sides, guessing at the likely victors and adjusting allegiances accordingly, swore fealty, broke oaths, betrayed one another, evaded, dissembled, decamped and took to the bush. Once neighbourly settlements became hostile to one another, and within villages people became divided among themselves. This was *sauve qui peut* in a landscape full of suspicion and terror, and it left a legacy of unforgiving bitterness.

There are glimpses of the ways in which all this affected Adeɛbeba people. At the end of the war, so witnesses recalled, some Adeɛbeba youths ventured south to Daban looking for lost friends. But on this expedition they were confronted with a sight so horrific that it entered village folklore. South of Daban on the Sɔkɔban path they found a man crucified to a tree (*bo asɛndua mu*) with a stake of the sort used in sacrificial offerings (*kɔnkumaa bɔfadua*). The dead man was known to his discoverers. He was a forager (*ɔbaafoɔ*) from Apaaso near Sɔkɔban and was often seen in Adeɛbeba where he tapped palm wine by agreement (*befaye*) with some farmers. Once they recovered from their shock the youths buried the remains by the side of the path. Kwaku Baako (later Samuel K. Baako, a Kumase timber contractor and lay preacher) was a member of this grisly burial party. In old age he recalled the experience as the 'very worst thing I saw ever in my life', adding that 'during my childhood days Ashanti was at war and bad things such as killings or kidnappings for murder were common'.[57]

Bitter memories of the civil wars were raked over well into the twentieth century. During the 1920s an Adeɛbeba girl was discouraged from marrying at Sɔkɔban because the people there were said to have stolen away an Adeɛbeba child at the height of the fighting and given her (or him) over to the custodians of the 'god' Sɔkɔban *nnannuro*. Suspicions of a like kind seem to have attached to the royal executioners (*adumfoɔ*) who lived at Kwanwuoma. In 1929 the then *Kumasihene* Agyeman Prempe was petitioned by Abena Wono of Adeɛbeba for restitution of monies seized by her ex-husband 'your Ahinkwa Adoo Buaboo of Kwanwoma'. She added that there was bad feeling between the two villages because during the civil wars Kwanwoma people 'stole away' unspecified people and property from Adeɛbeba. Abiding tensions were also apparent within Adeɛbeba. In 1938 the Adeɛbeba goldsmith Kwasi Pepra was asked to repay a loan to his fellow villager Samuel Badu who was then living at Adum in Kumase. He refused, giving as his reason the allegation that during the civil wars Badu's uncle had exploited his Saawua and Kumase connections to extort from his fellow villagers. Whatever the truth of this, opinions expressed by others do suggest a history going back to the civil wars of bad blood between Badu's kin and their fellow villagers.[58]

In 1896 Asante was still recovering from the civil wars when the British arrested and deported the *Asantehene* Agyeman Prempe and a number of his close kin and most senior office holders. This political decapitation was the prelude to the formal British annexation of Asante in 1901. It also occasioned deeply felt sensations of loss and disorientation among many Asante people. Such feelings crystallised into a politicised resentment and resistance among some – but by no means all – Asante and this exploded in the last Anglo-Asante war (1900–1), the failed military rising against the new colonial order that is known in tradition as the *yaa asantewaakɔ* (in commemoration of the *Edwesohemaa* Yaa Asantewaa, the symbol of its inspiration and spirit).

The removal of the *Asantehene* fractured the precolonial political order and had an immediate and profound impact on its members, most directly in Kumase. Tradition has it that the *Manwerehene* Kwaku Kra was a strong advocate among those who urged military resistance in 1896. But in the event Agyeman Prempe vetoed any armed response to his arrest. Whatever debates transpired, the stark fact remains that once the *Asantehene* was exiled the *Manwere fekuo* lost the last shreds of its residual focus and coherence. The *Manwerehene* himself was one of the officials of the inner royal household (*fiefoɔ*) and was defined in terms of his relationship of personal service to the occupant of the Golden Stool (*vide* Kwasi Brantuo and Kwaku Dua). Apart from other responsibilities he attended upon the *Asantehene* daily as a participant in the royal robing rituals. The suffix *were* (in *Manwere*) in one of its meanings connoted literal bodyguardianship, in the sense of a physical belonging to the substance of the royal person; indeed all of the *Manwere fekuo* office holders were bodyguards in that very same sense, symbolically constructed as 'eyes and ears' (*nsrafoɔ*: 'spies') attached to the *Asantehene*. Beyond this circle of proximity *Manwere nhenkwaa* were linked via their superiors to the ruler of Asante and their service was to his person. These were specialists – makers and menders of regalia, assayers who used the *fanfa* scoop to weigh and value gold dust, palace maintenance men, or keepers of elephant tails, clothing, sandals and all the rest. More distant still were generic *Manwere* subjects, physically remote from the *Asantehene* but still tied to his person by the filaments of office holding authority and hierarchy. In brief this entire edifice of place and identity existed only in relation to the person of the *Asantehene*. Once he was removed it was exposed to an interrogation that splintered it into self-questioning varieties of contradiction, disarray and redundancy. But anomie is not a programme for living in the material world. After the shock of 1896 people had to pick themselves up and adjust to a changed dispensation. Time fostered accommodation, for Agyeman Prempe was in exile for nearly thirty years (1896–1924) and the office of *Asantehene* was not restored until 1935.

In 1896 then the prospect of living a life defined through a functioning relationship to the *Asantehene* ceased to exist in any practical sense. For the thirteen-year-old *ahenkwaa* Yaw Dabo, an eyewitness to the arrest of Agyeman Prempe, the effect was shattering. A son of the *Manwere ahenkwaa* Kwame Manwere, the boy was summoned from his mother's kin at Adeɛbeba to Kumase as a ten-year-old to take his dead father's place. He was put to work in the palace to learn 'to portion and count' gold. An apt pupil, he was promoted to be bearer of the keys of office (*safo kasiawu*) belonging to the *Manwerehene*. Twice every day he accompanied senior treasury officials to 'the King's dining room' (*adidiase kɛseɛ*) and looked on as the *Asantehene* was given an account of household expenses. The business over, he and other trainees carried the leather bags containing the royal gold weights (*kotokuwaa*) back to the *dampɔnkɛseɛ* courtyard under the supervision of the *Manwerehene*. The work was demanding, for any error or breach of protocol was punished. But it was also rewarding, for 'I learned much of custom and was friends with other boys there for training.' This life, into which Yaw Dabo was born and upon which he was embarked, ended with shocking suddenness on the morning of *monodwo* (Monday) 20 January 1896 in Kumase when Governor Maxwell of the Gold Coast ordered the arrest of Agyeman Prempe.

In old age Yaw Dabo vividly recalled the emotional drama of the moment and the dissonant feelings that followed from it.

> I was afraid and shed tears when Nana Prempeh of blessed memory was taken away from us his people by the soldiers. I saw this with my own eyes. Nana and his mother and others were called by name and surrounded to be taken away. I hid nearby the palace with Akwasi Yamoah who was my own age hailing from Kokobin as a cook [*sodoni*] to Nana. What would become of us? I took myself and few things and returned to Adiebeba. I stayed at the village for long to see what I might do after this sad time. I had no means and could not know what I might do. At the end of this time I came back to Kumasi to see to my living.[59]

In the event Yaw Dabo was given work by a Yabe man as a carrier in the rubber trade to and from Ahafo. He was living there in the Berekum area during the war of 1900–1. Afterwards he again resettled in Adeɛbeba and then worked for the Public Works Department (PWD) in Kumase, first as a labourer and later as a motor mechanic. He married a Toase woman, had five children and retired to Adeɛbeba to farm in the 1930s. Subsequently he became a Christian and his faith 'helped me to see life and all the trials I have had in my life from when I was following on after my father in Kumasi'.

Testimony of a similar but fuller kind was given by Yaw Firempon. His father was the Kumase *Mpaboahene* Kwame Gyabo who came from Atasomaaso. His mother was a Nyeɛso woman who was the daughter of an *ahenkwaa* and his Adeɛbeba wife. Yaw Firempon was born in the late 1870s. In 1892 his father brought him to Kumase where 'I entered the King's service as a carrier of the King's sandals [i.e. followed his father as *ahenkwaa* in the *mpaboafoɔ* service group].' It was in Agyeman Prempe's palace that

> the young boys (Nhenkwaa) taken from various sections of Ashanti meet. They are boys very close to the King. Masters taught the children. On getting to the house [royal palace] I was placed in the school to learn. I entered as an 'Akontase' [*akontaaseni*: 'a counter up'; impl. pupillage]. The term is used to mean a student who is being started to count or learn the art of his service. The masters said 'Yerebɔ no "Akontase".' I learnt the names of all the twelve sandals of the King. I was also taught how to get the King to get his sandals off. It implied some dexterity because when he was on the move or coming down off a palanquin he should be 'sandled' expeditiously. Sometimes he may call a child to go and fetch him a particular sandal. The child should know this. It is a memory work. I learnt to recognise all the sandals. They were sandals decorated with gold. Some of these were Sika Mpaboa, Dwetɛ mpaboa, Mma-Nteaa, Aboa Kese, Ananse, Nsomor dwewa, Efa, Mfirifiriwa, Mmoammoa-womfa, Nfofoo, Sɛɛbɔɔkor.

After I had learnt to recognise these I was promoted Akontahene which is a teacher. I was too early in this advancement. I had not grown enough to be stopped from going to the 'Mmaamu' i.e. the women's household [the King's wives].[60]

Then Yaw Firempon's world turned upside down when the British came to Kumase and the *Asantehene* was taken away.

Afterwards 'all the "Henkwas" [*nhenkwaa*] who served Nana Prempeh had gone away to villages' as Kumase became an open city under foreign occupation. Yaw Firempon quit the capital for Atasomaaso. There he eked out a living by weaving mats and helping his father to farm. Then like Yaw Dabo (and the two probably knew one another) he became a rubber carrier and a seller of gin imported from Cape Coast – an unpleasant town to visit for 'we were insulted by the Fantis'. He took no part in the 1900–1 war and eventually went to labour in the Bibiani mines. He then traded kola from Sunyani to the north, married twice, had children and retired to Atasomaaso, when he developed rheumatism. There in the 1940s he severally recounted his life and times. If Yaw Dabo cultivated an air of Christian resignation in the face of life's trials, then Yaw Firempon retained something of the arrogance of the precolonial *ahenkwaa*. 'I was born in the reign of Osei Bonsu [the *Asantehene* Mensa Bonsu]. I served the late Ashantihene [Agyeman Prempe] and [I] was pleased with my service', he declared, adding that 'I have had a very bad temper in the past. I never could be appeased when offended.'

It is not at all easy to arrive at an understanding of what the removal of Agyeman Prempe meant to the ordinary folk of Adeɛbeba. Direct testimony is sparse, at least in the sense that recollections of 1896 seldom elaborate beyond cryptic or formulaic expressions of sadness and regret. Memory domesticated the event to wistfulness. Whenever people made unfavourable comparisons between colonial present and precolonial past they invoked the deportation of Agyeman Prempe as a key signpost that separated now from then. Distance lent nostalgia, but not necessarily at the expense of sincerity. In fact the arrest of the *Asantehene* did produce momentary alarm and confusion in Adeɛbeba, however much the passage of time allowed later recall to smooth the shock of the moment itself to a more amenable perspective.

Uniquely detailed evidence about Adeɛbeba in 1896 was provided by Kwabena Oben (J. K. Obeng), a dealer in valuable building timbers (*amire*; *ɔframo*). He was born about 1880 at Odumase in Ahafo. His father Yaw Amankwa belonged to a group of subjects that was settled at Odumase in the eighteenth century by Awua Panin, later the *Krontihene/Bantamahene* of Kumase. Kwabena Oben gave a very full account of his background, the circumstances that brought him to Adeɛbeba and what he saw there in 1896.

It is said that one Awuah Panin, a nephew of Adu Jambrah the then Bantamahene of Kumasi [*Krontihene/Bantamahene* Adu Gyamera, executed c. 1770] was stopping at Odomase on his way to Kumasi from a place called Kwatwima in Gyaman. He was a wealthy person [*sikani*] and had many followers. He asked the first settlers [at Odumase] whom they served. They in fear, for being killed by him, replied that they were subjects of Bantama Stool in Kumasi. Awuah Panin left his nephew with the then sub-chief of Odomase and proceeded on to Kumasi. The nephew was the chief headman of the people his uncle left at Odomase. The number of this people grew greater and greater and they were farming freely. But when the rubber trade came on my father Yow Amankwa left off farming and went as a tapper and carrier of rubber to the Gold Coast. He used to pass via Ashanti with his companions. When I was aged about twelve I joined my father in carrying. On one of his travels he met with a Kumasi man and they became fellow traders. This man was from Bedasi [Bedaase, near Afrantwo] and had people he stayed with when travelling anywhere in Ashanti. I was with my father and this man with cloth we brought from Saltpond when we were stopping in this village of Adiebeba. One day we heard that the Ashantihene Prempeh was taken off by the British to be put in prison. Panic gripped everyone from fear of what could happen to them, Gong-gong was beaten but there was no one to answer it. The people in Adiebeba had gone to bush. When the alarm was finished and the all-clear was sounded they returned. Many could not believe that their Great King was no more. Some put on mourning cloths and paraded the village. But in time life became the same once more. My father decided to remain here in trading with his Bedasi friend. We lived for a time at Ampabame and Kumasi. My father at the last settled in Adiebeba because he married there after a time of being a widower. I remained with him and did not go back to Odomase until I was grown and was making my own business in Kumasi. In 1928 I went to Odomase and made two cocoa farms. An elephant destroyed one! My father died without returning. I now live in Kumasi New Town but have kept this house here in Adiebeba.[61]

Panic was immediate, but whatever echoing fears or misgivings followed on from the arrest of Agyeman Prempe were quelled as people turned back to the business of getting a living. Perhaps the most visible sign of the passing of the old order in Adeɛbeba was the arrival of non-Asante strangers (*ananafoɔ*). Such persons now moved around Asante with a freedom denied them by the precolonial state. Roving hawkers (*akyinkyinfoɔ*), itinerant Fante preachers, demobilised Hausa soldiers and even a Pran conjuror who told fortunes and scared children all figure in Adeɛbeba memories of this time. Virtually all of these people were transients (*nea ɛnkye*), halting in a small village on their way to or from Kumase. A very few lingered for a while. Fewer still stayed on. One of this tiny minority became a famous figure in the small world of Adeɛbeba.

The village of Apire (or Apire Womaaso) lay three miles due west of Adeɛbeba via Fankyenebra. It contained subjects belonging to the Kumase stools of *Ankobia*, *Mamesene* and *Manwere*. In the late nineteenth century the wealthiest man in Apire was Kofi Manwere, possibly a son of the disgraced *Manwerehene* Kwasi Brantuo Kyei Kumaa and certainly an entrepreneur. From the 1880s on he and his business partners (including notably the father of 'Richman' Yaw Fin Boakye of Bekwai, a celebrated merchant of the 1930s) traded to north and south of Asante. They retailed local commodities (salt, meat, shea butter, kola) and imported goods (gin, gunpowder, cloth, beads). On one of his trading missions to the north Kofi Manwere purchased a young adult male slave (*ɔdɔnkɔ*). He was called Atinga Mosi but became known ever after as Pataku, a nickname given to him in Apire because of his long jaw (cf. *pataku*: 'hyena'). He proved astute and became Kofi Manwere's trusted lieutenant.

In the early 1890s Pataku was trading but also working oil palms on Apire land for his master. Then he saw a market niche that opened up when the political crisis of 1896 dislocated the circulation of goods and services around Kumase and its satellite villages. He switched to making distilled palm wine ('gin') and selling it to meet suddenly frustrated demand. Among his best customers were the African troops of the British garrison in Kumase. In their turn, soldiers and others supplied him with items needed for his new business. In very short order Pataku's ingenuity created a thriving and profitable operation.

> Gin was made at Apiri in big amounts. Pataku got metal pots and basins of every kind and iron and copper tubings from soldiers and Hausas in Kumasi as also Ewes from the coast. The pots all were half filled or more than this with a fresh palm wine and it was strongly covered without outlet for the air. Other pots were all filled with fresh water. The palm wine was set on a big big fire. When it was boiled a pipe was put into the part with air unfilled above the boiling liquid. This passed to the cold fresh water and out to pots and bottles at the side. The pipe was in a ring in the cold water. This ring was the secret. Vapours rose in the pipe and turned to liquid at the ring and fell out as gin into the small pots. In order to keep down low the bubble of the boiling palm wine from getting into the pipe and spoiling it palm nuts were cut into the liquid before it was ever set on the fire. The gin was sold in the Kumasi Asafu market and all over the district. Pataku's gin making was known near and far and he became rich. The business was not without hazard and sometimes when the pipe was punctured or broke the bystanders got scalded.[62]

Kofi Manwere had connections at Adeɛbeba and Pataku was well known there. In or about 1900 the master died and his kin freed the slave in return for help in settling their debts. Pataku now married an Adeɛbeba woman named Adwowaa Birago (who may have been of slave descent herself). At any rate he came to farm at Adeɛbeba, working land at 'Mosi Cottages' in an undeveloped part of *(n)tasu*. He grew plantain and cassava to sell in Kumase to add to the profits from his Apire business. It is plain from the tone as much as the content of recollections that Pataku came to loom large in Adeɛbeba village affairs. His influence derived from a formidable presence combined with a sure talent for making money. In the early 1900s he pioneered in hiring labourers to work his farms; he invested in the cattle trade; he became a firewood supplier, a builder and then a landlord in Kumase; and he loaned cash to his neighbours. By the 1910s he was raking in profits from the interest (*mfɛntomu*) on moneylending. When he died in 1931 (in the same month as Agyeman Prempe) he was owed a deal of money by Adeɛbeba villagers among others. According to Opoku Adade, his eldest son by Adwowaa Birago, Pataku died holding mortgages on six Adeɛbeba farms (as well as nine elsewhere) and many in the village were indebted to him for advances made to fund houses, to observe funerals or to service family debts. 'My father', said Opoku Adade, 'was owed £700 in all at Adiebeba at his passing.'

Disentangling Adeɛbeba attitudes to Pataku is revealing. When he first came to farm at the village he was an intriguing harbinger of the new order in Asante. He was welcomed none the less, for he seemed committed to the place in that he gave of his energy and enterprise for the benefit of his adopted community. We can well imagine that his moneylending began in a small way to oblige neighbours struggling with the cash economy. But as colonialism became embedded in and articulated through a commodification that extended into rural life, social relations were increasingly arbitrated by the flow and circulation of money. Pataku was a neighbour but also a businessman with his own need for cash. His interest rates on loans came to reflect this. To the standard *bɔsea* (a long-term, fixed-interest loan) he added the usurious repertoire of advances made to the importunate in the accelerated cash economy of early colonialism. This is why Pataku's posthumous reputation in Adeɛbeba was a mixed one. Some people recalled his arrival and enthused over his presence in and impact on community life; others remembered him as a man who specialised in the extortions of *fifiri* (lit. 'sweat') and *ohuruo* (lit. 'jumping'), short-term loans with interest rates set so high that the principal could never be repaid. In memory – and for better or worse – Pataku became a sign of the times. He was a phenomenon called into being by a new world that Adeɛbeba people dated from the convulsion of 1896.[63]

The precolonial political order ended with the removal of the *Asantehene* Agyeman Prempe. At first sight the *yaa asantewaakɔ* – the uprising of 1900–1 against British rule – seems like a straightforward act of redress, an attempt to turn the clock back. To some Asante it was just that, and there is no shortage of evidence that hatred of foreign domination and yearning for vanished power – and the certainties implicit in it – were widespread motives for fighting. But the nationalist mythology that came to encrust the war should not blind us to the understanding that many Asante chose not to fight, while others actively aided the British. In truth, the *yaa asantewaakɔ* was a struggle *against* the British and *between* Asante people. In both these aspects it was about the tension between past and present in defining the future. Where some saw the past as outmoded and looked to opportunities they discerned in the new dispensation, others saw the present as alien and looked to stabilities they identified in the old order. This is a broad division and accurate enough in its way. But it is ultimately unsatisfactory, for uncertainty and ambiguity clouded any such eminently simple choices. Thus individual motivation is difficult to tease out from an environment arbitrated by shifting contingencies and driven by contrary impulses. In sum, people found themselves pressed by contradiction. Most responsed situationally and notably so in the proverbial fog of war in 1900–1.

Some Adeɛbeba men fought the British and three or four, and perhaps more, died doing it. They were bivouacked as a company (*kuo*) with fellow insurgents from all over Atwoma and Mponoa, garrisoning one of the many barricades thrown up around the besieged British fort in Kumase. Their post was the *nsubinagya pie*, a log and wattle rampart by Kumase Akyere-made (near the present Kagyatia lorry park). They lived in temporary huts behind this wall, preparing and eating food brought by young boys from nearby farms, exchanging fire with enemy soldiers and enduring skirmishing forays from the fort or – fatally – close-range artillery fire. It was this last that wreaked carnage along the barricade, causing several deaths at once. Thus it killed 'Yaw Atie and his brother' from Adeɛbeba, recalled Kwadwo Konkori, and 'wounded my father in his side and leg so that he was taken away to Asukwa and came back to Adiebeba'. Unnamed neighbours of these men also perished or were injured at *nsubinagya pie*, and one man – Akuri (?) – made his escape to Bokwankye and only returned to Adeɛbeba 'after the railway reached to Kumasi' in 1903.[64]

It is hard to provide a satisfactory account of the volatile mix of inaction, purpose and emotional cathexis that gripped Adeɛbeba during the *yaa asantewaakɔ*. As a daily fact of life the war was inescapably present. Adeɛbeba was close to the fighting and heavy gunfire in Kumase was clearly audible. Every day, too, female relatives and supporters of the men at *nsubinagya pie* publicly sang and danced *mmobomme (mmomo(m)e)*, the customary ritual performed by women in wartime. In a small place like

Adeɛbeba *mmobomme* was impinging and unavoidable. The participants donned white clay (*hyire*) and paraded the village, commonly twice a day, banging brass pans and drums, yelling, gesturing, singing, dancing and generally acting in an aggressive – or even obscene – manner. Afua Tweneboaa recalled that 'twenty or more' took a part in the Adeɛbeba *mmobomme*, which was 'done by elder [*sic*] women including Abinah Chiah who took a lead also when Pua was taken off'. The reference is to *bra betɛn puaa* ('remove the tufts of head hair'), one of the customary injunctions given by adult women to girls undergoing their nubility rites (*bragorɔ*). Abena Akyiaa, at the forefront in arranging *bragorɔ* and *mmobomme*, was one of the Heman people and a person of consequence in village affairs. But like the rest of Adeɛbeba her own family was split over the issue of the war.

Abena Akyiaa's militancy was rejected by many of her neighbours including her only uterine brother Kofi Mensa. This man had left Adeɛbeba for the Gold Coast in unknown circumstances in the 1890s, had returned as a trader in cloth and salt, spoke some English and Hausa, and thought armed resistance to the British would lead to the destruction of Asante. Kofi Mensa and Abena Akyiaa quarrelled over the performance of *mmobomme*. 'This Mensah said that playing for war by his sister was a bad thing' that would lead to savage retribution when the British prevailed. The two appear to have exchanged an oath over this matter (and maybe others). The upshot was that people took sides. But in the end Kofi Mensa had his way and *mmobomme* ceased. What then happened is unclear except that Abena Akyiaa left Adeɛbeba and went to live at Kwadaso.[65]

How much weight should be given to this story? At the very least it suggests unease and disunity in Adeɛbeba about the wisdom of fighting the British. That divisions existed is confirmed by other evidence. Thus while some Adeɛbeba men took up arms, others steadfastly refused. Kwabena Dwumo was a goldsmith who became a cocoa factor and property owner in later life. He was opposed to the war on the grounds that it was 'a hopeless course' but also because 'the coming back to Ashanti of Ashantihene Prempeh would bring about severity as before of chiefs in taking off life and limb'. Traditional office holders were the foe, added Kwabena Dwumo, for 'big things always swallow up small things' (*obi so kyɛn wo a ɔmene wo*). Others declined to fight on the grounds that 'chiefs are the power absolute in Ashanti and wished to be as before the British'. Likewise it was said that malcontent office holders formed a 'gang of ruffians' round the *Edwesohemaa* Yaa Asantewaa and launched the uprising for their own selfish ends. Indeed one Kwabena Addai and his brother quit Adeɛbeba in disgust during the fighting and went to Akyem Kotoku 'so as to go on with trading in peace and quiet'. These two felt the war was bad for their business – which was dealing in guns.[66]

Kwabena (later Emmanuel) Osei was a youth in 1900–1. He was a great-grandson of the Adeɛbeba pioneer Yaa Atiwaa of Saawua. In later life he

became a Christian catechist, a schoolmaster and a sub-registrar of the
Native Authority (NA) Court in Bompata in Asante Akyem before retiring
to Adeɛbeba. He opposed fighting the British, and in reflecting upon the
reasons delivered himself of a quite remarkable peroration on Asante history
as seen from below.

> I wanted nothing at all to do with the fighting. My opinion was that
> Chiefs had had their day and would retard Ashanti if they again got
> back their old position. Many people here [Adeɛbeba] thought as I
> thought. In the former days of Ashanti's power and glory Chiefs were
> the Final Resort, the Power Supreme and the Sacred Leader. They
> had the Divine Right. It was the custom for Chiefs to have the final say
> in all matters affecting the state. A Chief sprang up from an ancient
> line. He was the descendant of the ancient line of Chiefs whose stool
> he was occupying. This was sufficient to get him the stool by which he
> was invested with the right of government. A descendant no matter
> how unfit in managing the affairs of state was considered fit. These
> Chiefs were always bragging 'Mete (such and such) Akonnua so.
> Menye abofra' [mete ... akonnua so, mennyɛ abofra: 'I hold such and
> such a stool so I am not a child']. This meant their position was high
> and gave them worthiness. But many Chiefs in fact were worthless.
> They led Ashanti into useless wars as in the Atwiriboana time [the civil
> wars of the 1880s] and they murdered and oppressed for no other
> cause but a high opinion of themselves. When the British came we
> rejoiced to see them laid low. They asked us to fight for them in Ya
> Asantiwa time [the war of 1900–1]. But they wanted only power and
> to revive traditions of the Decadent Past in our own days. At Adiebeba
> they said to us 'Fa Broni adwen to kyin na yenwin ho yin amanie
> kwanso' [fa broni adwen to nkyɛn na yennwen ho yɛn amannɛ kwan so:
> 'put aside European things and think only of our customs']. Then they
> said 'Yi ameto sa yiyi no sa nyiyie, ebeka' [yɛ meto saa yɛyɛ no saa
> nnyeye ɛbeka: 'we did not have those (European) things formerly and
> if we do so now it will not go well for we should stay as we are']. No
> one listened except a few who went to Kumasi to fight the Chiefs' war.
> I refused it. The Chiefs could do nothing. The days of their heedless
> power were over and done. It used to happen that a servant on the
> death of his master the Chief refused to live. He wanted to go along
> with him to serve him. This was superstitious stuff and nonsense and
> is now a thing of past history. The 'Good Old Days' are over and there
> is none but the Chiefs to mourn its passing.[67]

These are themes that will be returned to and discussed elsewhere. For
now let us note only and with regret that the evidence contains nothing
comparable setting out the views of those who fought the British in the *yaa
asantewaakɔ*.

As with all wars there are paradoxes, opacities and blanks in the record concerning the *yaa asantewaakɔ*. To a degree this is because it was fought by an aggregation of individuals (a popular front?) led and inspired by a medley of militant office holders and charismatic war captains. This force was a coalition of anti-British interests, partisan and dedicated but bearing only an approximate resemblance to the politico-military hierarchies of the precolonial state. It was an assembly of volunteers not a mobilisation of troops, and the campaign it fought was similarly improvised in planning and execution. Hence Adeɛbeba people who elected to take part did so as individuals rather than as a draft of subjects summoned to battle by the *Manwerehene*. In truth (and there is more than a hint of this in Kwabena Osei's testimony) the *Manwerehene* Kwaku Kra no longer possessed reserves of credible authority sufficient either to command or coerce subjects to do his bidding. He himself fought the British and, as has been seen, suffered imprisonment as a result.

The *yaa asantewaakɔ* revealed the extent to which office holders had forfeited any presumptive right to rule over a society their behaviour nearly destroyed in the 1880s. More particularly, the war and its aftermath pointed up the long-term decay of the *Manwere* in graphic terms. The *Manwere* stool itself suffered near eclipse after the arrest of Kwaku Kra and the formal British annexation of Asante. Colonial records show this with stark economy. Thus the first British review of Kumase stool organisation (1901) made no mention of the *Manwere fekuo*; and when a Kumase Council of Chiefs was set up to assist government (1905) *Manwere* was nowhere mentioned in discussions about its membership. Instead the erstwhile office holders of the *Manwere fekuo* were redistributed as subordinates in other administrative groups, while the *Manwere* stool itself was reassigned to the status of rank and file membership in the *Gyaasewa* sub-division of the *Gyaase fekuo*. In fact Kwaku Kra's British sanctioned successor was gazetted as being nothing more than the village headman of Heman.

In 1901 the British appointed their clients to or confirmed them in occupancy of a number of Kumase stools. These office holders were then given a fairly free hand to fill subordinate vacancies. Thus the *Gyaasewahene* Kwame Tua was authorised to find a successor to Kwaku Kra. A notorious extortioner (*ɔpempensifo*), Kwame Tua summoned Kofi Nti of Heman to Kumase and told him that 'he can have Maweri' for two *mperedwan* (£16). Kofi Nti countered that he was 'the proper person for the stool' by right as a nephew of Kwaku Kra and refused to pay. Kwame Tua then flew into a towering rage. He threatened that Kofi Nti 'can never succeed the stool' without his recommendation. Since Kwame Tua was esteemed and favoured by the British his outburst carried the argument. Kofi Nti paid up. He was given *Manwere*, but not before he had rendered a formal apology to the *Gyaasewahene* for his obduracy. Thereafter 'all the Maweri people' suffered the bullying exactions (*ahupoosɛm*) of Kwame Tua until his excesses forced the reluctant British to remove him from office in 1906. But relations barely improved under Kwame Tua's successor Kwabena Asubonten, a situation that may have had something to do with the nineteenth-century rivalry of *Gyaasewa* and *Manwere* for the control of treasury affairs. It was some relief therefore when *Manwere* was transferred to the *Ankobia fekuo* when that administrative group was detached from *Gyaase* by the British in 1911 and reconstituted in its historically autonomous form. But change was not restoration. The *Manwere* stool remained subordinate to the *Ankobiahene* until after the restoration of the Asante Confederacy by government in 1935.[68]

Two instances will suffice to illustrate the inconsequence of the *Manwere* stool in the early colonial period. First, in 1918 the *Manwerehene* Kofi Nti claimed title to subjects at Drobonso on the Afram plain within the Kumawu territorial division. The history of Drobonso was complex. The village emerged in the course of the eighteenth century from a hunting camp established by subjects of the *Tafohene*. In the mid-nineteenth century the then *Tafohene* Buadu Kwadwo gravely offended the *Asantehene* Kwaku Dua. He was fined £960 and was able to raise all but £240 (*mperedwan aduasa*) of this punitive amount. Kwaku Dua took the Tafo people at Drobonso in settlement and gave them to the *Manwerehene* Kwasi Brantuo. But when Kwasi Brantuo Kyei Kumaa was executed in 1872 these Drobonso subjects were confiscated from *Manwere*. Kofi Kakari awarded them to his favourite Kwaku Bosommuru Dwira when he promoted him (in circumstances already described) to the *Manwere fekuo* stool of *Akomfode/ Nyameani*. When Kwaku Bosommuru Dwira died in 1887 the *Manwerehene* Kwaku Kra reaffirmed overlordship. But once peace was restored following the civil wars, the *Kumawuhene* Kwasi Krapa asked for Drobonso as a reward for his services to Agyeman Prempe. His claim was stronger than that he entered for Kwadwo Bi and his kin (discussed above), for Drobonso was situated within Kumawu whatever its history of control from Kumase. The weakened Agyeman Prempe duly surrendered the *Manwere* subjects to Kumawu, preserving to himself no more than a fiction of royal authority. After 1901 the British – determined to devolve power away from Kumase – confirmed Kumawu in its overlordship. When at last Kofi Nti contested this arrangement in 1918, he did so chiefly at the prompting of Drobonso villagers who were disgruntled with the *Kumawuhene*. His hope of success cannot have been high and in due course the District Commissioner (DC) at Dwaaso upheld the earlier British ruling. The *Manwere* subjects at Drobonso remained under Kumawu control until after 1935.[69]

Second and more pointedly so than in the Drobonso case, the fate of the *Manwere* stool house in Kumase was symptomatic of a catastrophic loss of power and prestige. Until the coming of colonialism the blackened stool of Kwasi Brantuo was kept with regalia and ritual artifacts in either one of two stool houses at Heman and Adeɛbeba. However one of the indicators of achieved place and status within the emergent colonial order was the possession of a dedicated stool house – or failing that a room – of modern construction in Kumase itself. 'All the chiefs of Kumasi', it was observed, 'are eager to acquire a grand and imposing property for displaying their wealth in a good setting and for proclaiming to all and sundry the greatness of their ancient predecessors in fulfiling [*sic*] the Ashanti Nation in days of yore.'[70] Like others, therefore, but with a need driven on by the humiliating contrast between past position and present circumstance, Kofi Nti rented a stool room for £4 a month in a house at Kagyatia that belonged to the wealthy Fante cocoa magnate Isaac Mensah of Anomabo. All went well for years until in 1925 Mensah swore out a complaint against the then *Manwerehene* Kwasi Kyerapem for the recovery of a debt of £300 composed of long-standing rent arrears and a loan made to Kofi Nti. Kwasi Kyerapem agreed to settle the bill for the lease of the stool room but refused to meet his predecessor's obligation on the grounds that this was a personal rather than a stool debt. Mensah threatened eviction and prosecution. But when Kwasi Kyerapem stood his ground, the enraged landlord chose instead to throw the *Manwere* regalia out of his house into the busy Antoa road. Kwasi Kyerapem was informed and he set about gathering up the stool property before a jeering crowd. This ignominious state of affairs had arisen, so he recounted, because 'the stool of Manweri' was 'entirely lacking for helpers and without money'. Kwasi Brantuo's blackened stool was then taken from Kumase back to Adeɛbeba while the drums and other items were given temporary refuge in a padlocked shed near the railway yards along the lake Bosomtwe road. This demeaning episode was a nadir in the fortunes of the *Manwere* stool.[71]

VILLAGERS: MAINTAINING A COMMUNITY AT ADEƐBEBA, 1870s–1900s

Adeɛbeba village was founded in the 1840s. From the 1860s until the close of the nineteenth century it was buffeted by forces beyond its control. None the less it is clear that its response to pressure was solidarity (*nkabɔmu a gyina ade a nnipa ani gye ho so*), a realisation of belonging and an articulation of community. The concept of community – *nkabɔm(u)*, translatable as union or unity – was rooted in the practical ethics of a joining together for mutual advantage. As such it reflected historical experience going back to the seventeenth century. Asante people learned early that villages were built by work but sustained by cooperation. The successful community was a vigilant persuader to consensual accord (*biakoyɛ*) and harmony (*asomdwee*) between its members in every aspect of village life. Institutionalised structures and normative practices were directed to achieving this goal. But in the end success or failure depended upon people. Community leadership is difficult to particularise. Ascription commonly played a part in it, but so too did the reputation of a given individual. Entitlement to lead was a grant rather than a right, and it was bestowed on a person generally acknowledged to possess qualities that sustained a community by embodying its virtues. Remembrance is a useful guide here. When Adeɛbeba people reflected on their own community they accorded a central role in its maintenance to a woman named Amma Kyirimaa. The subject of a great deal of detailed reminiscence, Amma Kyirimaa of Adeɛbeba led a long and complicated life. Interpreting that life is similarly complicated. The first step is to understand the circumstances that shaped it.

Picture a small, oblong building at the westernmost edge of Adeɛbeba. It has red, baked-mud walls part faced with white stucco. The roof is branches and plaited vegetation and is steeply pitched. The building has no windows. It is divided by an internal wall. Entering from the public street the visitor finds a room, empty save for other people. The first room gives access to the second through a curtained doorway in the internal wall. This second room has a raised floor and steps lead up to its entrance. Visitors do not approach the second room until summoned from behind the curtain. They are usually called only one at a time. At the far side of the second room is a raised platform running the length of the external wall. Various items are disposed along or by this elevation. The centrally placed item is a chair. Set upon the chair is a brass vessel containing a brownish, viscous substance with a single long stick, twigs, feathers and bits of broken pottery protruding from its surface. Beneath and all about the chair is a miscellany of objects – cow tails, mirror glass, sticks, clubs, medicine bags and sheep skulls. Ranged on either side of the chair are numerous objects. Six wooden statuettes draw the eye. All six are anthropomorphic. Two, the smallest, are in the corner to the left front of the chair. They are suspended from the roof within a wooden box enmeshed in thorn sticks bound tightly together. These figures are *kwaku* and *awisaa*, a husband and wife. In the opposite corner to the right is *kramo*, a carving of a Muslim and clearly dressed as such. From the 1910s *kramo* is linked by wire and thread to a mound of stones heaped on the floor, and by this means he is able to receive and transmit telegraph messages. Hard by *kramo* in the 1920s is a representation of a transient sojourner. This is *afua brahua*, a woman whose effigy is stuck with knives. By the 1940s she is gone. The two largest statuettes stand either side of the chair. On the left is *amoa*, a male figure with scarred cheeks and a grinning mouth. On the right is a further male figure. This is *kurukoro (krukro)*, who is carrying a large club and wearing a messenger's cap.

This picture as given is in a generic ethnographic present, but it is a historical one none the less. That is, anyone entering the building in question between the 1870s and 1940s would have seen things more or less as they have been described. This small building was the dwelling place (ɔbosomfie) of the shrine of Adeɛbeba taa kwabena bena. Anthropomorphised most commonly as an extremely tall old man, taa kwabena bena was the manifestation of an ɔbosom (pl. abosom). The abosom, variously if loosely given in translation as 'gods', 'fetishes' or tutelary spirits, were assigned an identity by the Asante as the 'children' of onyame, the 'withdrawn' creator or supreme being. Their origins lay beyond the realm of human society, and their manifestations in the affairs of the Asante were unilateral and arbitrary. By definition, the abosom were powers in and of that nature that preceded culture. The Asante classified an ɔbosom with reference to its source or point of origin within the natural universe. Thus taa kwabena bena belonged to the category of atano, powers that derived from water, and principally rivers. This category was named for the Tano river in north-western Asante, which was in itself the source of numerous important manifestations of the abosom. Such manifestations, which were disseminated throughout Asante, were popularly known by the abbreviated term taa (der. Tano) and were further classified according to the day upon which they elected to reveal themselves. Hence taa (Tano) kwabena bena ('born' on a 'bad', i.e. dabɔne or ritually significant, bena or Tuesday) was a manifestation of the Tano river ɔbosom that appeared one Tuesday, in this case in Adeɛbeba.

Every Asante settlement contained manifestations of the abosom, for none was deemed to be properly or safely established without their presence. Thus it was the case that town or village abosom (as distinct from the myriad manifestations of these powers that 'belonged' to the Asanteman, to lineages or to individuals) assumed a central importance in the life of localised Asante communities. Many settlements accumulated numbers of these protective presences over the years as and when they manifested themselves. Others accumulated few. Thus and in brief, by the end of the nineteenth century Atasomaaso had no less than seven village abosom, Adeɛmmra had three, but Toase, Kaase, Santaase and Adeɛbeba itself had only one each. But enumerations of this sort must be treated with due caution. As indicated, abosom were a law unto themselves. They might choose to manifest themselves, but by corollary they might elect to absent themselves. The Asante could coax or conduce their presence but not command it. Thus settlements often contained the shrines of inactive abosom abandoned by their animating presence. Desertion might be permanent, but not necessarily. Some abosom simply became dormant. They were inactive over many years and then manifested themselves once more in the same or a nearby place.

Adeɛbeba taa kwabena bena first manifested itself in the reign of the Asantehene Kofi Kakari (1867–74) prior to the disgrace and death of the Manwerehene Kwasi Brantuo Kyei Kumaa in 1872. This was a matter of jubilant relief to the community for Adeɛbeba enjoyed the protection of no

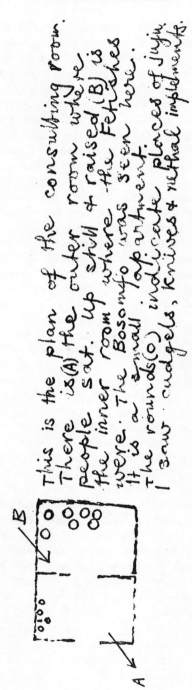

This is the plan of the consulting room. There is (A) the outer room where people sat. Up still + raised (B) is the inner room where the Fetishes were. The Bosomfo was seen here. It is a small apartment. The rounds (o) indicate places of juju. I saw cudgels, knives + metal implements.

Figure 2.1 Sketch Plan of the ɔbosomfie of Adeebeba *taa kwabena bena* in 1945.
(Source: Ashanti Social Survey Papers, Birmingham)

efficacious village *ɔbosom* before this time (or at least none that had elected
to stay). As has been seen, the shrine of *atwere* imported by the pioneer
Kwasi Yentumi in the 1840s was viewed with some scepticism by Adeɛbeba
people. Its failure to adjust to its new home – 'to lodge itself' – was severally
recalled and its capacities eventually weakened and dwindled away. But
from its coming until the mid-twentieth century (at least) *taa kwabena bena*
was a continuously active presence in Adeɛbeba. Indeed it was institution-
ally central to the daily life of the village. Its custodians and servitors were
perhaps the most influential voices in community affairs and their
reputations spread far beyond Adeɛbeba. 'All the villagers', so it was said,
'as well as those of the surrounding villages ascribed much power to the God
or Fetish Kwabena Bena.'[72]

The manifestation of *taa kwabena bena* was an epochal event in the history
of the Adeɛbeba village community and recalled as such.

> One evening in the days of Ohene Karikari (the *Asantehene* Kofi
> Kakari), in the little village of Adeɛbɛba, a globe of light was seen on
> a Gyedua Tree (Ficus) in the centre of the village.
>   Vultures flew about. There were noises and whistling in the air. The
> old people then rushed for drums which began to play. Voices began
> to cry out and a band of musicians set forth Akɔm nwom (Songs of
> Fetish Dances) [*akɔm mwom*]
>   The community was trying to capture an entity that wanted to come
> and stay with them and protect them.
>   They did not know the kind whether Tannɔ (*atano*), or Ɔbɔɔ (*ɔbo*)
> or Kobi (*kobi*) (River or Wood or Sky).
>   The power of something yet invisible was moving like a bird from
> place to place.
>   The King of Asante (Kofi Kakari) was informed. He sent sheep and
> long practised 'akomfo' (*akɔmfoɔ*: lit. 'ones who are possessed';
> conventionally 'priests') to help in welcoming the new Entity that was
> seeking to come down.
>   A brass pan was procurred [*sic*]. A little water was put in it. The
> noise in the (?) directed all these. The old priests called out for his
> name. He answered he came from River Tandoh & was called Tanno
> Kwabena Bena. Great balad [*sic*] singers were then sent for. They
> extold (sic) the phenomena in befitting phrase. The fetish then called
> out – 'Are you ready to receive me?' All this time drumming and
> singing and throwing of powdered clay (*hyire*), breaking of eggs and
> performing of ceremonies were going on.
>   At last after a good number of sheep & fowls had been sacrificed a
> meteor of light whistling through the air swiftly alighted and fell into
> the pan. It called out 'Who will come & receive me?'

One man, Kofi Ketewa went up, & embraced the pan to have it covered according to the orders. He was scalded all over the body from the chest to the belly.

He was reputed to be a very strong man. He did not live long. He shot himself.

The fetish then obsessed a woman who died in 1943.[73]

This description conforms to standard aetiologies about the manifestation of the *abosom*. The 'brass pan' – the locus chosen by *taa kwabena bena* – was the vessel eventually set upon the chair in the *ɔbosomfie*.

Issues of belief saturate this account, but no exegesis of them is offered here. The people of Adeɛbeba are the subject. They were the means by which *taa kwabena bena* effected its entry into history. Note that the *ɔbosom* first possessed or 'mounted' (*akɔm*) Kofi Ketewa. But it immediately rejected him. The result was his suicide with its hints of insanity.[74] Then *taa kwabena bena* 'obsessed a woman who died in 1943'. This woman was Amma Kyirimaa (also called Amma Anane, the fourth born) and she was said to have been over ninety years old when she died. She was an un-married adolescent when *taa kwabena bena* took possession of her and settled upon her as his conduit to the human world. She spent the rest of her long life as *ɔkɔmfɔ* to Adeɛbeba *taa kwabena bena*. As such she had custody of the *ɔbosomfie* that housed his shrine and served as mouthpiece of his communications and interpreter of his wishes. She was indispensable to interaction with him and he might only be consulted through her mediation. As a result Amma Kyirimaa was a figure of great consequence in Adeɛbeba for over seventy years.

Amma Kyirimaa's mother was Akosua Afiri, who belonged to the Heman group of subjects relocated to Adeɛbeba by Kwasi Brantuo. The details are imprecise, but Akosua Afiri seems to have been a uterine niece of Amma Donko, herself daughter of the Heman pioneer Afua Nimaako; as such she was a member of the lineage stirp in which the office of the Adeɛbeba *obaapanin* ('queen mother') was vested. Amma Kyirimaa's father was Kwadwo Atumtuni, a *Manwere* subject from nearby Apire. Born most probably in the mid-1850s, Amma Kyirimaa was the fourth of nine children produced by her parents. A little is known about one of her siblings (and this probably lodged in village memory precisely because of the nature of Amma Kyirimaa's own life experience). One of her younger brothers was called Kofi Donko (cf. *ɔdɔnkɔ*: 'a foreign-born slave'). This was because two of his older brothers had died in early childhood. Akosua Afiri consulted the shrine of *taa kwadwo* at Toase about this misfortune. There she was told that her bereavements were caused by a single child twice struggling and failing to live. Accordingly she was given 'staying' medicine (*gyina*) to help her next born boy survive and was advised to name him for a slave in order to deceive death about his worth. Hence her next male child was named

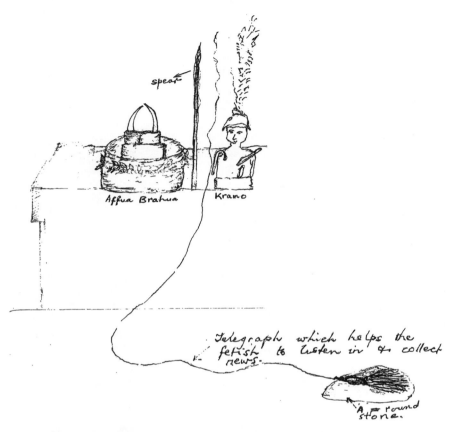

Figure 2.2 Sketch of *afua brahua* and *kramo* from information supplied by Kwasi Fi.

(Source: Ashanti Social Survey Papers, Birmingham)

Kofi Donko. He was *bagyina ba* ('a come and stay child') and *ɔbosom ba* ('an *ɔbosom* child', in this case of Toase *taa kwadwo*) and he lived into adulthood. Kofi Donko's story was unexceptional, a commonplace of Asante family life, but with hindsight it was combed for meaning because of his sister. Similar retrospective interrogations were directed at Amma Kyirimaa's own childhood. Her neighbours sought clues to her adult singularity in her early years. Thus Amma Kyirimaa was remembered as a solitary child. She was thought to be dumb (*mfum*), for she was notably slow in learning to speak. She was obedient and well mannered. She was quiet. She spent much time in the company of old women (*mmerewa*). She played little. In sum she was a child apart, at least in the mirror of memory. One other thing was widely recalled. Amma Kyirimaa was unmarried but ritually adult when she was

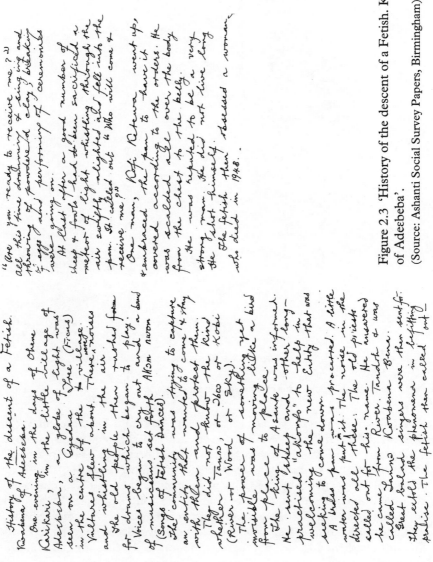

Figure 2.3 'History of the descent of a Fetish. Kwabena of Adeebeba'.

(Source: Ashanti Social Survey Papers, Birmingham)

first 'mounted' by *taa kwabena bena*, for she had recently undergone her puberty rites (*bragorɔ*).[75]

Amma Kyirimaa served as *ɔkɔmfɔ* to *taa kwabena bena* from the 1870s until her death in 1943. She and the *ɔbosom* swiftly acquired a reputation for accuracy in prophesying and efficacy in problem-solving. The building containing the shrine of *taa kwabena bena* was a site of unique power (*tumi*) in Adeɛbeba, and from it the *ɔbosom* directed the woman in the use of supernatural resources to address the needs and anxieties of her neighbours. Troubled individuals were summoned from the antechamber into the shrine room of the small building. There Amma Kyirimaa consulted *taa kwabena bena* on behalf of each petitioner.

> There is a pot [brass vessel] in which there are several things of pebbly nature. There is water in it. There is a stick. When people wanted to know certain facts (read their fortune) the old lady [Amma Kyirimaa] would seat [*sic*] on a chair near the pot. She would hold the stick and stir the pot of the contents. A little noise is made. Then after pausing for a time she would jerk the stick forward and tell the client all about him(self).[76]

Even more important in terms of community welfare and protection was the public role performed by *taa kwabena bena* and his spokesperson in Adeɛbeba. In this aspect of her calling Amma Kyirimaa was supported by the other servants of the *ɔbosom*.

> The fetish had a system of organisation such as a chief has. There was the medium *ɔkɔmfɔ* (sometimes referred to as *pɔnkɔ* the horse) or *ɔbosom yere* – Fetish wife. There was a linguist [*ɔkyeame*] also. There were other officers made up of males and females. There was an orchestra consisting of male drummers and female choreisters [*sic*]. The evening preceding a great day (Akwasi Dae, Awuku Dae, Fofiyie, Kwabena) was utilised in keeping a vigil. The choir sang and the drummers played upon the drums. On these occasions A[mma] K[yirimaa], the priest (medium, *pɔnkɔ*, *ɔbosom yere*) was often possessed by the fetish. She suddenly began to shake then shout out and collapse from which she got up a different fellow altogether. She then possessed wonderful power for she could jump and dance and whirl about in such a rapid succession that only a well-practised gymnastic student could emulate. She sang beautifully and foretold future events. Her oracles were known to be correct. Sometimes Kwabena Bena, the father fetish would obsess her. In this way all oracles were supreme. She spoke with authority and showed some maturity of judgement. All the attributes of a father featured in the period of this father fetish in her (AK's) behaviour.[77]

Close lineage kin of Amma Kyirimaa were prominent members of the group just described. Her sister Adwoaa Pomaa became ɔkyeame to taa kwabena bena. Her brother Kwasi Fi was responsible for the ritual besmearing or 'feeding' of taa kwabena bena with eggs (woredue ɔbosom).[78]

When publicly possessed, Amma Kyirimaa spoke with the voice of 'the father fetish' taa kwabena bena but also sometimes with those of 'the sons of the father god' amoa or kurukoro. The presence of these two was announced to Amma Kyirimaa by taa kwabena bena with the instruction that they be kept close by him and honoured as his 'children' and 'good helpers'. When Amma Kyirimaa was possessed by amoa she uttered an inflected, halting, slightly comical Twi. This was because amoa was understood to be of northern, non-Asante origins. The facial scarring and maniacal grin of his effigy conveyed Asante perceptions of the otherness of the non-Asante (i.e. non-human) savanna dweller. In consequence amoa was simultaneously risible and frightening, for his laughable uncouthness bespoke not only a lack of culture but also a belonging in that non-Asante nature that was the source of unknown and terrifying powers. Ambiguities of all sorts surrounded amoa. He provided helpful 'medicines', but his principal task was to exercise a 'severity in all measures of vengeance' when so directed by his 'father's fury'. His peer kurukoro stood in the same relationship to taa kwabena bena as did an ahenkwaa to the Asantehene. With his messenger's cap and club he functioned as the emissary of the ɔbosom. He was sent forth to appear to malefactors and to inhabit their thoughts with warnings and threats. Hence when Amma Kyirimaa spoke with the voice of kurukoro she declaimed in the rasping, quickfire, minatory Twi of the royal ahenkwaa. As chief lieutenants of the ɔbosom both amoa and kurukoro represented aspects of his awesome powers. All three spoke through Amma Kyirimaa, clothing her in the nimbus of taa kwabena bena. She uttered for and as the ɔbosom, and this conferred upon her an aura of privileged insight and a place of distinctive authority in the community.[79]

Amma Kyirimaa's connection to taa kwabena bena singled her out but otherwise she led the life of her fellow villagers. She had three husbands in all. The first of these was Poku Twumasi Ankra of Adeɛbeba by whom she had seven children. He died following a hunting accident. She then married Mensa Kwakwa, a rich man from Saawua and an intimate of the Asantehene Mensa Bonsu (1874–83). In fact Mensa Bonsu may have played a part in the meeting of Amma Kyirimaa and her second husband. Like his brother and predecessor Kofi Kakari, Mensa Bonsu often consulted Adeɛbeba taa kwabena bena. He sent messengers from Kumase to Amma Kyirimaa with his queries and his gifts for the ɔbosom. Be that as it may, Amma Kyirimaa's second marriage produced no children. Indeed Mensa Kwakwa effectively deserted his wife. He was an opponent of Agyeman Prempe, and in 1888 he fled into Akyem Kotoku with the rest of Yaw Twereboanna's defeated supporters. It is unclear whether or not he ever returned to Asante. However, at some stage Amma Kyirimaa 'cast him off' by divorcing him *in absentia*, an action that might have entailed complications if there had been offspring of the union or if Mensa Kwakwa had reappeared in Adeɛbeba. In or about 1890 Amma Kyirimaa married for the third and final time. Her last husband was Kwadwo Mensa, and like her first he was an Adeɛbeba man (from the Wono group). Two daughters were born in quick succession. These were Akosua Pokuaa and Abena Kraa (also called Abena Bima) and by the early 1900s they were Amma Kyirimaa's only surviving children.[80]

Amma Kyirimaa's name came up repeatedly and more often than any other in the narrative reminiscences of her fellow villagers. She was recalled as being a forceful personality in her own right as well as displaying the authority conferred upon her by *taa kwabena bena*. Her character and status together put her at the hub of the myriad transactions that made up the daily round of life in Adeɛbeba. In brief she was an important voice in and an acknowledged leader of her community. It is to be regretted that much of her impact – her quotidian presence – in Adeɛbeba is lost to the historical record, for it occurred within that everyday realm that so often leaves behind only indistinct or fragmentary traces. Adeɛbeba, to recap, was a small face-to-face community in which 'the inhabitants behaved as if they were all of one father and mother'.[81] Within this close-knit world Amma Kyirimaa knew everyone. She was both listener and adviser, a confidante of the troubled and a counsellor to the perplexed. She led her neighbours before the *ɔbosom*, consulted the 'oracle pot' (*nsuo yaa*) on their behalf and gave voice to whatever utterance was forthcoming. She was an arbiter in all manner of domestic disputes. She made and mended marriages. She presided over nubility rites. She organised women for communal work. She was the village midwife, greatly valued for her access to the supernatural powers that played such an imponderable part in childbirth. She aided the sick (acting on the instructions of *amoa*). These activities meshed with her public status and role. As the mouthpiece of the village *ɔbosom* she was looked to by the local political authorities – and by the *Manwerehene* – for advice on issues affecting Adeɛbeba. Farming, building, ritual and all of the many other activities and proprieties that calibrated the ordering of communal life were subject to the injunctions of *taa kwabena bena* as told through his servant *ɔkɔmfɔ*. In all, Amma Kyirimaa was a busily involved presence in shaping, directing and watching over her community.

But if Amma Kyirimaa was a leader among her neighbours then she was also set apart from them by the simple fact of having been chosen by *taa kwabena bena*. In Asante understanding this singularity clothed Amma Kyirimaa in a fearful aura of separation and distance. She had intimate traffic with hazardous supernatural power and this adept familiarity marked her as a person. It also affected her as a lineage member and mother, for her intercourse with the *ɔbosom* was interpreted as a disposition that inhered in her blood (*mogya*). Her intimacy with otherworldly powers might be activated in her close kin and children. In effect Amma Kyirimaa's experience defined her closest uterine relatives as being imbued *in potentia* with a receptivity to communication from non-human powers. As has been noted, both her uterine sister and brother were chosen as servants by *taa kwabena bena* and in time her children had like obligations placed upon them. Thus Amma Kyirimaa and her immediate matrikin had an ambiguity about them. They were powerful and important people. But the source of their distinction was an entity that was fickle, dangerous and alien, whatever its temporary disposition towards a cooperative domestication among the people of Adeɛbeba. Amma Kyirimaa herself was looked up to and admired. But the respect accorded her in the community was tinged with wariness and not a little fear.[82]

The understandings that framed Amma Kyirimaa's words and deeds – and enabled her emergence as a community leader – are difficult to describe economically. Like many *atano* Adeɛbeba *taa kwabena bena* was gendered in that it was believed to manifest itself in both a male and a female aspect. The male ('Father Fetish') manifestation resided in the brass vessel that sat on the chair in the *ɔbosomfie*. This was the shrine (*(a)yawa*) of the *ɔbosom*. It gave orders to Amma Kyirimaa as to which physical substances might be added to it or removed from it.[83] It was this that the possessed Amma Kyirimaa bore on her head when she paraded the village giving voice to 'his' utterances. The female manifestation was resident in the *nsuo yaa* or 'oracle pot', a clay vessel that was kept beneath the chair in the shrine building. The male *(a)yawa* was clamant, minatory and punitive (and was supported in this behaviour by his 'sons' *amoa* and *kurukoro*). The female *nsuo yaa* was sibilant, supportive and forgiving. The homologies with Asante readings of gender are clear, and they extended to encompass the antinomies inhering in all such modelled stereotypes. Thus, despite his aggression, the male aspect of *taa kwabena bena* might also act with masculine protectiveness and the compassion deriving from strength. By corollary, despite her empathy, the female aspect might also conduct herself with feminine duplicity and the malice arising from weakness. Much could be said in elaboration but our purpose here is to draw attention to the way in which *taa kwabena bena* was conceptualised by the people who heard it speak through Amma Kyirimaa. It was both projection and reflection of the basic biological, existential and intersubjective dimensions of Asante personhood. As such it offered up a forum for the interrogation and possible resolution of the many personal problems thrown up by those environments within which Asante villagers fashioned and made narrative sense of their identities. The imbricated expressions of *taa kwabena bena* – as personhood, gender, kinship, community, authority (with its ɔkyeame and nhenkwaa) and the rest – gave the lives of its constituents back to them as in a mirror, but refracted to an image of that more acceptable selfhood in which anxieties and problems dissolved. This was a therapeutic idiom of renewal to which Adeɛbeba people returned again and again so as to acquire the resolve to go on with their lives. Amma Kyirimaa spoke of resolution to the irresolute and cast a cloak of fixity over the community by relaying the protocols of an adequate belonging to its members.[84]

Adeɛbeba taa kwabena bena quickly gained a reputation for efficacy. Its area of special expertise was yadeɛfo. These were 'diseases' with physical symptoms but social and metaphysical causes. They were said to be occasioned by conflicted or antagonistic interpersonal relations and arose most commonly (but not exclusively) within the lineage or between the sexes. They were grave complaints in that they struck at the fundamentals of kinship, marriage and procreation. If untreated they might develop into abusua yadɛ, transmitted by and blighting ('spoiling') descent. Thus a daughter of the Asantehene Mensa Bonsu named Afua Ntimaa was treated by taa kwabena bena for repeated stillbirths (abaawuo) and subsequently bore a son. Other yadeɛfo were brought to the ɔbosom and Amma Kyirimaa dispensed its diagnoses and prescriptions. Cases of female infertility (awoo), male impotence (kɔtewui), premature delivery (nyidwuo; also spontaneous abortion), menstrual irregularities (deepua), adherence of the placenta (awodɛ) and breech delivery (akwaada na atendaabere) are all reported. Matters other than yadeɛfo were also brought to Amma Kyirimaa. Note has been made of her role as village midwife (wogyefo), a job that involved obstetric knowledge. In stubborn cases of childbirth village women knew that Amma Kyirimaa could enlist metaphysical aid in support of her practical skills. Thus in the matter of Takyiwaa Benya, an Adeɛbeba mother of eight dangerously weakened by childbearing, Amma Kyirimaa was able to bring about an end to conception (ye twa no awo: lit. 'we cut her birth') through the advice of taa kwabena bena.[85]

It is important to point out at this stage that yadeɛfo and similar problems having a metaphysical dimension were not necessarily attributed to the malign operations of witchcraft (bayi). Like many atano abosom, Adeɛbeba taa kwabena bena had no particular specialisation in witchcraft matters. Few recorded cases of this type were brought before it. Those that were either remained undecided (in the sense that witchcraft was ruled out) or they were transferred from the jurisdiction of taa kwabena bena to a neighbouring shrine with an acknowledged competence. Thus Adeɛbeba people looked to the nearby shrines of afaawo at Adeɛmmra or apeapa at Nye ɛso for help with bayi. Recollection claims that witchcraft was not a serious problem in Adeɛbeba until the 1890s. Thereafter it burgeoned 'as a plague on us to be resisted to destruction' to the point where (about 1921–2) 'Brahuah (*afua brahua*) came to add her power on to us.'[86] Witchcraft in Adeɛbeba is discussed more fully in due course.

By the 1880s the efficacy of the *ɔbosom* and the charisma of its *ɔkɔmfɔ* together endowed *taa kwabena bena* with a reputation that extended far beyond Adeɛbeba. Individual manifestations of *abosom* operated within a pluralist economy of belief that was porously open to new revelations. As a result, shrines functioned within a jostlingly competitive 'market'.[87] Admired specialists in *yadeɛfo*, *taa kwabena bena* and Amma Kyirimaa achieved – to pursue the same metaphor – enviable niche marketing. Thus the sources record that from the early 1880s ever-growing numbers of Asante travelled to Adeɛbeba to consult the *ɔbosom*. Most were from Kumase itself or the towns and villages of Amansie and Mponoa. But people also came from more distant Kwabre and Sekyere and even from as far away as Asante Akyem.[88] If *taa kwabena bena* increased its reputation then it was at the expense of other shrines. To take only the case of *atano abosom*, there were manifestations of these within easy walking distance of Adeɛbeba at Adeɛmmra, Atasomaaso, Daban, Akyease, Apraman, Toase and Kaase. There was also *taa kwadwo*, whose eighteenth-century shrine was in the nearby Asokwa ward of Kumase. But in the closing twenty years of the nineteenth century 'Taa Bena eclipsed all other of the Fetishes around by prophecy and understanding' of the many problems brought before it.[89] Whatever allowance is made for local chauvinism, the fact remains that Adeɛbeba *taa kwabena bena* was very successful. Nor did the turbulence of the mid-1880s decrease the flow of anxious supplicants. If anything, their numbers increased and went on growing throughout the crises of the 1890s. In the process *taa kwabena bena* – and Amma Kyirimaa – became prosperous from a steady stream of offerings, gifts and bequests. By the time of the *yaa asantewaakɔ* in 1900–1 Amma Kyirimaa was possibly the wealthiest and certainly the best-known person in Adeɛbeba. Her position as a community leader was assured. It is only with hindsight that we can see that this was the zenith of her prestige.

3

ADEƐBEBA LIVES:
CONTEXTUALISING COMMUNITY
AND IDENTITY

REFERENCE, INFERENCE AND COMMUNITY

In 1908 a body was discovered near Adeɛbeba on the path leading to
Santaase. An investigation was carried out by the British magistrate Capt.
H. A. Kortright. The identity of the deceased was readily established. He
was the pedlar Kofi Asare Bediako, a well-known figure in the villages
around Kumase. His mother Afua Kyim belonged to the Heman group at
Adeɛbeba and was still living there. But his father Kwasi Agyei was dead.
Whatever else people knew or thought about Kofi Asare Bediako, the
scandalous circumstances surrounding his father's death clung to him and
fuelled talk about him. Kwasi Agyei was from Suame just north of Kumase.
He was in service to the *Asantehene* Agyeman Prempe as head of the royal
hammock bearers (*Asoamfoɔhene*). But in 1895 he was revealed to be having
a sexual liaison with Akosua Berenya, a daughter of the Kumase royal Yaa
Afere and so a uterine sister of Agyeman Prempe's defeated rival Yaw
Twereboanna. This was prohibited, for in a calculated move to extinguish
dynastic competition Agyeman Prempe made it a capital offence to have
intercourse with any of Yaa Afere's daughters. Kwasi Agyei was tried,
convicted, tortured and publicly beheaded. His remains were cast into the
bush and mention of his name was forbidden (*popa*: lit. 'wiped away').[1]
Memories of the heinous crime and terrible fate of the father exacerbated
disquiet in people's minds as they pondered the equally sudden and
unexplained death of the son. Was there a connection? Who was responsible
for Kofi Asare Bediako's death? The British were of little help with these
conundrums. Kortright found no evidence of foul play, and so Kofi Asare
Bediako's death was attributed to heart failure or to some other natural
cause. Officialdom declared the matter closed and duly released the corpse
into the custody of Afua Kyim and her kin for burial. But the Adeɛbeba
community refused to inter Kofi Asare Bediako until such time as it had
exhausted its own procedures for establishing the cause of his death.

Kofi Asare Bediako's remains were tightly bound in cloth, placed on a litter
of palm branches and borne around Adeɛbeba by his lineage kin. This was
the custom of *afunu soa* ('carrying the corpse'), a divinatory inquest during
which the dead were implored to identify anyone responsible for killing or

otherwise harming them by wish, thought or deed. The 'apprehensive inquisition' involved was conducted in the following way.

> A stick of an average size was planted at a distance varying from 6 to 12 yards from the dreadful load and its bearers. The head of the family took his stand behind the fixed pole, and in a loud voice enquired in these words: (Let us assume that Yao was the name of the deceased and Mensah the head of the family). Mensah took his stand before the pole and cried aloud, 'Yao! I, Mensah stand before you, and in the name of all the members of my family of which I am the head enquire from you whether I or any person among my family is the cause of your death. If I or any one in my family is guilty of your death knock at this pole: if not Yao should signify.' The innocence of any family was testified and indicated by the corpse bending once to the right and to the left. This sign is called 'Thanksgiving by the Corpse.' The inquiry went on till the name of a suspected family had been mentioned. At this instant the pole would be knocked three, four, or five to six times consecutively with the corpse. The carriers of the corpse were supposed to be driven on to knock at the pole by the spirit of the deceased. After this the corpse would be carried back home, and the person or the door of the suspected individual in that unfortunate family would be knocked by the load. At some places the dead body would be left with the supposed malefactor to be washed, dressed and interred.[2]

This procedure was not always conclusive. Kofi Asare Bediako's corpse 'swayed to one side and then to another', pointing out 'several possible culprits'. Asked to interpret, the ɔkɔmfɔ and community leader Amma Kyirimaa stated that the dead man kept whispering 'worms will eat your flesh, whatever you do' (*nkanka be di wo nam, be di wo nam*), a sign that he held the village collectively responsible for his fate. The phrase itself was troubling. It was an imprecation (*ɔdome*) commonly hurled by victims – like Kofi Asare Bediako's father – at their executioners. The complex of alarming ambiguities arising out of the *afunu soa* called for clarification and resolution. This was sought in the cleansing ritual known as *mpata*, a measure intended to secure communal expiation by exposing and reconciling intersubjective antagonisms. It was anticipated that those with malice towards Kofi Asare Bediako would be revealed if Adeɛbeba people confronted all of the hostile undercurrents subversive of harmony between them. Accordingly, the villagers assembled and Amma Kyirimaa

> collected together 'Odwen' [camwood] root and put same into a pot. She put into it palm oil and ground the root into soft paste. When this was done she put in 'Kankabi' [a centipede] and 'Bogya' [a glow worm] and 'Tamiriwa' [a snail] with a black shell together into the

pot. These three living creatures are opposed to each other in some ways. The glow worm attacks the snail stings it and tries to eat it and the centipede has its meal on the glow worm itself and the snail is deadly poison to the centipede. When the three were all in the pot they caused commotion together. It was a big fight. But they realised all too soon that they were in danger of dying from the sticky paste and so they stopped their fighting to climb up the pot. A[mma] K[yirimaa] spoke to the three and lifted them out while informing all present that if enemies such as these might only save themselves by not fighting then how much more should the people of A[deɛbeba] help themselves by strict cooperation. She asked that everyone tell by their mouths why they are unwilling to live at peace amongst each other.[3]

An outpouring followed during which villagers confessed their ill feelings towards relatives and neighbours. In the course of this Kofi Asare Bediako's uterine nephew Kwabena Tabiri produced a scrap of blue yarn (*bibiri*). He announced that this was from the haft of one of the knives used to kill Kwasi Agyei. It had been given into his safekeeping by Kofi Asare Bediako with the solemn injunction not to lose it. But the two had quarrelled, and when the uncle died the nephew looked for but could not find the yarn. Kwabena Tabiri 'therefore admitted he was the one who brought about the tragic death' of his kinsman through a wilful neglect born of spite. It was only 'on this day' of *mpata* that he determined to confess. Once this decision was taken he immediately remembered where the yarn was hidden and recovered it. Uproar followed this speech. The crowd took up the chant 'send our child away' (*fa abofra no kɔ*), meaning that Kwabena Tabiri should be expelled from Adeɛbeba to atone for his behaviour and 'to save our village from any further threats from backbiting amongst ourselves brought forth by his evil presence'. Amma Kyirimaa appealed for quiet but was shouted down. In fear of his life Kwabena Tabiri 'turned on his heels and fled into the bush'.[4]

Some days later a British officer accompanied by a policeman arrived in Adeɛbeba and ordered the villagers to assemble. He announced that Kwabena Tabiri was in Kumase and had given an account of his treatment to the authorities. Government was unconcerned with the rights or wrongs of the case, the officer continued, but it was determined to punish any breach of the peace arising out of the observation of 'native customs, rites and worship'. Accordingly, under the provisions of the Ashanti Native Customs Ordinance (1908) Adeɛbeba was fined £8, required to desist from practising *afunu soa*, *mpata* or 'rituals of a like kind that are liable to inflame feeling and threaten public order', and ordered to bury Kofi Asare Bediako. Kwabena Tabiri would not be returning to Adeɛbeba, the officer concluded, and the matter was now closed.[5] Adeɛbeba people who were present at this meeting later recalled that the British officer was listened to with mixed feelings.

> Some became ashamed of how they treated Kwabina Tabri in making him a scapegoat. It is not a right thing to do to blame one person for all of the hardships of living; people are always ready and willing to think bad of each other in this life and this is true here [Adeɛbeba] as everywhere. In the same way some people said that in the Glory Days of Ashanti Kingdom before the coming of British Empire then such as K[wabena] T[abiri] should have paid the debt of nature with his head for bringing a bad behaviour as an example. If one person is quarrelsome then others follow suit Mako Mako [*mmako mmako*: 'one after the other'] until the town is spoiled. If the wrongdoer had come back some would have extended the hand of forgiveness to him. It is better that he stayed away as he did because a town is All for One and One for All. Evil thoughts of a guilty kind cannot be kept hidden. They spread over all and one bad person can bring about the ruin of a town when left unchecked. The smooth running of affairs needs a constant attention to find out the bad before it spoils the good.[6]

Like many another, the story just recounted is much concerned with debating and describing the nature of community. It is structured around conceptual proprieties. Its narrativity is driven by the acknowledgement and attribution of deontic statuses (commitments and obligations, entitlements and rights) as the essential denotations of how community was made and mobilised in Adeɛbeba. Conceptual proprieties are themselves normative statuses in the sense that they are performed correctly or incorrectly according to the protocols and calibrations of rules or practices. Thus rules or practices combine the ontological with the deontological, the model itself with instructions for its use. I have argued elsewhere that Asante custom conflated rules with practices at the epistemological and performative levels.[7] Be that as it may, we are still left with the problem of identifying the descriptors relevant to the Asante understanding of community. Their historical articulation clearly resided in and was secreted as narrative, a configuration now much discussed in Africanist and other historiographies.[8] But how was narrative sourced and accessed? If the narrated representation was constructed by means of reference to and inference from rules and practices, then what ways of worldmaking lay behind, enabled and conditioned strategies and procedures?[9] This is important, for the selves in all of our Adeɛbeba testimonies have an autobiographical autonomy (*l'histoire à soi*) that was circumscribed and arbitrated by communal determinations. Adeɛbeba lives were quite literally self-interested, but were also recognised as being – in Deleuze's sense – shared ontologies or collective properties that 'passed through' individuals by intersubjective subscription.[10] If Adeɛbeba people existed alone and together, then how was synergy achieved between personal and communal identities? The answer lies in what narrative and other articulations reveal about the nature of embodied understanding and discursive practice.

The capacity to refer to and to infer from agreed rules and practices depends *ipso facto* upon a shared ground of intelligibility. How is this inscribed and sustained? Rules and practices compose the ethnographer's custom, or what the philosopher Taylor (following Wittgenstein and Bourdieu) terms 'background understanding'. This

> underlies our ability to grasp directions and follow rules [and] is to a large degree embodied. This helps to explain the combination of features it exhibits: it is a form of understanding, a making sense of things and actions; at the same time it is entirely unarticulated; and third, it can be the basis of fresh articulation. As long as we think of understanding in the old intellectualist fashion, as residing in thoughts or representations, it is hard to explain how we can know how to follow a rule, or in any way behave rightly, without having the thoughts to justify this behaviour as right. We are driven to a foundationalist construal, which would allow us to attribute only a finite list of such thoughts justifying an action from scratch, as it were. Or else, abandoning this, we are forced to conceive of a supporting background in the form of brute, de facto connections. This is because intellectualism leaves us only with the choice between an understanding that consists of representations and no understanding at all. Embodied understanding provides us with the third alternative we need to make sense of ourselves. At the same time, it allows us to show the connections of this understanding to social practice. My embodied understanding doesn't only exist in me as as individual agent, but also as the coagent of common actions. This is the sense we can give to Wittgenstein's claim that obeying a rule is a practice. He means by this a social practice.[11]

Embodied understanding translates to collocative enactment during which persons make sense of and for themselves by making sense to and with others. This meets the propositional criteria and dispositional ordering of Adeɛbeba testimonies, but a still more precise cultural and historical specificity can be added in amplification. In Asante the constituents of embodied understanding were spoken but not written down. The result was that cultural actors made extensive use of a panoply of non-verbal technologies in support of speech. Communicative efficacy depended upon acquiring and inhabiting normative synergies between speaking and its appropriate situational, behavioural and temporal environments to a degree unnecessary among people with access to a written mnemonic of reference and inference. The absence of a written record imposed structural limitations (of a Weberian kind that is much debated in Asante historiography), but it cannot be equated with an impoverished communicative order. As I have argued in other contexts, exuberant incorporations characterised the Asante hermeneutic. Embodied understanding was expressed in and through the protocols of this encompassing imaginary. Speech acts and their circumstantial determinations were oriented to explore and assimilate interlocutory properties inhering in the material and non-material worlds. Place and landscape were constituents of embodied understanding, and rootedness in or alienation from them were experienced in dialogic exchanges with them. 'The bush possesses ears and a mouth' (*wura mu haban wɔ aso ne ano*) encapsulated the understanding that nature and everything in it vibrated with communicative capacity. The realm of the supernatural was also alive with talk, and Asante constructions of belief hinged on an embodied understanding that admitted non-human entities to the competencies of address and response. Thus, Adeɛbeba *taa kwabena bena* spoke to and through Amma Kyirimaa. Its utterances might need interpretation, but they were intended for all. Like everyone else the *abosom* talked, and like everyone else they expected a hearing and sought a response.

Embodied understanding describes the process by which Asante people became interlocutory participants in a shared ground of intelligibility rooted in language and its supporting technologies. The realisation of intelligibility as community depended upon a public sphere of conceptual proprieties and their deontological applications being interpreted through discursive practice. Encounters between practitioners presumed common terms of reference and inference. But engagement in discourse required that participants exercise some latitude in acknowledging one another's dispositions. In sum, discursive communication had intensional but also extensional dimensions. These defined an arena of commitment in which – and here I follow Brandom – contracting parties made things 'explicit'.

> Interpreting the members of a community as engaging in discursive practices is interpreting them as binding themselves by objective, shared concepts whose proprieties of use outrun their dispositions to apply them. There is no answer that could be given in advance as to how much one must be able to get right in order to be interpreted as hooked up to one concept or another. Massive individual differences in inferential dispositions among interlocutors are compatible with interpreting them all as nonetheless governed by (answerable to) the same set of conceptual proprieties. For it is compatible with interpreting them as talking about the same objects, answering to the same set of objective facts.[12]

It is apparent that discursive practice in a community is a form of intersubjective scorekeeping. It is incumbent upon contracting parties that they adopt intensional and extensional stances towards one another. By doing this they 'can appreciate the inferentially articulated pragmatic significance' of their own speech and actions as well as entertaining the 'claims' and 'nonlinguistic performances' of others.[13]

Since the consequence of succeeding in all these procedures is the naturalisation (or conventionalisation) of community over elapsed time, it is hardly surprising that there are deeply felt first-person Adeɛbeba accounts of deviance but only ethically generalised individual testimonies to conformity. No one rehearsed their adherence and devotion to normative proprieties in detail. Any such stance was a given, and in any case attributions of virtuous conformity were properly made by community members other than oneself. But transgressors subjected to opprobrium and duress often rehearsed their offences with a minute attention to the empirical facts of the case. Motives for this doubtlessly mixed together fear and guilt with a desire to end ostracism and regain acceptance by and inclusion in the community. Whatever prompted such statements, their content took the form of a running commentary on the speaker's betrayal of self and others as a result of the willed misuse of communication. That is why the preamble to penitent disclosure was formulaic: 'I am now going to confess through the words of my mouth so that I may regain my life and henceforth thrive' (*nana mere bɛka manum asɛm na ma nya aduan adɛ*). The habitual deformation of discursive practice – by innuendo (*akutia*), backbiting (*ntwiri*), slander (*asɛm a wɔka de seɛ obi din*), lying (*twa nkontompo*), and all the rest – was acknowledged to be a deadly subversion of community. Recognition of the great power for good or ill that was locked up in the web of words sometimes led malefactors (discursive malpractitioners) to discern in their specific offences a larger intention to undermine all conceptual proprieties. Such people characterised their offending selves as the very negation of community. In an eagerness to make amends they confessed to being active citizens of and sedulous proselytisers for an inverted communal order. Purgation took the form of talking about this counterlife, and redemption lay in offering up its counterfeited version of community for comparison with the real thing.

The language of witchcraft confession is an extreme case in point. Five statements of this sort are contained among the Adeɛbeba testimonies. One was made by the petty trader and seamstress Abena Gyebi in Twi and recorded in the original (with its sentences numbered in parallel with those of an English translation set down in the same hand). Abena Gyebi was one of the Wono *nkoa* at Adeɛbeba. She was a uterine niece of Adwowaa Bemba, whose own daughter Yaa Kuruboaa's tragic death in the 1870s has

already been discussed. Amma Kyirimaa's brother Kwasi Fi described
Abena Gyebi as being 'known all her days as a woman who is keeping a
Bayie Kukuo (*bayi kuku*: 'a witch's pot')'. By her own admission, Abena
Gyebi made her first confession of witchcraft as a young girl 'before Nana
Prempeh was taken away out of Ashanti' in 1896. Over the years she made
further confessions of the same sort. In 1945 she 'suffered visitation of evil
influence' once again and unburdened herself before the *kankanmmea* shrine
at Ankaase. It was immediately after this that she gave an account of her
many confessions. She said that they all repeated the same story of seizures
and thoughts 'that come over again all the same to make me every time do
bad in my dealings'. Asked to explain, she made the following illustrative
statement. Attention should be paid to the circumstantial structuring and
unfolding of the narrative in terms of the interrelationship between
conceptual proprieties, discursive practice and community.

> I am a proper witch. I am misleading people by concealment when
> talking with them in a sly manner of deception. I know I must not do
> such a thing as it wrongs people and leads me on to my downfall. But
> I am a witch. I have devoured 99 people. At our meetings every one of
> us brings one victim to be sacrificed. I have a black mamba snake in
> my genitals that I keep there. Any man whom I do not like in any way
> is bitten during embrace. I have removed the ovaries from many
> women even including my two sisters. I have roasted them so that
> none may bear children and can only weep. I put people into a very
> dangerous state of health. I wish I got rid of the influence that takes me
> off at nights to a place that is like here [Adeɛbeba] although it is only
> looking like it. It is an evil place. My grandmother Y.T. gave me the
> power herself from her cordial dislike of her sisters and her own
> trusting neighbours. She was rancrous [*sic*] person who told lies to get
> people into difficulty. She worked like I am working nowadays to end
> any smooth feeling in the town. Because of her I got into a habit of
> dreaming some peculiar dreams. These developed some more until
> the presence of other people in them called me away all the time to the
> true home. I was wanted there to help make the town. In this world
> where we are meeting there is an organisation just as we have in
> ordinary life. We have means of locomotion. Our town has been
> divided into three quarters by mystical rivers. The elders sit us down
> to eat and talk over improving the town by capturing people to its
> population. My challenge is to bring over new people so I set out to
> deceive all those I know in life when I fly back here [to Adeɛbeba]. I do
> impose a dying condition on this place by diabolical talk of cursing
> others and nursing grudges and setting people at odds. In time all will
> be convinced that the true home is the town of the Satanic Fraternity
> and so accompany me there riding on the back of Osebo [*ɔsebo*: a

leopard]. They will be happy to leave – Sa tena bea yiye yare [? *saa tena bia yi yɛɛ yare*: ? 'to remain here in such a state is a sign of ill health']. I am doing this work wholeheartedly but it is under an evil influence. This is the reason I have come here to you to beg of you [the shrine being addressed] to hear and give up to me your help for restoring my good health.[14]

REFERENCE, INFERENCE AND IDENTITY

In 1931 the future Asante and Ghanaian politician Joe Appiah was thirteen years old. He was living in Kumase Adum and preparing to go to Mfantsipim school.[15] In the evenings he and his friends used to go to a playing field to flirt with the girls who gathered there to sing and dance. One night the girls chanted a new song that 'bowled us over' because it was 'profane in the extreme' and 'constituted the most daring challenge to our manhood and courage'. The girls declared that 'an uncircumcised penis is detestable' and avowed that they would 'never marry the uncircumcised'. This 'taunting' was repeated night after night and during the day as well. Appiah and his friends held 'long deliberations' and decided to heed the 'plea' of their 'future sweethearts and wives'. Accordingly, they inquired at the Kumase Government Hospital but were told that circumcision was only performed on medical grounds. So they went to a Muslim Hausa 'circumcision surgeon' who plied his trade in the Kumase Zongo. Appiah volunteered to go first. His account of the procedure – knife, blood, pain – is a picaresque vivid with daring and fright. But his recollection of the aftermath is altogether more reflective. Circumcision brought

> approbation from the girls but scorn and contempt from the adults – male and female – of Adum. The song of scorn was never repeated again by the girls in their nightly frolics, for we had proved our mettle as worthy scions of our brave ancestors.
>
> But, alas, we were to lose our rights to be elected as 'chiefs' in the future because we had forfeited those rights by our decision to become 'half-alive and half-buried' through our circumcision. We had eaten of the forbidden fruit, and were to pay the penalty for so doing. It was the fast traditional rule that no man could occupy a stool once he was circumcised. Happily, like many other traditional usages and rules, this rule has been relaxed and it is suspected that today [1990] many occupants of stools are our comrades in affliction.[16]

In Asante custom male (or female) circumcision (*twa twetia*) was prohibited as 'an abominable thing' (*akyiwadeɛ*), for bodily incompleteness of any kind was deemed to be physically offensive and metaphysically dangerous.[17] But young Appiah and his friends were not alone in their transgression. After the

First World War 'many young men and boys ran to embrace the deadly
fashion of being circumcised'.[18] By the 1930s the Chief Medical Officer of
Health in Kumase felt impelled to comment on the practice because of 'the
great number of infections we see resulting from this operation. It is
frowned upon by older Ashanti on religious and other grounds but young
men flock to have it done by northerners in Kumasi and other towns in spite
of the risk from unhygienic conditions.'[19] All the evidence indicates that
male circumcision was a major source of conflict between old and young
throughout colonial Asante. In Adeɛbeba disputes about it generated
partisan opinion and heated exchange. However, it is clear that a wider
spectrum of antagonisms hovered about the issue of male circumcision and
were articulated through it. Adeɛbeba people themselves ruefully admitted
that 'talk about the thing itself (male circumcision) got little result because
complaints of every kind were heaped up on top'.[20]

Mention has been made of Kwabena Oben of Odumase who resettled at
Adeɛbeba with his father in the 1890s and later became a dealer in timber.
About 1900 he married Afua Amponsaa, a descendant of the Adeɛbeba
pioneer Yaa Atiwaa of Saawua. The couple had two sons and then two
daughters. The boys were Yaw Awua and Yaw Asare and both were born
before 1905. At the end of the First World War Kwabena Oben used his
contacts to find his teenage sons jobs bagging and carrying wood chips at a
sawmill in Kumase. All went well until one day when the brothers returned
to Adeɛbeba and Yaw Asare 'fell down in a faint as if dead' while talking to
his father. His clothing was stained with blood and investigation revealed
that he was circumcised. Kwabena Oben became enraged and in the row
that followed Yaw Awua admitted that he too was circumcised. 'It was a bad
evil thing that they had done', Kwabena Oben recollected,

> because no Ashanti man is to be cut in this way. They had gone against
> me. I was looking out to find wives for them as a father ought to and
> they understood that the watchword in life was 'Ti Egya Asem' [*tie
> agya asɛm*: 'obey the words of father']. I questioned them why they did
> this bad thing. They gave no explanation but that it was the new
> Kumasi custom. I knew this to be true because young men here
> [Adeɛbeba] and there were at the time running to do it. It was a
> fashion because boys and young girls said it made the act of sex
> [coition] better [more satisfactory] to all concerned. They thought it
> was an enlightened thing for the upkeep of health given out by the
> Europeans. [Laughs] Boys did it all together to make themselves brave
> in showing courage as men and so each of them pushed on the other.
> It was a profitable business for the people charging 1/- each. The cause
> behind it was sex. All boys and girls were taking their opportunity that
> would not have been formerly allowed to them by their parents. A girl
> especially was kept in a private state before she went to marry the one

picked for her. But now Ashanti is full of Tootoo women (*tuu tuu*: slang for a prostitute; der. *atuu*: 'embrace, grip tightly'). Young boys go to them and their appetite increases. It is a big change since former days. Children do not obey their elders as formerly. They go about with a motto of pleasing yourself that is 'Ninkyin Dodo' [*nyinkyin dodoɔ*: lit. 'changing oneself repeatedly and excessively'].[21]

Other Adeɛbeba adults echoed Kwabena Oben's views.[22] Male circumcision was condemned as being symptomatic of an encompassing moral economy in which parents were losing control over their children because normative proprieties were being eroded and were leaching away. Reference to rules and practices was being overcome by inferential dispositions that privileged personal autonomy in novel ways promulgated and foregrounded by the inscriptive power of the colonial order. The limits and boundaries of discursive practice were in process of reformulation as radically different perspectives were brought to bear on conceptualisations of the relationship between the individual and the community. A great deal more will be said about these issues in due course when discussion is focused on questions of 'due recognition' under the colonial dispensation. But for the present let us look a little more closely at the matters just adumbrated.

Kwabena Oben used the phrase *nyinkyin dodoɔ* to encapsulate his view of what the fashion for male circumcision meant and intended. Other Adeɛbeba people – most volubly the loquacious Kwasi Fi, brother to Amma Kyirimaa and a servant of *taa kwabena bena* – condemned colonial youth in much the same terms. As he saw it, the problem was *mboroso* – literally excess, but with a sense of striving always to change so as to surpass and impress others.[23] It is clear that people like Kwabena Oben and Kwasi Fi feared that they were living through a deleterious shift in the conduct and aspirations of young people. They thought that youth flitted about in haphazard pursuit of novelties (*adefoforo*) like male circumcision. They sensed provocation and challenge in the ways that young people dressed and comported themselves. They detected signs of turpitude and aggression in youthful attitudes that they felt to be instrumental and irresponsible (*nea ɔnhwɛ n'abrabo so yiyɛ*). Above all, they held the young responsible for mounting assaults on received order through their radical readjustments of the terms of discursive practice. In this view young people were *mbasafoɔ*, quite literally those who spoke a language full of new words, usages and concepts (*abaso twi*). Their use of slang (*kasa a abɔfra kasa bi mu a gye wɔn a wɔka nkoto na ɛte ase*) purported their intention to exclude all those not privy to it. This argot of invention, reformulation or borrowing (from English in its British and later its American forms) also symbolised a shift in the pattern of intersubjective address and exchange. Conventions of deference to older people were being eroded by rising tides of discursive familiarity that took their cue from dissociation or hostility on the part of the young. Girls as well

as boys practised a newly explicit frankness (*pae mu se*), expressing alien
views in offhand ways to adults with an unprecedented directness. People
like Kwabena Oben and Kwasi Fi sensed, resented and feared this shift.
'Youth of today talk to their elders without respect. They lack discipline for
keeping themselves in check. They say anything of offensive kind. Even the
manner of speaking up when talking this disgraceful [*sic*] is not as before
being harsh and strange in the ears and not the proper thing at all.' Older
people saw habit and its certainties dissolving in flux because 'young people
today have no fear' (*nnɛɛ mmafoɔ nsoro biribi*) of the sanctions implicit in
established norms.[24] What young people themselves thought will be
discussed in due course.

Presented with an account of the sort just given, any analyst concerned to
identify the dialectical means by which Adeɛbeba people were inserted and
interpellated as historical subjects would point to deference as the crucial
ideological technology that kept inference subordinate to reference. She
would then go on to argue that the developments that alarmed Kwabena
Oben and Kwasi Fi arose out of the novel rhetorics of power that were
inscribed in Asante life by colonialism, westernisation and modernisation.
She would continue that young people – whose valorisation of the past was
pedagogically instilled rather than experientially acquired – were most
susceptible to a conscious identification with these potent new instrumenta-
tions. She would conclude that the consequences of inscription and identification were implicit in the configurations (the hegemonic intent) that
described and drove the rhetorics of power. That is to say, since the imbricated triumvirate of colonialism, westernisation and modernisation proposed European models of individualism (with their persuasions towards
realised autonomies of selfhood), it was to be expected that inference would
overcome deference as it uncoupled from reference.[25] There are countless
variations on this theme, dialectical and otherwise. It is conventional to
argue that twentieth-century colonialism and its ideological partners implanted individualism (inference) at the expense of community (reference)
all around the globe. But this prescriptiveness needs to be qualified in two
obvious and related ways. First, a reading of the evidence suggests that in
Asante (and presumably in many other societies) the binary relationship
between individualism and community has a recuperable history that
antedated the twentieth century and bore directly upon developments
associated with it. Second – and by corollary – while there can be little doubt
that the twentieth century raised the stakes in the matter of Asante
individualism by widening horizons of instruction and opportunity for the
realisation of selfhood, these radical developments (which will be discussed
in due course) must be analysed in relation to complex legacies of
precolonial identity formation.

Some help with these matters is provided by work done in Akan philosophy. Thus, in a robust but scrupulously argued discussion of Cartesian existentialism the Akan philosopher Wiredu has given an account of the 'ordinary language' meaning of *cogito ergo sum* in Twi. He writes that

> the most relevant fact regarding the concept of existence in Akan is that it is intrinsically spatial, in fact, locative; to exist is to be there, at some place. 'Wo ho' is the Akan rendition of 'exist.' Without the 'ho', which means 'there', in other words, 'some place', all meaning is lost. 'Wo', standing alone, does not in any way correspond to the existential sense of the verb 'to be', which has no place in Akan syntax or semantics. Recur, now, to 'I think, therefore I am', and consider the existential component of that attempted message as it comes across in Akan. In that medium the information communicated can only be that I am there, at some place; which means that spatial location is essential to the idea of my existence.[26]

Wiredu's point about spatialised existence is well taken. It answers to many of the reflexive denotations employed by Adeɛbeba witnesses to harness the individual to community. But does it meet the conditions of all cases or possibilities? Do rules of language use offer a comprehensive or even adequate transparency in clarifying the meaning(s) affirmed through the historical record?

I think that Wiredu (like other philosophers trained in the Anglo-American analytical tradition) would urge some such version of linguistic parsimony. Thus, in treating the verifiability or otherwise of the claim that 'exemption from the possibility of error is nothing short of infallibility' he again looks to the Twi language use to see what such a proposition might mean to the Akan.

> In this language to say 'I am certain' I should have to say something which would translate back into English in some such fashion as 'I know very clearly' (*Minim pefee* or *Minim koronyee*) or 'I very much know' (*Minim papaapa*). For the more impersonal locution 'It is certain' we would say something like 'It is indeed so' (*Ampa*) or 'It is true' (*Eye nokware*) or 'It is rightly or very much so' (*Ete saa potee*) or 'It is something lying out there' (*Eye ade a eda ho*). None of these turns of phrase has the slightest tendency to invoke any intimations of infallibility. To suggest that in order to say of something that *eta saa potee* I must claim exemption from the possibility of error would strike any average or above average Akan as, to say the least, odd in the extreme.[27]

This is fine as an account of communicative efficacy among like-minded individuals committed to a discursive practice objectified in and refereed by the third party of language rules. But historical actors seldom (if ever) possess this level of self-conscious identification with a struggle for clarity; motives for speaking are always interested, and inhibited by awareness of the interlocutory motives of others. In a like manner, historical subjects seldom (if ever) manifest this degree of dedicated identification with an edificatory pedagogy; resources for speaking are drawn from an individual's capital, and deployed tactically as investments rather than displayed altruistically for the common good. Thus, while the philosopher has significant and sometimes helpful things to tell us about the existence of regulatory protocols and conditional circumstances, he has less to say about the actual historical uses – and abuses – made of these by individuals in a community like Adeɛbeba. Empirical practice is not exact, but fuzzy. It is not programmed, but constructed historically out of negotiation involving individual and community. Confusion between the two perspectives can give rise to varieties of ahistorical idealism, a matter to which we now direct our attention.

In an analysis cued by communitarian critiques of liberal individualist social theory, the Asante philosopher Gyekye has discussed 'the notion of personhood from the normative perspective, highlighting a moral conception of personhood' in which he distinguishes 'person from individual, regarding the latter as socially detached and the former as embedded in, but only partially constituted by, the community'. Casting community as a reality and a value in and of itself (in MacIntyre's sense), he enlarges upon this distinction by observing that in Akan–Asante society, 'social success and economic achievement will by themselves not – from the perspective of the wider community – confer personhood on an individual, *if* [emphasised in original] that individual's conduct frequently falls short of the moral expectations of the community, if he fails, for instance, to demonstrate moral sensitivity to the welfare of others.' Thus 'achieving economic success or status is one thing'; but 'achieving personhood is quite another'. Now, Gyekye is too subtle a philosopher not to see obvious problems with his 'moral conception' of the Asante person as distinct from the Asante individual. In plain terms, how does an individual become a person, what are the criteria for measuring this, and who validates these criteria? 'I have a difficulty', Gyekye writes,

> not with the notion of moral achievement per se, but with how to bring it about, how, as it were, to achieve moral achievement. If moral achievement is the actual consequence of the successful exercise of an individual's moral capacity, how is it that some individuals succeed in this enterprise and so attain the status of personhood, while others fail in their moral endeavour and, thus, fail to attain that status? Since achievement here clearly involves a dynamic interplay between potentiality and actuality, the problem relates to the actualization of the potential. An examination of this problem, within the context of

morality, would involve a discussion of such concepts as trying, moral will, and moral weakness, which is beyond the scope of my present purposes.[28]

But there are teleological dangers here more serious than this cul-de-sac. Gyekye's notion of the individual – someone whose being is ontologically innate but whose personhood is ethically earned – does admit choice, for it sites ego in relation to degrees of responsibility or irresponsibility towards communally sanctioned moral aspiration. That is why (and how) some individuals succeed while others fail in the endeavour to achieve personhood. That no explanandum can follow on from this arises from Gyekye's use of a conceptual apparatus that is divorced from historical process. His 'potentiality' and 'actuality' take no account of dispositions outside of a closed circuit of ethical striving (just as Wiredu supposes that communication is naturalised to transparency by an analogous order of linguistic striving). There is an ahistorical idealisation at work here (inspired by the desire to make restitutive claims about Asante, Akan and African oral philosophical practice?). This is not to say that no processual contextualisation is on offer. It is, but it is similarly idealised to timeless generalisation – a stasis (read as an index of folk wisdom) rather than a kinesis (understood as an interrogation of historical evidence). In sum, it is all reference and no inference.[29]

Perhaps the problems described are insoluble, or amenable only to interrogation in part along the lines pursued throughout this chapter. But if areas of unknowing are conceded because of lacunae in the evidence, it still remains possible to pose – if not fully to answer – nagging questions about the precolonial Adeɛbeba community and the individuals who composed it. It must be acknowledged that the framework of inquiry here relies as much on the sense conveyed by the evidence as a whole as it does on any of the empirical information distributed across its parts. Critical reading of this kind is generated by intensively harrowing the same materials over and over again. It is the root of an informed reflection that provokes speculation about possibilities inhering in the sense, thrust or shape of the evidence and makes such thoughts resonate with experiential and other kinds of understandings. There is nothing arcane about this (given saturation in the relevant materials and milieux), and indeed it is a scholarly commonplace.

Consider the following. Many commentators have noted the potential for conflict implicit in the ordering of Asante society through prescriptive matrilineal kinship structures. A predictable consequence of such arrangements was gender-defined differences over the goals of marriage and reproduction. Men and women brought dissimilar priorities, investments and expectations to marrying and having children. These structural ambivalences and antagonisms spilled over into personal relations between the sexes. One expression of all this was the historical sedimentation of gendered stereotypes of otherness. Men and women affirmed and confirmed their suspicions of one another by drawing upon a folk tradition that cast difference as a given and disposed individuals to frame expectation and surmise with reference to its accumulated understandings. When Adeɛbeba people spoke of such matters they filtered personal experience through generic presumption to produce accounts freighted with a dissonantly jarring mix of passion and resignation. Abraded feeling and a lack of surprise at being its victim found focus and voice in bitter narratives that rehearsed the offences of the opposite sex as manifested by one or another of its members. Tales of gendered dereliction – emotional, sexual, financial and the rest – are recounted in the next chapter. But once explicit narratives of this sort are set on one side, it is striking just how many Adeɛbeba testimonies about matters other than gender are inflected by discursive preoccupation with its metaphorical power and reach. Thus, the farmer Kwaku Atuahene compared the will-o'-the-wisp nature of money to female duplicity; 'like woman it [money] is fickle to show you the back of the hand (*nsaakyi*; impl. *nsaakyinsayaamu*: 'two-faced, deceitful') in coming and going when it likes.' By corollary, the seamstress Adwowaa Yamoaa complained that work like marriage involved attentive commitment for uncertain reward; 'care to get ahead in this life is needful on every occasion just as vigilant outlook is for men to meet the promises they give freely only to neglect them after a time'.[30] It is conventional to read such remarks as evidence of gender relations made newly complex, dissonant or sour by colonialism. That may well be the case, but it is an argument that complements rather than contradicts another. In brief, there is an elusive yet palpable sense in the twentieth-century Adeɛbeba evidence that relations between men and women were conducted with an unease that long antedated colonialism.

Other ways of reading the evidence as a whole suggest other possibilities. Kwame (Amos) Mensah of the ASS research team scribbled a few lines on 'Homesickness for Village Life'. In this he noted a 'nostalgia' (*angyina*) among 'young immigrants to the towns both male and female but especially the former' for village friends, but not for the authority 'wielded over them' by parents and elders; young men particularly resented the controlling intrusions of fathers, 'distant and foreboding [*sic*] individuals as these are to many of them'.[31] Fortes took up hints of this sort and mulled them over in the light of his academic training in both psychology and anthropology. He wrote much on intergenerational relations understood within the conflicting contexts of matriliny and marriage. Thirty years after the ASS research, he reaffirmed his finding that 'the conjugal bond tends to remain relatively insecure in contrast to the bonds of matrilineal kinship for the partners'; a 'husband-father', he added, exercised only limited influence over 'directing the activities of wives and children'.[32] From such arrangements Fortes drew inferences that were later enlarged upon in a close rereading of his work by Horton. The 'situation of the individual in Ashanti society', so Horton concluded, 'would seem to be complex, conflict-ridden and generally disturbing'. This was because he (but also she) was brought up

> in a setting where one of his most important relationships, that with his father, lies outside the matrilineal nexus, and where the affairs of his matrilineage are still remote from him. Because of his parents' divided loyalties, moreover, he experiences feelings of insecurity which make for restless status-seeking later on. As an adult, the same person is asked to centre his life on the matrilineage, and, in so doing, to abstain from any aggressive competition therein. In short, the demands which society makes on him in later life conflict at several points with the desires and inclinations planted deep in him through early upbringing. And the whole of this later life is one long struggle to reconcile the demands of society with his individual aspirations.[33]

Whether or not we elect to follow this particular line of psychological reasoning is beside the point. What is pertinent is the overarching argument that problematises the contradictory situation of the single person (*obiakofo*) in relation to matrilineal, marital and parental bonds. Again, the Adeɛbeba evidence considered as a whole contains much that points towards the dynamics of affect and personhood being qualified by structural cleavages of the sort described. The example of father–son relations is a case in point. In several testimonies men characterised their fathers as being remote or unfamiliar figures who none the less expected unquestioning respect and obedience. 'My own father', recalled the Adeɛbeba palm-wine tapper Kwame Sefa, 'had as his motto self reliance. When he called us to him he might chastise us then order us to be good and work hard. He advised us always to rely on ourselves for every thing. I cannot say much more about him because children passed little time with their fathers.'[34]

Now the trend of such remarks (and of reciprocal complaints by fathers about their disobedient sons), when taken in conjunction with similar expressions of reserve concerning the drawbacks of marriage and the pitfalls of kinship, delineates a world of ensnaring intersubjectivities. In this, the individual struggled to gain some purchase on distance and emancipation. But here again, colonial developments – whatever the novelties of imperative or opportunity that helped to shape them – are linked to structural features of precolonial Asante society. Clearly, twentieth-century Adeɛbeba evidence speaks with its own voice. But it does so out of and with regard to a discursive inheritance freighted with all manner of equivocal irresolutions about the referential and inferential nexus that framed relations between individuals and the community. Gyekye himself goes some way towards conceding this very point about identity. In urging that social thought

attempts to strike a 'balance between individualism and communalism' in
Asante, he admits none the less that there is 'an enduring tension' between
personal goals asserted by the individual (inferential dispositions) and
normative values invested in the community (conceptual proprieties).[35]
Adeɛbeba witnesses help us to say things – fewer than we might hope, more
than we might expect – about the history of these 'enduring tensions'.

WITNESSING TO THEN AND NOW

On 1 January 1946 'Baafoɔ Manwerehene of Ashanti, elders and supporters
came down from Kumasi to Adiebeba to pour special libation' to thank *taa
kwabena bena* for 'assistance given during the dark days of the war now
ended'. This was a festive occasion that attracted sponsorship from various
Adeɛbeba people living in Kumase. The leading donor was Kwaku (Edward)
Ketewa of 'Bosumprah House, Old Ejisu Road, Fanti New Town-Kumasi'
who gave £10 'to buy rum' and the loan of a five-ton Bedford lorry to ferry
celebrants. He was present, dressed in a blue suit, shirt and tie. He gave off
an 'air of consequence' as various people greeted him 'and thanked him for
his generosity'. The ASS researchers who were there to record events had
never seen him in Adeɛbeba before and hastened to introduce themselves.
Kwaku Ketewa proved 'an affable man'. He explained that he was a
Kumase contractor who dealt in bulk metals and wire. In 1944 this business
had taken him to Takoradi on the Gold Coast and he had only just returned
to Asante. He had not visited Adeɛbeba since 1941 when he had come to
help perform the funeral rites for his mother Akua Badu, a sister of the
Wono *abusua panin* Kwadwo Konkoma. He 'politely asked after the work'
being done by the ASS and invited its researchers to visit him in Kumase.
This was serendipity indeed, for Kwaku Ketewa turned out to be most
cooperative and obliging. When he met Steel he expressed the 'warmest
support' for research that he thought would 'benefit the Ashanti and bring
improvements in their circumstances'. Be that as it may, among other things
Kwaku Ketewa allowed the ASS to conduct an intensively detailed
economic study of his household in Fanti New Town.[36]

Kwaku Ketewa's house was a sprawling, single-storey dwelling (since demolished) on the right-hand side of the Old Ejisu (Edweso) road where it ran
east from central Kumase towards Amakom. It was built to a traditional
design. Four sides pierced by entrances at the front and rear surrounded a
central courtyard. The side facing the street was made of whitewashed
concrete over a brick rubble fill. Kofi Ketewa, his wife and their three
youngest children lived there. The other three sides were of swish, but with
additional supports and other embellishments in more modern materials.
Four other 'quasi-households' (as the ASS termed them) occupied this
dwelling space. These were: Kofi Ketewa's unmarried sister Abena

Adarkwaa, who looked after another dead sister's two daughters; Kofi Ketewa's mother's sister's son Kwame Apea, his Fante wife Rebecca and their seven children; K. Ahenkora, a schoolteacher originally from Asuboa and unrelated to Kofi Ketewa, who rented with his wife and five children but also had living with him his younger sister and her own two children; and Akosua (Dora) Nketea of Kumase, a divorced (or long separated) cloth trader who rented with two of her unmarried daughters, each of whom had a small child of her own. In addition, two rooms by the rear entrance to the compound were rented out to single men. These were Kwaku Tawia of Obo in Asante Akyem who worked in the motor trade in Suame; and Yaw (Michael) Wiredu from Mampon Adwira whose uncle had apprenticed him to a carpenter and furniture maker in Manhyia. Finally, at any given time the house 'gave temporary shelter to relatives and friends who were in the town [Kumase] for one reason or the other'. In 1946 Kwaku Ketewa presided over a dwelling that accommodated thirteen adults (including himself), twenty-one children and young adolescents, and a floating population of visitors. This was a large number of people, even by the crowded standards of urban Kumase.

Kwaku Ketewa both inherited and made money. His father Kwasi Serebuo was a member of the celebrated Saawua *kuo*, a company of traders from that town who grew wealthy from the late nineteenth-century coastal trade. Kwasi Serebuo had three wives, but the youngest Akua Badu of Adeɛbeba was his favourite because she bore his only son Kwaku Ketewa. Thus, father and son were unusually close (in part too because Kwasi Serebuo quarrelled with his Saawua kin). About 1912 Kwasi Serebuo enrolled his boy in a Kumase school run by a Mr Easmon so that he might acquire writing and accounting skills. Kwaku Ketewa duly became his father's secretary and then his junior partner when the two of them began to put money into Kumase property. Kwasi Serebuo built and leased houses behind the Kumase railway station in Bompata; he put up a warehouse and other storage facilities at Asokwa; he bought two buildings at Amakom; and he purchased rights to several building plots in Manhyia. Then, in 1927 he acquired and began to put up a house for himself on a plot on the Edweso road. This dwelling was unfinished when Kwasi Serebuo died in 1931. Kwaku Ketewa inherited the property because his father 'swore [an oath] before Chief Frimpon [the Kumase *Adontenhene* Kwame Frimpon] and witnesses that the house in question was solely for his only begotten son and not for his ingrateful [*sic*] family [his Saawua *abusua*]'. Kwaku Ketewa finished building in 1933 and took up residence. The compound house cost £1,200 in total and had fourteen rooms.

In 1946 Kwaku Ketewa estimated that he might expect to realise £288 a year from the house if all the rooms - bar the two composing his own family quarters - were leased individually at an (admittedly maximum) economic rent of £2 a month. But his actual income from sub-leasing was only £72 per annum, and this was further diminished by annual maintenance costs of £12. In reality he was earning less than 25 per cent of potential rental income. Furthermore, while the young men Kwaku Tawia and Yaw Wiredu paid regularly (15/- a month each), the trader Akosua Nketea (£2 a month) and the schoolteacher Ahenkora (£2-10-0 a month) were behind with their rent. The last owed an accumulated deficit of five months rent (£12-10-0) in March 1946 and this was the subject of rows with and pleas to the landlord. But the real problem was Abena Adarkwaa and Kwame Apea. These two were Kwaku Ketewa's matrilineal kin from Adeɛbeba, and as such they paid only occasional or token sums on the six rooms they and their dependants occupied. Kwaku Ketewa found the whole situation irksome, and his irritation at his tenants was aggravated by money worries. He was reticent about his finances but the problem was centred around his need (or desire) for liquid capital to invest in business. He was much more forthcoming about his personal dissatisfaction with those living in his house and returned to this matter again and again in conversations with ASS researchers. Kwaku Ketewa's concerns were echoed by many another Adeɛbeba witness, but for whatever reason his capacity to situate them in a larger historical perspective was unusually acute.

Kwaku Ketewa described himself as 'a modern Ashanti man', and offered as proof his memberships of the Wesleyan-Methodist Church, the Society of Oddfellows and the Hudson Reading, Discussion and Debating Club of Kumase, together with his subscriptions to *The Ashanti Pioneer* (2/3d per month), the *Government Gazette* (£2 per annum) and *The Timber Traders Journal* (£2-2-0 per annum). He believed that the future of Asante depended upon 'education, education and again more education' in tandem with the 'responsibility for one's own path in life that is vouchsafed through Our Lord'. In line with his faith in 'progressing the Ashanti man and woman', Kwaku Ketewa paid school fees for various children living in his house or in Adeɛbeba; all received 'a course of regular instruction at school' and on Sundays attended Wesleyan-Methodist services in Kumase. He was especially proud of the fact that his sponsorship of 'relatives who were too grown up to attend school in their time' meant they were now able to 'read with tolerable fluency books written in their mother tongue'. Kwaku Ketewa had clients other than kin. Thrice he had paid over a 'craft fee' of £12 to apprentice 'promising and hard working young men' to master tradesmen. He explained all this in terms of the need for 'industry to get ahead' in life. His father was an 'illiterate' but had embraced Christianity 'in his adult life' and so had achieved much by dint of faith and hard work. 'I myself followed in his footsteps but learned reading and writing,' said Kwaku Ketewa, and so 'I have achieved the goal of life by a big effort.' But there were flies in the ointment of this self-fashioning.

Kwaku Ketewa complained that his philanthropic gestures were all too often seen by their beneficiaries as a right. His Adeɛbeba lineage kin and especially his sister Abena Adarkwaa were notably guilty in this regard. 'In the past', he reflected, 'we were all for one and one for all. Money was unknown. There was no need being few goods and the rule was you helped others of your family and they helped you in your turn.' This system he defined as 'of Communistic tendency and suitable for Ashanti then'. But 'nowadays money is here as the needful thing and so you must work to get your daily bread'. The problem was that 'in any family circle some will come to prosper by their efforts though others do nothing but [laughs] expect to eat sweet things – Sikyiri (di asikyire: 'to eat sugar').' Kwaku Ketewa saw himself as a progressive and a benefactor, yet much resented the burdens he had placed upon himself. Asked to explain these contradictions he condemned his sister and cousin for quitting Adeɛbeba and coming to live off him in his Kumase house, but added that there was little he could do about this situation. The reason for his own contradictions, he continued, lay in the contradictory condition of Asante society itself. 'I cannot send my own people away out of here', said Kwaku Ketewa,

> as if I did it I would suffer and get a bad name. They would say that I refused help to them when in necessity. The same if I refused to help with school fees for my younger nephews and nieces. In this Ashanti of now you must look to your own talents to go ahead and progress in your affairs. Village people are farmers and farming is not a very paying occupation. Still they bear the stamp of the influence of a need for money and so come to beseech me as I am their Big Uncle. It is my Christian duty to offer succor [sic] when asked though too many bear on me for this help with funeral expenses or schooling as for other reasons. In many a family of today to be wealthy means that you can be asked to support everyone from elderly people down to babes in arms. I do not like it as it shows lazy attitude by many who are thinking always to live by the sweat of the brows of others. It is a relic of the past to hinder the progress of Ashanti. All of these things are out of date and will surely vanish with time. But until the happy day arrives I cannot help but do as I am doing now.[37]

Kwaku Ketewa's witnessing makes it plain that the transit from the pre-colonial to the colonial was not a rupture with the past but a metamorphosis from it. This was an uncertain process, appearing profound or superficial in its effects depending on the angle from which it is viewed. Even so, we still need to form some conceptual understanding of the kind(s) of process involved. There are a number of ways to go about this. Let us begin with a summary recapitulation. This book is concerned with biographical experience, closely observed, over the century between roughly the 1840s and

1940s. One specific focus of this concern is to illustrate through an exploration of life histories – interlinked narratives of witnessing – some of the substantive contents and consequences of the shift from conditions of precolonial autonomy to those of colonial dependency. Empirical data from Adeɛbeba relevant to this process are analysed in the next chapter. Discussion there takes account of the legacies of the past, but it also looks to newly emergent themes in the lives of twentieth-century Adeɛbeba people. Our immediate concern here is to get some processual grasp on these themes by considering the knot of explicit practices and implicit understandings that is usually (and often promiscuously) collapsed together under some such rubric as colonial modernity. A caution needs to be entered and duly emphasised. African modernities (and postmodernities) of various kinds are the subject of a large and ever growing body of scholarship. A problem with much of this writing is that it is really a hermeneutics of the present-day, feebly or only very generally rooted in historical evidence. There is an obvious or even misleading limitation to understanding if one writes about, say, contemporary witchcraft in an African society without documenting the history (as opposed to the ethnography) of the practice. The present day has a past, and is comprehensible only in terms of a substantive account of what happened empirically in that past.[38]

The problems of arriving at some working definition of modernity and of assessing its impacts in a historical context like colonial Asante are legion. In due course we will look to this matter, and to possibly distinct but clearly related processes like modernisation and westernisation. But first let us simply take modernity as a given and explore how it can be historicised as processual event. It is nigh impossible to present any adequate sequential or linear account of its workings. This is because of the complexity of the issues in play, but also because of their elusiveness. The trace or signature of modernity in Adeɛbeba lives is partial and fragmentary, and often contradictorily at odds with discernibly historical protocols of reference and inference. Hence it is difficult to provide any generalisation about the strength of the forces at work, the degree of their penetration, the responses they elicited, or the consequential adjustments that did or did not ensue. Nor is this very surprising. Wherever modernity has impacted, it is agreed that it has been experienced as an unstable continuous present in the form of a gale blowing against the bulwark of the past. As such it is a solvent of past histories, but not in any predictable way. This liminality both assures and menaces by its transfigurative power. In its guise as disenchantment of the world – a new being promised or threatened but deferred in its precarious becoming – it is by turns exhilarating and frightening as (in Marx's wonderful apophthegm) 'all that is solid melts into air.'[39]

The environment generated by the process described inspires and/or terrorises just because it is ceaselessly mobile, a palimpsest of erasure and accretion. An obvious but complicating problem is that different changes move at different speeds, and with variable levels of visibility. Modernity in process is simultaneously present and absent, pervasive but evasive, engrafted yet uninscribed. Its tempos are multiple and fluctuating (here speeding up, there slowing down), just as its chronologies are friable and indistinct (here leaching into the past, there advancing into the future). Philosophers often give modernity the character of an 'unfinished project' and this has mundane as well as other significances.[40] That is, a constituent of its opacity is the vexing uncertainties that surround not only how it is realised but also when it is achieved. How do people – in Adeɛbeba or anywhere else – gauge their status within it? How much and what sorts of modernity are required before a subject can think of herself as being modern? There is no plausible answer to this question other than the historically conditioned. In any society the historical cadaver of modernity, so to speak, is revealed by sectioning its organs rather than labelling them. Slicing into its empirical history at any and/or every promising angle is the procedure required, for the components need to be fully exposed to view before the processual narrative can even begin to be glimpsed in dimmest outline. Dissection by slicing is messily promiscuous in its revelations, and so expectation is constantly surprised. This is entirely as it should be, for the history – the process – of modernity in Asante is comprehensible only as the sum of its parts.[41]

In attempting to recuperate the specificities of Adeɛbeba people's lives within the parameters of such a palpable but slippery conjuncture, we need to address some of the conventional objects of social history with radical suspicion. The unvoiced premiss of historical treatments of biographical narratives is dialectical, in the sense that subjectivities are acknowledged to be situational while the concept of identity itself is granted a privileged given-ness or even immutability. Identity is conceptualised as a vertical axis, the spine running through a lifetime that permits the historian to draw up a retrospective characterisation. The technique involved appropriates the data of existence, few and fragmentary as these commonly are, and then uses induction to reveal that spine and attach it to a larger social reality. Resulting explanations privilege conjunctures over disjunctures. Now this can be represented as a robust common sense (especially when accompanied by ritualised hand wringing over lacunae in the data), but it masks as much as it reveals.

The quest for the vertical axis of identity is limiting. It proposes a reconstruction grounded in identity understood as a host of irreducible singularities. But identity needs to be seen as a horizontal axis that opens into connectivities. This is not situational identity, but a recognition that what we term identity has no privileged given-ness. It is sited in negotiations conducted over a lifetime. That is, the quest for identity is the thing itself. It is constructed rhizomatically from connectivities of becoming and not foundationally from singularities of being. Hence, life histories are to be read through an optic of connectivities that presupposes neither core nor boundary. If lives derive and impart significations by making meaning in this way, then it is helpful to see modernity as a seismic intrusion into the field of rhizomatic connectivities. We might say that Asante connectivities to historical practice were destabilised and/or reconfigured through their entanglement with the injunctions and seductions proposed by modernity. Identity and agency in this situation were guesswork, deductive inferences drawn from the loudest messages received. The endless self-fashioning involved composed the empirical stuff of modernity, the transit from the precolonial to the colonial (and through it to the postcolonial).[42]

A useful way of looking at this and linking it to previous discussions of reference and inference is to consider the reconfiguration of communicative resources by and in modernity. Recall that in preliterate Adeɛbeba talk or speech (ɔkasa) was the primary instrument of affecting-the-other intersubjectively. But under the impress of modernity the cognitive and expressive framework of this 'interworld' (Schutz) or 'lifeworld' (Habermas) was increasingly structured through and determined by cross-purposes. Communicating parties may or may not have shared in meaning at the same level of efficacy or with the same degree of confidence (vide Kwaku Ketewa and his kin), for the pre-existing cultural message system of reference and inference was compromised. The voice of modernity was loud and heteroglossic. It forced attention and demanded interpretation. But Adeɛbeba people interpreted insistent polyphony in divergent ways. Such interpretations had to be synergised with or somehow reconciled to lived historical experiences. Relentless interrogation undercut assumption and led to an unstably busy privileging and disprivileging of the pre-existing message system. Volume increased to threaten communication as diverse readings of the new enjoined newly diverse readings of the old. Efficacy and confidence in affecting-the-other diminished in fact or in perception as the workings of modernity made the 'interworld' ever more 'baroque'. Confusion here was compounded by innovation. Literacy was a new communicative resource and its significance extended far beyond its regulatory role in the making of colonial subjects. Administrative documents, legal records, newspapers, letters and all of the rest furnished an archive that was deployed and/or fetishised in the arena of reference and inference. The written word (in Twi as well as English) was a potent instrumentation for identifying the self and affecting-the-other. Its iconic status in modernity was acknowledged by a majority who could not read or write. People enlisted its communicative authority by proxy. The notary, the letter writer and the literate school pupil were key mediators in colonial Asante, individuals who formed a bridge between writing and speaking in the quest for communicative efficacy in a shifting world.[43]

The fetishisation of literacy was a two-way street and as such it supplies an insight into the Asante reception of modernity. People acknowledged a power (*tumi*) in writing that made it ambiguously desirable and dangerous. The Adeɛbeba produce buyer Kwadwo Asaaman (we will meet him again) put the matter in the following equivocal terms.

> I cannot write but if needful for my business I ask a friend to do it for me. You ask me to know if I would prefer to write. I do not think I would like it. In this day and age it is the fact that writing has come but if you do this thing it may cause harm. An Ashanti man lived long time with no writing and where is the harm? Is life sweeter today than yesterday!? You cannot say so. Money is the master now and if writing gave you the wherewithall [*sic*] without spoiling you then I would do it. People in the village do not like this writing. It takes something of you by going to school. It can affect the health but some more than others. Schoolboys are learning about every kind of thing that will stop them from being Ashanti as formerly. This writing is coming from outside 'Poakye' (*nea ɛwɔ po akyi*: 'from overseas'). It never was in Ashanti before. It is MODERN TIMES [capitalised in text] we are living in and without peace or harmony.[44]

Others demurred, but even so it is striking how slowly Asante people came to trust literacy as opposed to using it. Naturalisation of new powers took negotiation, and negotiation took time.

Literacy was a technology alien and arcane enough to suggest occult hazard. The Christian religion dealt in the supernatural by definition. In the next chapter we will see how certain Adeɛbeba villagers tried to negotiate a selfhood that took due account of their understanding of both Christian revelation and Asante belief. This was often a tortuous – and indeed a tortured – process. But if we step back from the deeply engaged musings of such individuals we can see another aspect of the matter that speaks directly to issues of reference and inference. Adeɛbeba people sometimes looked to Christianity to reaffirm and renew their threatened sense of community and belonging. This was a discontinuous process marked by waves of enthusiasm rather than any sustained investment in Christian practice. One peak occurred in 1921–3 when the self-styled prophet Opon Asibe Tutu (Samson Opon) temporarily recruited thousands of Asante to Wesleyan-Methodism.[45] One convert was Abena Asantewaa, an Adeɛbeba girl who went on to become an adviser to women with 'problems of infertility'. She heard Opon Asibe Tutu preach in Kumase and recalled the following about the experience and its aftermath.

I was then young when I went to see Oppong preach at the present
Asafo market. A crowd was gathered. I remember some of the things
he said to us. He told us of Christ Jesus saving the sinners ... [not
legible] ... the means of salvation was in our hands. The Community
in Christ Jesus (Our Lord) was come and we should join with friends
in saving our Immortal Souls in company together. I felt this word
much. I became a firm Christian and looked for Christian fellowship
to be as a mother and father both and as my family. My own mother
was a heathen (Fetish Worshipper) and disapproved. I stayed with it in
Kumasi for some years in the bosom of the Christian Family. Since
that time I have fallen into a heathenish way of serving the Fetish from
time to time. I am still a Christian at heart. It is my true family that I go
back to whenever the Fetishes are failing me. Christians share and
share alike as we are meant to do always with friends and relations who
are helping us.[46]

Communication reflected the circuits and environments that were symptomatic of modernity and strove to make sense out of them. But there were
many spheres of encounter in addition to literacy and religion. Historians of
different societies have deliberated over modernity in relation to conjunctural
inscriptions that include time, monetisation, consumption, corporeality,
health, politics, ethnicity, subalternship and a range of others.[47] Such matters
are discussed below as and when they arise in the testimonies of Adeɛbeba
witnesses. In the meantime it is pertinent to recall that the crucible of
modernity's insertions and experiments in Asante – as across the globe – was
urbanism in versions amenable and answerable to colonialism and capitalism.
Twentieth-century Kumase brought into sharpest relief that intangible
pedagogy of feeling and sensibility, that questing after purchase upon and
place within the new world of power and money and their kaleidoscopic
representations, that is a benchmark of the installation and reception of
modernity. In this regard Adeɛbeba people and their fellow Asante were kin
to those revenant sojourners in Benjamin's *Passagenwerk*, in Bachelard's
durées, in Lefebvre's *rhythmanalyse*, in Bakhtin's discursive anatomies, in de
Certeau's *culture pluriel*, in Foucault's genealogies of the present, or in
Pred's carousels of consumption.[48] All dreamed the sense of modernity in its
salient urban form, framed that sense as speech, and tried to communicate it.

I use the term modernity in an extensional and not an intensional way. That
is to say, I employ it (*vide* Frege) to denote that class of historical features to
which it might make reference and not to connote the sense or property of
the term in and of itself. The principle at work is inclusive plausibility in
practice and not exclusive singularity of definition. An adequate account of
modernity needs to be framed in terms of a naturalised epistemology;
understanding cannot be based on trying to justify our knowledge of it, but

instead must produce a causal account of it in its historical situations and transactions. Unfortunately, many accounts of modernity are so divorced from these historical conditions that they give it the character of an *a priori* rather than an empirical phenomenon. Disfigurements of this kind are especially prevalent in accounts that discuss the sense and property of modernity by subjecting the term itself to sub-division. This compounds the original problem by multiplying the objects to be defined. Thus, modernisation and westernisation are employed in ostensible refinement of the definition of an originary term that is itself intensionally suspect. Confusion increases when modernity (or modernisation or westernisation) is separated out from its particular histories and accorded free-standing status as a conceptual programme. A common tic of this form of reading is to laud or revile modernity's historical implementations as substantiations of or as deviations from type, thereby preserving intact its notional essence. The result is a sociology of becoming, a writing about modernity that thinks its effects good or bad in relation to presumptions about the intensional sense or property of the term. Any such move is ahistorical, for it works to dissolve rather than resolve the extensional past by addressing itself to the intensional future. Shuffled in this way, the cards yield a new game.

Gyekye for one (among many, but an Akan) devotes much space to modernisation and westernisation so as to draw out to his satisfaction distinctions between the two. His account is one version of the intensional sociology of becoming, for his technique of preserving modernity in principle by sub-dividing it in practice is a way of reassuring Akan (and African) people that it can be instantiated by instrumental rationalities that stand over and above the inconvenient historical effects produced by its earlier beginnings in colonialism. 'Modernity' itself, Gyekye writes,

> whatever else it involves, certainly involves a transition to a new era; the transition is borne partly on the wings of the elegant or worthwhile features of a cultural tradition, and partly through the production of new ideas and the invention of new techniques of far-reaching consequences. The latter may involve whatever can usefully and suitably be appropriated and adapted from outside a given culture in addition to what can be acquired from within the culture itself by way of the exercise of the indigenous intellectual, evaluative and adaptive capacities. The former will require the abandonment of what I call the negative features of a culture as well as the maintenance – albeit through refinement – of what I call the positive features. The creation of modernity in Africa will be a function of both methods of transition.[49]

All well and good, but the past does not afford a *tabula rasa* amenable to any such edificatory inscription. Neither is modernity an intensional blueprint still awaiting its true realisation in the overcoming of its own history.

Colonialism authorised but did not author the effects of modernity. It was complicit in producing them but occupied no position of privileged detachment from them. Like Asante subjects, British rulers were caught up as actors in the processes they set in train. Oversight was disallowed in a context that yoked metropole to colony; rulers and ruled both swam in the sea of modernity's effects. These were at once self-fulfilling and self-justifying in that they operated to create persons – British or Asante – conditioned to understand the directed circumstances of their becoming as an effect of choice. In Europe and Africa, modernity 'aspired to create persons who would, after the fact, have wished to have become modern'.[50] That said, it must be added that a 'real' modernity in itself could never be installed anywhere (*pace* Gyekye), because its substantiation depended on effects that were produced relationally and contingently in time and space. In short, modernity in Asante was about the authorisation of culturally specific historical conjunctures of enunciation and address, and within this project the exercise of colonial power acted upon pre-existing terms of reference and inference and set new ones. Modernity's processes and effects were determined by historical authorisation but not predetermined by epistemological authorship.

Authorisation is complicated in that it can be both direct and indirect, inculcated by inscription but also disseminated by example. The effects of colonial modernity in Asante were produced alongside analogous developments among the Akan and other peoples of the Gold Coast Colony. Chronological sequence is important here. Even before the Colony was created in 1874 – but with an ever accelerating speed thereafter – its inhabitants were exposed to processes of colonial modernity and adjusted themselves to take active or passive account of their effects. Meanwhile, after defeat by the British in 1873–4 the Kumase government steadily surrendered its historically tight controls over movement in and out of Asante. Thus, over the last quarter of the nineteenth century interactions between Gold Coast and Asante people became unprecedentedly frequent. Travellers from the Colony carried ideas into Asante along with trade goods; and Asante visitors to or exiles in the Colony were exposed to new ways of living as they went about their business. Part of this story is well documented. That is, much is known about the effects of Gold Coast colonial modernity on certain Asante individuals who were prominent in commerce or politics.[51] More difficult to recuperate are the consequences of the numberless chance encounters that took place between ordinary Asante and their counterparts from the Gold Coast. References to these inter-actions abound, even if they lack the circumstantial detail necessary for precise reconstruction and analysis. That said, it is incontrovertible that countless Asante individuals came into contact with representatives of colonial modernity in its Gold Coast incarnation over the quarter-century before British overrule was formally installed in Kumase in 1901. Here we can see a prehistory to the history of colonial modernity in Asante, an indirect form of authorisation disseminated by example.

4

ADEƐBEBA LIVES:
THE TWENTIETH CENTURY

INCITEMENTS: ADEƐBEBA PEOPLE, MOBILITY AND MONEY, 1900s–1940s

The new colonial order materialised in the daily lives of Adeɛbeba people with the coming of the railway to Kumase. By 1902 the line ran north from the seaport of Sekondi to the gold mining centres of Tarkwa and Obuase. In 1902–3, as a matter of urgency following the *yaa asantewaakɔ*, the track was driven north again into Asante over the forty-four miles from Obuase to Kumase. Adeɛbeba people joined the large gangs of Asante wage labourers (*apaafoɔ*) recruited to work flat out to complete the last twenty miles of line from Bekwai into Kumase. Women and men from Adeɛbeba laboured on the stretch of track around Kaase junction, barely a mile east of their homes. This was recalled as arduous toil, involving bush clearing, carrying, grading and trackbed laying over long hours in the hot sun. But it also offered the excitement of novelty. Working on the railway took people out of the village, away from the daily round of farming, and paid them a wage. Those who took part remembered the experience as their initiation into the emerging colonial regimes of mobility and money.[1]

Afua Nsoro, Afua Dinkyim and Abena (later Mercy) Kwansa of Adeɛbeba were all adolescent girls when they went to Kaase with a Fante man named Tewiah 'to carry stones for making the railway'. Tewiah was one of many labour contractors authorised by the British to hire workers. He appeared in Adeɛbeba in early 1903 and recruited seven youths and the three girls. The girls were age-mate friends. In old age they agreed that the decisive inducement for them was the adventure of being away from home. Their parents were not so enthusiastic but were won over by the prospect of income and the reassurances that the girls 'would look out for one another' and return to sleep in Adeɛbeba every night. Once this was settled, Tewiah issued the girls with employment cards. These stipulated that they were to work as general labourers for a period of twelve weeks, renewable thereafter at his discretion. The girls worked a ten-hour day for six days in seven. Saturday or Sunday alternated as rest days in the schedule imposed by management. The three disposed of brush, soil and rocks, carried stones and rubble for the grading engineers, and suffered from the sun and in the mud created by downpours. On workdays they left Adeɛbeba to come on site by six. Then they laboured until four with a break for a midday meal provided by Tewiah. Afua Dinkyim recalled that the work was very hard but no worse than weeding farms. At the end of the working week Tewiah handed over their wages. They were paid at a daily rate of sixpence each.

Railway work introduced Adeɛbeba youth to industrial work time and discipline. It also opened windows onto the emergent worlds of earned income and personal consumption. Thus the three girls contributed to household budgets in Adeɛbeba but also purchased pieces of cloth, headties and trinkets for themselves. Labour mobility was indispensable to railway building, and beyond that to realisation of the larger economic project of colonialism. Mobility then was a respatialisation of people called into being by the structural conditions of British rule. But immediately to the people concerned railway work was a conjunctural milieu in which strangers encountered one another, shared experiences, exchanged views and first became aware of the possibility of conducting lives beyond the inherited horizons described by natal villages and communities. Thus people from all over south Asante worked at Kaase junction. Adolescents, temporarily freed from family or lineage oversight, flirted and had love affairs. Permanent relationships also developed. Afua Nsoro married a fellow Kaase worker who came from Apenkra near Kokofu, but only after a battle to get her parents and the Heman lineage head at Adeɛbeba to give their consent. They agreed when she threatened to leave home and never return. Once things were decided the newlyweds settled in Kumase. There Afua Nsoro lived by petty trading and seamstressing while her husband found work as a cook. But they had no children and divorced. Thereafter Afua Nsoro remained in Kumase, for 'I could not gain my living in this place (Adeɛbeba).' She married again and bore two children. When her second husband died in 1937 she decided to retire. Only then did she return to Adeɛbeba to live with her younger sister's daughter Akua Tipaa. Like her friend Afua Nsoro, Afua Dinkyim also decided after working at Kaase that village life was constraining. She too decided to seek her fortune in Kumase. Her parents tried to stop her but she defied them and left Adeɛbeba after a row. She married in Kumase Adum, ran a 'chop bar' there (patronised by soldiers from the Kumase garrison), and then lived in Suhum, Saltpond and Accra in the Gold Coast Colony before finally returning to farm at Adeɛbeba. Abena Kwansa never lived in Kumase, but on a visit there 'to see the town' after working on the railway she was converted to Christianity by a Fante catechist named Adjaye. Baptised 'Mercy' in 1907, she was a staunch Wesleyan-Methodist and in due course a pillar of that denomination in Adeɛbeba.[2]

Afua Nsoro, Afua Dinkyim and Abena Kwansa were modest pioneers of the mobile capitalism and consumerism of the very early twentieth century that

then stood on the threshold of effecting sweeping adjustments throughout
Asante society. All three were enthusiasts of the new, or at least were prepared in some measure to consider its many possibilities, experiment with
its opportunities or respond to its blandishments. In recollection they
stressed the range of goods made available to their younger selves by the
colonial economy. Kerosene lighting, cooking oil, metal pots and pans,
clothing (especially underwear), soap, cosmetics and tinned food were all
listed as being among 'the sweet things of life' in colonial Asante. Afua
Dinkyim described these items as 'Kan Dodi', an easily recognisable
transcription of the term *akɔndɔde* (pl. *nkɔnnɔde*). The word is derived from
akɔnnɔ (der. *kon dɔ*), meaning a desiring appetite for something, and *ade*,
signifying the thing itself desired. Hence in the colonial context *nkɔnnɔde*
were consumer goods. However, consumption of this sort required cash.
Afua Nsoro expressed the view that while *nkɔnnɔde* improved ('sweetened')
life, unrestrained pursuit of the money needed to acquire them was a social
evil that destroyed lives, families and communities. Her argument for a
balanced approach to consumption reflected widely shared ambiguities about
its benefits and drawbacks. Like other Asante people the three Adeɛbeba
girls embraced colonial incitements to mobility and money with a studied
enthusiasm tempered by flashes of disquiet and suspicion.

In some Adeɛbeba people suspicion of the new order predominated and
it led them to reject its values. In old age Kwasi Fi, servant of Adeɛbeba *taa
kwabena bena* and brother to Amma Kyirimaa, bemoaned the changes that
had occurred during his lifetime. These had 'spoiled Ashanti' for 'money is
now the King paramount'. Adeɛbeba was no longer 'a sweet place for
everybody lives as for himself' and 'no respect is any longer given grey hairs'.
His sister's apprehensions fixed upon the anxiety that the pursuit of money
would lead to neglect of the *abosom* and that this in turn would have dire
consequences.[3] In part these views were ethical. Like devout Christian
Asante (though the comparison would have shocked them), both Kwasi Fi
and Amma Kyirimaa saw *nkɔnnɔde* in terms of unbridled worldly desires that
gratified the individual at the expense of the community. This resonated
with the historic understanding that the propensity to *akɔnnɔ* (as with generic
'lust' in the Bible) needed to be checked to prevent the fragmentation of the
moral order into greedily destructive interpersonal antagonisms. From this
perspective money in a community was said to be like 'feathers in a fire' (*hyɛ
takraw gyamu*), an element that destabilised the whole by overexcitation of
its parts. But it would be misleading to interpret such views as uncom-
plicated nostalgia for the assurances of a receding past. The moral high
ground could be occupied with sincerity but still partake of instrumental
considerations of power and prestige. Kwasi Fi and more particularly Amma
Kyirimaa were important personages in precolonial Adeɛbeba. They had a
heavy investment in continuity and much at risk from change.

Figure 4.1 Adeɛbeba village in 1905.
(Source: Manwere Stool Papers, Kumase. Photographer unknown, but said to have been a Wesleyan–Methodist pastor)

The three girls by contrast were on the cusp of embarking on adult lives when they went to labour on the railway. The excitement they felt arose from an exhilarating sense of empowerment and agency, feelings that were still fresh in the memory some forty years on. Novelty was part of this but so was possibility. The horizon of Adeɛbeba life that described their childhood was simultaneously breached and extended, suddenly and by their own initiative. Their testimonies show that they knew they had led lives unimaginable (because unavailable) to women of earlier generations in Adeɛbeba. Their adult selves were formed by objective changes in material conditions but also by subjective interrogations of established norms. It is apparent that within this context of openings to new models of autonomy and enfranchisement any consideration of the future invited judgement on the past. The three Adeɛbeba girls weighed their gender-ascribed roles in the balance (ballasted though these were by family and familiarity) and saw a past deficient in possibility. By analogy Amma Kyirimaa and her brother Kwasi Fi looked to who and what they were and saw a future pregnant with threat. Both views were incited into being by colonialism and foregrounded by its interventions. In the middle ground many people oscillated between optimism and pessimism as they strove to reconcile retrospect with prospect.

According to Abena Kwansa the coming of the colonial order produced generalised consternation (*abotutraso*) as Adeɛbeba people waited to see what it might mean. In this atmosphere unusual happenings took on the character of portents. Thus in October 1903 the Obuase–Kumase railway link was formally inaugurated. The first train to steam into Kumase station carried among its official passengers a number of British-appointed office holders. Included among these was an invited party of Kumase chiefs that boarded the train at Kaase for the final stage of the journey. This was a signal moment in the instantiation of British power in Asante. The link to Sekondi, as CCA Fuller noted, would give Asante trade 'an impetus and scope hitherto unknown', while the railway itself was a strikingly brute incarnation of imperial presence and purpose. Accordingly the first train steamed out of Kaase along a route lined with onlookers and towards a terminus where officialdom with its guard of honour and military band awaited it amidst a large crowd. But in the course of the short journey from Kaase the Kumase *Nsumankwaahene* Yaw Kusi literally went mad and never recovered his senses. The symbolism was perplexing. Yaw Kusi was a British appointee to the stool that had custody of the talismans, amulets and charms (*nsuman*) belonging to the exiled *Asantehene*. This conjunction made Yaw Kusi's fate a sensation in Adeɛbeba and throughout Asante. On the one hand his abrupt descent into insanity crystallised ideas that Asante was in the process of forfeiting its historic identity to an alien present and imponderable future. The legacy of the past was profaned, or so it was said, and *sika dwa* and *abosom* alike had visited their insulted wrath upon the head of a usurper. On the other hand Yaw Kusi's madness focused thoughts that Asante was in the process of acquiring a new identity in a changed present and hopeful future. The legacy of the past was bankrupted, or so it was said, and *sika dwa* and *abosom* alike had demonstrated their corrupted incapacity in civil war, suffering and anomie. The message was loud but ambiguous in the ears of people who were already riven by equivocal uncertainties. 'Yaw Kussi became mad because of helping the British to rule over the country,' recalled Yaw Afriyie of Adeɛbeba. But his neighbour Afua Nsoro looked back on the same episode and reflected that 'this Yow Kussi was not a good chief and was a Fetishist having no place in this modern Ashanti. This is why he suffered his superstitious misfortune.'[4]

For those travelling any distance the railway was the optimum means of transport in and beyond Asante until the later 1920s when its primacy began to come under serious challenge from roads and motor vehicles.[5] At first disprivileged by colonial planners, an integrated road network began to make an impact on Asante life just before the First World War. In time the infrastructural development of a modern road system enabled the same liberation into mass mobility as had the railway. But before then, making roads – just like making the railway – opened up new horizons for people from Adeɛbeba and all over Asante.

In 1918 Kwaku Anti of Adeɛbeba, his brothers Kofi Donko and Kwadwo Abane and their friend Kwasi Nimaako of Toase were members of a work gang labouring to upgrade 'The Great North Road' that ran from Kumase via Mampon to the Northern Territories of the Gold Coast. They were based first at Gyamaase, some twenty-two miles north of the Asante capital, and then at nearby Daaho (Odaho). These were young, single men and they succumbed to the legendary charms of Mampon girls.[6] In recalling that 'Mampong women were exceedingly beautiful', Kwaku Anti added a revealing postscript about his travels. 'They were much more beautiful than those in other parts of Ashanti I had then seen,' he stated, listing visits to or sojourns in Manso Nkwanta, Asante Akyem and the Ahafo towns of Bere-kum and Kukuom. His elder brother Kofi Donko courted one Kyiriwaa, 'a short dark strong woman' from Daaho. In the same village Kwaku Anti encountered 'tall slender dark Akosua Nkwanpa who captured my heart'.

Kwaku Anti's romance was a creation of the new mobility. Thus before consenting to marriage the girl's kin demanded information and reassur-ance, not only about the prospective husband's character and lineage as was customary, but also about distant Adeɛbeba itself. Daaho in Mampon was in Sekyere in north Asante while Adeɛbeba was in Kumase district just south of the capital. In precolonial terms these were worlds apart. No one in Daaho knew anything about Adeɛbeba or had any personal or historical link with the place. For his part Kwaku Anti confessed that he and his mates thought Daaho 'poor' and 'backward', a reflection no doubt of the lack of amenities in north Asante as compared to colonial penetration in and around Kumase. But be that as it may, Kwaku Anti was set on marrying Akosua Nkwanpa and subsequently recounted the formalities he went through. The step-by-step detail of his narrative suggests not only a rigid adherence to custom as this was understood in Sekyere but also the circumspection of his prospective in-laws. In their eyes he was a stranger from afar, a suspiciously unknown quantity among people whose historically conditioned preference was for suitors who were fellow villagers or inhabitants of nearby settle-ments. Who knew or could speak for Kwaku Anti? In the end his suit was declared by his brothers, by other kin from Adeɛbeba and by a delegation of friends who were 'well dressed Kumasi men'. All these supporters argued Kwaku Anti's case in formal meetings with Akosua Nkwanpa's lineage head, uncles, parents and 'others of Odaho'. Their efforts were eventually crowned with success and Kwaku Anti and Akosua Nkwanpa were married.

This tale had a dénouement that mixed the old with the new. By the mid-1940s husband and wife were living in their respective natal villages, in and of itself not an unusual outcome. But they were still in touch despite distances that would have inhibited any sustained contact prior to the twentieth century. In the course of the marriage Kwaku Anti, who was employed by the Kumase Public Works Department (PWD), had liaisons with several other women. None the less, in an idiosyncratic variant of the theme of distance lending enchantment, he felt able to sum up his marriage as being 'very satisfactory'. In explanation he added parenthetically that 'I lord over her. My wife Akosua Nkwanpa does not make bones of my misconduct in many things.' A very sanguine view, but then the wife's side of the story is not recorded.[7]

After the First World War rail and road facilitated ever widening circuits of mobility and spheres of sociability as Asante villagers moved around looking for work in the cash economy. Kwaku Anti's brother Kwadwo Abane typified this peripatetic life. In the 1920s he left Adeɛbeba with two friends to seek employment in the Obuase gold mining complex and also 'to see the Obuasi camp of which I heard much from youngmen who went there'. The three were hired as firewood cutters in Obuase town itself. They felled and stacked timber and then head loaded it to the rubbish incinerators operated by the Ashanti Goldfields Corporation (AGC) behind Ram's Hill near the Gyimi river. The work was tiring but it paid a regular wage. Obuase itself possessed novel attractions and amenities. It was a multi-ethnic town of some three thousand plus miners and other wage earners. Dance halls and bars abounded as did makeshift brothels (nguamannan). Kwadwo Abane recalled that Obuase was full of prostitutes. These were mainly girls from the north who came south with their menfolk. When the men returned home with their earnings to farm these women 'refused to go and stayed for their comforts and sold themselves to get them'. By his own account Kwadwo Abane 'never went with any such sort of woman' from fear of affliction with 'Kotupee' (kɔtepie: lit. 'a disturbed penis') as a result of contracting venereal disease (generically babaso). Whatever the fact of the matter, Kwadwo Abane found plenty of other things to interest him in Obuase. He had a relationship with a girl from Fomena in Adanse, made friends with some Akyem men, played cards, saw electric lighting for the first time and never forgot the sight of Europeans playing golf on the AGC course. He liked the life as well as the money and returned three times after his first stay. On his fourth visit in the mid-1930s he found 'a job that paid more than any before' laying water pipes from Obuase through its Zongo to the new company housing estate at Nsuta west of the town.

In between his Obuase sojourns Kwadwo Abane was briefly involved in the cattle trade and travelled to Pran in the north. He went to Ahafo with some Adeɛbeba neighbours who were looking to lease land to farm cocoa. He journeyed by rail to Sekondi where he did casual work around the docks and saw the sea for the first time. He went east to Konongo in Asante Akyem

Figure 4.2 Roadmaking in Mampon, Asante about 1920.
(Source: Kumase Fort Photographic Collection)

and again laboured on building and maintaining roads. His testimony
makes it clear that his experience of travel was far from unusual. Many of the
younger people in Adeɛbeba, he said, 'travelled out' to 'earn money and see
the world'. One of his childhood friends called Kwame Fin had gotten as far
as Nigeria and settled there. But in the end, he admitted, he himself had
come home 'to settle down to marry'. His wife Abena Oforiwaa was from
Anyinam just south of Adeɛbeba. Pressed to explain his decision to return at
last to the village in which he was born, he offered the following explanation:

> You see Ashantis like to wander. The social life at Kumasi and Obuasi
> is preferable to that of the village. There is money to be made there
> and various amenities of life. Even at Obuasi camp [the] water supply
> is on the very door steps and available at any time. Big places are
> tempting to live in for this reason. But it is not always quite rosy. At
> Obuasi we [Adeɛbeba men] were Nyisa Kuo [nyisaa kuo: 'a band of
> orphans'] who missed the family and home comforts. It was as if being
> a soldier is now [i.e. in the Second World War]. You come to miss
> what is your old life and greeting your friends from childhood days.
> You are pining but money is the King [laughs]. It is a hard hard choice
> to make. But tiredness makes you come to settle. A wife and children
> are better in the village where there is no temptation. They help you
> farm. You eat for yourself and enjoy peace. When I was a young man
> I travelled about the world. Everyone did this. But all came back to live
> by the family and on the land of their childhood. Even now people
> from here live at Kumasi. But they come from there on every oppor-
> tunity. It is not far. Kumasi is rich and everything is there. But here
> [Adeɛbeba] there is peace and quiet. It is home. An Ashanti man will
> like to live at home at last and be buried near to his ancestors. Life in
> this modern time is money and need of money means moving back
> and forth not like olden days. It is interesting to travel all about and
> come back at last. We are all here of this opinion now.[8]

Colonial capitalism both impelled and invited its subjects to practise mobility in the pursuit of money. Incitements to this end camouflaged compulsive
structuration in seductive commodification. But Asante people soon
learned that the engine of the new order was a pervasive monetisation, the
reconfiguration of life and labour in terms of exchange value. Thus 'the
pressure of cash' became a commonplace and strategies for acquiring this
now indispensable resource were as various as the many narratives that
bemoaned its scarcity.[9] 'Money is a tyrant set over us in this life,' said Yaa
Buoho of Adeɛbeba, a sentiment that echoed through the testimonies of
most of her neighbours.[10] Complaints of this sort reflected a harsh reality
but not a supine passivity. Precolonial Asante society possessed ideologies
of wealth and technologies of accumulation. In the twentieth century this

legacy was drawn upon, reconfigured and mobilised to join with innovation in meeting the challenges posed by colonial capitalism. Nowhere was this dynamic combination of expertise and originality more apparent than in the introduction of cocoa into Asante by its own people. The history of this sovereign cash crop is well understood in general terms and much debated as to its macroeconomic effects over the longer term. An awareness of these larger issues informs the discussion here.[11] But our specific concern is with the somewhat atypical history of cocoa in Adeɛbeba, and more precisely with its role and effects in the matters of mobility and money.

As early as 1902 cocoa was introduced into Adeɛbeba from the Dwaben town of Konongo in Asante Akyem. The chain of events that led to this can be recuperated in detail. In 1875 Kumase sent troops to discipline the secessionist *Dwabenhene* Asafo Agyei. Fighting ensued and Dwaben was defeated. Asafo Agyei and large numbers of his subjects fled from Asante into Akyem. There they established the town of New Dwaben (Koforidua) and rejected all requests to return home. Then in 1896 British rule was installed in Kumase. In these changed circumstances the *Dwabenhene* Yaw Sapon sent an embassy to press the refugees to come back. Kwame Asare Nimo of Konongo was appointed to head this mission because his uncle Kofi Agyaakwa was an influential figure in the exile community. In the event negotiations were inconclusive but the embassy did not return empty handed.

> In 1896 or thereabouts, the Juabenhene sent a batch of delegates, among whom were Kwami Nimo, Kwodwo Mma and Kofi Otin Abeng, to interview the Chief of Koforidua on State Matters. (It should be remembered that the people of Koforidua are Juaben people who emigrated into that part of the country after one of the Ashanti Wars in which they fought the Ashanti army. The Koforidua Chief therefore owns [*sic*] the Juaben Chief allegiance.) These delegates from the town of Konongo saw the seeds of the newly introduced Cocoa and from what they saw and heard from their fellow Juaben People, they bought some of the seeds and sent them over to their homes for experimental purposes. Traders and other travellers from Ashanti Akim returned later on with some more of these seeds and by 1900 the first Cocoa plantations had started producing at Konongo. The Konongo Cocoa planted just north of the town became very famous and the demand for it led farmers to come from all over Ashanti. The farmers returned with Cocoa seeds to plant on their own account and grow the crop.[12]

Among those who visited Konongo was Kwabena Ba, a grandson of the Adeɛbeba pioneer Kwasi Yentumi of Asoromaso near Dwaben. Proud of his reputation as the man who introduced cocoa to Adeɛbeba, Kwabena Ba

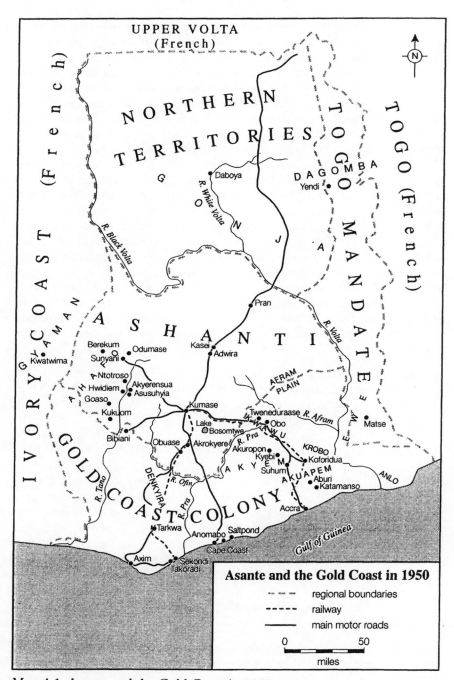

Map 4.1 Asante and the Gold Coast in 1950

claimed with hindsight that he was 'a scientific farmer' who had travelled to Konongo in a spirit of inquiry after hearing tales of the crop. Be that as it may, Adeɛbeba testimonies other than his own are agreed that he imported cocoa seeds from Konongo in 1902 and planted them on his farm at *(n)tasu*. But this experiment was not a success. Some of the seedlings became waterlogged in poorly drained soil; others perished from lack of adequate shade cover; but most died because they were planted out too closely together. By 1910 Kwabena Ba's initiative had foundered. In the process Adeɛbeba people learned fundamental lessons about the problems of growing cocoa in their community. Perhaps drainage and shade were amenable to solution but little could be done about acreage. Imitators of Kwabena Ba who tried to intercrop cocoa at Adeɛbeba were stymied by a lack of sufficient land. Neighbouring cocoa farmers at Ahodwo and Toase faced the same inhibiting difficulty and this led to endemic disputes with Adeɛbeba over marginal boundary adjustments. However, none of this prevented people in Adeɛbeba from trying to share in the profits to be made from cocoa. In 1912 a man named Adu Asabi 'pioneered' the crop for the second time in Adeɛbeba. He was a blacksmith (*ɔtomfo*) as well as a farmer and had lived for a time in Asante Akyem. His cocoa farm was situated at *(n)tasu* on bottomland along a branch of the Nsuben river. He persevered throughout the First World War but land scarcity embroiled him in disputes with local authorities at Apraman to the south. But in the 1920s he found a solution to the problem of limited acreage. To grow more cocoa he rented uncultivated tracts around Mfensi, to the north-west of Kumase, and in the Kukuom area of Ahafo. When he died in 1937, his property included a house in Kumase Asafo, a respectable amount of cash and five cocoa farms located far from Adeɛbeba.[13]

From the 1920s on the practice of 'stranger farming' by migrants to Ahafo became widespread throughout Asante. Ahafo was the cocoa frontier, an area of plentiful land and relatively low population densities. Adeɛbeba entrepreneurs participated in emulation of Adu Asabi and others. By the 1940s the wealthiest cocoa farmers in Adeɛbeba were Kofi Nyame of the Heman settler group and his three younger brothers. They went first to Ahafo in 1923 and leased land between the villages of Ntotroso, Hwidiem, Asusuhyia and Akyerensua, some fifty miles north-west of Adeɛbeba. Their choice was dictated by availability, but also by the fact that this part of eastern Ahafo had ready access to the Sunyani–Kumase motor road. The brothers were based at Hwidiem to the south of their farms. Kofi Nyame gave an account of the matter.

> In Hwidiem now (1945) there are living five or six hundred people. At first when I came (1920s) there was not a big number. I have a swish house and food farm. But when I am visiting I sleep on the farms to check the cocoa. The population in recent years has increased to a big

extent. These people who have immigrated into the village consist of
mainly Ashanti, NTs (people from the Northern Territories of the
Gold Coast), Gyaamans, Kwahus and some Akuapims. The NTs
come for the buying of kola and labour. Gyaamans for taking up work
as cocoa caretakers. I myself have Gyaamans as caretakers as well as
Ashantis. The Kwahus are robbers. Kwahus know Ashantis' interest
and desire for idols and deem it an advantage to bring over some of
these mysterious idols from the French territory to rob people of
money whenever they go to consult them. I go to Hwidiem two times
in a year to inspect the cocoa. There is a big market on Thursdays and
Sundays where all the necessities of life can be obtained.[14]

By the 1940s the brothers had eleven Ahafo cocoa farms. All followed the
same pattern of development. Kofi Nyame and his kin cleared and planted
the land with the help of hired labourers. While the trees matured one or
more of the brothers stayed at Hwidiem and bivouacked in the fields. After
the trees began to bear but before they fruited – between three and seven
years after planting – the farm was given over to a caretaker (ɔhwɛfo). This
practice was widespread. It liberated the owner from frequent inspection
trips so that he (or she) might clear more land to farm, pursue other business
interests or simply spend more time at home. Thus by the 1940s Kofi
Nyame spent little time in Ahafo. His twice yearly visits were of short duration. His youngest brother Benson Anane described him as a 'gentleman
farmer' who 'passes his days now at home in Adiebeba and Kumasi'. This
witness described the system of 'caretaking of cocoa farms' (kookoo nhwɛso)
as practised by the four Adeɛbeba brothers.

All the farms have caretakers now. They are Ashantis excepting two
who are from Ivory Coast. Before the farm is given to a caretaker he
must be honest and hardworking for obvious reasons. Caretakers are
usually strangers sometimes Krobos or Ewes as well as Ashantis. The
usual thing is Abusa System [abusa: sharecropping in return for one
third of the product] but in a farm that needs much work then Abonu
System [abunu: sharecropping in return for one half of the product] is
demanded. This is too much profit and only one farm at Ntotoroso
[Ntotroso[is Abonu System. If a caretaker fails in maintaining the
weeding and thinning then you take the farm back. Caretakers are not
hard to find among old men and even farmers who are in debt. A man
might mortgage his own cocoa from need and be a caretaker to
another. Agreements are not written down. Witnesses are called and
Apensa [apɛnsa: a small validation fee] and some drinks stamp it. It is
better not to use relatives for this job. They are difficult to remove
when they do not give satisfaction. Strangers are disposed of more
easily. Caretaking is done by those who have failed in their cocoa

business. Cocoa farming is not so profitable and it is easy to fall into debt. It is better to have some other thing to do on top of cocoa for getting money.[15]

Benson Anane insisted that diversified business interests 'on top of cocoa' were the key to making money. Thus, he and his brothers owned a small sawmill at Daban and a workshop in south Kumase that stripped out copper wire for resale. Most significantly, Kofi Nyame was a *rentier* landlord who owned two houses in Kumase. One of these was a dwelling at Oforikrom just east of the city centre. It contained seven sleeping rooms, two of which were no more than curtained off hallways. In 1945 this building housed no fewer than eleven adult tenants and seventeen 'and maybe more' children. Kofi Nyame's other Kumase dwelling was close by in Amakom and was also leased out for multi-occupation. Rents, claimed Benson Anane, were a useful source of profit for they had risen steeply to meet accelerating housing demand in Kumase during the Second World War. The buildings and the plots they stood on were valuable in and of themselves. The Amakom house alone was reckoned to be worth well over £2,000 in 1945, a healthy return on an original investment of £350 in 1931. But the real value of Kumase properties did not lie in rents. Nor did it reside in convertibility, for such buildings were sold off only in a liquidity crisis amenable to no other solution. It was situated instead in the aura of substance that possession of such assets conferred upon the owner.

> Money is scarce and costs are big. Everyone must borrow to make ends meet. But where is this money coming from? It is not coming from cocoa. Cocoa farmers are in debt. No one wants a cocoa farm as surety against [a] loan because how is money to be made? Cocoa is a poor return. But money can be very readily borrowed if you have buildings at Kumasi for it is known that when kept to good standard such utility [sic] is always increasing financially. A Kumasi house is a good thing when you approach someone to loan money. They will give you because you are financial [sic] and you can meet repayment in one way and another. When you take loan you put it to something but not any more cocoa. Cocoa farmers are struggling to make ends meet and have no means to get loan any more.[16]

Real producer prices for cocoa lessened greatly after 1917, a trend that only began to be reversed after the Second World War. The reasons for this decline and the protests that ensued need not concern us.[17] But the steadily downward trend of returns created a particular problem for cocoa farmers because of the nature of their crop. Cocoa growing was a long-term business. As noted, trees took an average of five years to fruit. Thereafter 'only a proportion of the cocoa comes into bearing before ten years old', and then 'the maximum yield is produced about the seventeenth or eighteenth years'.[18] Scholarship pays tribute to Asante initiative, rational forward planning and deferral of gratification in the making of the cocoa industry. But given the absence of producer control over prices, the time lag between investment and unpredictable return, and the long-term illiquidity of capital tied up in farms, cocoa growing was something of a poisoned chalice. Thus, by the 1920s putting money into cocoa on any scale was economically realistic only for those – like Kofi Nyame and his kin – who had other ways of generating income, ready liquidity, borrowing capacity and the resource base to wait and gamble on profit taking some ten to twenty years into the future. For anyone else cocoa farming was a matter of falling returns and rising debt. Against the indicators, the great mass of farmers clung to cocoa for two main reasons. First, it gave them a foothold – however precarious – in a world of money that they might only enter otherwise by selling their labour on the open market. Second, and simply, they were trapped. Such capital as they had was tied up long term. In a variant of the triumph of hope over experience they could only sit tight and wait for things to improve. But they did not. The result was wholesale borrowing against equity to keep afloat. But mortgaged cocoa farms lost value and then appeal as they glutted the market. Institutional lenders were scarce so the whole process was a tale of spiralling indebtedness to richer neighbours.

In 1945 nine people in Adeɛbeba other than Kofi Nyame and his brothers identified themselves as cocoa farmers. Six of these were men and three were women. All were 'stranger farmers' in Ahafo or Atwoma. Two of the men and one woman had two farms apiece. The other six had one farm each. None had a reliable source of income apart from cocoa. All complained about cocoa prices and bemoaned their lack of money. All were in debt to a greater or lesser extent. The most indebted was Kwame Aboagye, a sometime palm-wine tapper who established a cocoa farm around 1930 on land at Goaso in Ahafo. He bumped along by borrowing and other measures until events overtook him. Thus, in 1942

> my mother and sister died. I was without any means for making their funeral and providing for [his sister's] children. I owed Nyantakyi already and some others for expenses made in connection with family matters. I approach N[yantakyi] again at Kumasi but he said he did not want any cocoa farm. I begged him and he took it on loan of £80 with an interest of £40. I took some and made the funeral. Kwami Dikyi heard of my pledging the farm and requested me for my money owed to him. I was unable to meet his request. This was Fafafiri and not usual loan. The amount was too much. It was a millstone around my neck of £320 on £40 given [as a loan]. I could not repay even a part. I went to Kojo Mosi at Kejetia [in Kumase] and pledged the farm once again. I was given £64. I had a short time to pay – Femm. Mosi

sent to me after hearing the farm was pledged before. He asked for his money. He abused me as I cannot give him. He swore against me and N[ative] A[uthority] Bailiff Mr Obeng summoned me to court to answer his charge of fraud. Before I was pleading one Yaw Fodjuor with the Fanti Koomson also brought a summons against said Mosi for arrears. They were saying that he is a rich man but tells them of his bad luck in his business to stop him paying up rent. He owes £32 (to them) and £10–6 to a former landlord. My case came on but is not yet settled. I paid £3–10 court costs. I am despairing on the money matter and pray for any relief. Even the farm if it was for me [i.e. if it was not mortgaged] would not be able to lift my crushing burden of debts.[19]

Kwame Aboagye was an extreme case of debt, but of degree rather than kind. All Adeɛbeba cocoa farmers struggled to sustain borrowing capacity to meet needs and obligations. Testimonies reveal lives spent juggling scarce money. Commonly the sums involved were small. Thus, in the late 1930s Afua Pirabon surrendered a share in her cocoa crop to her kinsman and neighbour Kwasi Dabo of the Heman lineage at Adeɛbeba for an £8 loan. She contrived to pay off £6 in accumulating interest over several years. But in 1945 the debt was still outstanding and relations between creditor and debtor were soured.[20] The continuum that led from Afua Pirabon to Kwame Aboagye was 'the pressure of cash'. Dwindling producer prices, a failed crop, unexpected expenses, improvidence, bad luck, or any combination of these and a myriad other things might escalate the small debt of the one into the bankrupting entanglements of the other. At some point in this process the man or woman would fall into the world of the moneylender (ɔkyekyefo: lit. 'he who binds'), a radically different place from the village community with its good or ill feelings among individuals about modest sums of money.

Gold was scarce in precolonial Asante and interest rates on loans made in it were correspondingly high and sometimes punitive.[21] However the market rate was tied to a theoretical norm. This was *bosea* – an 'ordinary loan', due for repayment after one Asante year at the conventionalised interest rate of 50 per cent. But *bosea* was the province of state office holders and other rich individuals [*asikafoɔ*] who trafficked in gold. It was beyond the ken of ordinary people. Instead, loans among villagers were mostly in kind and were called *nsa*, literally the 'drink' of palm wine or other alcohol that served as 'thanks' (*aseda*) or 'interest' on repayment. Loans of this sort had no fixed term but were customarily paid back within one Asante month (*adaduanan*). Shorter settlement times were simply agreed on a case-by-case basis between contracting parties. Twentieth-century Adeɛbeba witnesses tended to idealise or even sentimentalise *nsa*, mourning it as a token of lost neighbourliness. This was because the colonial economy recast *nsa* in monetary terms.

It became known as *fɛm*, a revealing usage that implied the sense of being pressed upon or squeezed. The transition from *nsa* to *fɛm* was a shift from a compact between kin, friends or neighbours to a commercialised business transaction between lender and borrower. Only the principle of short-term repayment was retained as interest in cash replaced the older form of *aseda*. But *fɛm* – as in the case of Kwadwo Mosi's loan to Kwame Aboagye – was only one among a repertoire of similarly usurious devices employed by moneylenders during the colonial period. The remote model for all of these mechanisms was *bosea*. Precolonial levies on loans in scarce gold were now universalised and adapted to meet a growing demand for equally scarce money.

One of Kwame Aboagye's loans was *fɛm* ('Femm'). Another was *fifiri* ('Fafafiri'), literally 'sweating'. By the terms of this a moneylender reserved the right to revise interest or repayment conditions every three months. Borrowers 'sweated' over an outcome that rarely if ever involved reducing charges or extending credit. Similarly punitive was *huru*, literally the 'jumping' loan in which compound interest might be charged at an extortionate rate of 50 per cent every six days. Worst of all loans was *afaaseduru* – the 'laxative' – an agreement that imposed such high interest charges that trying (and failing) to repay them 'purged' the borrower of all money without ever reducing the principal. People who borrowed on such terms hoped against hope that something – anything – would interrupt and delay scheduled repayments. Thus, a moneylender's death often brought respite for a period of time as the heir(s) struggled to master accounts seldom committed to paper in any transparent way. Debtors called such periods of relief 'sweetness' (*ɔdew*), and referred to their temporarily suspended loan obligations as 'ghosts' (*asaman*). But in time matters were rectified and accumulating repayments fell due.

Several Adeɛbeba people were in debt to moneylenders. Most loans were for sums under £30. But four villagers other than Kwame Aboagye were seriously indebted. These were Osei Manwere and Kwabena Anini, cocoa farmers in Atwoma; Abena Afre, a cloth and bead trader whose unfinished Kumase house collapsed in 1936; and Yaw Amoaten, a cocoa broker and property speculator with a long history of unsound investment. Each of these people accumulated loans in excess of £350 exclusive of interest. Each resorted to a range of lenders. But all borrowed some money from the same person. This was 'Nyantakyi', the moneylender mentioned by Kwame Aboagye and a man well known in the Kumase of his day. In his youth, Owusu Nyantakyi was a junior member of a famously successful cohort of Saawua entrepreneurs. This group grew rich from the late nineteenth century rubber trade, from gold dealing, and from importing goods into Asante.[22] Owusu Nyantakyi's mother was sister to the Saawua brothers Kwabena Nketia and Kwabena Akyem, prominent figures in this commercial network. But his father was a subject of the *Saamanhene* from Atonso near Kaase and had some kinship connection with the Heman people at Adeɛbeba. In the early colonial period Owusu Nyantakyi settled in Kumase. A man of substance already, he invested in property and deployed much of the profit in moneylending. Some light was shed on these dealings in the mid-1930s when his role in financing the factional politics of the *Mampon* stool came under British scrutiny. According to this investigation Owusu Nyantakyi was a 'big moneylender' with over £2,300 out on loan to seventeen people; among the sureties he held were mortgages on thirteen cocoa farms.[23]

Adeɛbeba people turned to Owusu Nyantakyi for help because he was known in the village. Whether or not this was because of his father's connections is unclear. But whatever the prior relationship, no sentiment entered into Owusu Nyantakyi's dealings with his Adeɛbeba clients. Abena Afre pledged gold jewellery to him in exchange for a loan of £100. After three years she still owed the principal but had paid £48 'Mfentun' (*mfɛntomu*: interest) when he raised the interest rate. All her protests fell on deaf ears and 'I could do nothing but pay.' Kwabena Anini secured a loan of £75 by mortgaging his Ofoase cocoa farm to Owusu Nyantakyi. He failed to meet the interest payments, whereupon the terms of his debt were made more stringent. It will be apparent from these Adeɛbeba cases that moneylending was not a simple matter of giving out on interest pending eventual return in full. Most borrowers had multiple obligations and no prospect of clearing them. So why did people like Owusu Nyantakyi lend money, even on an unsecured basis? And why did they accept such economically marginal sureties as cocoa farms? Certainly, all the evidence suggests that moneylenders seldom if ever showed much interest in cropping the cocoa mortgaged to them.[24]

The business of moneylending was not about the return of loaned capital or, failing that, foreclosure on mortgaged assets. Cleared debts or impounded possessions marked the end of the arrangement between a creditor and a debtor. Moneylenders did not welcome this. Their profit (*mfaso*) derived from ensnaring needy borrowers in servicing debt for as long as possible. Interest charges were the point of lending money. These ensured cash flow, often interrupted but virtually never ending. But there were other factors in play. 'Money is lifes [*sic*] blood,' declared Abena Afre in a comparison echoed by many others. Both substances were vital to existence and in preciously finite supply. Blood supported life by pulsing through veins and arteries (*mogya ntini*), just as money guaranteed it by flowing between people. In both instances the key mechanism at work was circulation. Lending and borrowing scarce money was necessary to the working of Asante colonial society. Because of this circumstance, the circuit defined by moneylending inflected the economics of exchange with palpable sociabilities.

Creditor and debtor were both subjected to the incitements proposed by money. Both wanted and needed it, and so in their shared persuasion wanted and needed each other. From this joint recognition there emerged the naturalisation of moneylending within the ordering of colonial society. It was a social relationship as well as an economic one. Moneylenders sometimes claimed to be social benefactors. By corollary, Abena Afre observed that 'usurers are needful to everybody here (in Adeɛbeba) and are good helpers with the trials of life'.[25]

INVOLVEMENTS: ADEɛBEBA PEOPLE AND KUMASE, 1900s-1940s

Above all other places colonial Kumase was magnet to and focus of the residential, occupational and affective dimensions of mobility. The capital was at the cutting edge of the processes of modernity in Asante, a restless, ever shifting landscape of hybridised urban forms and styles of living. It drew many people, Asante and otherwise, to its bustling array of opportunity and spectacle. A social history of Kumase in the first half of the twentieth century remains to be written, but it is beyond present concerns. The task at hand is to explore the many involvements of Adeɛbeba villagers with the colonial city. But before considering specifics, three preliminary points need to be made.

First, and to reiterate, in its foundation Adeɛbeba village was intimately linked to precolonial Kumase. The two were closely situated and within comfortable walking distance of one another. Thus, whether as *nhenkwaa*, *Manwerefoɔ* or visitors for whatever purpose, Adeɛbeba people had a degree of intercourse and familiarity with the city that was far from being the norm in precolonial Asante. Adeɛbeba was a small place but its inhabitants saw themselves as *kumasefoɔ*, and they viewed remoter Asante through the sophisticated and contemptuous eyes of their borrowed urban identity. This historic self-definition imparted a particular flavour to twentieth-century Adeɛbeba testimonies about Kumase. The colonial city was represented all at once as a commonplace, something already known and thus nothing special, and as a revelation, something completely new and hence wildly exciting. Recalled in tranquillity, much Adeɛbeba evidence about the experience of colonial Kumase was framed as autobiographical adventure, a narrative blend of the knowing and wide eyed; the result was sometimes picaresque.[26]

Second, the majority of twentieth-century Adeɛbeba people spent some time in Kumase and a sizeable if unquantifiable number sojourned for extended periods of their lives in the city. Old and New Asafo, Adum, Kagyatia and Ashanti and Fanti New Towns were all areas of colonial Kumase that housed Adeɛbeba residents. Such locational connections were important, for it was to them that the itinerant visitor gravitated in search of

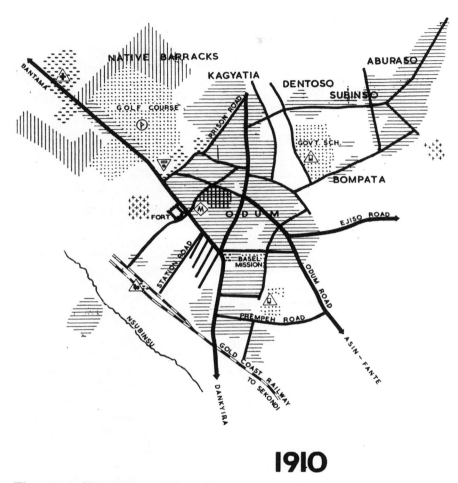

1910

Figure 4.3 Sketch Map of Kumase in 1910.
(Source: F. A. Abloh, *Growth of Towns in Ghana: A Study of the Social and Physical Growth of Selected Towns in Ghana.* Department of Housing and Planning Research, Faculty of Architecture, University of Science and Technology, Kumase. 1967. Opposite p. 26)

food, lodging and help from fellow villagers with jobs and other concerns. Thus specific locales, dwellings and named individuals recur in many testimonies. For example, it is clear that from the 1920s house number D.117 in Adum was a multi-occupied building largely inhabited by Adeɛbeba people. It belonged to Kwaakye Sei, a small-scale *rentier* and moneylender from Adeɛbeba who had first become wealthy from the 1890s rubber trade. He was a business associate of Adu Abankro of Sɔkɔban, a famously rich trader, cocoa magnate and city landlord. When Kwaakye Sei died in the mid-1930s the house passed into the ownership of his nephew Solomon Amoateng. In 1946 there were seventeen adults living in the building, of whom eleven including the landlord were from Adeɛbeba.[27] Another dwelling of this sort was located at the north end of Lake Road in Asafo. It was the property of Daniel Amponsah, a building contractor from Asuyeboa just west of Kumase. In the 1920s he married Amma Pimpim, a descendant of the Adeɛbeba pioneer Yaa Atiwaa of Saawua. By the early 1930s his Asafo house was full of Adeɛbeba tenants. One of them was a sawyer and lay preacher called Isaac Antwi. He recalled the advantages of living in Kumase with friends and fellow villagers.

> People belonging to a Kumasi household such as this feel that they are not alone here. There are people from home with whom they can talk over their sorrows and griefs. A man may not be overpowered by trouble for the resources and counsel of the various members of the household can be employed to free a member from trouble. Life in a household such as this tends to check the very rapid prosperity of an adventurous individual but it does not allow one to be destitute. It tends to make the standard of life equal for all.[28]

Third, Adeɛbeba testimonies considered collectively furnish a sense of the evolving organism that was the city as this presented itself to perception. Although a great deal might be said concerning this matter only one general comment is offered now. This concerns perceptual chronologies. The thrust of the Adeɛbeba evidence suggests that early colonial Kumase possessed a somewhat chaotic and incoherent identity up until about the mid-1920s. Before this time the city was a palimpsest, embroiled in the contradictory impulses that inhered in the inscription of colonialism within a ruined but remembered historic urbanism. Early colonial Kumase was governed by and filled up with non-Asante people for the first time in its long history, a sort of overwriting that occluded its mnemonic power without erasing it. As a result perceptions were ruled by a ghostly sense of liminality. Some things were changing while others were not, but there was little discernible pattern in this process. This bred a sense of instability that encompassed seductive familiarity and threatening novelty in equally uncertain measure. But from about the mid-1920s the equivocations that attached to this envisioning began to diminish. Adeɛbeba accounts concerning the 1930s and 1940s suggest a greater ease and confidence in dealing with the quiddity of a city more settled, more routinised and more predictable than in its earlier colonial incarnation. In part this shift was institutional. The repatriation of the *Asantehene* Agyeman Prempe as the Christian literate Mr Edward Prempeh in 1924 and the concurrent rationalisation of urban form, planning and administration for the very first time with the founding of the Kumase Public Health Board (KPHB) formed a watershed. But in larger part the change was generational. By the later 1920s ever increasing numbers of villagers venturing into Kumase were children of the colonial dispensation. Their memories included neither direct experience of precolonial Asante nor any participation in the traumas of 1896 and 1900–1 that ushered in British rule. Their understanding of precolonial Asante was indirect, derived and in itself literally historical.[29]

For obvious reasons of space parsimony is required in giving biographical details in substantiation of the foregoing. Let us then first consider the illustrative case of Kwabena Bonsu, who was born in 1912. His mother was Yaa Yeboa of the Heman connection at Adeɛbeba. His father Kwaku Dwumo was from Adwuman Kobiri, three miles north of Kokofu. Kwaku Dwumo was the son of an *Asantehene*, most probably Kwaku Dua Kumaa, who died in 1884 after only a month in office.[30] Thus Kwabena Bonsu styled himself *ɔhenenana* ('grandson of a chief'; i.e. a patrilineal descendant of an *Asantehene*) in all of his autobiographical declarations.

Kwabena Bonsu spent his 'early days' with his father Kwaku Dwumo in a house at Kumase Kagyatia. This house belonged to the then Kumase *Atipinhene* Kwaku Dua Agyeman, who succeeded his uncle and patron Osei Bonsu as *Mamponhene* in 1931.[31] A British client and a political intriguer, Kwaku Dua Agyeman was inordinately proud of his birth as a royal of the Mampon *botaase* lineage and his consequent right of access to a stool that was second in rank only to the *sika dwa*. He was self-consciously aristocratic and maintained a Kumase household commensurate with that image and status (*dibea*). For reasons that are unknown Kwaku Dwumo was a client or dependant of Kwaku Dua Agyeman, and his son was set to work as an *ahenkwaa* in his patron's house. In one of his recollections of this time in his young life Kwabena Bonsu reminisced in detail about his training 'in the old school' and about Kumase shortly after the First World War.

> We were taught the court manners of Ashanti. Kumasi had not been developed as at present. I have in my mind's eye the picture of an insanitary town, with tufts of grass and bushes here and there. There were pit wells all about. There were no tarred streets and no stalls for a crowded slippery market where on wet days people slipped and fell thus calling forth hootings all over. Bompata was a farm area. The area behind the Fanti New Town was a farm of sugar cane plantation owned by immigrant Fanti traders. The only parts of sanitary outlet were, the Cantonments, the area around the Fort, the Ridge, the Post Office, BBWA (The British Bank of West Africa) and the European buildings. It was not easy to go from place to place. One would have to walk across another's farms thus raising trouble. The lighting of the

town was restricted to important streets of European offices or residences.[32]

These were the conditions that gave rise to an outbreak of bubonic plague in 1924 that killed nearly one hundred and fifty people in Kumase, caused mass panic and led to the overdue creation of the KPHB to regulate local government.[33]

Kwabena Bonsu was schooled in the etiquette of speaking, dressing and eating, and in all of the other accomplishments of the traditional *ahenkwaa*. Then one day he found himself in attendance at a funeral. He was sent, as he often was, to a bar in Kagyatia to buy 'rum' (*aworɔnte*) for the adult mourners. He brought the alcohol and many 'courses of wine went round'. All present became more or less drunk, grievances were aired and things got out of hand. Eventually a man named Mosi, a former slave and member of the *Asantehene* Agyeman Prempe's *kete* musical ensemble, stabbed another man to death. The victim, Dahenease, was also a 'slave' (and that is the term used) of Kwabena Bonsu's father, Kwaku Dwumo. Uproar ensued; crowds gathered in Kagyatia; and Kwabena Bonsu and the other young boys present were locked for safety into a cupboard. When Mosi was arraigned and the murder investigated, Kwaku Dwumo smuggled his son out of Kumase to Adwuman Kobiri. After two weeks there the boy was sent on to his mother Yaa Yeboa at Adeɛbeba.

By his own testimony this incident 'produced a great impression' on Kwabena Bonsu's youthful mind. But on reflection he conceded that it was not all that unusual as 'murders and all sorts of wildness' took place in Kumase at that time. The early colonial city during Kwabena Bonsu's sojourn there was 'crowded with Ashantis and strangers', many of them unemployed or itinerant, and at night it was notoriously 'dangerous'. The inhabitants 'were up to all kinds of tricks' and theft, assault and 'other bad things' occurred on a daily basis. Withal, Kumase was then 'exciting for a boy' and a place in which money was made and 'fine things' could be bought. On the other hand many people struggled to survive in a city that was clearly Asante but also 'seemed to change all the time'. New roads and buildings impressed but in their shadow immigrants led anarchic lives trying to find their bearings in a shifting landscape. The city was a dreamscape of juxtapositions and contrasts and this is the underlying motif of Kwabena Bonsu's recollections.

There is a last telling footnote to be added to Kwabena Bonsu's account of his boyhood. For reasons that need not detain us here, Kwaku Dwumo and Yaa Yeboa separated and disputed the custody of their son. Kwabena Bonsu was removed from Adeɛbeba and sent again to Adwuman Kobiri. There his life was an idyll of play and comradeship but in a village environment still largely untouched by the twentieth century. 'A typical village life I led,' he recalled, and having dilated on this theme, he ended by observing that 'the village life was a definite contrast to what I saw in Kumasi'. Narratives that perceived ever growing differences between the experiential rhythms and textures of city and village are common to Adeɛbeba as elsewhere. The felt reality of this contrast became reinforced by exaggerations. In articulation its dialectic required that the city be all motion and the village all stasis. In Kwabena Bonsu's perception Kumase changed all the time but Adwuman Kobiri was changeless. The idea struggling into early focus here was that in their respective presents the urban incarnated the future while the rural memorialised the past. As this understanding spread, it sanctified partisanships and prejudices that exist to this day with effects that lie beyond immediate concerns.[34]

Kwabena Bonsu's recollections were of Kumase life around 1920. By contrast Yaw Aprutwum of Adeɛbeba lived in Kumase for the five years 1938–43. He was born in 1922, the last of the seven children of Abena Mmurosa and Kofi Baa, both of whom were Adeɛbeba residents. Kofi Baa was a blacksmith by trade and had worked for some time for mining companies in both Tarkwa and Obuase. Prior to this he had lived for a period as a young man in Tetrefu two miles east of Saawua and was there during the *yaa asantewaakɔ*. Described by his youngest child as having a 'traditional Ashanti outlook', Kofi Baa opposed his wife's ambition to have their children educated. But Abena Mmurosa was supported by her senior brother Yaw Dabo, and Yaw Aprutwum was sent at his uncle's expense to a peripatetic school run by an Akuapem man in Fankyenebra and then in nearby Danyaame. The boy learned to read and write basic English, but his education was intermittent. He was often removed from school by his father and this was apparently one of the reasons why his parents divorced in 1935.

In 1938 Yaw Aprutwum apprenticed himself to a metalworker in Kumase. At the outbreak of war in the following year he was taken on by the greatly expanded Kumase Public Works Department (PWD) and there he learned panel beating and some general and electrical engineering. For most of his stay he lived just down the hill from the Wesleyan-Methodist church in that house number D.117 in Adum, already noted as being full of Adeɛbeba people. In Yaw Aprutwum's estimation Kumase was 'a nice place in which to live and had all the modern conveniences of life'. These included many amenities that had been introduced since Kwabena Bonsu had lived in Kagyatia: electric lighting in some public areas (first installed 1927); macadamised main roads (1927–30) and a steady upgrading of street surfaces thereafter; Kingsway, a new business and commercial thoroughfare (1929); the lorry park to cope with the growth in motorised transport (1930); the beginnings of a pipe-borne water supply (1934); the opening of Jackson Park (1935) and Prempeh Hall (1939); the building of public latrines with septic tanks (1939); and the organisation of a much needed

Figure 4.4 Colonial Kumase: Kagyatia in 1941.
(Source: P. Redmayne, *The Gold Coast Yesterday and Today*. Cape Coast: Methodist
Book Depot. 1941. p. 74)

municipal fire brigade (1942). These were among the most visible signs of
colonial improvement, but the key developments were less palpable infrastructural shifts. The year 1937 witnessed an unprecedented building boom
and thereafter – in a process radically accelerated by wartime population
growth – Kumase grew to annex its peri-urban periphery. The leading edge
of this unplanned but inexorable growth took the form of ribbon development along the improved arterial roads to Cape Coast via Obuase (1936)
and to Accra (1938), but by 1941 fevered if patchy building was going on
elsewhere around the city's edges.

Yaw Aprutwum took note of aspects of all of this as and when they im-
pinged on him. Thus he often took lorries back and forth to Edweso along
the Accra road and south-east to Kuntanase by lake Bosomtwe. He played
football with a PWD works team in Jackson Park on Saturday afternoons.
For a while he pursued a girl from Bantama in the north of the city and they
used to meet in the Central Market and in his room at Adum. With two
male friends, the one a Kumase man and the other from Adeɛbeba, he
sometimes went to a makeshift open-air cinema operated by an Indian
trader between the Zongo and Ashanti New Town (his favourite films being
westerns, adventure serials and gangster movies). He patronised an Ewe
tailor in Manhyia, had his hair cut and styled by a barber at 'Prempeh's
Farm' and went to dances in the Rialto in Adum. He belonged to a group of
friends who drank together in bars in and around Kagyatia. In the midst of

this busy urban life Yaw Aprutwum often returned to Adeɛbeba to visit with kin. In fact urban growth was closing a cognitive gap; 'Adiebeba and Kumasi are the same' in the precise sense that the village was in process of being engulfed by the city.

In 1943 Yaw Aprutwum broke his leg and went to Adeɛbeba to con-valesce. He was still there in 1945 when he summed up his experience of living in Kumase in the following terms.

> It is quiet here. Adiebeba is near to Kumasi but the two are different in all regards. I am not liking to stay here for I am not making any living. People here go to farm and keep close to each other's affairs. This is a bad thing as it means you are at all times being overlooked in what you are doing. In Kumasi it is different. In living there I was working and having money to please myself. I eat 'Arkasa' [akasa: maize porridge] here [laughs] but in Kumasi there is everything good to chop. There is no clean water in the village and the night lighting is bad. People don't have much light here. They retire early and go to farm early. But Kumasi is busy at all times. I miss the friends I moved with in Kumasi. There is nothing to see now. No stalls and shops and no beautiful girls [laughs]. There is not even a proper church built yet. I tell you [i.e. the interviewer Edward Nyantakyi] you come here from Kumasi and you do not live here. You could not live here for more than one day. You can stay and begin weeping for all the good things you do not have. I am not happy with my lot in life [laughs]. In Kumasi there was every thing and not a moment to loose [sic] in life. It is sad this change. I will go up to Kumasi as soon as I am able to live my life again. I am not any more a real village boy.[35]

What do the tales of Kwabena Bonsu and Yaw Aprutwum say about the evolving relationship between Adeɛbeba people and Kumase? In sifting and pondering their memories and those of others one reply that suggests itself seems to reside in the progressive installation of a sense of ease. In 1920 Kwabena Bonsu inhabited a colonialism still in process of wrenching manu-facture. Its temporal signature was literal dis-ease, a disjunctive rawness produced by a scraping against the tectonic plate of the precolonial order. That order dwelled within – for it had formed – most Adeɛbeba people then living. But by 1940 Yaw Aprutwum inhabited a colonialism of established insertion. Its leitmotifs were familiarity and tractability, for it had accom-modated the receding precolonial order to a landscape defined through its own expectations and cued by its own desires. In implanting itself the colonial order sought mastery through solvent technologies of erasure, amnesia and fervent reinscription. The instantiation of normality offered up by this palimpsest arose not simply from the passage of years, nor from the fading of memory, but rather from the engineering of masterful points of

view. Colonial Kumase was the most visible of these, potency disciplined
and routinised to a spectacle of concrete order. The colonial city proclaimed
its mastery by endlessly rehearsing its inevitability. This was a praxis of repetitions that defined progress as the increment of subscription to guidance.
As such it functioned as a persuasion to adherence, an invitation to ease in
all those called upon to inhabit its improving effects.[36]

One effect that impacted on Adeɛbeba people was the disciplinary
rationalisation of market commerce. A demonstration of order and an
insinuation of improvement were combined together in the evolutionary
implementation of this colonial project. It will be recalled that Kwabena
Bonsu remembered the makeshift state of the main Kumase market about
1920. An earlier witness of long experience gave a graphic description of
market conditions throughout the decade of the 1900s. This account shows
colonialism deploying its battery of disciplinary regimes in a first attempt at
realising its visions of order and improvement.

> Various foodstuffs such as plantains, cocoyams, palm nuts, cassava,
> corn, yams, eggplants, firewood, drink and other commodities are
> brought along these [eight main] routes to the Kumasi market for sale
> every morning. The foodstuffs start arriving from about seven in the
> morning until nine. Palm wine begins to arrive in the market between
> ten and eleven-thirty. The foodstuffs market closes at noon. Due to its
> large size and the large number of people who meet there, fights, mis-
> demeanours, intimidation and stealing are rampant in the market.
> Consequently, the British government has appointed some policemen
> to be responsible for guarding the market from morning till night, in
> order to forestall any misbehaviour likely to tarnish the market's
> reputation. Hardly a day passes without people being arrested in the
> market and taken into custody.
>
> When foodstuffs are scarce the police are ordered to assemble all the
> women who bring food and drink into the market in one place. When
> they are all gathered together a policeman follows them into the
> market in order to enable everyone to get enough goods to buy ... The
> cheapest commodities in the market are foodstuffs. The only slightly
> annoying thing is that one has to pay Simpowa [simpɔwa: a weight of
> gold equivalent to threepence] for practically every item, be it pepper,
> eggplants, pineapples, or bananas; all are sold in lots of (i.e. costing)
> Simpowa. It is only recently that the government has forced them to
> use Kapre [kaperɛ: a British copper penny]. But this decision was
> strongly debated before being finally accepted. Initially some people
> objected to the use of Kapre and were punished with imprisonment,
> thereby weakening resistance to it. Now the populace are contented
> because anybody, rich or poor, can afford to buy from the market. Can
> the poor be happy or afford to live within a state or town where one can

only have a meal at a cost of Simpowa? So with regard to food, Kumase is now without comparison.[37]

Colonial planning wanted a single central market with fixed stalls so as to control sanitation and police revenue collection through surveillance. The first site chosen in 1902 was in Adum, but congestion there steadily eroded order and eventually produced the conditions noted by Kwabena Bonsu. In 1924 the newly empowered KPHB removed the central market to its present site at Kagyatia-Asafo, behind the railway station in the drained marsh of the central Nsuben river valley. Thereafter, the market steadily expanded as new sections were sanctioned and traders took up the leases. Thus, by the 1940s 'a great part of the Kumasi market is supplied with sheds which the sellers hire and sell in; this gives the place a clean, tidy and modern appearance'. The market itself was 'divided into three distinct parts – the wholesale market, the retail market for foodstuffs and vegetables, and the section for imported goods'. The whole was 'a well ordered place and a first class market that villagers are comfortable in using. Keenness is strictly observed in all matters of cleanliness and hygiene and in contributing to the ease of sellers and buyers in the place.'[38] In short, the Kumase central market was an exemplary realisation of the colonial project. It was also the part of the city most frequented by Adeebeba people. Their various involvements with the market were passages in the reception of capitalism and in the domestication of the colonial order guaranteed and served by it.

The 'section for imported goods' was located 'through the Main Gates which are opposite the Railway Station'. The 'stores' here were outlets supplied by European and African import houses in Kumase. Thus,

> women and men in the market stores have invested in the firms some money or gold trinkets and they are being supplied with goods at the end of every month, after paying for the past month's goods supplied to them by the firms. They sometimes make their own choice of goods, and sometimes the firms add other things which have been in the wholesales [sic] for a long time, which one cannot easily sell in the market; so in order to get rid of these things they reduce the prices and sell them at a loss, and then increase very highly the prices of other things which are very hard to get from the stores. By doing this they gain what they have lost on the other goods and even get some profit. This way of trading is not often safe, for most of them get into debts and their Pass Books are being closed down by the firms.[39]

This business called for initial risk capital, good contacts, entrepreneurial skills and a knowledge of consumer preferences. Unsurprisingly, therefore, it was dominated by Kumase traders, and by other Akan, Ewe, Hausa and Yoruba urbanites. Few if any villagers participated. The only Adeebeba person known to have done so was Yaa Dente. From 1934 to 1936 she and

her two women partners from Kumase sold cloth supplied by the United
Africa Company (UAC) from a 'firm store' on 'the western side of the main
market entrance'. Yaa Dente volunteered no information about the source
of the capital the trio deposited with UAC. But from what happened to the
business it can be inferred that the partners resorted to a moneylender from
the outset. Unlike their supplier, they sold cloth by the yard rather than the
whole or half piece. This appealed to villagers with little money and trade
flourished. But the three were bankrupted within two years by their neighbourly custom of extending credit to kin, friends and 'good customers'.
They borrowed cash at the market rate but 'customers were not paying and
this became our debt'. In the end they could not settle accounts with the
moneylender or with UAC. In consequence of this second dereliction,
'every outstanding amount left unpaid was deducted from our money (the
initial deposit) which decreased the amount till it was all washed out'. At
this point UAC cut off the supply of goods and the business folded. Yaa
Dente reflected that 'generosity in giving credit' caused 'my going down'.
She added that this congenial but unbusinesslike practice was 'the downfall
of most women' who failed as traders in the Kumase market.[40]

Adeɛbeba people frequented Kumase central market. They lingered
around import stores of the sort run by Yaa Dente. These businesses were
open fronted and their stock spilled out before them. This cornucopia of
piled-up goods was an image of colonial urban plenty. Some people bought,
but all were exposed to and instructed in the pedagogy of consumerist
desire. Confirmation of this comes from the fact that when Adeɛbeba
people talked of their encounter with this world they resorted to listing
goods. 'In the firm stores', said Kwaku Amponsa, 'are cloths in pieces of
every size, hardware, stationery, ready made dresses, hats of all sizes, head
kerchiefs, beads, pomades, soaps, plates, etc.' Benson Anane, already cited
in the matter of cocoa farming, listed 'imported goods of every kind and
description. But especially cotton cloths, hardware, books and paper, tinned
fish, kerosene, china, medicines or drugs, ready-made clothings, singlets,
shirts and unders [sic], tools, footwear, pans, baskets, handbags and everything else good.' Josephine (Akua) Asabi listed 'household items of every
kind, and cloth, sewing machines, needles, thread, buttons or all other
necessaries of seamstressing'.[41] The point need not be laboured. In the import stores of the Kumase central market Adeɛbeba villagers – and others
like them from all over Asante – came face to face with the abundance of
colonial capitalism. Order and improvement were implied by the
accessibility and novelty of the goods displayed. But the real issue was
money. It alone could close the gap between desire and consumption.

Adeɛbeba people were widely involved as buyers and sellers in the 'foodstuffs and vegetables' section of the Kumase market. This lay at the heart of

the Kagyatia-Asafo site and it was thronged to overcrowding. People from Adeɛbeba made the trip virtually every day to buy food, because the weekly market in their own village was small and 'poorly supplied with even the necessaries of life'.[42] In addition to buying, many Adeɛbeba people went up to the Kumase market to sell. Most were women who vended a range of raw produce and cooked food. Testimonies about this are complexly detailed concerning the minutiae of business arrangements and personal relationships. The general portrait that emerges from them is of people caught up in a world ruled by money but transacted in sociability. Foodstuff selling was a business, but it was also a way of life.

Mention has been made of the specialist growing of shallots at *dodow* and *(n)tasu* in later nineteenth-century Adeɛbeba. In the colonial period Adeɛbeba people went on cultivating this plant for sale in Kumase. The farming was done by women on small tracts of well-watered land. Shallots cropped twice a year, and at Adeɛbeba they were planted out in sequence to forestall shortages and meet demand. Selling was done by groups of two to three women. Abena Asisiwaa was in business with her younger sister and a friend. 'I bring the shallots to Kumasi', she said,

> tied up in bundles. I sell and do it in the sun in the big market. I am in the open (no shed at all) beside a friend from Amakom. She sells cassava along with a Pankronu woman. Traders come in from Pease, Kodaso, Abobooso, Aforekrom, Ahudjo and Kumasi farms etc. I know them and go round greeting when I arrive. I take pains to see the shallots are washed and in good condition. If people think it does not look well they do not buy. Kumasi people like this [shallots] but the Kwahu traders cheat and Anlo people charge much money. I do good trade except in the rains as fewer people come out to buy. It is too cold then and it is muddy all about. I used to sell on a table but the leg broke off. I sit down on the ground now [laughs]. There is always someone who buys shallots. It is a popular food and I never return home with any of them unsold. Sometimes my profit is 3 shillings a day [laughs]. But a small basket of fish is 3 shillings too. I could stay on the farm and eat but money from the trading buys foodstuffs and other things. I like tinned fish [laughs] and buy cloth from a woman Adjua Kum who is well known to me and sells me cheap. I have done this thing for many years. I do not want always the village and going to farm for I would miss the life here with my friends. My sister who is helping me also sells cooked food. Her son my nephew goes about the country making Konko.[43]

Like other people in the cash economy, Abena Asisiwaa did several things to make ends meet; and like them too she relied on group solidarity, in this case close kin who pooled at least some of their earnings with hers.

Apart from shallot selling and food farming, she sewed and peddled clothing, sold kerosene and traded in bottled palm oil. Her younger sister Afua Akromaa sold cooked yam, plantain fried in oil, cassava slices and other 'snacks'. She was one of five women who bought yam in bulk from a Tamale man in 'the wholesale market' in Kumase so as to cut costs. The yam was divided up between the women, washed, cut up, boiled and sold in halfpenny slices. Sometimes she sold oranges, buying them at three for a penny and retailing them for a halfpenny each. But her son Kwadwo Asaaman was the entrepreneurial money maker in the family. He worked out of the Kumase market as a middleman (*konkosini*) in any business that paid. Thus, he travelled around Ahafo and Amansie buying up 'corn in bags and bringing them to Kumasi market on lorries'. He sold this on to Ga and Fante food sellers. Each bag cost 'from £1–6 to £1–10 and the profit on it is up to 7/-. When I am without funds I get the corn on commission as the farmers at Sunyani and Bekwai know me.' For a time he had an arrangement with some Fante fishermen. They sent their catch up by rail from Sekondi and Kwadwo Asaaman sold it on to Kumase fishmongers on a commission basis; 'I am selling 100 smoked herrings at 12/6 and I take 1/6 from this amount.' He also procured old lorry tyres for a 'Lagosian (Yoruba) sandal maker' who had a stall behind the railway station; 'he sells a pair (of sandals) for 1/6 up to 2/6 and he makes £1 profit from using a tyre. I am paid for each tyre at 2/-.' Kwadwo Asaaman's silence about where the tyres came from is eloquent. He was a village boy who lived by his wits in the urban cash economy. There were many like him, prototypes of those 'verandah boys' who were to play a significant role in Asante politics during and after decolonisation.[44]

Adeɛbeba people had much to do with the Kumase central market. To many it was a metaphor for the city itself and for the relentless monetisation of life. Take the matter of fuel. Firewood was in short supply in precolonial Adeɛbeba for reasons that have been discussed. Villagers knew this, but chose to blame scarcity on the demands of the capital. The growth of the colonial city reinforced this perception. In fact twentieth-century Kumase did consume more and more firewood; and ever rising demand did mean that fuel had to be brought into the city from further and further away, with predictable implications for its cost to consumers. Adeɛbeba villagers understood all this, but it was what they chose to make of it that compels interest. The matter of fuel was employed as a device around which were woven narratives about past and present life, identity and money. Villagers revealed much when they dilated on this issue. Kwabena Mensa was a prolix man. His testimony was fuller than most, but it echoed with opinions held by others.

> There is no firewood here now in Adiebeba. It is all used up by the Kumasi people. Now only Breman, Kanyasi, Asu Yeboa and Sipe have wood. Women from these places carry firewood from their husbands'

farms or their brothers', uncles' or cousins' farms into Kumasi on to the market to profiteer. A short bundle of firewood is sold at Kumasi market at 1/6 and 1/9. Men from the NTs [Northern Territories of the Gold Coast Colony] go all around and about the bush villages taking firewood as it pleases them in the night so as to join in profiteering. Such people are over all Ashanti now and think to use the country like the sea as if it was free to all fishermen. This did not happen in past times. Firewood was free to all on their own land and Ashanti was not yet oppressed by the TYRANT MONEY (capitals in original). Kumasi market is vagabonds, thiefs [sic] and criminals few of which are Ashanti bred. The Fanti and Hausa charcoal makers are low people. They steal the trees in villages near Kumasi to burn them into charcoal to sell at market. Ashanti people would not do this thing. Ashantis have enough work to do therefore they do not like this kind of dirty work. They are interested in farming. Now slaves have money such as those NTs and Fanti people. Firewood is dear and charcoal is even more. It costs much to cook food. This is a common thing nowadays. Every thing in life costs money and how are people here (Adeɛbeba) to live when strangers are all about us? Kumasi is a bad place. It is money and money again. It is only us who are suffering from this. Ashanti is open season to all and the native born are forced to make way for emigrants (sic). The TYRANT MONEY is King in Kumasi and is ruling us with an iron rod.[45]

Anxieties of the sort expressed by Kwabena Mensa were not uncommon. In some villagers involvement with the colonial city inspired a fearful repulsion. When they beheld Kumase they saw a juggernaut in chaotic motion. They would not – or could not – penetrate its surface anarchy to the circuits of order and opportunity that lay beneath. Owusu Gyebi sometimes went to Kumase in the 1930s to visit his 'older sister', the pioneer railway worker Afua Nsoro. He disliked the city and detested the central market.

Kumasi is a dirty dirty place. Too many sick people roam about in the market even some lepers. Blind people are there and many with skin diseases and open sores. All are beggars and go about begging all the time and rubbing with the healthy people. There are nuisances all about committed by the market traders. The smell is bad. Worse [sic] of all is the crowds of people. Shoutings and jostlings are the order of the day and hurrying about to and fro. Where foodstuffs are is a noisy crowd of men, women and young boys and girls. These boys come from Ashanti and all over the Gold Coast. They live by stealing and cheating people of money. Even schoolchildren who come to the market to buy cooked food after 12 o'clock have no respect for anyone. They think as they are Kumasifoo [kumasefoɔ: 'the people of Kumase'] that they can swagger about shouting and disturbing all others. They are the byword for rudeness of behaviour. Offences of all sorts take place every day in this market. Policemen are there but few and stay by the overseer's station to do nothing. They are loafers as bad as the common element. From the market up to Adum smell is everywhere. The noise is tremendous. Kumasi people are daring to do any bad thing. The motto is the bird must fly about any how to stop itself from starving [lit. *anoma antu a bua da*; impl. 'nothing ventured, nothing gained', a saying applied to those of notably bold and aggressive character].[46]

An extreme view? Perhaps. What is clear is that attitudes of this sort implied a contrast between the disorienting city and the tranquil village. For some Adeɛbeba people the difference was explicit and expressed as such. Amma Porowaa was a tomato seller at Kagyatia-Asafo and then at Bantama when government sanctioned trading there in 1941 to relieve pressure on the central market.

I go up and down to Kumasi when I want to sell. I was for a time selling tomatoes with others but I am now selling for myself. I sell in Bantama and also by the Zongo roadside. I go and greet Yaa Brenya who is a trader at Fuller road. Kumasi is a hard place. The people there live by robbing and cheating strangers. They are Kroomfo men [*akrɔmfoɔ*: thieves] there. Kumasi is too big. You can get lost there and no one will lift a hand to help you. I prefer to stay in this place [Adeɛbeba]. I spent girlhood days here. My mother lived in it till she died and three of her sisters are still living here. It is better to be here than at Kumasi. The village is clean and quiet and no one troubles you with stealing. You can sleep in peace and quiet and go about untroubled in the place. People are kind as neighbours and you know you will get every assistance when needful. I go to Kumasi because there is no one here to buy. But even as I am going there I wish to come back here. The village is home for me. I know every one who is living in it and all my families [*sic*] are buried in their cemetery by the Toase road. What is Kumasi to me? I tell you nothing at all. I went to Mampontin once a time ago as my uncle was trading kola. Even it was better than Kumasi though small with only a market set down on the ground. It is full of NTs people. Mampontin is better than Kumasi but more spoiled by strangers than here. I want to go on living here to my days end [*sic*] without troubles.[47]

Was the encounter of Adeɛbeba people with Kumase different in kind or degree from that experienced by other Asante villagers? A difference of kind is doubtful and there is some evidence on that head.[48] But a difference of degree is another matter. To recapitulate: Adeɛbeba was near Kumase,

developed in relationship to it, and in the end was engulfed by and later
(1954) incorporated into it. Proximity and history involved Adeɛbeba
villagers in the city to an unusual extent, and the intensity of this exposure
worked to sharpen and complicate their attitudes and opinions. Extremes of
liking or loathing have been noted. But irrespective of these responses,
Adeɛbeba testimonies in general voiced a feeling of apprehension and ambiguity about colonial Kumase and all of its works. In part this may have been
the result of historical imprinting. In its precolonial incarnation Kumase
represented power. The mandate of authority devolved downwards from
the city to the village. So although Adeɛbeba people might choose to
identify themselves with Kumase, no such affinity was acknowledged in
return. The inhabitants of the capital were *kumasefoɔ*, sophisticated and
worldly denizens of the realm of power; to them all others beyond the capital
– even those living as close as Adeɛbeba – were generic *nkuraasefoɔ*, uncouth
and uninformed village dwellers separated the one from the other only by
risible tics of comportment, dress or speech.[49] Then in its colonial incarnation Kumase still represented power and authority. But to Adeɛbeba
people this proposition was harder to grasp than it had been in the
nineteenth century. Precolonial power was all of a piece with the society and
culture it ruled over. But colonial power was in the hands of non-Asante.
Furthermore it expressed itself in innovation and flux, not custom and
hierarchy. The gap that separated village and city was still there, but the
latter was now receding from view into the future. To Adeɛbeba people this
accelerating Kumase was as palpable as it was difficult to describe. It was
also unsettling at levels that people often found hard to articulate. Those
who liked Kumase commonly spoke with a nervous bravado; and those who
disliked it often testified with a repelled fascination.

The things about colonial Kumase that bothered Amma Porowaa and those
men and women like her were the same as those that intrigued or excited
Kwabena Bonsu and Yaw Aprutwum. For all of them the city was a preci-
pitate of the present, a piling-up of experiences in the existential moment.
Recuperated as memory the anxieties or exhilarations of such moments
were domesticated in the light of a retrospection that made them seem
predictable, but only *after* they had happened. Personal memory was patin-
ated to a narrative nostalgia of the moment, recollected from when it was
first experienced as a shock of pleasure, horror or the rest. This was how
Adeɛbeba and other people naturalised the relationship between colonialism
and autobiography. As a technique it liberated the experience of colonialism
into personal sampling and speculation, the parcellisation of likes and
dislikes into a placating narrative that one could tell oneself and others. It
also (re)produced epiphanies, the signposts of a mnemonic ordering.
   Many Adeɛbeba people recalled their first encounter with electric light in

Kumase, a striking thing indeed when villages were still plunged into darkness by night. It is all too easy to overlook the shock this produced. But Adeɛbeba witnesses did not forget, and 'vanquishing of the dark at night' featured in many reminiscences. European stores and shops in Kumase inspired a similar astonishment at first sight and the experience lodged in the memory. Adeɛbeba people recalled plate-glass frontages, window displays, counters, tables and piled-up consumer goods. Three people made particular mention of encountering mannequins. Their fascination and bemusement were a general phenomenon. During the First World War an Agogo schoolboy accompanied his father to Kumase for the first time. Over half a century later he recalled seeing

> a big shop (F. and A. Swanzy Ltd) opposite the Kumasi Post Office, with an enchanting local name: OSAMAN AFIADE (A Ghost's Shop). At a conspicuous place in the shop stood a mannequin. That (?c)lay figure placed in the room for display of clothes was, in the native belief in the transposition of the spiritual being into corporeal form, a ghost in physical human form. It went without saying that the shop was a principal centre of attraction for several villagers like I was, who went to Kumasi to do shopping ... I stood at a respectable distance, right arm akimbo, staring sheepishly at the 'Ghost', quite oblivious to all that went on in the big shop.[50]

In colonial Kumase the shock of the new was endlessly renewable and it struck people as such. Adeɛbeba villagers grasped after intention and meaning but were reduced to notation. In retirement Afua Nsoro declared that Kumase was a crucible of 'changes' in which 'someone who has gone away will not see it the same when coming back'. Kwasi Fi disliked Kumase, for there the Adeɛbeba visitor 'loses of himself in wandering all about' in its shifting landscape.[51] Perspective was needed to fill out such notations. Adeɛbeba villagers lacked the comparative and rhetorical tools (and the distancing trick of ironising memory to evoke nostalgia). But the sense of their imaginings was not so far away from the articulations of the Kumase-born intellectual K. A. Appiah. His musings on change would certainly have struck some chord in their understanding. 'Back in the 1950s', so Appiah recalled of his childhood in Kumase Mbrom,

> the cinema at the end of the street in Kumasi, the Odeon, brought us musicals from India, kung fu movies from Hong Kong, westerns from Hollywood. In those days before television, the Odeon was our (but whose?) periscope into a wider world. It was owned by a Lebanese family. The last time I was at home, I was reminded that the Odeon is no longer a cinema – cinema in Kumasi has been destroyed by the video clubs – but a church, one of those evangelical Protestant denominations that are spreading throughout Africa. I wonder what Max Weber

would have said about this triumph of Protestantism over the Protestant ethic of the Muslims who built the Odeon.[52]

Let us conclude here with a Kumase that is the same place in the same era but at a remove from the city of the villager or the intellectual. In 1930 some thirty-nine Asante businessmen, 'loyal subjects and tax payers' – including one Kwasi Heman, whose mother was Nana Akua Afrantwo of Adeɛbeba – petitioned the Chief Commissioner of Asante (CCA) to forestall any attempt by chiefship to resurrect the precolonial system of death duties. In their communication they gave *inter alia* a retrospective of colonialism to date. This was framed as a witnessing to the evolutionary ordering of Kumase in the early twentieth century. In substance this was a list, a balance sheet of the materialisation of the colonial project distributed in space and implanted over time. 'In Your Honour's time', they informed the CCA,

> Kumasi is almost part of London, whatever institution is in London is in Kumasi; Kumasi has big mansions, Banks, Churches, Lights have defeated Darkness, wills making and letters of administration have sunk capricious chiefs freebootering (plundering) deceased's estate and we are tax-payers to the British Government to help to make the Electric Lights, Water Works, Schools, Churches, Roads and other comfortable things.[53]

Here was the CCA's Kumase mirrored and reflected back at him. But everyone had a version of the city. The carpenter Kwaku Antwi of Adeɛbeba and Kumase Adum put the matter with unimprovable economy. 'Kumasi town', he observed, 'is all things to all men.'[54]

INTERSUBJECTIVITIES: ADEƐBEBA WOMEN AND MEN, 1900s–1940s

In the 1920s Rattray committed to his ethnographic notebooks an enumeration by occupation and task of the Asante sexual division of labour. Exclusively male and female responsibilities were listed. There followed a description of 'the combined work of men and women'. Under this heading was a single entry; men and women customarily shared in the work of 'making' and 'cleaning' food and cocoa farms. Having neutrally recorded this observation, Rattray left matters there.[55] He made no mention of gendered rights in farming or of money. Someone who did was the Adeɛbeba farmer Kwabena Buo.

> Land for farming is made ready in two ways. First way is by weeding the grass and burning it when dry. The second is without burning too much. You take off the stumps and go about your business. I like the first way as better. It cools the land down after Gyahyibere [*gyahye brɛ*: 'the time of sparks'; i.e. dry season grass burning]. When the man and wife are working the farm together they do not each own the crop

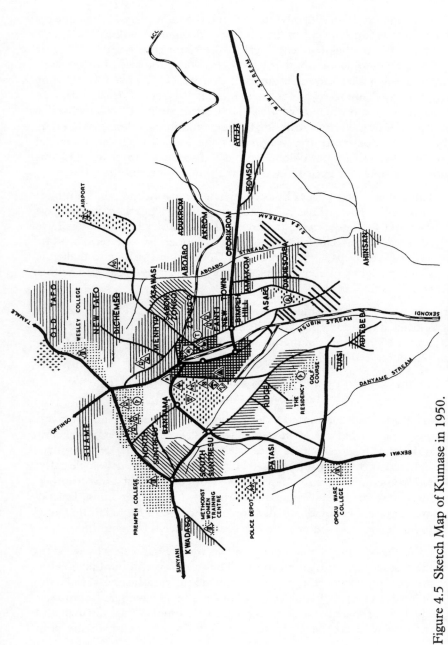

Figure 4.5 Sketch Map of Kumase in 1950.
(Source: F. A. Abloh, *Growth of Towns in Ghana: A Study of the Social and Physical Growth of Selected Towns in Ghana.* Department of Housing and Planning Research, Faculty of Architecture, University of Science and Technology, Kumase. 1967. Opposite p. 26)

together. The man has to bear the cost of labour and so he plants the
first crop. When this germinates then the woman's share comes in.
She plants vegetables or some plantain or cocoyam. In the harvesting
the wife helps the husband. But the man does not help the woman in
getting hers harvested. The man can sell the crops without ever
consulting the woman. But the woman must consult the man when
she wants to sell any of the crops. Similarly whenever the crop is sold
the woman should inform the man when she wants to use any of her
share of money on anything. If she wants to buy cloth or any jewellery
the man is to be consulted. Cloths, beads, earrings, and meat is provided to the woman by the man. But this does not mean the woman
should not use any share of money she realises from the farm on the
man. The woman must provide things when necessary such as soap,
sponge and towel, dishes and buckets, cooking pots and salt. She must
buy her own cutlass. The farm is for the man and afterwards for the
woman. Women nowadays say this is not right as their God Supreme
is Money. They are abandoning themselves [sic] to go after this thing
and leaving their duties.[56]

Other men supported Kwabena Buo's views and enlarged on his complaints. Kwasi Fi, brother of the ɔkɔmfɔ Amma Kyirimaa, said that women
had become wilful, disobedient and promiscuous. They disrespected their
husbands, and they 'liked money over much and went to any man' who had
or promised it. Young girls were turning away from village life and domestic
responsibility, marriage was not what once it had been, and desertion and
divorce were rife. It was maybe less trouble now, he said with strained levity,
to embrace the unmarried state.[57] Yaw Tenten, uncle of the beauteous Afua
Tweneduaase whose marriage against the wishes of her kin has already been
discussed, was scathing about 'the women of today'. In Adeɛbeba, he said,
wives used 'to help their husbands in farming willingly and without troubling them'. But now the descendants of these very women were 'hot headed
and no longer to be trusted'. They used their wiles 'to snare men in' and then
refused work and demanded money. Divorce was 'the burning issue of the
day' because women forsook their responsibilities out of 'a selfish opinion'.[58]
Yaw Dapaa, a farmer at (n)tasu, was bitter rather than angry. 'I have had no
very good dealings with women in my life,' he declared, and went on to
explain that his wife Afua Mpobi had left him when 'I could supply her no
more money.' During the marriage she 'refused to go to farm', bore him no
children and 'played freely with other men'.[59] To a greater or lesser extent
Adeɛbeba men in general expressed views of this sort. By corollary – as we
shall see in due course – Adeɛbeba women had their own stories to tell.

The opinions just adumbrated can be taken to suggest a palpable if con-
fusedly articulated male fretfulness about the shifting ground of gender

relations in the colonial era. Others have explored aspects of the anxiety or 'chaos' that overtook relations between the sexes in colonial Asante in consequence of rapid changes in economy and society. Inexorable monetisation of the relations of production was at the root of this development. The implications were pervasive and far reaching, and scholarship has begun to address some of them.[60] Analysis here, however, is confined to the Adeɛbeba evidence.

Testimonies concerning the context and content of marriage in colonial Adeɛbeba provide confirmation, at the impressionistic level, that both women and men felt themselves to be in a shifting, negotiable moral economy *vis-à-vis* relations with the opposite sex. Some care is required in assessing this dimension, however, for whereas some of its constituents were unarguably new, others appear historically rooted. At the systemic level it might be argued that monetisation of the relations of production, accomplished under the political aegis of colonial overrule, simply exposed the configuration of precolonial gender relations for what it was; that is, an ideological determination constructed by a male office holding power in its own – and *ipso facto* its gender's – interest. By the terms of this construct, the kinship ordering premises of matrilineality were guaranteed, overseen and mediated by a state authority that was vested in a hierarchical male elite. As in other societies, matriliny did not preclude patriarchy. This is not at all to suggest that women were bereft of statutory rights or recourse in precolonial Asante. But it is to suggest that individual women who tried to venture autonomy outside the perimeter of ascribed jural rights as defined by matriliny were commonly and prejudicially disadvantaged in their encounters with both the explicit facts of male political power and the implicit understandings and assumptions of patriarchy. Thus, adultery requiring compensation (*ayɛfere sika*), construed as a transaction between an offended and an offending male, reduced female agency to a sexual signifier in an exclusively masculinist construction.[61] Admittedly adultery was the extreme case. It raised in acute form for men the issue of proprietary rights in marriage and the fathering of children, and inflected these with anxieties about female sexuality. In consequence resolutions were achieved in law that effaced or otherwise discounted any concept of female autonomy or agency.

The Asante state set the agenda strictly in matters like adultery, but such evidence as there is suggests that in daily practice precolonial marriage was a processual construct rather than an unrelenting system of legal domination. In the sphere of intersubjective relations that lay below the level of the state's oversight wives and husbands were caught up in negotiations around conjugal rights and reciprocities. It was these interpersonal understandings, as well as more public issues, that were destabilised by colonialism. In brief, the following occurred. First, the role of the Asante state as ideological arbiter was abolished, but male chiefship and patriarchy remained to contest for their historic prerogatives over women. Second, relations of production were monetised, investing labour – including farm work – with a value reducible to cash. Third, the British outlawed slavery and pawning and so radically diminished the reservoir of biddable labour. Fourth, all these developments took place in conjunction with the embedding of cash-crop agriculture. Fifth, in their struggle to maintain food farms and create profit-yielding cocoa farms Asante men exploited their wives and children as the principal surviving source of free labour. Sixth and last, as colonial capitalism tightened its grip it led exploited wives – and women generally – to feel resentment at exclusion from the profits of their labour. The result was that many women looked at their needs and possibilities and then set about trying to forge economic autonomy and security for themselves in a world driven by money. Marriage and gender relations came under unprecedented interrogation as established norms and emerging practices were inscribed together in unstable protocols of behaviour and expectation. In broad terms men strove to re-create the *status quo ante*, while women elected – or felt compelled – to explore new horizons.

Mention has been made already of the Adeɛbeba cocoa 'pioneer' Adu Asabi who died intestate in 1937. Most of his cocoa farms were far from Adeɛbeba around Mfensi and Kukuom. But one of them lay along the confluence of the Awawia and Kokroma streams only three miles west of Adeɛbeba near Santaase. At his death this land bore 'cocoa trees and stems' intercropped with plantain. Along with the rest of the estate, the 'Awawah farm' was claimed under the customary laws of inheritance by Adu Asabi's uterine nephew (*wɔfase*) Osei Agyekum, supported by both men's lineage head (*abusua panin*) Kofi Manwere of Adeɛbeba. However, Adu Asabi's widow Akosua Gyankumaa of Anyinam disputed the ownership of this particular farm. The couple had married in the late 1880s and had produced seven children. As a child herself Akosua Gyankumaa had been removed from Anyinam and resettled at Adeɛbeba as a pawn (*ɔwowani*), as surety for a debt owed to the *Manwerehene* by the Kumase *Anamenakohene*, the overlord of her natal village. In Adeɛbeba she was assigned to the lot of the Heman *abusua* of Afua Nimaako to which Adu Asabi belonged.[62] Thus when Adu Asabi married her she was 'a pawn wife' (*awowa ɔyere*), in service to *Manwere* through her husband's lineage. Such an arrangement was a commonplace of precolonial Asante life.

When her husband of half a century died in 1937 Akosua Gyankumaa argued that she and her surviving children should inherit his Awawia-Kokroma farm on the grounds of her sustained contribution to its creation, upkeep and profitability.

> Self and children walked in the sun to Wamasi to make (this) farm. I lived there in a hut in weeding the estate to grown [*sic*] foodstuffs.

When cocoa was coming in it was put out to the boundary of a tree (Odangya) separating from Atta Mensah's farm. Late Asabi planted stems and I planted with him together. He got sick for a time and the farmwork was carried on by self. Now my children are left without any share or fruits. We are not now living as before in the past times and now the fact (is) that the one who works will enjoy the benefit. Agyakum [Osei Agyekum] is now claiming all this farm for himself but he was young when it was made by me and (my) son Asare for the children. He who did not sow cannot in any case reap and the farm is for me.[63]

Osei Agyekum and Kofi Manwere responded by asserting that Adu Asabi's farm belonged 'by all established rights' of inheritance to his lineage kin. In extension of their argument they stated that Akosua Gyankumaa's claim was illicit, for 'no one is to succeed excepting the family which are the rightful heirs'. They went on to insinuate that Akosua Gyankumaa, being an unredeemed pawn (a status long since abolished by the British), was somehow without full legal rights. They also impugned her moral character. The late Adu Asabi, they urged, had sometimes thought of divorcing her. Akosua Gyankumaa had abandoned her husband and lived for several years with her children at Kotei in irregular circumstances. Despite the clear implication of adultery here, Adu Asabi had perversely chosen to overlook the defects suggested by his wife's many detractors. In large part, they concluded, this was because Akosua Gyankumaa exercised an unspecified but malign power over her husband.[64]

The outcome of Akosua Gyankumaa's dispute with her husband's kin is unknown. But the substance of her case was symptomatic of the resentments felt by women towards the terms and constraints of customary marriage. Adeɛbeba testimonies echo her protest against inequities, and several widows voiced dissatisfaction at being excluded from a share in a dead husband's property by the enforcement of customary lineage claims. Yaa Pirabon, widowed in the early 1930s, encapsulated a widespread sentiment when she observed that following her husband's death the man's *abusua* had 'stood fast upon' the marital property 'without referring any to me'. The lineage demanded everything as of right, irrespective of the failure of its members to make any contribution 'to making the farms when he (her husband) was yet in the land of the living'. The widowed Yaa Ankyewaa stated bluntly that her husband's kin had 'stolen away' his farm at *dodow*. Afua Dinkyim, widowed when her husband was killed in a road accident in 1940, said that his 'sisters and brothers' had left her after a lifetime of labour 'without the necessary means of support'.[65] Affines countered that such claims overstated the case, for widows were themselves legatees through their own *abusua* affiliations. The argument was that Asante custom proposed equity, for women as uterine sisters, aunts or nieces shared in lineage property bequeathed by their deceased brothers, nephews or uncles. But this line of reasoning failed to satisfy complaints or staunch the angry sense of grievance that fuelled them.

The underlying problem was structural and it produced stress in both women and men. Precedent balances and equilibria in the fundamental matter of engendered expectations of marriage, as in so much else, were destabilised by colonialism. Marriage was subjected to 'the pressure of cash' and the ideological effect was to leach away consensual subscription to the *status quo ante* as a given of life. When commentators talk of shifting, conflicted gender relations in the twentieth century, of anxiety or of 'chaos', they are referencing a profound attitudinal flux. The terrain of relations between women and men was tilting because of shifts across the entire landscape in which negotiated understandings of the subjective and the intersubjective were grounded. In this tectonic upheaval the abrasive issue of inheritance from marriage was clearly visible because it was critically important and amenable to litigation and hence documentation. But it arose like a peak above a submerged cognitive and affective iceberg. Below the waterline gender relations were in an uncertain process of reassessment marked by contradiction, revision and instability. Unsurprisingly, sexuality was a key area in which women and men rehearsed their views. Of basic importance in its own right, sexuality also served as a topic onto which were displaced wider anxieties about the past and future in light of the present.

Male sexuality in the testimonies of Adeɛbeba women appears as a scalding indictment levelled at a perceived construction and self-image of Asante manhood. The follies and crimes of that manhood, a catalogue of sexual inadequacies and derelictions, were represented by women as the narrated facts of – and so as an explanatory metaphor for – widespread female dissent from both the institutional structurings and interpersonal facets of marriage. This was sometimes framed as bawdiness, but more often with a directed, quite unmistakable edge. Thus, in the 1940s a number of Adeɛbeba women confided that their husbands were 'unable to meet' them in sexual intercourse (i.e. impotence), or complained of their being afflicted by *ɔpe soro rekɔ* or 'a shortened retention' during coition (i.e. premature ejaculation). According to A.A. of Adeɛbeba sexual acts 'plunged into' with her husband were 'not at all the thing itself'. His 'retension [*sic*]' was 'not of a lengthy duration', and so his lovemaking was unsatisfactorily 'too quick'. Other complaints by Adeɛbeba women ranged over penis size, erectile capacity, failure to wash, bad breath, various infringements of understood sexual etiquette, and above all men's relentless promiscuity with its risk of transmitting venereal disease.[66]

Several comments can be made about this confessional evidence. First, all of the Adeɛbeba wives involved confided that they had taken one or more

lovers during their marriages. Those who expressed themselves on the subject of the stringent norms governing female adultery in precolonial Asante
conceded the error of their ways, but offered in justification the argument
that 'men do every thing like this and suffer nothing about it'. Second,
criticisms of men's sexual performance were commonly linked to another
sort of behaviour connoting male irresponsibility. This was the practice of
marital birth control, which village men were notably reluctant to countenance. 'Children come into this world,' said Y.K. of Adeɛbeba, 'but the
money is lacking. Men go all about and around here or there in spending
every thing with girlfriends.' It was remarked by Adeɛbeba women that their
men neither took contraceptive measures before or during marriage, nor
expected to pay for subsequent extra-marital promiscuity and lack of
precaution. Men went after girls, spent money on them, got them pregnant,
married one such, and then moved on to other costly liaisons. The tone in
which women recited this litany was resentful not resigned, and though
some blamed 'young girls' most held men responsible. That mores slowly
seemed to be changing in nearby Kumase only deepened female anger in
Adeɛbeba. 'Men's commitments', it was observed,

> are so very little in connection with conception that there is no known
> method by which they can prevent conception. They [men in the villages]
> freely conceive with their girlfriends and they have the right to let them
> go after delivery if they are not financial enough to marry them.
> Sometimes the man may pay from ten to twenty shillings per month.
> Usually parents do not go to contention about a conceived woman.
> People who live in large towns however are brought within some rules
> of discipline. In Kumasi the Ashantis are affected by a strict law of
> Fanti morality. One cannot conceive with girls and hope to go freely as
> in the case of a village community. School children and young educated
> men resort to pessaries, rubber sheaths and interrupted coital action.[67]

Furthermore, close reading in Adeɛbeba women's testimonies shows
that their gendered strictures about marriage, coition, adultery and reproduction were all referenced to a moral economy of male privilege in spending and hoarding. Men 'spent' selfishly, heedlessly, imprudently – in the
sexual act itself, in promiscuous pursuit of women, in lavishing money on
girlfriends, in fathering children. But men 'hoarded' in a like fashion – in the
denial of sexual gratification to women, in discounting their marital obligations, in discarding inconvenient partners, in failing to provide for offspring.
This perception of gender relations as a negotiation built around spending
and hoarding reflected the early twentieth-century monetisation of customary norms of obligation and reciprocity. Women recognised the problem
and felt disprivileged. British men enforced their economic participation,
but Asante men denied their economic autonomy.

Unsurprisingly male views differed, although they were also shaped by the forces of change. Female sexuality in the testimonies of Adeɛbeba men was historicised. That is, the male view was that the conditions of colonialism operated to render explicit and uncontrolled a dangerous female sexuality that formerly had been kept implicit and controlled by regulatory norms mediated by the Asante state. In the precolonial order female sexuality was subsumed in marriage. Uncontrolled female sexuality was anomalous, and female promiscuity was *nea edi afra* (lit. 'that which is out of place'). Men feared the female genitalia, the site of pleasure but also of a metaphysical power with the potential for wilful harm.[68] In the colonial era, many Asante men correlated the rising stridency of women's economic and other demands with decreasing social – that is, male – control over female sexuality. This perception fused together unbridled sexuality and rampant capitalism in an image of woman as a predatory mistress to and servant of her own unbiddable powers. In the male view, women gave instrumentally and took ruthlessly in a new circuit of genital commodification.[69]

A pointed version of this view was provided by Kwame Agyapon of Asumagya, a shoemaker by trade who lived for a time in Adeɛbeba. He had three wives. His senior wife was from Kokofu and she was 'fond of sexual indulgence'. Kwame Agyapon himself was 'used to frequent practices in sex matters'. In 1941 he enlisted in the army and was absent in India and Burma for five years. He 'found it difficult to be without women when overseas', but also realised that his senior wife 'could not remain without man' in his prolonged absence. On his return to Asante he discovered that she had 'got a child with another man'. He forgave her because he still desired her. He accepted a 'pacification fee' from her lover and resumed sexual intercourse with her. Unfortunately he proved impotent. Then he was presented with 'a bill amounting to £113–6–8 being the senior wife's claim for subsistence for the five years he had been away'. This claim was itemised in respect of puberty rite (*bragoɔ*) expenses for three of their daughters, school fees for their sons, and 'daily maintenance at 1s' for his wife. Kwame Agyapon offered two interpretations of this. First, he stated that these demands were 'a manifest sign of the wife's desire to go away' because he was 'a victim of impotence'. But second, in a confidence fuelled by drink, he berated his wife for 'making use of the vagina (*twɛ*) to captivate' him. She was sexually voracious, and in their marriage she employed 'her powers of allurement [*sic*]' to procure money from him. 'Wealth is her God,' he asserted, and her sexual and monetary needs, reciprocally driving each other on, were parasitic upon his own substance. She had made him into 'an empty vessel', a hollowed-out sexual and economic being.[70]

Education modified the tone in which such opinions were expressed, but it seems to have done little to alter their content. Kwaku (Charles) Frimpon Mensa was the son of Adwowaa Frimpon of Adeɛbeba and E. O. Gyimah,

a Kumase businessman who came originally from Fomena in Adanse in
south Asante. Kwaku Frimpon Mensa was educated at the Kumase Government School and then sent by his father in the mid-1930s to Kyebi in
Akyem Abuakwa to complete his schooling. He became a teacher himself in
Akyem but returned to Kumase in 1943. He gave up schoolmastering and
opened a furniture-making business 'so as to have money sufficient unto the
day and satisfy my needs'. A Roman Catholic like his father, he devoted a
deal of time to looking for a suitable wife. Disappointed in this quest, he
reflected on the reasons for his failure. He wanted to marry a literate Christian and for a time courted Emily B., an educated girl who taught type-
writing. But she was sexually unresponsive and financially demanding. She
denied Kwaku Frimpon Mensa 'full satisfaction' but 'constantly inquired as
to money'. Tiring of this, he embarked on a relationship with another girl.
She was 'an illiterate' but was 'keen in meeting me sexually'. Kwaku Frimpon
Mensa still wanted to marry Emily B. but balked at what he saw as her
mercenary attitude to sex. Marrying her 'will cost more than £25 under the
(Government Marriage) Ordinance', he thought, and even then she might
still not be 'compliant in the sex act' unless he continued to meet her
demands for money. He remained undecided, but in the meantime entered
into a liaison with yet another girl.[71]

There is considerable contextual evidence showing that Kwaku Frimpon
Mensa's views were widely held. Educated men wanted to marry literate
girls as a matter of prestige. But they subscribed to a common belief about
the problems involved. All women were sexually charged beings, and all
used sex as a bargaining counter to 'enslave the man' into meeting their
financial demands. Illiterate village girls did this by seduction, compliance
and availability. Educated girls did it by withholding their favours until 'the
publicity of a wedding to show the whole world', and then by rationing sex
to extract money from their husbands. Thus men were caught in the bind of
women's instrumental sexuality. Village girls were 'the most active and
willing as partners in sexual acts of coition', but they were unsuitable wives
for any educated male aspirant to status. Educated girls were sexually unsatisfactory because 'their charms are used to further their advantage', but they
were socially desirable spouses. It is interesting to note that in this stereotype men blamed the coldness of such women on their educationally
enhanced appetites for money and position – that is, on contemporary
refinements of their essential nature.[72]

The resentful sub-text in all this male anxiety was alarm about proving
inadequate in meeting female demands that were now limitless because
women were believed to be beyond control. For the individual husband,
genital commodification assumed the form of a permanently dissatisfied
wife. Thus Kwadwo Anane of Adeɛbeba separated from his first wife because
'she made complaint about copulation', demanded cash from him, and

refused to cook his food out of spite and 'in saying I was unfit for her'. His fellow villager Kwabena Manu married a Sɔkɔban woman much younger than himself. Her kin insisted that he settle a debt on their behalf (*tiri ka*) before they consented to the marriage. He confessed with hindsight that this had been a mistake, for his young wife and her relatives proved 'hard-hearted and greedy'. But Kwabena Manu was infatuated, for his wife had 'great sexual appetite'. She was a petty trader and absented herself in Kumase and Bekwai for lengthy periods. Kwabena Manu was suspicious, but he continued a willing dupe of his wife's 'deceitful wiles'. She pestered him for money and he 'gave her whatever I could'. Then Kwabena Manu heard that his wife had a young lover in Bekwai. He confronted her and she confessed to 'playing at sex' with several men. He decided in his heart to forgive her, but she abandoned him and went to live in Kumase. Y.A. of Adeɛbeba's wife went 'astray' and left him because 'she felt a satisfaction more than before' in sex with her Toase lover. From a male point of view, Kwaku Atakora of Adeɛbeba's relationship with Ntraafi of Kaase was an object lesson in the dissatisfied fickleness of women. His version of events, told to and recorded by another Asante man, painted her as unreliable, opportunist and self-interested.

> Kweku Attakora married Ntrufi of Ekaase who had only just left off another marriage with a railway locomotive engine driver. They were getting on fairly well when the girl befriended the wives of some soldiers. Kweku Attakora was then a painter. At one time Ntrufi advised Kweku Attakora to join the army. He wanted very much to know the motive behind that good piece of advice. He could not fathom the mystery behind this. After a while the girl began to show disinterest in Kweku Attakora who had not yet gone through in a strict sense the customary payments of Ashanti. He had sent two bottles of rum. There was not the usual 'tiri nsa' in money given (head rum). The girl had been selling palm wine and had been taking it to the 'lines'. She made friends with a soldier. Unsuspecting Kweku Attakora counted on errant Ntrufi who eventually broke free saying she would rather have a soldier for a husband than anyone else. Most probably she was desirous of having 'allotment' paid out to her. The girl packed off and got married to a soldier. Kweku Attakora made no bones about it. She often asks Kweku Attakora to visit her at Ashanti New Town where she is working as a cook to a Syrian who had employed her husband as that before he became a soldier. She is being paid £2-10-0 a month. Her husband is away overseas.[73]

It would be misleading to suggest that tension inhabited every single relationship entered into by Adeɛbeba men and women. It did not. But estranged, antagonistic gender relations are an insistent theme in the narratives of most

Adeɛbeba lives. To reiterate: women sought to negotiate autonomy within the new colonial order of economic opportunity and individual mobility. Men sought to prevent this, and to restore the *status quo ante* in which women were sexually and economically controlled through marriage.[74] So far, so good. But now analysis must shift from praxological dynamics to a consideration of gender relations as a field of meanings. What did men and women intend by their statements about one another? What precisely did they want?

Running like a thread through all of the testimonies supplied by Adeɛbeba women and men, but most visibly in their opinions about gendered relationships between self and other(s), is the question of what has been termed 'due recognition'. Some variant of this is a sociological constant of historically complex societies, and it proposes itself as an agitated interrogation of self in relation to other(s) in periods of rapid, stressful and disorienting transformation. During such a time interiority is challenged by external circumstances to internal review, and to a consequent grasping after approbation within the intersubjective frameworks of a socio-cultural order in process of reformulation.[75]

As we have seen, there can be little doubt that in precolonial Asante there existed unresolved tensions between the injunction to conform to communal norms, rooted and enshrined in the jural definitions of matrilineal personhood, and the ego-inspired goals of individualism, forged in and by the experiential transit through life. The historical evidence concerning this is complex but unambiguous.[76] It is a generalisation, but a considered and just one, to say that the resources available to precolonial Asante individuals to attain to any 'due recognition' in their own right were limited and constrained. During the eighteenth and nineteenth centuries, intersubjective networks were embedded overwhelmingly in the fields of localised kinship and community. This reflected an achieved synergy between organisational principles and the material realities that had given rise to them. Precolonial Asante life was lived as a form of endogenous sociability. This 'communalism', to use Gyekye's term, was ideologically articulated by the state in order to preclude any intentional action by individuals outside of sanctioned patterns of belonging. Now 'communalism' was a comfort because it was a necessity, a bulwark of security in a challenging environment, but it was doubtless oppressive in many ways. It acted to inhibit any sustained individualist aspiration to 'due recognition', for it persuaded away from the valorisation of interiority. Untrammelled expression in self-fashioning brought an individual uncomfortably face to face with all of the many situational contradictions already described. Persistence along these lines risked intersubjective opprobrium and ultimately courted investigative attention by the state.[77]

The quest for 'due recognition', for a grounded interiority that might command and secure acknowledgement from others similarly engaged, was a leitmotif of Asante lives during the colonial period. Nor is this surprising, for as has been made plain the socio-cultural order was in process of a reconfiguration enjoined by colonialism and capitalism. In this passage of Asante history the individual was conspicuously foregrounded. The spheres of action and agency hitherto arbitrated by community were now exposed to the constellation of rights and obligations that located the social in the personal. Mobility and money, as noted, were instruments of this new dispensation. But life was far from easy for the individual staking a claim to 'due recognition' on personal terms. In terms of personhood, colonialism and its works ran counter to Asante historical experience. The unsurprising consequence was that the individual's impulse to 'due recognition' was at once powerfully felt and strongly contradicted. It is overstating the matter to say that people consciously lived this suspension, but the evidence shows that they lived *with* it. Attitudes and behaviour, themselves often contradictory and erratic, reveal the oscillations and irresolutions involved. The most salient foci of self-interrogation were, so to speak, the investments of the personal in personhood. This is why gender relations, and all that they encompassed and implied, were supremely a matter of concern, a site of engagement and an arena of conflict.

The Adeɛbeba evidence throws glancing light on the autobiographical becoming of the individual life. Two lives are considered here. Both are dense with event and circumstance. Both are inflected by the issue of gender relations. Both say things about the struggle for 'due recognition' and the impress of history. Both illustrate lives in process of existential becoming rather than achieved being. One is a man, the other a woman. The analytic objective is to read people with and against the grain of their behaviour and their justifications for it.

The *ɔhenenana* Kwabena Bonsu's boyhood experiences in Kumase around 1920 have already been discussed. It will be recalled that when his parents separated his father Kwaku Dwumo removed him to Adwuman Kobiri. He was living there when he reached puberty and his father 'advised me to learn some trade'. He apprenticed himself to a cloth weaver at Bonwire, worked at that craft for a time in Akuapem, and then returned to Kumase.[78]

Urban life greatly appealed to Kwabena Bonsu. He saw 'many attractions' in the 'modern city'. It is evident from his several testimonies that he fashioned out of self-conscious acts of *bricolage* a version and vision of himself in fluid interaction with the urban milieu. These acts fused together a variety of normative behaviours with a miscellany of popular images of what city life was all about. The resulting construct was redolent of that modernist archetype, the *flâneur*.[79] Kwabena Bonsu abandoned weaving and fell into a restlessly peripatetic life of 'moving up and down' in Kumase. There is a *jouissance*, a pleasurable surrender to the city as texture, in his recollection of living 'a sort of communal life' and of roving about Kumase with 'a set of young friends whose sex appetite was very keen'. This immersion in the quotidian was economically marginal and heedless of the future. But it derived from potent stirrings to 'due recognition'. Kwabena Bonsu thought chiefship irrelevant – 'all fudge' – and railed against 'the reprobates' who demanded that 'modern Ashanti people' should 'cast aside European ideas' (*fa broni adwe to kye*). By corollary he believed in personal autonomy and choice, now that 'Kumasi is up to date more than in former days.' In particular, he construed his sexual adventurism as a series of encounters between individuals, and remembered it as an odyssey undertaken in search of 'a true love'. In pursuit of this vision of sexual love between two persons – the individual's quest for 'due recognition' from others distilled to an irreducibly bonded dyad – Kwabena Bonsu knew that he was flying in the face of received mores. He must have expected trouble (from father, from mother, from kin, from elders, peers or others), and he got it.

Kwabena Bonsu's accounts of his impregnation within the space of a month of an Akuapem girl living at Kumase Mbrom and an Asante girl residing at Kumase Asafo vary in tone and emphasis. A bald narrative of complex events is paralleled by two less structured, more rawly emotional testaments. There are lacunae in all three statements, and evident contradictions between them. The narrative is taken up with Kwabena Bonsu's *braggadocio* about evading the pitfalls and snares created by his sexuality. In this, the two girls and their kin appear as occupational hazards of the urban life. But in the two intimate testaments this veil is thrown aside to reveal that Kwabena Bonsu and one of the girls had a consuming passion for each other. The flat detachment of the narrative is a rationalisation. It is an *ex post facto* attempt to put a brave face on thwarted love. The testaments on the other hand pick hesitantly at the emotional scars of what was really at stake. Taken together, these three autobiographical fragments cast light on the individual's struggle for 'due recognition'.

Kwabena Bonsu lied about the Asante girl. He denied responsibility, paternity was unproven, and her angry kin simply 'went away'. His behaviour in this matter was instrumental, for the Akuapem girl 'F and good self loved each other.' However, this girl's relatives demanded swingeing compensation, for she had been promised in marriage to a man who had already incurred expenditure 'on her maintenance'. Kwabena Bonsu refused to pay because he had no cash.[80] But he did offer 'to look after' the girl. This was not good enough for her kin. They 'caused uproar' and the girl fled from this 'persecution'. So Kwabena Bonsu and 'F' started living together in his single room, 'penniless' and 'in poverty'. Still her relatives pursued the matter, claiming that the lovers were residing together 'as if married', but without the customary formalities and prestations by 'the husband'. The girl's kin chose to involve the *Ahenkurohene* as arbiter. He and Kwabena Bonsu quarrelled after the chief spoke 'so imperatively' and behaved 'in a haughty way'.

'F' soon became a burden on Kwabena Bonsu, for she was afraid and 'weeping'. But he struggled to overcome their problems, for 'I felt her [sic] and she too loved me.' The pair grew ever more isolated and anxious. They were pressed by both sets of kin, either to regularise their relationship in the customary way or break it off. The lovers would not contemplate the second solution, and Kwabena Bonsu lacked the money for the first but also the willingness 'to give up in surrender'. 'As for us we did not want at all for any separation,' recalled Kwabena Bonsu, adding that 'in this modern age of Ashanti who are old men and women to say if things are right or wrong. We are not any more living in former days to be told this or that by grey hairs and illiterates [sic] chiefs.' However 'F' grew depressed and ill because of the pressure to the point where 'one day she told me she was going to hang herself'. In the event she ran away but then returned to Kwabena Bonsu. He himself was now 'the figure of a wrecked wretched soul indeed'. Then one night 'F' slipped away again. Kwabena Bonsu chased after her.

> I took the way to Sipe [Sepe Owusu Ansa, now in north-east Kumase]. I saw her sitting in a sugar plantation by the side of the road. It was about 4a.m. The moonlight was on. I sat by her side and effort to get her home was not spared. No word moved her. I wept bitter tears of regret. She remained a fixture where she was. I was compelled to keep by her side. Day dawned on two [of the most] wretched lovers ever seen. I appealed to all the passersby of whose advice she did not make anything. We kept on. At 4p.m. I was famishing. She had only 2d with which she had bought me 1d worth of bananas and a penny worth of sugar cane. She refused to take in something in the nature of food. At 6p.m. the repeated advice of many people induced her to come home with me.[81]

'F' calmed down but the situation remained the same. Eventually the strain grew too much for her again. She fled Kumase for Agogo and then Aburi. Once home in Akuapem she gave birth to a daughter. In his retrospective narrative Kwabena Bonsu recalled his simple relief at being suddenly freed from intolerable anxiety. And in a coda he recalled how at a later date he again encountered 'F', but she 'was severe and told me vehemently that I had been the cause of her downfall'. Elsewhere however Kwabena Bonsu reported a differently nuanced outcome. 'I saw her once again in Kumasi,' he stated, 'and both of us wept at our misfortune.' Then 'F' told Kwabena Bonsu that she still reciprocated his love for her, but that the forces opposed to their relationship were too strong. He pleaded with her, but she worked herself up into a highly emotional state. Regrets and recriminations left nothing further to say. She walked away from him. They never met again. 'It did not go on as it was before,' he concluded. Kwabena Bonsu blamed Asante custom and the traditionalists who upheld and enforced it for his misfortune. They 'never seek for a change in marriage or any other thing'. Their 'arrogance' was 'set out against any person who tried in his life for himself'. His countrymen, he opined, still had much to learn about 'living in changed times'.

In 1944 Adwoaa Tweapon, aged sixteen, spent a great deal of time sitting before a sewing machine in Mrs Mansah's Academy for Seamstresses in Kumase Adum, just down the hill from the Wesleyan-Methodist church. She had been a boarder in the hostel attached to the Academy for less than a year. When she first arrived she had with her, by order of Mrs Mansah, a sleeping mat, a pillow, two pillow cases, two blankets, two towels, two plates, a cup, saucer, knife and fork, a bucket for washing, a chop box and a small trunk containing a sponge, soap and personal keepsakes. These items were mandatory, for the Academy was dedicated to the fashioning of 'the modern Ashanti woman'.[82]

In pursuit of this goal Adwoaa Tweapon and her eleven fellow boarders followed a curriculum of sewing, domestic science, home management and child welfare, with evening classes in English and arithmetic. On Saturday evenings the girls held musical concerts or were instructed in ballroom dancing. On Sunday mornings the girls dressed in white uniforms with blue trim, a hat in the same colours and black shoes. They then went to morning service, most commonly an Anglican one, for Mrs Mansah was a member of the Church of England. On Sunday afternoons the girls were taken to visit the government hospital or to private clinics to listen to talks on hygiene, midwifery, obstetrics and infant care. On Sunday evenings they attended Bible classes led by Mrs Mansah. The girls invariably rose at 5.30a.m. and went to bed at 8.00p.m. They cooked and ate their food communally, and did their laundry in a like manner. At no time were they permitted to leave the hostel unaccompanied, and talking to men in the Kumase streets was strictly forbidden. Indeed any sort of unsanctioned association with the male sex was punishable and repeat offenders suffered expulsion from the Academy.

The course at Mrs Mansah's Academy cost £1-5-0 a month and lasted two years. At graduation the girls received a certificate and help with finding employment. Adwoaa Tweapon graduated in April 1945 and found work as a seamstress at St Monica's College in Mampon. But in north Asante she was immediately homesick for her mother 'Yah Agyapong and family at Adiebeba'. So she left. She returned to live in Adeɛbeba and found seam-stressing work at nearby Nyeɛso. This cured one problem but soon created others. Glad to be with her mother, the seventeen-year-old missed Kumase. Her kin pressed her to marry but the kind of husband that Adwoaa Tweapon had in mind did not exist in the village. She wanted a 'proper man' with a white-collar job in Kumase. They would marry, live in a new house (in the new housing development at Kwadaso?), and have three or four children. She would not work as an employee but instead would look after the children, manage the household, immerse herself in a circle of like-minded 'ladies', and from time to time sew dresses commissioned by friends. She would take up choir singing and go 'European dancing' with her husband. The prelude to all this was to be a fashionable Anglican church wedding, with ushers, pageboys, bridesmaids and Adwoaa Tweapon in an ivory silk dress designed by herself. She avowed that she had made a mistake in returning to Adeɛbeba, for she felt she was no longer suited to 'the simple life of the village'.

A complex family history underlay these reveries. Adwoaa Tweapon's mother Yaa Agyapon was a daughter of Akua Timpomaa of Fankyenebra, who was pawned as a child about 1870 in settlement of a debt owed by the *Baworohene* to the second *Manwerehene* Kwasi Brantuo Kyei Kumaa. Resettled at Adeɛbeba, Akua Timpomaa grew up and married her fellow villager Kwaku Dabini. Yaa Agyapon was their third and youngest child. The family was poor and Akua Timpomaa felt stigmatised by her status. She talked of 'going home' to Fankyenebra. Yaa Agyapon recalled that she grew up in this atmosphere determined to become wealthy. But about 1917 her parents married her to Osei Baane, a lowly Adeɛbeba charcoal seller. He did this 'dirty work' in partnership with a gang of Fante immigrants. They bought up trees a few at a time, burned them in pits at Toase and head-loaded the charcoal into Kumase. Profit margins were high, but the sums involved were small. Charcoal selling was no way to get rich. So in 1919 Yaa Agyapon took up petty trading. Through an acquaintance she became involved in fish retailing with women from Abono on lake Bosomtwe. She prospered and in 1925 was one of the first licensed traders in the Kumase central market. By this time Yaa Agyapon and Osei Baane had three children – Kwabena Amponsa, Abena Nsiah and Amma Akoto. Their fourth and last child Adwoaa Tweapon was born in 1928. Yaa Agyapon then deserted Osei Baane and the two were divorced. All four children stayed with their mother.

Yaa Agyapon wanted the betterment of all her children, but was especially keen to launch her favourite Adwoaa Tweapon upon the world. The child was sent to a fee-paying Kumase school run by an Axim man. She proved able and reinforced her mother's hope that she would 'do well in her life'. To this end Yaa Agyapon dressed her daughter in clothes copied from imported European styles and enrolled her in a course in deportment given by a Miss Veronica Mends, a self-styled tutor in 'modern manners'. Then about 1941 Adwoaa Tweapon passed the menarche. Her older sisters had already undergone the nubility rites (*bragorɔ*) associated with this event. In

both cases the celebration took place presided over by the elderly women of
Adeɛbeba headed by the now very aged Amma Kyirimaa. Abena Nsiah, Yaa
Agyapon's eldest daughter, had a lavish *bragorɔ* in 1937. Her mother, by
then a fairly wealthy trader, expended a deal of money on food, clothes and
gifts. She paid for the same levels of display and consumption when her
middle daughter Amma Akoto underwent her nubility rites in 1940. Both
these celebrations excited comment. By the 1930s the full panoply of
traditional *bragorɔ* was on the wane across rural Asante. It was costly. Many
thought it redundant for that reason and self-styled progressives saw it as a
barbaric anachronism. Notwithstanding, Yaa Agyapon insisted on the full
customary rites, in large part – so Abena Nsiah said – to show her Adeɛbeba
neighbours that the daughter of the Fankyenebra pawn had made good in
life. But the two celebrations were not wholly successful. In that passage of
the rites in which the initiate was physically inspected by the village
matrons, an occasion for ribald comment, chaffing, intrusion and even
insult, both of Yaa Agyapon's daughters were roughly handled. In the case
of Amma Akoto it would seem that this went beyond acceptable norms. Her
physical development was the subject of wounding criticism and she was left
feeling humiliated.[83] All accounts suggest that Abena Nsiah and Amma Akoto
became, quite literally, sites of contestation between their assertive *nouveau
riche* mother and the disapproving hierarchy of senior Adeɛbeba women.

In any event, when Adwoaa Tweapon reached menarche her mother
refused her a traditional *bragorɔ* like those of her sisters. Instead, the girl
underwent the greatly abbreviated and much less showy 'enlightened' Fante
nubility rite (*nka kye*: the 'invocation'), and she did so in Kumase not
Adeɛbeba.[84] This was a snub to the village. But it was also resented by
Adwoaa Tweapon herself. Brought up as the cynosure of her mother's eye,
encouraged to an exalted understanding of her own destiny, and then
arbitrarily denied her turn as the centre of attention after her sisters, Adwoaa
Tweapon reacted by rebelling against her mother. She fled and went into
hiding in Kumase. Whatever her intention, she produced an effect.
Adeɛbeba tongues wagged, saying none of this would have happened if
Adwoaa Tweapon had been allowed to celebrate a modest rite in the village.
It was all the mother's fault, for Yaa Agyapon had 'become as a Fanti
interested in money only'. She had forgotten she was an Adeɛbeba villager,
an Asante like her neighbours, but was this altogether surprising? After all,
her mother was a pawn. What else could one expect, whispered the tongues,
from a family descended from someone who was paid over to settle a debt?

Then, as Yaa Agyapon searched Kumase for her missing daughter, an
Adeɛbeba woman named Afua Ntim quarrelled publicly with Adwoaa Tweapon's sister Abena Nsiah. This row arose out of the malicious innuendo
(*akutia*) that now enveloped Yaa Agyapon's family. In the heat of argument
Afua Ntim outrageously proclaimed that Abena Nsiah's grandmother Akua

Timpomaa had been scarred like a slave (*eye twa*).[85] This was going too far. It breached the prohibition against speculating about the origins of another person (*obi nkyere obi ase*). But Afua Ntim went even further. She asserted that Abena Nsiah's father Osei Baane had been bought as a child from the army of the Almami Samori. This was why he sold charcoal, a 'dirty' job fit only for a slave.[86] By custom Abena Nsiah should have sworn an oath so that duly constituted chiefly authority might investigate these calumnies. But she declined to do so. Instead, she announced that her mother's Kumase lawyer Mr Agyemang would be instructed to prepare a case. He would then move to sue for damages for defamation in a British court. The writ would be served on Afua Ntim and also on an unspecified number of Adeɛbeba 'liars and troublemakers'.

Yaa Agyapon found Adwoaa Tweapon in a matter of days and enrolled her in Mrs Mansah's Academy as a place of safety and discipline as well as improvement. Abena Nsiah never acted on her threat. But the terms of that threat made life very difficult for her family in Adeɛbeba. The quarrel brought into the open all of the villagers' whispered dislike of Yaa Agyapon and her offspring. Then Abena Nsiah compounded the problem. Words said might not be unsaid, as everyone knew, but there existed customary norms that framed resolutions to such problems, and did so in the interests of restored harmony, solidarity and community. By perpetrating the solecism of rejecting oath procedures in favour of colonial law, Abena Nsiah offended against Adeɛbeba's image of itself as a community. She publicly tore up the charter that allowed compromise, and so exposed the fracture lines that lay beneath circumstantial negotiations of the everyday. The village could not forgive her aggressive dismissal of its methods of handling its problems. So the quarrel hung in the air unresolved, and because of this no reconciliation was achieved. By the time that Adwoaa Tweapon returned from Mampon her family were ostracised and isolated. Thus, in October 1945 Yaa Agyapon moved with her children to a rented property in Kumase Kagyatia.

The family broke apart almost immediately. Abena Nsiah blamed her mother for the troubles that had befallen them all and went to live elsewhere in Kumase. Adwoaa Tweapon thought that in the city she could set about looking for an ideal husband. But she was sadly disabused. Men, she found, were interested in 'sex play' rather than homemaking. But when she unburdened herself to her mother, Yaa Agyapon flew into a towering rage and said 'men were evil beings' ruled by their sexual passions. She decried the morals and status of her long-vanished husband Osei Baane and told their daughter Adwoaa Tweapon that she had paid for her training and accomplishments so that she might meet and marry 'some gentleman of good breeding'. When Adwoaa Tweapon replied that 'gentlemen' were every bit as bad as other men, her mother thrashed her with a stick and locked her up.

It was soon after this that the two reflected on their situation, on the nature of men, and on gender relations.

Yaa Agyapon said her life had been 'a struggle' to escape poverty and the 'insults of others' about her background and marriage. She made money, and this meant 'I never had any more to look for a(nother) man to marry with me.' This was just as well, because men were 'on the look out for themselves' and 'why now should I share the fruits of my labours with a man who give [*sic*] out to girlfriends every penny'. She had warned her daughters repeatedly about men. She had paid for lavish nubility rites for two of them and 'a polishing training' for the third so that they might find husbands in Kumase 'possessing money already'. But all her plans had been 'brought down' by the enmity of others and finally ruined by the wilful behaviour of Adwoaa Tweapon. Her youngest daughter, she said, had perversely failed to use her expensively inculcated charms to secure an appropriate husband. For her part Adwoaa Tweapon claimed her mother had misinformed her. She had been led to believe that she would meet and marry a Kumase man who would give her children, provide for her needs, and not 'stray away' to other women. But the sorts of men Yaa Agyapon approved of were promiscuous seducers just like their village counterparts. She now despaired of marrying at all because she was unable to reconcile her expectations with her experience. Her mother, she concluded, was 'bitter' because of the money invested without any return.

Multiple factors are at work in the histories of Yaa Agyapon and her daughters. It seems churlish to complain, but one would like to know more about certain things and have a clearer sight of others: Yaa Agyapon's business and income; Adwoaa Tweapon's middle-class British ideas of the 'feminine'; Abena Nsiah's volatility and motives. But all that is known about them in terms of money, status, interpersonal and especially gender relations revolves around the quest for 'due recognition'. It would be otiose to rehearse matters already discussed, so let us break off analysis here with the simple observation that the intersubjective complexities of self and other(s) are recuperable to historical understanding – in part, and up to a point.

SUBJECTIVITIES: BEING, BELIEF AND THE TRAVAILS OF AMMA KYIRIMAA, 1900s–1940s

The mobilities implicit within the unstable continuous present of colonialism were also – even primarily – a matter of beliefs and ideas. Here of course the historian struggles for purchase on all the masking indirections that bore upon narratives of self-fashioning and the quest for 'due recognition'. First-person ontologies were conscious and unconscious. They also lacked clear boundaries where they leached away into intersubjectivities. Furthermore, in making themselves within the jarring contexts of the precolonial past and the colonial present individuals experienced a complicated distancing from any transparent calculus of choice. Whether they acknowledged it or not, their consciousness was always ambushed by another history, an alternative ordering of the world.

Now there is an honourable place in the reading of these matters for institutional histories – schools, churches, workplaces and all the rest – but this approach is eschewed here. It is too limiting for present purposes in the sense that it tends to schematise lived experience in protocols of adherence to or deviation from ideas cast as formal structures or prescriptive trajectories. This sociology of the person is useful but overly general. Adeɛbeba people lived not in structures or trajectories but rather in the interstices of such grand narratives of idea and belief. Sampling in self-fashioning is again the key to autobiography. The promiscuous *bricolage* involved can only be untangled by beginning with individual lives. Structures and trajectories are best illuminated from the inside, from the histories of persons living with and through them. Such histories lie like impasto over the plain ground of action and are notoriously difficult to separate out and expose. Accordingly, in the highly focused discussion that follows, attention is confined to a handful of persons concerning whom the evidence is such as to permit transits from the sociological to the subjective. Historical generalisation remains the goal here, but not as a substitute – as it too often is, *faute de mieux* – for the substance of people's lived experience.

It will be recalled that at the close of the nineteenth century Amma Kyirimaa the *ɔkɔmfɔ* of Adeɛbeba *taa kwabena bena* was a pre-eminent figure in the life of her community. She remained a singular presence, not least because of her longevity. She was over ninety years old when she died in 1943, and more than one witness to her passing saw in it the conclusion of an era. At the funeral, mourners hoped to conduce the *ɔbosom* to indicate her successor by visiting *akɔm* on someone who was present. Experienced *akɔmfoɔ* from Adeemmra, Atasomaaso, Saawua and Kumase were in attendance to help 'assist the god to appear', and to interpret any sign that might be vouchsafed to those assembled. The 'brass pan', the locus chosen by *taa kwabena bena* about 1870, was taken from the *ɔbosomfie*, bound in white cloth and set upon a chair in the midst of the mourners. Kwasi Fi, Amma Kyirimaa's aged brother, 'fed' (*woredue*) the *ɔbosom* while others drummed and sang. At first nothing untoward happened. Then, a 'young boy' showed signs of being seized by *akɔm*. The *akɔmfoɔ* took the lead in trying 'to strengthen the presence of the god'. This involved three hours of strenuous application, but then they 'gave up' when it was clear that 'the boy was not obsessed'. The prognosis was that *taa kwabena bena* 'did not like the boy' and so had withdrawn. All 'the worshippers set to making a possible choice' of an *ɔkɔmfɔ*, but this too failed for lack of conclusive evidence about the wishes of the *ɔbosom*. In the end, and with 'heavy hearts', the assembly returned the 'brass pan' to the *ɔbosomfie*. It was decided to appoint a 'caretaker' until such time as *taa kwabena bena* elected to choose an *ɔkɔmfɔ* . After several villagers had declined to act in this capacity, a youth named Yaw Mensa volunteered for the task. Two years later he was still 'sitting by the god', for *taa kwabena bena* had remained 'mute' and declined to 'name' a successor to Amma Kyirimaa.[87]

· In 1945 Kwasi Fi was led to reflect upon what might have happened. His sister Amma Kyirimaa, he said, had 'faithfully served' *taa kwabena bena* but latterly she had lost her way. In part this was due to age, but more importantly it was because of family worries and changed times. None of her descendants or younger kin, she felt, were wholly devoted to the *ɔbosom*. Her daughter Akosua Pokuaa was a particular disappointment. She had fallen into 'the slavish afflictions of witchcraft now prevailing as never before' and in moments of respite tried to 'rid herself of these evil imaginings'. It was Akosua Pokuaa who talked her mother into acquiring the anti-witchcraft shrine of *afua brahua* in the 1920s. Not only had this signally failed to cleanse Akosua Pokuaa, but the 'presumptuous' *afua brahua* offended *taa kwabena bena* by her very presence. This 'woman' was talkative, interfering and unwilling to concede the seniority of the 'male' *ɔbosom*. Amma Kyirimaa used to hear the two of them quarrelling in the night, just as Adeɛbeba people themselves were now much more prone to dispute than in 'former days'. Then, at some point in the later 1930s, *afua brahua* 'announced her leaving' and 'vacated' the village. Harmony was restored, but the *ɔbosom* had been 'weakened' by his bruising encounter with 'the snares of Affuah'. In the final years of her life Amma Kyirimaa was increasingly fearful about the future of Adeɛbeba. She became convinced that after her death the villagers and the *ɔbosom* would abandon each other. Kwasi Fi remarked that events at Amma Kyirimaa's funeral confirmed her perspicacity.

· Kwasi Fi ended his reminiscence of his sister by drawing out and contextualising its broader meanings. For some time, as Amma Kyirimaa knew, the 'god' had been 'thinking to leave' the village. This was because many Adeɛbeba people had 'now deserted his worship'. The old man blamed a number of things for this destructive apostasy. 'Morality' had broken down. Thinking perhaps of his sister's comments on *afua brahua*, Kofi Fi declared that women had forgotten their duty and become disobedient. This had infected family life and children were now disrespectful and heedless of any 'advice given by (their) elders'. Amma Kyirimaa herself, he added, had suffered in this regard. The 'greed for money' was the primary cause of this ethical disintegration, and education and Christianity were particular inspirations and symptoms of its progress. There were no schools in Adeɛbeba (the first was opened in 1949), but some villagers sent their children daily to be educated in Kumase and elsewhere. This was 'a poisoning thing', for individuals exposed to schooling became dissatisfied with Adeɛbeba. They abandoned the place to lead rootless lives of self-gratification in Kumase. Christians were even worse, for they had betrayed Amma Kyirimaa's trust. With the blessing of *taa kwabena bena* she had done nothing to forbid people from embracing Christianity, because 'all are serving the Creator Onyame together as one person'. But this ecumenical tolerance was not reciprocated. Once the various Christian denominations in Kumase had gained some converts in Adeɛbeba they threatened to exclude any member who did not renounce *taa kwabena bena*. At first this was not a great problem. There was only one 'church' actually located in the village (a Wesleyan-Methodist chapel in a dwelling converted to this purpose in 1913), and there was no resident pastor. Christians 'indulged the Obosom' for a time. But in the end they turned their backs on it, partly because they were ordered to do so, but chiefly because Christianity was the faith of the whites and so offered 'astonishing power to be rich in this world of nowadays'. Most Christians, said Kwasi Fi, were simply after money. The proof of this he derived from another alarming development. This was witchcraft, which was morally destructive and now unprecedentedly widespread. Adeɛbeba and other Asante people both practised witchcraft and were victimised by it. This was because witchcraft – like education or Christianity – was about getting wealth and power at the expense of others. Many Adeɛbeba villagers, and especially those of 'the rising generations', oscillated between Christianity, witchcraft and 'anything else of a known supernatural power' to gain competitive advantage over their fellows in the pursuit of money. These lamentable imperatives had led people away from the guidance offered by *taa kwabena bena* and Amma Kyirimaa into an immoral world bereft of cooperation and community. 'Ashanti men and women of now', Kwasi Fi concluded, were 'mostly lost to their past consideration of others.' The message in all this was plain. The consequence of deserting history was social and personal incoherence.[88]

As we have seen already Amma Kyirimaa had two daughters by her third and last husband. Akosua Pokuaa and her sister Abena Kraa (otherwise Abena Bima) were born about 1890, and by the turn of the century they were Amma Kyirimaa's only surviving children. Both went on to have lives that alarmed their mother and many others. Both were in Kwasi Fi's mind when he testified about the travails that had blighted his sister's middle and later years. Let us look first then to Abena Kraa, the younger of the two girls.

Amma Kyirimaa was a traditionalist and she insisted that her daughters undergo full nubility rites (*bragoɔ*). She was notably strict in this matter in the case of her younger daughter, for Abena Kraa matured early and was generally judged to be beautiful. In custom a girl who was seduced and became pregnant prior to her *bragoɔ* had committed the offence of *kyiribra* (lit. 'the hate of menstruation') and she, her lover and her family were

excoriated. Moreover the purification rituals for *kyiribra* were always
conducted by the senior *ɔkɔmfɔ* in a community.[89] Thus, in or about 1905
the precociously desirable Abena Kraa was hastened through her nubility
rites. Her mother was anxious to avert the disgrace of a *kyiribra* daughter.
But Amma Kyirimaa also wanted to avoid the added humiliation of having
publicly to cleanse her own child of the shame she had brought down upon
Adeɛbeba and *taa kwabena bena*.

After undergoing her *bragorɔ* a girl was considered ready for marriage.
With her looks and connections Abena Kraa did not lack for suitors. Prominent among these was the *Manwerehene* Kofi Nti. But Amma Kyirimaa
flatly refused to countenance his suit. She had very precise reasons for her
refusal. Amma Kyirimaa felt that her uterine descendants had a special
destiny that was known only to *taa kwabena bena*. When possessed by the
ɔbosom she was advised not to allow Abena Kraa to marry Kofi Nti. Any
such 'marriage with a chief' (*ɔhene aware*) would expose Amma Kyirimaa's
matrilineage to a future of 'slavish compulsion'. This was the customary
right of *ayetɛ*, whereby chiefs might claim stool wives in perpetuity from
lineages married into by their predecessors in office. Whether or not Kofi
Nti was privy to Amma Kyirimaa's thinking, her rejection of him insulted
and enraged him. He was after all the *Manwerehene* and Amma Kyirimaa
was his subject. Hence in or about 1906 he summoned Amma Kyirimaa
before the Native Clan Tribunal (NCT) presided over by his associate the
Saamanhene/Gyaasehene Kwabena Kokofu.[90] The hearing that ensued was
an embittered clash between the historic prerogatives of chiefship and Amma
Kyirimaa's determination to follow the instructions of *taa kwabena bena*. 'It
was during the time of (CCA) Fuller', recalled Amma Kyirimaa's grandson,

> at a time when the chiefs had established a borrowed power out of the
> ruins of defeated Ashanti. The 'manwerehene', Kofi Nti, whose resi-
> dence was at the old Asafo (the site of KPHB) was very much angry
> when he got back the message that A(mma) K(yirimaa) had refused
> marriage of her daughter, A(bena) K(raa), to him as there was no 'ayetɛ'
> in her family. The case was decided at the Gyasehene's court. He was
> Kobina Kokofu. The case went against AK. The court was composed of
> many other chiefs, representing the Abrempongs (*abirɛmpɔn*) of Kumasi.
> These chiefs were filling the gap created by the absence to Seychelles
> of the Ashantihene. It would appear that the courts of Kumasi chiefs
> were not fair. It was a question of the upper class extorting the lower
> class of the community. The Ashantis had not forgotten the time when
> subjects were subjected to the will of the master. The court which
> decided the case against A(mma) K(yirimaa) explained that 'ayetɛ' as
> a system of marriage must start somehow under ordinary conditions
> before its establishment. It was not reasonable for AK being a subject
> of the 'manwere' stool to refuse the occupant (of the 'manwere' stool)

her daughter in marriage. The girl had not been espoused to any man. If even that was the case it would be a case of refunding the moneys [*sic*] expended by the prospective husband.[91]

Amma Kyirimaa was ordered to give up Abena Kraa to marry the *Manwerehene* Kofi Nti. She was also assessed for court costs in the swingeing sum of £9 by a vindictive Kwabena Kokofu as punishment for her temerity in challenging chiefly authority. The family appealed the judgement before the DC (Kumase). He reversed it, presumably on the common-law grounds of infringement of individual rights. But at the same time Kofi Nti abandoned interest in Abena Kraa. It had been 'brought to his attention that her powers of fetish deriving from the mother herself were of a dangerous purpose'. Abena Kraa with her challenging reputation was now 'left free to choose her own partner in life'.[92]

Abena Kraa's choice fell upon someone we have already encountered. This was Yaw Firempon of Atasomaaso (and Nyeɛso), the royal *ahenkwaa* who became a weaver of mats after 1896 and then a rubber carrier, gin trader, mine labourer and kola retailer. The implication of all the sources is that this was a love match despite the discrepancy in age. Be that as it may the age gap between husband and wife was a customary norm and probably appealed as such to Amma Kyirimaa. In other respects too Yaw Firempon had much to recommend him as a son-in-law (*ase*). He was from a nearby village and he and his lineage were probably known to Amma Kyirimaa and her relatives.[93] An *ahenkwaa* by ascription, he had shown initiative and enterprise in dealing with the vicissitudes that had befallen him after 1896. He himself claimed that these problems had deterred him from marrying at a younger age. But this in itself was an advantage for he was now a mature man. He was said to be a hard worker and had farmland at Atasomaaso. Both personally and economically Yaw Firempon was equipped to fulfil the basic obligation required of an Asante husband – *bɔ no akɔnhama* (lit. 'to maintain her with food'; i.e. to support a wife and her children).[94] Perhaps we can permit ourselves the further speculation that Amma Kyirimaa saw in Yaw Firempon a steadying influence over Abena Kraa, a young woman whose sexual attractiveness and singular reputation had already complicated her own life and that of her mother. But all of these were supplementary considerations. The decisive factor in Amma Kyirimaa's approval of the match was that *taa kwabena bena* 'spoke his permission' to her.

Abena Kraa and Yaw Firempon were married in or about 1908. A son called Kofi Abanase was born shortly thereafter. Then Abena Kraa 'could not conceive' until a second boy named Kofi Manwere was born to her in 1911.[95] But soon after this Yaw Firempon preferred adultery charges against his wife. They were proved to his satisfaction and he secured a divorce. Now it has already been seen that Yaw Firempon was by his own admission a quick-tempered and unforgiving man. He was perhaps unduly suspicious of his beautiful young wife. Equally, Abena Kraa may have committed adultery or behaved in some way that convinced her husband that she had done so. But whatever transpired, the evidence suggests that there were undercurrents in the marriage that frightened Yaw Firempon and that these had to do with Abena Kraa's membership of a kin group that trafficked with occult powers.

Yaw Firempon's anxiety centred on his second son. Kofi Manwere was born light skinned and sickly. His behaviour from birth was sufficiently odd to excite alarmed comment. Some in Adeɛbeba said *taa kwabena bena* had sent him to punish people for submitting to the British and their alien ways. Others argued that his task was to call his grandmother personally to account for failing to deflect foreign rule and the changes wrought in its name. Yet others saw him as harbinger and exemplar of a new and better world conjured into being to redress the iniquities of the past. A tragedy then deepened rather than clarified these mysteries. When Kofi Manwere was still an infant his divorced mother Abena Kraa 'stumbled behind her house and died outright'. This was very shocking – a 'bad death' – and Adeɛbeba villagers talked of maleficence. Could Kofi Manwere have killed his own mother? Related anxieties also surfaced in people's minds. Amma Kyirimaa was in service to and under the protection of *taa kwabena bena*. That being the case, why had eight of her nine children predeceased her? And why had the young and beauteous Abena Kraa, last of the eight to die, perished in such abominable circumstances? Amma Kyirimaa offered no explanation. She exhibited resignation in public and deflected speculation about the deaths of her children with the formulaic phrase *safo nsa neho* (colloquially 'physicians can't heal themselves'). Her stoicism was admired, but, nervously, as if it masked appalling truths. Was *taa kwabena bena* angry with her? Alternatively, was its power weakening? The enigmatic infant Kofi Manwere was somehow linked to all this flux and foreboding. Then in the midst of all this uncertainty Amma Kyirimaa's only surviving child Akosua Pokuaa began to behave in ways that sharpened fears for the wellbeing of the community.

Akosua Pokuaa showed early signs of being favoured by *taa kwabena bena* as an adept. As a child she was obsessionally interested in *kaatipo*, the ring used by her mother to help conduce speech during possession. But the child grew up into an adolescent who was given to fits of melancholy (*awerɛho*) that alternated with frantic glossolalia and a quite unnatural talent for involving others in anti-social behaviour. Crucial to her youthful development was a visit she made to Kumase in 1907. There she was caught up in the frenzied accusations and confessions that surrounded the witch-cleansing cult of *aberewa* ('the old woman').[96] Convinced that all Asante was 'filling up with

Figure 4.6 The Witchfinding cult of *aberewa* in Kumase in 1908.
(Source: Smyly Collection, Royal Commonwealth Society Papers, University of
Cambridge Library)

a rising tide of witches', she tried to introduce *aberewa* to Adeɛbeba. The
village needed protection from herself and her kin, for they all trafficked in
supernatural power and so 'she and (her) whole family were witches who
should confess to all their wrongdoings'. Amma Kyirimaa demurred, and
with the advice of *taa kwabena bena* and the hesitant support of a thoroughly
confused community she banned *aberewa* from Adeɛbeba. But Akosua
Pokuaa now believed herself to be a witch surrounded by witches. She wished
to confess and be cleansed, but felt that her mother, relatives and their allies
in Adeɛbeba were unrepentant in their own witchcraft and so were trying to
kill her. She also believed that *taa kwabena bena* was now weakened 'in his
strength for good' and was being held captive in the *ɔbosomfie* by evil forces
of immense destructive power. Akosua Pokuaa's behaviour became ever
more erratic and alarming. She harangued her neighbours by day and stalked
the village at night. On occasion her mother had to use all of her accumulated prestige to prevent her daughter from being turned out of the community.

In the 1920s Akosua Pokuaa was at the centre of a public scandal in
Adeɛbeba that proved to be a watershed in her life. She took the lead in
involving herself and two other women with an itinerant herbalist (*odunsini*)
from Akuapem who pitched up in Adeɛbeba. This man claimed a conversa-
tional intimacy with *mmoatia* ('little people') and access to the power of *atia
apirede*, a supernatural source of money, health and peace of mind for those

who followed its directions. In addition to this repertoire the *odunsini* also possessed a mystical ring named Tat which had been bestowed upon him in a dream by a Pharaonic priest. This item was exclusively for the benefit of women. By looking into the ring its owner could remove the power of witchcraft over a female client. He could use it to conduce sexual satisfaction, pregnancy or childbirth. But the ring's prescription of last resort for the spiritually, sexually or reproductively troubled was intercourse with the herbalist. In the event, Akosua Pokuaa, Akua Foriwaa and the Adeɛbeba *obaapanin* Akua Frempomaa all had sexual intercourse with the *odunsini*. There is no doubt that Akosua Pokuaa took the first step and then persuaded the others to this course of action. Little or no attempt was made to conceal what was going on. Akosua Pokuaa herself had sex with the Akuapem man in the bush outskirts of the village (itself a prohibition, *akyiwadeɛ*), and they were observed by a number of people.

Apart from anything else, all three of the women were married. In the specific case of Akosua Pokuaa this status was only technical, but still binding in law. She was married around the time that she witnessed *aberewa* in Kumase, but her husband took fright at her behaviour and the two were estranged almost immediately. His name is unknown. He went to live in Obuase but, significantly, he seems never to have bothered with formal divorce proceedings. Certainly Akosua Pokuaa clung to the fantasy that she had a husband and it would appear that the villagers indulged her in this belief. Now they acted on their indulgence. The women were all charged with committing adultery. Their defence was not denial but amnesia. They claimed they remembered nothing of what transpired. The villagers were incensed by this, and with two outraged husbands in the lead they demanded that Amma Kyirimaa summon her daughter and the others before *taa kwabena bena* to determine their guilt or innocence. Faced with communal obloquy, the three women confessed to their adultery. They said they had been seduced by the supernatural arts of the *odunsini* who had since decamped from Adeɛbeba. In later years Akosua Pokuaa recollected how her mother had led her and her associates before the *ɔbosom* to confess and be ritually cleansed. In the atmosphere of hostility that accompanied this process a further culprit was named.

> When we went up to swear each of us had an egg in our hand. I first spoke out cursing myself and striking the egg against the wall. Akua Frempomaa did hers. As soon as Akua Foriwaa finished hers she fell down on the (her) back. She was not able to move a few steps back. Then one of the men in the village, Kwabena Affum gave her a spanking in the face. She then cried out 'Why do you strike me? Your sister Mɔbi and I are companions in the game of adultery. We are the two persons with whom the man has had sexual connection.' Then the husband of Mɔbi who was Akwesi Si of Asokwa charged [an] adultery

fee of six pounds (£6). Akua Foriwaa was asked to pay for it is a law that no one is to confess the adultery of one other than oneself. The 'odunsini' paramour escaped. He had given some herbs squeezed which Akua Foriwaa had placed into her mouth. This is called 'dinsi anwu' (odunsini) medicine.[97]

After this things went from bad to worse for Akosua Pokuaa. She sat silent for days on end and endeavoured to 'shut things off from the inside of my head'. In the intervals between these bouts of catatonia she experienced passages of violent derangement. Her Adeɛbeba neighbours now agreed that she was suffering from malevolent possession by witchcraft. This conferred an unusual status on Akosua Pokuaa. She was seen to have been right all along, and remarkably prescient in her understanding of the ever growing power of witchcraft in society. Accordingly, she was taken to a range of shrines that specialised in treating this affliction, travelling as far afield as Koforidua in Akyem to consult bra kunde, the famous 'witchfinder'. But episodes of the sort described continued to recur and by the 1940s Akosua Pokuaa was said to be 'lost' and 'notorious as a witch of outstanding character' who had been 'caught by several witch finding cults more than once' but never cured.[98] By this time too her mother had long given up hope for any permanent recovery. Amma Kyirimaa had lost her two surviving daughters to maleficence of one sort or another. She became despairing and began to entertain those fears and anxieties about Adeɛbeba reported by her brother Kwasi Fi.

The life of Amma Kyirimaa's grandson Kofi Manwere is very fully documented, for he supplied a number of frank autobiographical statements.[99] After his mother's death he was raised by his grandmother and other female kin. Clearly intelligent but physically weak, Kofi Manwere continued to excite comment because of the singularity of his person and the sheer oddity of his behaviour. Before he was five he suffered badly from yaws and then from life-threatening ulcerations of his legs. As a result he was puny and slow to grow. He did not play with other children and practised the disconcerting habit of staring at people. Notwithstanding all this, a bond developed between the boy and his grandmother. They spent hours closeted together, during which she recounted tales of the abosom and other supernatural powers. Otherwise – and within the limits set by his family and personal histories – Kofi Manwere led the unremarkable life of an Adeɛbeba village boy.

When Kofi Manwere was nine his father Yaw Firempon told Amma Kyirimaa that he wanted to send his son to school. There is a suggestion that what lay behind this proposal, which was still an unusual one for an Asante father to make at that time, was Yaw Firempon's conviction that his son's future wellbeing depended on exposing him to something that would offset

. Figure 4.7 The Famous 'witchfinder' *bra kunde* at Koforidua.
(Source: Ghana National Archives, Koforidua: Photographic Collection)

the baleful influence of his matrilineal kin. Amma Kyirimaa consulted *taa kwabena bena* and was told that Kofi Manwere would die if he was sent to school. A bitter argument ensued, but Yaw Firempon prevailed with the aid of some influential Kumase and Adeɛbeba associates.[100] So in or about 1920 Kofi Manwere 'went over the ridge' to the Kumase Government School as a day boy. What he did not know, and did not discover until he was an adult, was that after his father won the argument over schooling he had thought it prudent to propitiate *taa kwabena bena*. This act of appeasement proved ambiguous. It remained unclear as to whether or not the *ɔbosom* had relented by accepting the offering made at its shrine. Yaw Firempon thought so, but worried about other supernatural forces abroad in Adeɛbeba. Amma Kyirimaa thought not, and worried about the life of her grandson. Be that as it may, Kofi Manwere was taught to read, write and count by teachers from Cape Coast and Accra. In 1923 he passed easily into Standard I. He was accepted by his fellow pupils, but remained isolated because of his fragile health. His underdeveloped physique meant that he could not play games. He also found the daily four-mile round trip to school very taxing. None the less on Saturdays he helped Amma Kyirimaa on her farm at *(n)tasu*.

As he grew older Kofi Manwere began to reflect on his bifurcated life. In particular he contrasted the rootedness of Adeɛbeba with the fantasies that Kumase bred within him. Life in the village was familiar and cocooning, but the city opened into a world of dreams. He imagined himself growing up to be a medical doctor who was also a powerful ɔkɔmfɔ. He imagined himself a rich man (sikani) with a motor car and many fine houses in Kumase. He fantasised limitless sex with the beautiful girls that he saw everywhere in the city. All these imaginings were produced in nights punctuated by vivid dreams. During the day he often lapsed into exhausted reveries. By his own account he entertained fanciful ideas and exaggerated hopes. In school he learned about other countries and became fascinated by India and the USA. He thought these places the sources of ultimate wisdom and power. So he determined to master and command their metaphysical resources, and then use them to realise his dreams.

With the help of a schoolmaster and then on his own account Kofi Manwere wrote to addresses in India and the USA to secure information about talismans, charms and rings that conferred wisdom and power. A 'Professor De Laurence', a self-styled 'magus', sent him catalogues and pamphlets from the USA. Among these were treatments of the *Pseudepigrapha* and discussions of the esoteric meanings concealed in the Psalms as explicated by the (lost) Books of Moses.[101] All of these various influences fused together with the stories told by Amma Kyirimaa. Spiritual forces from across this syncretic constellation guided and aided Kofi Manwere in his schoolwork, imparted magical numbers to protect him, and haunted his waking and sleeping selves. He resorted to cemeteries and there unburdened himself to conclaves of imaginary presences. He talked with beings he saw carried along by the wind (*mframa*). He constructed 'number boards' and spent hours divining their hidden meanings. He incorporated parts of the Christianity taught at his school into his personal philosophy. Later, in adulthood, he took instruction at the Anglican church (now cathedral) of St Cyprian the Martyr in Kumase and was confirmed. The rite of this church was High Anglo-Catholic and Kofi Manwere was drawn to its hushed air of mystery and initiation.

At one level there was nothing very unusual in Kofi Manwere's eclectic mysticism. Many in colonial Asante responded to capitalism and its fetishised commodification by mixing education and autodidacticism in philosophies of personal enablement. The pressure to survive and succeed was clearly bound up with money. But money itself was something more than substance. It was both reified and mystified as the indispensable idiom and icon of the wholly inhabited self. Kofi Manwere and those like him ransacked past and present technologies of every kind in order to conduce monetary essence out of the capitalist ether and into being, fixity and possession. In pursuit of this grail – the quiddity of wealth rather than its tokens – people looked everywhere for metaphysical devices to circumvent accumulation and deliver up the thing itself.

> The general belief among the literate community of this country is that there is another means [other than by learning] for acquiring knowledge. This may be a talisman [King Solomon type], a ring with some magical signs of the Eastern countries, pills [phospherine], lotions, pomades for oiling the hair etc. The worst is there are pens, blotting papers, powdered stuff for making ink and many things of stationery type which are represented by some vicious individuals as possessing power for helping candidates to pass. When a teacher complains to an educated man about his son's lapses he is often shocked by the fact that a ring, a box of pills or something is being ordered for the boy. Many school children are dealing with some mystical overseas organisations to which remittances are made regularly. Their parents help them in this economic squandor [sic] of wealth. The belief in American rings and Indian talismans is very great. Also some charlatans who call themselves 'professors of magic' take a number of school children especially of Std. VII class [their Primary School leaving certificate examination period] to the grave yard where some spirits are invoked. Of course confederates well draped in white emerge from the thickets and throw off peculiar rings with some signals of ancient magic lore. Then the would be candidates keep these rings, charms and talismans for learning. The springing up of crooks (rogues or charlatans) of all grades might be put down to the rampant financial stringency. It is helped by the mental attitude of the G.C. society all classes of which have a belief in something supernatural – superstition it is![102]

Kofi Manwere forged for himself a belief in 'a very personal God in the midst of myriads of agents'. This deity, he claimed, 'is assisting me at all times of the day and night to gain success in my life and reach the sea of calm'. Three identifiable props underpinned this syncretism. First, there was orthodox High Anglicanism. Kofi Manwere wore a pectoral cross given to him by the priest of St Cyprian the Martyr, treasured a votive medallion of the Madonna and Child, and slept with an annotated Bible and Missal under his pillow.[103] Second, there were self-fashioned borrowings from the hermetic tradition, an eclectic mixture of Christian, sectarian, occult and magical influences. Kofi Manwere possessed books on numerology, pamphlets on the all-seeing eye and the golden cubit, and a host of gleanings from the writings of 'the occultist wizards'. He kept a secret notebook, coded in red, blue and green ink. In this he entered mystical numbers; formulae for conjuring up wealth, health and power; protective invocations deriving from the 'Rosicrucian mysteries' and the 'Masters of the Pyramids'; and drawings of kin, neighbours and acquaintances in threatening or

Figure 4.8 Sketch of 'An Evil Attack' from a notebook kept by Kofi Manwere.
(Source: Ashanti Social Survey Papers, Birmingham)

submissive poses, embroiled with snakes or hung about with charms. Third, there was the Asante tradition of his upbringing. He attended to the rites and obligations incumbent upon a follower of *taa kwabena bena* whenever he stayed in Adeɛbeba with his grandmother. But he developed a conviction that his natal village was 'fading away' into darkness and oblivion. Witches hovered in the air and swooped between the dwellings. Every night they met together in the same dwelling – that of Akosua Pokuaa. There they helped his aunt to 'drain out lifeblood' from his grandmother. When they finally killed Amma Kyirimaa the village would vanish 'altogether and utterly' until such time as he had wealth and power sufficient to vanquish them and 'bring every person (back) to life'.

Perhaps unsurprisingly, Kofi Manwere's spiritual and intellectual formation proved to be difficult to sustain in any kind of equilibrium. It first came under interrogation with his transit through puberty. It is clear from his testimony that Kofi Manwere's Christian understanding of the doctrine of original sin collided in guilt and anxiety with his adolescent sexuality. Unfortunately, his already confused feelings about these matters were compounded alarmingly by medical problems. These were real enough but their nature conjured up dire speculations in their victim. In 1929 Kofi Manwere developed genital ulceration and associated this with masturbation (*sɔ obi goro ne kɔte anaa ne barima ho maɛ sɔre*), a practice censured in both Asante and Christian morality. In fact he was suffering from reinfection by yaws and was successfully cauterised in the Kumase hospital. He remained convinced, however, that he had induced the complaint through 'constantly thinking of the sexual act'. He struggled thereafter to maintain continence of mind and body, for 'spiritual infections via evil thoughts' as well as coition might produce deadly diseases.

Akosua Pokuaa became convinced that her nephew's recurring complaints were the result of witchcraft practised by herself and others. Malefactors were legion, she thought, for 'since the time of Ashanti Kingdom (i.e. the precolonial period) the great evil done by Witches has greatly increased'. Her diagnosis was persuasive. It allowed Kofi Manwere to displace anxieties about his carefully crafted self onto agencies and persons that he already thought pervasive, and that – importantly – were beyond his powers to control. If his illnesses were self-inflicted, then the self in question was manipulated by something and someone external to it. Since the someone in question was her-himself powerless to resist that something, then his aunt was only dangerous because of her own helpless victimhood. Accordingly, Kofi Manwere and Akosua Pokuaa began to consult witchcraft-cleansing shrines together. A visit to Anwomaaso east of Kumase relieved Kofi Manwere's anxieties for a time, but when his symptoms returned in greater force Akosua Pokuaa took him off to the famous shrine of *senya kupo* at Twene-duraase in Kwawu south-east of Asante.[104] Both received treatment there. But when Kofi Manwere was exposed to 'protection mysteries' *senya kupo* 'reared up' and declared him a practitioner rather than a victim of witch-craft. He was called upon to confess he was a wizard (*ɔbonsam*) and, like his aunt, an adept of 'hot' or maleficent witchcraft (*bayi boro*). But no cure was effected in either case and the two returned to Adeɛbeba. Amma Kyirimaa was forced to admit to herself that *taa kwabena bena* could not help her kin. In desperation she sent Kofi Manwere to a succession of healers of every sort and persuasion. He was even for a short period an out-patient at Agogo Hospital. Then in 1939 Kofi Manwere was induced to drink an infusion that Akosua Pokuaa purchased from an Asen woman herbalist in Kumase. He vomited immediately and prodigiously, developed a high fever and weeping sores, but shortly thereafter his lesions healed and he ceased to hallucinate, hear voices or have nightmares.

This 'cure' was still in effect when Kofi Manwere recounted his experi-ences six years later. In the end his aunt Akosua Pokuaa had helped him, he said, but had failed to be helped herself. His grandmother Amma Kyirimaa too had died in a state of fretful anxiety at the declining efficacy of the *ɔbosom* she served. Like her, Kofi Manwere felt that the world was now consider-ably more complex, more difficult and more dangerous than in the past. The life of the community and the individuals within it was subjected to fragmenting pressures 'in this age of changes'. The prevalence of witchcraft was at once a cause and a consequence of this state of affairs. Kofi Manwere had given up his dreams of success in favour of a quiet life in Adeɛbeba. Individuals, he thought, were now beset with problems 'from every side'. As a result, people viewed each other with understandable suspicion in an increasingly atomised world.

There is much to ponder in the lives of Amma Kyirimaa and her kin. Let us begin with witchcraft. At first glance this seems a predictable matter. After all, everyone discussed had unusually intense structural and subjective predispositions towards awareness of and traffic with the supernatural. Hence witchcraft appears to be an obvious idiom in and through which Amma Kyirimaa's kin interrogated anxieties born of the changes wrought by colonial capitalism. But beyond this small circle Adeɛbeba people generally were preoccupied with witchcraft. It played a part in many lives and featured in many testimonies. All witnesses acknowledged it was endemic to Asante society but believed it had increased greatly in the twentieth century. It was agreed moreover that its effects were felt by everyone and not just by those like Amma Kyirimaa's kin 'whose very business in life is to make contacts with the shadowy Abosom and other sorts of supernatural entities on behalf of us all'.[105] Witchcraft embodied its own facticity and people saw it all around. But at the same time witnesses accorded it the fuzzy explanatory status of metonymy. In many cases brittle subjectivities attached themselves to its dramas of cause and consequence in the hope that life's troubles might have an identifiable source. To identify that source was *ipso facto* to deal with life's troubles. But this failed to convince even as people went through the motions.

Why was this the case? In the twentieth century witchcraft became semi-detached from issues of instance and event. It was launched upon a career as a diffused and arbitrary signifier. This is not to claim that it was emptied of its rhetorical content. But it is to say that its carrying capacity was inflated. Thus one reason why people saw witchcraft increasing was because they enlarged its ontological status so that they might use it to categorise a widening spectrum of intractable anxieties. This manoeuvre was a significant cognitive shift. Precolonial Asante people addressed witchcraft as an occurrence, and endeavoured to frame specific resolutions to its manifestations. Colonial Asante people interrogated witchcraft as a category, and tried to deduce generic meanings from its manifestations. This shift was caused by overloading. Colonial instrumentalities bore down, not only upon conceptions of witchcraft, but also upon the entire range of situating technologies bequeathed by historic Asante cultural practice. People experienced colonialism as acceleration in that messages came thick and fast. Uncertainty was produced by this relentless flow. There was no respite to assimilate information and erase contradiction. In consequence, past and present fell inwards on one another. As people grasped after some purchase on their lives, some moment of surcease, of subjective fixity and certifiable identity, they meditated on plausible reconciliations between old and new questions and answers. This drive to generate meaning was a striving to close the gap between two information systems. But in trying to integrate the past with the present people came to various forms of grief. Incommensurable rationalities resisted unification, and the clash of their evaluative criteria was just as likely to discourage as console. The escape valve from all of this was resolutely to hedge one's bets. Amma Kyirimaa refused to do it. Akosua Pokuaa failed to do it. Kofi Manwere did it, but only eventually and at great cost.

In the circumstances hedging one's bets about witchcraft or anything else was a rational response. It was also very difficult to sustain. Dialogical selffashioning between the pressures of past and present meant no clear boundaries and no sure footing. Some insight into the price to be paid for walking this tightrope was given by J. C. Frimpong, a man with family ties to Adeɛbeba, Asumagya and Bekwai. A self-described 'Christian literate and Asante traditionalist', he gave utterance to widespread dilemmas with mordant acuity in a transparently personal text.[106] This was entitled 'Sitting on the Fence', and reading it one is reminded of just how precarious, unstable, uncomfortable and difficult is the position described by that blandly conventional phrase. It is cited here in full in light of its intrinsic interest, but also because it gives a voice to those less well equipped to marshal similar thoughts or articulate similar feelings.

> Born in superstition and initiated into the rites arising therefrom the Gold Coast literate native has yet to tear himself free from the limpethold of beliefs which his early associations with the family circle have indelibly written on his subconscious mind.
>
> As the impressions of early childhood are deep so are those of later experiences faint belated as they are against the time when the growing mind is more receptive.
>
> The literate native of the Gold Coast has not the boldness of a plainspeaking man of candour to face the question as to whether he does not share, in common with his illiterate brother, the beliefs – legendary, mythological or superstitious – which make the basis of all traditions.
>
> He feints to be a christian which to the world around is another term for one a little higher on the scale of culture – one whose mental state is free from the odd (is it uncanny?) beliefs in witchcrafts, fetishes, ancestor-worship, propitiation and other upshoots of superstition. A christian has his own line of belief – his creed. He does not believe in the existence of witchcraft; in the power of juju; in ancestral worship etc. As they occupy the front seats of the church room, pay in to support the church, join in the devine [sic] service they draw the attention of their priests to their extreme respectability which stands out in such

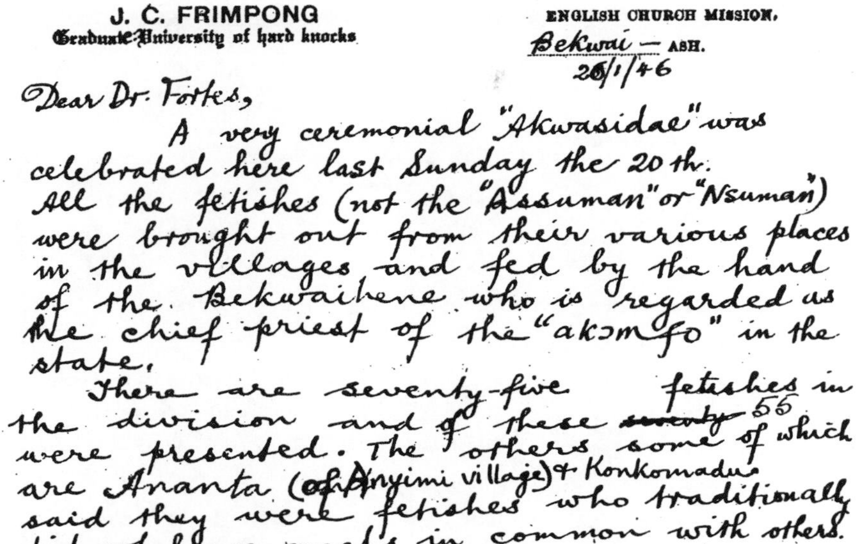

J. C. FRIMPONG
Graduate University of hard knocks

ENGLISH CHURCH MISSION,
Bekwai — ASH.
20/1/46

Dear Dr. Fortes,

A very ceremonial "Akwasidae" was celebrated here last Sunday the 20 th. All the fetishes (not the "Assuman" or "Nsuman") were brought out from their various places in the villages and fed by the hand of the Bekwaihene who is regarded as the chief priest of the "akɔmfo" in the state.

There are seventy-five fetishes in the division and of these 56 were presented. The others, some of which are Ananta (of Anyimi village) & Konkomadu said they were fetishes who traditionally did not have meals in common with others. Their part was therefore sent over to them in their villages.

The scene of this ceremony, I am informed, was exceedingly grand, and the rites as captivating and impressive.

The fetishes were brought to the "Ahemfie" where they were lined up according to their order of importance which is calculated from the point of view of their time of coming and potence. There were a great many fetishes, varying in sizes, some tall, others short; some covered in muslin, others bare; some small others big. Some claimed to have been as old as the stool Tradition.

Figure 4.9 'Graduate: University of hard knocks': J. C. Frimpong to M. Fortes, 1946.
(Source: Ashanti Social Survey Papers, Birmingham)

a pronounced contrast with their secret beliefs. Their innocent seeming appearance, their undoubted outward probity and rectitude conceal some secret musings.

Are not a great number of literate christians daily visiting centres of witchcraft finding cults to look for protection against the evil one that

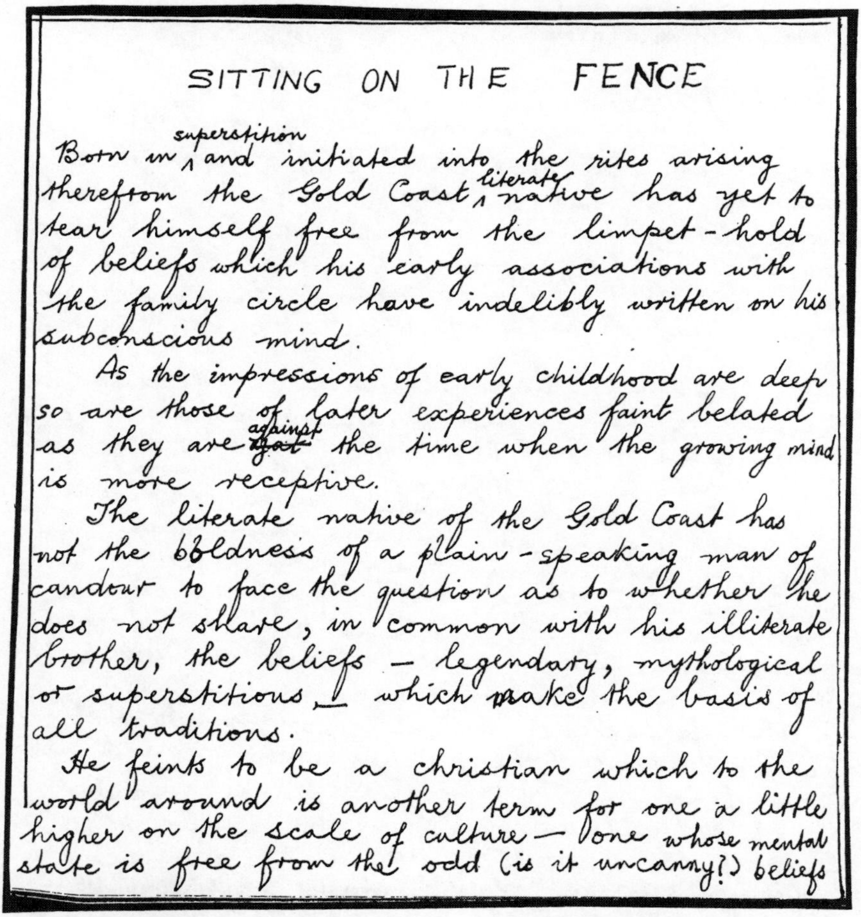

SITTING ON THE FENCE

Born in ˄superstition, and initiated into the rites arising therefrom the Gold Coast ˄literate native has yet to tear himself free from the limpet-hold of beliefs which his early associations with the family circle have indelibly written on his subconscious mind.

As the impressions of early childhood are deep so are those of later experiences faint belated as they are ~~against~~ the time when the growing mind is more receptive.

The literate native of the Gold Coast has not the boldness of a plain-speaking man of candour to face the question as to whether he does not share, in common with his illiterate brother, the beliefs — legendary, mythological or superstitious, — which make the basis of all traditions.

He feints to be a christian which to the world around is another term for one a little higher on the scale of culture — one whose mental state is free from the odd (is it uncanny?) beliefs

Figure 4.10 'Sitting on the Fence' by J. C. Frimpong, 1945–6.
(Source: Ashanti Social Survey Papers, Birmingham)

does not allow their getting money or getting on in life or getting children and other desirables?

Are not the so called literate christians owners of jujus kept under their beds?

Are not the successful literates – the heads of certain branches of services affianced to certain fetishes or juju men who have to take care of their welfare. Don't some employ, maintain and pay special mahommedans? Is it true that the literate christians are sincere? Do they accept the articles of Christian Religion? I am sure these are best in witchcrafts, fetishes, ancestor-worship, propitiation and other upshoots of superstition. A christian has his own line of belief – his creed. He does not believe in the existence of witchcraft; in the power of juju; in ancestral worship etc. As they occupy the front seats of the church room, pay in to support the church, join in the devine service they draw the attention of their priests to their extreme respectability which stands out in ~~bold contrast with~~ such a pronounced contrast with their secret beliefs. Their innocent seeming appearance, their undoubted outward probity and rectitude conceal some secret musings.

Are not a great number of literate christians daily visiting centres of witchcraft finding cults to look for protection against the evil one that does not allow their getting money or getting on in life or getting children and other desirables?

Are not the so called literate christians owners of jujus kept under their beds?

Are not the successful literates – the heads of certain branches of & services affianced to certain fetishes or juju men who have to take care of their welfare. Don't some employ, ~~maintain~~ and pay special mahommedans? ~~Is~~ it true that the literate christians are sincere? Do they accept the articles of Christian Religion? I am sure these are best answered when in the negative. The priests of the churches continually preach against these lapses. They are the experience which come to them from "spies".

The young struggling literate is equally ~~also~~ anxious to get a charm or a juju or the services of a mahomedan to help him ~~to~~ get employed, to get the favour of his head of department (boss) and to protect him from "poisoning by juju" by other competitors. The middle class man may enlist ~~the assistance of a physician~~

of a physician, a ~~fet~~ mahommedan ~~or~~ a fetish. He
may get a cow-tail juju (NKabɛɛ) for tying up
all wishes. [A PANACEA for all wishes). Another is
a lock for locking up all wishes. There are
other forms of little charms or juju to
which ~~an~~ ~~a~~ literate may repeat his wishes
the first thing in the morning, even before
prayers. He serves ~~this~~ whatever juju he
keeps with perfect secrecy. On great days
he may kill a fowl and daub it with its
blood. Some have boxes and boxes of these
nauseating jujus (besmeared with blood now
and then). There is that kind called
"AGBA - LA - GBA" which attained considerable
vogue a few years ago. Those who keep
such idols are christians who think themselves
better cultured than their illiterate brothers who
differ from them in one chief point:

    (a) Literate natives practise their native belief
       in secret, dreading to be seen.
    (a) The illiterate in the open and conscious
       that there is some truth in his native cult.

The literate native is sitting on the fence
unable to assess the real value of the two
faiths he is practising. He becomes a contradiction
to himself. It is a question of looking into a
bottle with two eyes. He dreads to be referred to
as superstitious but he sees he cannot get on
in life trusting in Christian prayers alone.
The illiterate is clear on the point. This can
set out the state of mental wavering effect
which may be readily seen in those literates
who have secret jujus of the kind described
above. They have a mentality bordering on
madness. I know a lot of people, who after
hesitating between such conflicting states of belief
have steadily worsened into a demented state.
It is an accepted fact that those who "DEAL IN
JUJU ~~often go~~ mad." "Nnuro tutuo ma onipa bo dam."
Often educated people who are seen going mad are
~~referred~~ to as such. The illiterate jujuman does not suffer.

answered when in the negative. The priests of the churches continually preach against these lapses. They are the experiences which
come to them from 'spies'.

The young struggling literate is equally anxious to get a charm or a
juju or the services of a mahomedan to help him get employed, to get
the favour of his head of department (boss) and to protect him from
'poisoning by juju' by other competitors. The middle class man may
enlist the assistance of a physician, a mahommedan or a fetish. He may
get a cow-tail juju (Nkabrε) for tying up all wishes. (A PANACEA for
all wishes) [sic]. Another is a lock, for locking up all wishes. There are
other forms of little charms or juju to which a literate may repeat his
wishes the first thing in the morning, even before prayers. He serves
whatever juju he keeps with perfect secrecy. On great days he may kill
a fowl and daub it with its blood. Some have boxes and boxes of these
nauseating jujus (besmeared with blood now and then). There is that
kind called 'AGBA-LA-GBA' which attained considerable vogue a
few years ago. Those who keep such idols are christians who think
themselves better cultured than their illiterate brothers who differ
from them in one chief point:

(a) Literate natives practise their native belief in secret, dreading to
be seen.

(a) The illiterate in the open and conscious that there is some truth
in his native cult.

The literate native is sitting on the fence unable to assess the real
value of the two 'faiths' he is practising. He becomes a contradiction to
himself. It is a question of looking into a bottle with two eyes. He
dreads to be referred to as superstitious but he sees he cannot get on in
life trusting in Christian prayers alone. The illiterate is clear on the
point. This can set out the state of mental wavering effect which may
be readily seen in those literates who have secret jujus of the kind
described above. They have a mentality bordering on madness. I know
a lot of people, who after hesitating between such conflicting states of
belief have steadily worsened into a demented state. It is an accepted
fact that those who 'DEAL IN JUJU often go mad.' 'Nnuro tutuo ma
onipa bɔ dam.' Often educated people who are seen going mad are
referred to as such. The illiterate jujuman does not suffer.[107]

Few people could articulate J. C. Frimpong's powerful vision of ambiguities in the inscription of colonial selfhood. His view was personal, but
also a sociological statement forged from unusually high levels of dis-
passionate intellection. But for Adeεbeba people generally the myriad inter-
sections between subject positions and the many environments that framed
them were much less clear cut. An anxious sense of *carpe diem*, at once
confused and confusing, inflected the presentation of self in autobiograph-

ical narratives. It is tempting to comb such testimonies for rhetorics of
sincerity or mimicry, but this presumes subjectivities self-consciously stabilised to some recognition of their own authenticity. Rhetorical moves were
certainly made, but they existed in an echo chamber of identity where
thought and deed boomed loudly but dissonantly, and commonly without
obvious connection. Self-description was not self-recognition; or, as Kwasi
Fi put it, 'We are all here (Adeɛbeba) the same as ever before only times
have changed.'[108]

5

CONCLUSION

'SCRAMBLING FOR MONEY': KUMASE AFTER 1945

The expansion of Kumase after 1945 has already been discussed in general terms. We turn now to the details of that process as it affected Adeɛbeba. This is a very involved story in its own right. It is complicated further by the fact that surviving witnesses are reticent about discussing certain transactions in which they played a part because these still bear upon arrangements that are current today. Equally, and for much the same reason, I know of the existence of relevant documentation that I have been able to access thus far only in part. That said, I would urge the overall accuracy of what follows while acknowledging that amplification of some of the arguments might yet be forthcoming.[1]

In October 1945 a town-planning exhibition was held in the Prempeh Hall, Kumase. Admission was free and Asante people came in large numbers. On the first day eager crowds thronged Jackson Park next to the exhibition hall to watch the Chief Commissioner of Asante perform the official opening. On the second and third days additional police were drafted in to control the crowds. On the fourth and final day invited parties of schoolchildren blocked traffic along Maxwell Street as they queued to enter. Fortes and Steel visited the exhibition twice and a number of ASS researchers also came to look at it.[2]

The scale of the planning described for Kumase was unprecedented. The pamphlet published by government as a guide to the exhibition acknowledged this in its self-conscious attempt to defuse anticipated alarm. It was prefaced by an 'Explanatory Note' addressed to the people of Kumase. This was a mix of emollient reassurance and didactic paternalism that sought to cast the urban project as a disinterested exercise in high-minded improvement. The aim was to beckon Asante towards the progressive modernity that awaited it in the benign pedagogy of post-war colonial tutelage.

> Town Planning is the concern of all people in Kumasi, and this Exhibition is being held to show you how your city could be properly developed. To produce better and fuller lives, your city must possess healthy conditions, good communications and beauty. This is what

Figure 5.1 Programme Cover, Kumase Town Planning Exhibition, 1945.
(Source: Ashanti Social Survey Papers, Birmingham)

Town Planning can do. Except in connection with the slum clearance the plans do not suggest large scale demolitions either of houses or other buildings, but provide for a continual ordered development throughout the future years. It will of necessity be a gradual process and its success will rely to a very great extent upon the goodwill of the citizens both of today and tomorrow. It is hoped that the Exhibition will explain to you the meaning of Town Planning. It should be directly understood that the exhibits referred to in this programme illustrate proposals for Town Planning which are not necessarily in their final form, and are at present under consideration by the Government. No rapid or violent changes are contemplated, and whenever schemes are put into effect the interests of all those concerned will be given the fullest consideration.[3]

Government gave its tentative approval to an ambitious programme that was to be given 'priority during the first ten post-war years'. Earmarked work included the completion of the Asawasi housing scheme 'for the labouring class'; the clearance of 'slums' in the Old Zongo and elsewhere in the inner city; the execution of an improved road and bridge layout to expedite traffic flow; the construction of a new general hospital, asylum, recreation centre, open-air cinema, swimming pool and other amenities; the upgrading of the main food market; and the redevelopment of Stewart Avenue into an imposing 'Whitehall' for the colonial administration.[4]

All these building projects were expensive but piecemeal. More problematic was the choice of an integrated planning scheme to give visionary shape to the future city. The exhibition displayed the two proposals under consideration. Plan 'A' was radical; it envisaged the complete resiting of the railway away from south-central Kumase to permit redevelopment there. Plan 'B' was pragmatic; it envisaged the partial rerouting of the railway around south-central Kumase to achieve the same end. Both plans anticipated a phased expansion of the town to meet existing and projected demographic pressures on housing. The removal or reconfiguration of the railway liberated building land in the inner city. More importantly it abolished the bottleneck that inhibited what the plans called the 'natural growth line' of Kumase along the east Nsuben river and out into the southern and eastern peripheries of the city. In this regard both plans drew attention to one particular document in the exhibition. This was prosaically titled 'Diagram 15: Proposed New Housing Areas'. To the casual glance it was a spider's web of inky lines. But to the discerning eye it disclosed an impending building boom – and hence rocketing land values – to the south and east of Kumase.[5]

The 1945 exhibition arose from planning work on the post-war development of the Gold Coast and Asante ordered by Lord Swinton, who was appointed the Resident Minister for British West Africa in 1942. A sometime Secretary of State for the Colonies (1931–5), Swinton held Cabinet rank and his brief was to oversee and implement coordinated policies for the infrastructural improvement of British West Africa. By 1945 development in all its forms was a cornerstone of Colonial Office thinking.[6] Thus, planning schemes were drafted in 1945 in the Gold Coast for the capital of Accra, the historic town of Cape Coast, the deep water industrial port of Sekondi-Takoradi and the mining centre of Tarkwa in addition to Kumase in Asante.[7] The principal authors of all these plans for the Gold Coast and Asante were the husband and wife architectural partnership of E. Maxwell Fry and Jane B. Drew. It was their vision of tropical urbanism that gave substance to Swinton's directive. Fry and Drew shared exclusive responsibility for the Kumase Draft Town Planning Scheme (KDTPS) that was submitted to the Resident Minister in August 1945 and that then formed the blueprint for the October exhibition.[8]

In hindsight it can be seen that by 1945 Fry and Drew were already on their way to becoming significant figures in the modern movement in British architecture. The pair were important theorists of the emerging post-war concern with effective and humane town planning in both the metropole and the tropical colonies.[9] Fry, the more experienced of the two, co-founded the modernist MARS group in Britain in the 1930s and for a short but decisive period in 1934–6 he was associated with the *Bauhaus* exile Walter Gropius in the execution of eight innovative commissions in and around London. Thus, important for Fry's plans for the Asawasi housing estate in Kumase was his experience of executing with Gropius in London the R. E. Sassoon Flats (1936) and the Kensal House Flats (1936). In both these buildings *Bauhaus* concepts were adapted to address the problem of constructing low-cost rental housing that aspired to meet humanitarian socialist criteria in the context of a modernist aesthetic.[10] Drew, thirty-four in 1945, had designed only one building in her own right when she was appointed Assistant Town Planning Adviser under Fry in West Africa in 1944. Fry and Drew, of course, went on to design and build many commissions in the Gold Coast and Nigeria, and in 1951–6 they participated with Le Corbusier in the internationally publicised construction of the new city of Chandigarh in the Punjab.[11]

Fry and Drew were socialist idealists, but fairly hard-headed ones. They combined a belief in betterment through the planned improvement of the built environment with a sensitivity to the need to 'harmonise' the totality of 'the human and climatic conditions of the humid West African tropics' in the making of satisfactory urban forms. In this task it was the duty of the town planner to temper 'reasoning' with 'moral' criteria in assessing human needs.[12] This *engagé* approach was practised as a kind of visionary problem solving. It was manifested in the way in which Fry and Drew tackled their

1945 Kumase brief. Their KDTPS was rhapsodic over future possibilities in the Asante capital but sober in its detailing of basic enablements like a pipe-borne sewerage system. Aware that their reach might exceed their grasp, Fry and Drew none the less aimed for a planned comprehensiveness that was admirable if sometimes naive. Thus, for example, they devoted time to debating the 'design of street furniture' in Kumase and worried at the problem of choosing a colour scheme for such items.[13] Their concern in this and other matters was that extreme care should be taken in design so that modernity in all of its forms might become readily accepted into the quotidian texture of Asante urban life. Fry and Drew were well meaning and conscientious, but as the enlightened agents of a sovereign colonial power they tended to privilege their ideas over Asante realities. Their vision of the good life of tropical urban modernism subsumed or discounted Asante historical experience in the quest to plan and deliver a brave new post-war world.

Fry and Drew were aware of the significance of Kumase in Asante history but their understanding was limited. In their deliberations they tended to acknowledge the symbolic value of the past rather than engage with its legacy of ideological and material expressions. History for them was a secondary consideration. They were more attuned to the exciting develop-mental opportunities presented by the 'open character' of 'the Garden City of West Africa'. Indeed, there was some justification for this other than professional or personal preference.[14]

Briefly to recapitulate: Kumase in 1945 was an ever growing but minim-ally planned city. When the British annexed the precolonial Asante capital it was little more than a shell. Devastation and depopulation begun by civil wars in the 1880s halted only after the last Anglo-Asante conflict in 1900–1. Thereafter, colonial planning was more tactical than strategic. Problems were addressed on an *ad hoc* basis, more or less as and when they arose. The result was unplanned hybridity. A haphazard colonial urbanism overlay an older order, masking but not erasing it, for despite its shattered fabric and the exile of its ruler (until 1924) the precolonial city continued to resonate as a site of meaning and memory for Asante people. Rooted in this, life went on for the most part on its own terms and out of sight of a remote and often baffled imperial power. Kumase citizens tended to regard the spasmodic directives and interventions of government with suspicion, and they responded to regulation with evasion or subversion. Colonial Kumase grew in a barely planned and lightly administered way. Its sociability was con-ducted as a thing of houses, streets and quarters, in a palpably vibrant manner, but without benefit of any larger vision of a cohering urban design.

Such conditions posed an alluring challenge to Fry and Drew. The very fluidity of Kumase as urban form suggested that the resolute planner might

Figure 5.2 (above and opposite) Present Realities: three views of Kumase in 1945.
(Source: E. Maxwell Fry (FRIBA) and Jane B. Drew (FRIBA), 'Draft Town Planning Scheme for Kumasi: Report', August 1945)

impose the future upon it. Indeed, so little strategic thinking had taken place that everything seemed possible. The physical prospect of the city presented itself in terms of a radically unrealised landscape, a thing of inherited bits and pieces and open spaces available to willed mastery and direction. Kumase was 'in fact a beautiful town' in 'the open character of its development', for it possessed 'large areas of luxuriant greenery' awaiting responsible urban improvement.[15] In sum, the quiddity of the planner's Kumase was inscribed in its future possibility as biddable landscape and not in its past instantiation as unsystematised environment.

But, as always, the devil lay in the details. As we have seen, the KDTPS offered two plans to remove or reconfigure the 'railway loop', which 'helped to limit the southward development of the town'. Fry and Drew thought the

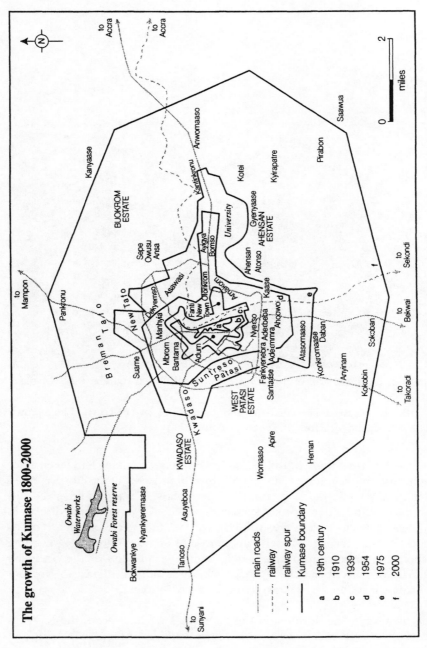

Map 5.1 The growth of Kumase 1800–2000

logic of expansion in this direction irrefutable, a marriage between organic planning and environmental opportunity. Furthermore, most of the newer housing stock built since the 1930s was 'spread over the eastern and northern parts of the town', but open land was plentiful in the south along the line of the Sekondi railway and the Bekwai road. This might be used to relieve inner city congestion and so meet 'the great need for house building in Kumasi'. The villages south of the capital already formed a semi-urban periphery. Fry and Drew suggested their formal incorporation into Kumase. But extending the metropolitan boundary in law was not the same as realising the practical possibilities opened up by such a measure. Clearly, there would be a time lag, pending the necessary legal and fiscal clearances for a sustained programme of housebuilding within the newly incorporated southern arc. Anyway, addressing the problem of the railway was the KDTPS's first priority, and this promised to be a long and costly business.[16]

Drew later recalled the pressure to produce interim solutions consonant with the KDTPS's longer term proposals. Basic demographic facts prompted this sense of urgency. As we have already seen, the curve of upward population increase was worryingly steep in that it placed immense strain on limited housing stocks and on infrastructural resources generally. By 1945 British colonial officials and Asante office holders alike were alarmed by this pressure of numbers and the clear trend towards a future of spiralling growth. Now Fry and Drew intended to place a huge but incalculable strain on already stretched provision by expanding Kumase so that many additional people would be entitled to lay claim to its services and amenities. But the nub of the problem was non-existent housing, and its seriousness can be gauged by the fact that there was already a shortfall in 1945 when the population of Kumase was 45,133; but by 1948 there were 71,313 people living in Fry and Drew's expanded urban enumeration area. Building new dwellings was essential to the success of the KDTPS. The proposed Asawasi housing estate was one attempt to address this problem by providing affordable accommodation away from the overcrowded city centre. But much more needed to be done, at least until such time as construction got seriously under way in the south. Fry and Drew knew this and suggested earmarking land to the east of Asawasi along the Accra road so that an interim building programme there might 'conveniently follow on to extend' the housing estate to provide short-term relief. Indeed, they judged the need for new dwellings to be so acute that they recommended sub-division into standardised plots of modest size (3,600 sq.ft.) so as to accelerate surveying and allocation and maximise building and occupancy. In a like manner, they urged that people be encouraged to use intermediate building technologies (stabilised swish walling, shingle roofing) so that a swift increment of housing stock might be gained by not 'making it too expensive for ordinary people'.[17]

Figure 5.3 (above and opposite) Future Possibilities: four planning sketches
of Kumase by E. Maxwell Fry, 1945.
(Source: E. Maxwell Fry (FRIBA) and Jane B. Drew (FRIBA), 'Draft Town
Planning Scheme for Kumasi: Report', August 1945)

The KDTPS was complex in detail but its basic points were simple to understand. Most fundamentally Kumase was to be extended in an ordered manner, first and in the short term to the east and then systematically to the south so as 'to wrap new African housing areas around the centre'.[18] The message was plain, but there was a problem. Fry and Drew presumed that implementation would take place in an uncontentious atmosphere. Government would approve, fund and oversee their plan either in whole or in part. This duly happened. The cheaper, less disruptive Plan 'B' was selected, urban expansion was sanctioned, rapid housebuilding was encouraged and grants-in-aid and other incentives to construction were offered. The goodwill of Asante people was simply taken for granted. The KDTPS had been carefully 'explained to its intended beneficiaries', and so their cooperation and support were guaranteed. Drew recalled that 'at the time we were thinking things through' she and her husband paid insufficient heed to 'the difficulties surrounding ownership of land. This turned out to be a mare's nest.'[19] Indeed it did.

The *Asantehene* Osei Agyeman Prempeh II identified this problem right away. He was given a presentation copy of the KDTPS bound in embossed green leather. He read it carefully and annotated it extensively in its margins and on interpolated sheets of notepaper.[20] He understood that Kumase was soon to be enlarged 'by one means or another', whether or not government chose to act on the specific recommendations of Fry and Drew. The inevitability of expansion troubled him and he committed his reservations to writing and confided them to intimate associates. He predicted that the expansion of Kumase would lead to unprecedentedly litigious struggles over rights in land as people tried to assert title to potentially valuable building plots. East and more particularly south of the capital, he minuted, there existed a 'complicated picture' of historic landholding patterns that the KDTPS seemed to think 'will be of little importance to the making of changes'. In this the planners were greatly mistaken. In the south 'many servants of the Golden Stool' and the subjects of numerous other office holders were dispersed across a range of small nucleated villages that stood on land 'sacredly held in trust by the Kumasi Divisional Chiefs since the beginning of Ashanti'. Rights in this area were 'held up with pride and dignity' and in consequence had already been the subject of much dispute throughout the earlier colonial period. Conflict would now intensify to 'an unbearable extent', for despite its proximity to Kumase the southern periphery still contained much exploitable land for building in the form of small farms and even open 'forest tracts'. Official encouragement to put up buildings all around south Kumase, the *Asantehene* concluded, would unleash a 'battle royal' driven on by a relentless 'scrambling for money' by everyone concerned.[21]

Osei Agyeman Prempeh II's presentiments were widely shared and they proved to be accurate. Through their plans for expansion, Fry and Drew unwittingly opened a door onto a long history that was vital and contested rather than annulled and forgotten. Their proposals also suggested an opening to the future that invited the involvement of new men as well as established power in the construction of post-war urban modernity. From the later 1940s and into the 1950s conflict over land rights around Kumase escalated hugely as did applications to build. In this very convoluted process some foregrounded history and rehearsed versions of the past in order to assert present advantage. Others denied the relevance of history and mounted claims as representatives of an emerging order that looked increasingly to decolonisation and the achievement of independence in one guise or another. The template for the struggle over building land was Ayigya immediately east of Asawasi, recommended by Fry and Drew as an interim housing site pending the development of the southern periphery of Kumase. Disputes over rights to build in Ayigya became endemic, following the pattern described by the *Asantehene* in his prescient forecasting of events. But personalities and events in Ayigya also had a direct bearing upon the affairs of Adeɛbeba. It is to this matter that we now turn our attention.

Ayigya was an old settlement. It was founded in the 1690s following the victory of the first *Asantehene* Osei Tutu over Amakom (presently located in east-central Kumase). The *Amakomhene* was incorporated into the nascent Asante state and Osei Tutu seized or otherwise assumed rights of disposition over tracts of Amakom land. One of these tracts was awarded by Osei Tutu to his wife Abena Maanu. She was the female head (*obaapanin*) of the Amma Gyata *aduana* lineage, resident at Asakyere near Bekwai in the Amansie area. Osei Tutu settled her on the Amakom land with, it is said, thirty followers. This settlement became Ayigya village and its people served the Golden Stool.

The males of Abena Maanu's lineage supplied the chiefs of Ayigya. In memory of their origin these office holders assumed the title of *Asaky-erehene*. They served the *Asantehene* in the ritual capacity of 'soul washers' (*nkradwarefoɔ*). Moreover, in commemoration of the union between Osei Tutu and Abena Maanu successive *Asantehenes* married *ayite* or stool wives from the Amma Gyata lineage.[22] In the eighteenth and nineteenth centuries Ayigya was never a large place but it steadily if modestly increased in population. In the 1830s the *Asantehene* Osei Yaw settled a displaced Dwaben lineage in the village as players of the royal *amoakwa* horns. Again, during the 1880s Ayigya became home to refugees who fled Nkuntaase in Mampon because of the civil wars. The village survived the disruptions of the later nineteenth century, and in 1902 it was an early target for proselytisation by Basel missionaries. Cocoa came to Ayigya in the 1900s. Local farmers cultivated it on intercropped land but the only substantial

plantation belonged to the celebrated Kumase businessman Kofi Sraha.[23]
Up until nearly mid-century Ayigya remained a backwater. Aerial photo-
graphs of 1948 show a cluster of dwellings encircled and dwarfed by
farmland and scrub bush. In that year the census recorded that Ayigya
contained 387 residents distributed between 35 compound houses. Until
1951 Ayigya's main street formed part of the Kumase–Accra trunk road,
but it was a place that people passed through on their way to somewhere
else.[24]

However, from the later 1940s Ayigya began to change with an ever
accelerating momentum. As we have seen, it was earmarked by Fry and
Drew (as to a lesser extent were the settlements of Bomso, Sisaaso and
Kantinkronu contiguous to it) as a priority site for relief construction and
development. This proposal was given an additional urgency by strictly
local demographic pressures. In the late 1940s immigrants from the Kwabre
and Mponoa areas of rural Asante began to flood into east Kumase in the
hope of securing work in the urban economy. Ayigya was a magnet for such
people. It had open land, was at the growth point of east Kumase and was
well served by passing road transport. Thereafter, about 1950, existing
Asante immigration was swelled by an influx of Muslim northerners in
search of jobs. By 1953 Ayigya had a makeshift mosque and a rapidly
growing Muslim quarter or Zongo sited to the north-west of the original
village. Already by this time Ayigya was densely crowded with incomers,
and by 1960 it had in excess of two thousand residents. It was a 'bustling,
disorderly place' with a thriving informal economy, but with strained
amenities servicing what was in effect a huge building site. This was a
fulfilment of KDTPS intentions, at least of a sort.[25]

The expansion of Ayigya was accomplished in a welter of alliances,
confrontations and litigious dealings. Owners and occupiers, squatters and
speculators, or indeed anyone who hoped to cash in on the building boom
pitched into battle over rights in land. The lineages that made up the
precolonial population fought each other over historical prerogatives and
split internally over issues of family or personal control over prime building
sites. Office holders from outside – the *Gyenyaasehene* and *Ayeduasehene* –
claimed slender or even fictive historic title to Ayigya land. In addition, the
Kumase *Akyempemhene* asserted that Ayigya had been gifted to his stool
around 1800, and that subjects of his from nearby Kantinkronu were the
rightful owners of the land. The *Asantehene* Osei Agyeman Prempeh II
refuted this in person and sought an apology. Beyond this circle of office
holders, a bewildering mix of Asante entrepreneurs, Syrian businessmen
and Kumase Muslims all involved themselves in Ayigya affairs. By the early
1950s the Kumase Town Council (KTC) was exasperated by its inability
either to control or direct runaway construction in Ayigya.

Unauthorised or otherwise unregistered development was so anarchic in Ayigya that in 1953–4 the *Asantehene*, in consultation with the *Asakyerehene* and with officers of the KTC and its successor the Municipal Council (1954–62), sent in teams of surveyors to demarcate building plots while all housing transactions were theoretically suspended. On paper these plots generally followed the suggestions of Fry and Drew as to size. But almost immediately the ongoing impetus of housing demand and its profitability led to an uncontrollable process of random sub-division. The housing sector was overtaken by rental sub-lettings on a huge scale as those individuals with clear title to plots sought to optimise their returns. Indeed, rental payments from tenants to landlords living in the same dwelling swiftly became a major source of revenue in Ayigya's booming building economy. By the mid-1950s gross overcrowding and an increasing pattern of absentee landlordism had created slum conditions amidst continued expansion. As a result, in 1959, building began to the west of both village and Zongo in an area that came to be known as West Ayigya. This was a planned development of better quality housing on larger plots. It was put up to accommodate wealthy and influential residents who wanted to remove from Ayigya proper to a more exclusive site.[26]

In theory, those wishing to secure title to an Ayigya building plot paid allocation, registration and other legal fees to the Kumase metropolitan authority, and then customary 'drink money' (*sika nsa*) to the *Asantehene* as landholder to 'stamp' (i.e. confirm) the arrangement. As late as 1948 the latter was commonly a token sum. But by 1950 the building boom had created inflation, and the *Asantehene* told his representative the *Asakyerehene* to assess customary fees at the going market rate (the highest figures being to seal stay-of-rent agreements for a fixed term of initial occupancy). The Golden Stool profited from this increase, but the basic reason for its imposition was to try to claw back revenues of all kinds that otherwise would have remained unpaid. The *Asantehene* had (re)established historical title to Ayigya and was a considerable landlord there in his own right (albeit through nominees). But even he could not hope to control third-party involvement in the building boom or monitor and collect the monies owed to him. The supreme Asante office holder found it well nigh impossible to keep track of the explosive post-war growth of a village only two miles from his palace.

'NANA, YOUR FIRE DOES NOT BURN ME': ADEƐBEBA AFTER 1945

As a part of defending his rights in Ayigya in the early 1950s, the *Asantehene* tried to secure writs for restraint of trespass against many people. He was especially exercised by the activities of a group that became known as 'the auctioneers' or *awuɔsɔnfoɔ*. The nickname arose from the group's practice of

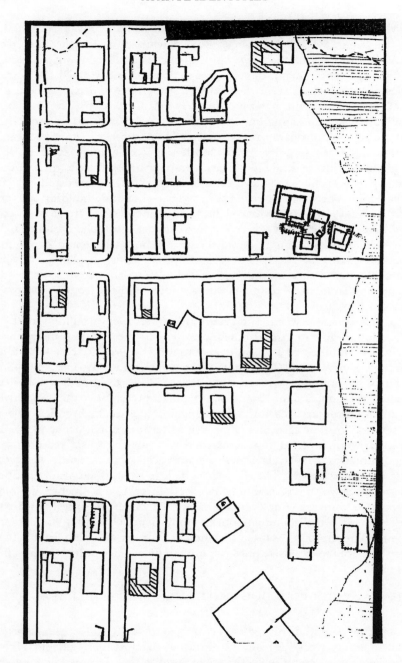

Figure 5.4 Fragments I: incomplete sketch plan of Adeɛbeba in 1945.
(Source: Ashanti Social Survey Papers, Birmingham)

declaring rights over plots in Ayigya (and elsewhere) and then 'auctioning' them off to the highest bidder. This was profitable, but also illegal. Yet the *Asantehene* moved against this group with uncharacteristic caution. He issued writs against its members but then declined to pursue them through the courts. The reason was that 'the auctioneers' were activist opponents of the Golden Stool with support and connections in and beyond Asante. Their principal backer was (J. E. A.) Krobo Edusei, a sometime debt collector and newspaper reporter, a leading light in the Ashanti Youth Association (AYA), a rising star in Nkrumah's Convention People's Party (CPP), and a long-time opponent of Asante chiefship. Krobo Edusei's connection to 'the auctioneers' went back at least to 1948 when he spear-headed Asante participation in the Gold Coast-wide boycott of imported goods. Feeling ran high against inflationary prices, and in tandem with nationalist aspiration this made for a highly charged and volatile situation. As Chairman of the Ashanti Boycott Committee, Krobo Edusei recalled that he

> set up 'illegal courts' which tried offenders who committed a breach of the boycott rules and that a fine of £7 10s was imposed on each. He asserted that he had his own 'policemen' and that he paid them £2 10s from each fine of £7 10s and kept £5 for himself. He asserted further that during the boycott period, he toured the whole country, that the chiefs and people gave him money and that by the end of 1949 his total receipts were £20,000.[27]

The present relevance of this testimony is that the 'policemen' recruited by Krobo Edusei became his clients and some among them went on to form the core of 'the auctioneers'. These included Ata Ababio and Mensa Bonsu (later activist CPP foot soldiers in Adanse), Arthur Takyi (a Kumase-based Fante from Cape Coast who became a buyer and accountant for Krobo Edusei) and – most importantly here – an Adeɛbeba man named (John) Kwasi Manwere.

Kwasi Manwere was born about 1910. His mother Abena Takyiwaa was a great-granddaughter of the Adeɛbeba pioneer Amma Donko of Heman. His father was Yaw Brantuo, a son of the second *Manwerehene* Kwasi Brantuo Kyei Kumaa, who was executed by the *Asantehene* Kofi Kakari in 1872 in circumstances that have already been discussed. Yaw Brantuo left Asante for the Gold Coast in the 1880s, returning to Kumase only after the removal of Agyeman Prempe in 1896. By then he was a wealthy trader, and he later became an agriculturalist and a *rentier* with several properties in Kumase. Although the details are unclear, it would appear that he tried but failed to secure the *Manwere* stool in 1901 when it was more or less sold to Kofi Nti by the *Gyaasewahene* Kwame Tua. Again, in 1926 he wrote to the

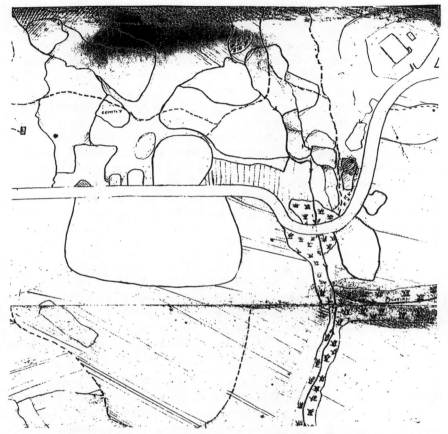

Figure 5.5 Fragments II: incomplete sketch map of Adeεbeba farmland in
1945.
(Source: Ashanti Social Survey Papers, Birmingham)

repatriated Agyeman Prempe to protest that the incumbent *Manwerehene*
Kwasi Kyerapem was a usurper.[28] The evidence suggests that Yaw Brantuo
was an unfulfilled and embittered man with grudges against established
authority that originated in the humiliation and death of his father. He died
during the 1930s and there is only one passing reference to him in the ASS
materials. At some point in the 1920s he was asked to supply a sheep to
'wash' Adeεbeba *taa kwabena bena* 'as royals of the [*Manwere*] stool were
obliged to do'. He refused point blank and this minor scandal was still
recalled some twenty years after the event.[29]

   Yaw Brantuo was a Wesleyan-Methodist and his son Kwasi Manwere
was baptised and educated by that denomination in Kumase. He later

attended a vocational school in Mampon. By the early 1930s he was back in Kumase and employed as a clerk. There his life took a decisive turn when he became the client and associate of a conspicuously politicised individual. This was E. C. Bobie Ansa, acknowledged as a leader among Kumase 'youngmen' (*nkwankwaa*) because of his education and distinguished patrilineal descent. His father was the *Ankobiahene* Yaw Kyem, a son of the *Akyamfoɔ Dumienuhene* Kwaku Bobie, himself a son of the *Asantehene* Osei Tutu Kwame.[30] Such an ancestry commanded respect, but it conferred no access to office except by royal favour. Consequently, in the colonial era well born, newly educated and often moneyed men like Bobie Ansa experienced resentment when their sense of ambitious self-esteem was frustrated by exclusion from the power and status of chiefship. They became the fiercest critics of a hierarchy that denied them membership, and in that role they attracted a following of less advantaged *nkwankwaa* whose grievances they articulated. Kwasi Manwere became a follower of the sort described. He identified with Bobie Ansa, imbibed his equivocal dislike of chiefship, and refined it in the light of his own background into a hatred of the *Manwere* stool, its chief and elders. But in 1936 the British exiled Bobie Ansa from Asante for taking a part in a conspiracy against the *Asantehene* Osei Agyeman Prempeh II. Widespread claims that Kwasi Manwere was among those involved on the periphery of the plot are unproven.[31]

Kwasi Manwere kept a low profile after 1936 and nothing certain is known about his activities. Then in 1941 he secured employment as a typesetter at the Abura Printing Works in Kumase. There he met Krobo Edusei who was a fellow employee. Like Bobie Ansa and Kwasi Manwere himself, Krobo Edusei was an *akwankwaa* – but not a well-born one. However, he more than made up for this with a forceful personality that combined political and oratorical skills with a renowned daring (*nea ne koko yɛ duru*) in challenging chiefly authority. Like many another, Kwasi Manwere fell under the spell of Krobo Edusei's charisma and attached himself to this rising star of Asante and Gold Coast politics. Then in the late 1940s Kwasi Manwere became one of Krobo Edusei's agents in a series of confrontations with the *Asantehene* and his chiefs. The violent history of these exchanges remains to be written, but the activities of 'the auctioneers' in Ayigya were one episode from it. Indeed, rights in building land and the income to be gained from them was a key locus of conflict between chiefship and its opponents in this period. The objects of groups like 'the auctioneers' were to attack chiefly authority by challenging its rights in land; to accumulate money from such activities for political and personal use; and – perhaps above all – to expose to public gaze the corrupt self-interest of the *Asantehene* and his associates in profiting from the building boom through their insistence on historic prerogatives of access to and control over land.[32] Ayigya was a cutting edge of this struggle, but it rapidly spilled over to

Figure 5.6 Adeɛbeba today I: the Bekwai road at Adeɛbeba.
(Source: Photograph by Anna McCaskie, August 2000)

embrace much of the potentially valuable building land scattered around
south Kumase. This included Adeɛbeba, where Kwasi Manwere mounted a
highly personal campaign against the then incumbent *Manwerehene*, the
fourth Kwasi Brantuo. In the course of this, as we shall see, the nationalist
politics of decolonisation and independence came to Adeɛbeba with a
sudden and direct urgency. Such concerns had still lain over the horizon
when the ASS researchers quit Asante in 1946.

In 1935 Osei Agyeman Prempeh II was reinvested with the title of
Asantehene as head of a restored Asante Confederacy. Thereafter, he
worked to return Kumase to its place of historic pre-eminence. As part of
this effort he determined to restore the dignities of the *Manwerehene*. An
early opportunity for restitution concerned the *Manwere* subjects at
Drobonso. As we have seen, these people were first lost to *Manwere* in 1872
and finally confirmed as Kumawu subjects by the British in 1918. But in
1935–6 the Committee of Privileges set up by the British to review matters
at dispute between Confederacy members reopened the Drobonso case. In
giving evidence the *Manwerehene* identified himself as a 'sub-chief' in
Kumase *Ankobia* and entered a claim for the restoration of his Drobonso
subjects. He was supported by the *Asantehene*. Importantly too, he was
arguing his case before a British officialdom that was responsive to Kumase
claims in a way that it had not been prior to the inception of indirect rule in

Figure 5.7 Adeɛbeba today II: entrance to old Adeɛbeba village.
(Source: Photograph by Anna McCaskie, August 2000)

Figure 5.8 Adeɛbeba today III: section of main street of old Adeɛbeba village.
(Source: Photograph by Sue Benson, August 2000)

1935.[33] The hearing rehearsed the history already recounted, adding details
such as the fact that in 1924 the people of Drobonso sent elephant hide via
the *Manwere* stool to the returned Agyeman Prempe in token of their true
allegiance as Kumase subjects. In the end the CCA transferred the
Drobonso people back to *Manwere*. His ruling was a policy decision that
took advantage of a technicality. The Kumawu cases as presented in 1918
and 1935 were found to be at odds with one another, and so the earlier
judgement in favour of the *Kumawuhene* was declared unsound. The
contradiction came to light, said the CCA, when he looked through his files
and fortuitously 'found' a Kumawu letter that had been overlooked when
submitted in 1918. In the event this sympathetic British decision endured,
though Kumawu claims were resurrected from time to time.[34]

In 1941 – 'on a great day in the History of Manwere Stool' – the
Manwerehene was ritually reinvested with the rank and title of *fekuo* head
originally bestowed upon the first Kwasi Brantuo by the *Asantehene* Kwaku
Dua.[35] At the same time the *Akomfode*, *Asabi* and *Ayebiakyere* stools were
reconfirmed as 'supporters' of the *Manwere fekuo*; the *Nyinahin*, *Nkawie
Panin*, *Asrampon* and *Nkontonko* stools were transferred to its jurisdiction;
and the newly created *Omanti* and *Nkabom* stools were added to it. The
foundation of *Nkabom* was a signal of Osei Agyeman Prempeh II's purpose
in reviving *Manwere*. The stool was named for the political concept of
nkabɔm(u), translatable in this context as 'unity' or 'union', but also
carrying implications of joining together for mutual advantage.[36] Thus, the
Nkabom stool symbolised the (re)joining together of Asante under its

Figure 5.9 Adeɛbeba today IV: beauty parlour.
(Source: Photograph by Sue Benson, August 2000)

Figure 5.10 Adeɛbeba today V: new house.
(Source: Photograph by Sue Benson, August 2000)

restored ruler in 1935, but also affirmed a return to the *status quo ante* of Kumase 'unity' and therefore primacy.

The programmatic was linked to the personal in Osei Agyeman Prempeh II's vision. An empowered Kumase was inseparable from a *puissant Asantehene*. Politics and wealth were historically sanctioned arenas of royal action, and in the 1940s Osei Agyeman Prempeh II involved himself fully in both. The issue of land united politics and wealth in a salient way. After the Kumase lands were formally reinvested in the Golden Stool in May 1943, the *Asantehene* set out to interpret trusteeship as a means of reasserting control in matters pertaining to their (re)allocation. But, as has been seen, tracts of this land became so potentially valuable after 1945 that Osei Agyeman Prempeh II found himself confronting an army of self-interested litigants prosecuting a chaotic scramble after rights and profits. Battle was joined, with the *Asantehene* fighting a war for control by proxy through clients of his like the *Manwerehene*. But this struggle was no longer conducted as an exclusive affair between office holders as had been the case historically. A constellation of new actors now took part. Activists of an emergent Asante and Gold Coast nationalist politics and entrepreneurs of a developed colonial economy redefined the axes of conflict. Thus, by the later 1940s – in Ayigya as elsewhere – the attempt by chiefs to affirm historic title to suddenly profitable land was intertwined with a wider struggle over the role of chiefship itself throughout Asante and the Gold Coast. The *Asantehene* was in the eye of this storm, but every other Asante office holder was caught up in it. This included the *Manwerehene*, only recently restored to his historic status but now plunged into new as well as old types of dispute.

On 19 February 1951 the *Manwerehene* Kwasi Brantuo IV wrote to his patron the *Asantehene* Osei Agyeman Prempeh II. He described a serious dispute between his own stool and that of the *Saamanhene* (the Kumase *Gyaasehene*) concerning the overlordship of Adeɛbeba. This first letter was followed by others and by the sworn testimonies of Adeɛbeba villagers. Conflict had arisen, said Kwasi Brantuo, because in the 1920s a part of *dodow* was leased to cassava farmers from nearby Toase. Adeɛbeba people (including Benson Anane, who spoke to ASS researchers about cocoa farming) testified that the arrangement had come about because 'part of this land in question was left idle by those absented to work [*sic*] elsewhere at the time'.[37] Whatever the case, the Toase tenant farmers were *Saaman* subjects. Their presence on the land first encouraged *Saaman* claims to *dodow* and then to suzerainty over Adeɛbeba itself. This dispute simmered over the years and caused ill feeling. Then in 1949–50 a steep rise in theft and burglary was recorded in south Kumase, a phenomenon blamed by all affected on the encroaching city. Ostensibly to combat this problem, Toase now proposed a merger with Adeɛbeba so that the two villages might petition for the creation of a joint local community authority. Immediately thereafter, however, Kwasi Boakye of Toase – a *Saaman* subject and *dodow* tenant grown rich from property development in Kumase – declared himself Adeɛbeba village head. Simultaneously, the *Saamanhene* pressed his case for tenurial authority over Adeɛbeba. Kwasi Brantuo refuted these claims absolutely and sought the aid of the *Asantehene* to 'defeat the plot'.

Kwasi Brantuo appealed to history. He attested to the indissoluble bond between *Manwere* and Adeɛbeba; thus, 'if two legs of a duyker are hanging out for sale, the price of one determines the price of the other'. Adeɛbeba was 'sacred' to the *Manwere* stool because 'it was given to my great grand uncle Brantuo'. So, argued Kwasi Brantuo with a fine rhetorical flourish, 'Where is Brantuo without Adiebeba? It is the original place you honoured me.' Reflecting upon the misfortunes of his stool he added the coda that, 'for a long time the house of Manwere has failed and irregularities have taken place in its management'. But because of the revival of *Manwere* since 1935, 'I am now beginning to take interest in Adiebeba.' Six weeks later he reiterated his argument. Adeɛbeba, so he assured Osei Agyeman Prempeh II, was 'for Manwere by itself alone' because it was the place where the first Kwasi Brantuo 'was put down to honour and obey Nana Adjiman [Kwaku Dua] and did serve him there with all loyalty till the end of his days'.[38] Kwasi Brantuo's letters and petitions were addressed to the *Asantehene* in person and made appeal to a shared history. They echoed the dependence (*danwoman*) of the first Kwasi Brantuo on Kwaku Dua, and invoked this in terms of *boa* – an idea that connoted the abasement of an inferior before a superior so that a seemingly hopeless problem might be resolved (lit. 'brought into order'). In soliciting aid, Kwasi Brantuo also employed the phrase to 'honour and obey' from the Christian marriage service. These words resonated with *danwoman* by calling attention to the historic conceit that assigned the favoured stool holder the idealised role of a submissive 'wife' to the *Asantehene*.

In truth Kwasi Brantuo needed aid from the *Asantehene*. Whatever the resurgence in his status, he had large debts and little income. By his own admission, he owed £1,600 to the Kumase lawyer Ofei Awere for legal work undertaken on his behalf. His Kumase house in Ashanti New Town was mortgaged in the sum of £700 plus interest to the infamous moneylending brothers Kwaku Adeɛ and Yaw Abebrese of Mampon Apa. Kwasi Brantuo had no liquid capital and his stool had no reserve of cash. Indeed, *Manwere* was despairingly trying to recover an advance of £175 made to the Suame goldsmith Kwabena Domeabra for the repair of stool regalia. But the goldsmith denied knowledge of the transaction and defied Kwasi Brantuo to summon him to court. Here was the nub of the problem. Kwasi Brantuo could ill afford to go to litigation with Kwabena Domeabra. He certainly lacked the means to take the *Saamanhene* through the courts in what would doubtless be a long and costly battle over Adeɛbeba. He told the *Asantehene* as much, laying emphasis on his indigence while appealing for intervention and support.

In May 1951 Osei Agyeman Prempeh II responded to Kwasi Brantuo. He expressed agreement that the Adeɛbeba dispute should not go to court. Instead, he proposed to arbitrate personally and in private.[39] In fact, the *Asantehene* had reasons of his own for wanting to avoid publicity. It was widely rumoured and as widely believed that he had commissioned his own surveys at Adeɛbeba, Toase and elsewhere in south Kumase with a view to acquiring development sites on his own account via nominees. In 1949 this story and others of a like kind surfaced in a court case concerning disputed land at Ahodwo near Adeɛbeba. Feelings ran high, and the *Asantehene* withdrew from the hearing amidst jeering and uproar. He was furious, blaming disaffected 'youngmen' for his humiliation and for circulating calumnies about his business interests and those of his kin and associates. Worse followed almost immediately.

A rumour arose that Osei Agyeman Prempeh II's greed was such that in addition to manipulating land transactions in south Kumase, he was also conspiring to sell the sacred lake Bosomtwe to European speculators. People wearing mourning cloth gathered at the palace in token of approaching calamity (*mmusuo*). In this charged atmosphere the *Asantehene* was once again obliged to convene his court, this time to hear destoolment charges brought against the Kumase *Adontenhene*. This was a constitutional case involving a major stool, and on the opening day in June 1949 the court was full to overflowing. Proceedings were barely under way when an outrage occurred. A man produced a shotgun and fired on the bench. He was overpowered before anyone was injured. In the confusion a visibly shaken Osei Agyeman Prempeh II was hurried away, losing his sandals in the process. An unshod *Asantehene* was a serious violation of custom. The shaming tale of royal flight spread like wildfire through Kumase. By report, Osei Agyeman Prempeh II raged at his entourage for failing to protect the palace, told the hapless *Adontenhene* that he deserved to be beheaded and ordered the *nhenkwaa* to throw every office holder into the street. When tempers cooled it was found that the gunman had paid over lavish bribes to Kumase stool holders to find in his favour in a land dispute at Santaase. But he had gotten nothing in return for bankrupting himself and so had taken the law into his own hands.[40]

These tensions and alarms formed the background against which Osei Agyeman Prempeh II opted for confidentiality in settling the Adeɛbeba dispute. In June 1951 he summoned the *Manwerehene* and *Saamanhene* to secret talks in the palace. No one else was present and there is no record of what transpired. But this meeting was inconclusive, and in July another private discussion took place. This time the conversation ended with summary action arising from royal anger. The reason was the revelation that the *Saamanhene* Ofori Kan Ababio was £1,700 in debt to his wealthy subject Kwasi Boakye of Toase. This money was borrowed after 1945 at a usurious interest rate to enable Ofori Kan Ababio to stockpile building materials pending an anticipated boom in demand for them. But the *Saamanhene* had other large debts and bought off insistent creditors with his reserves of cement, bricks, shingles, rods and planking. Having no means anymore of repaying Kwasi Boakye, he instead offered a deal. This hinged on Ofori Kan Ababio's claim that Adeɛbeba belonged to the *Saaman* stool. The proposal was that in exchange for relief on his debt the *Saamanhene* would sign over rights to survey, develop and lease building plots at *dodow* and elsewhere to Kwasi Boakye, and in confirmation he appointed him Adeɛbeba *odekuro*. Two Adeɛbeba villagers testified to the existence of this arrangement in January 1951. But it was only in early July – when *Saaman* elders in Saawua lodged a formal complaint that Ofori Kan Ababio was alienating stool land for personal gain – that the *Asantehene* looked into the matter. He confronted Ofori Kan Ababio with these allegations in the presence of Kwasi Brantuo at the second round of palace talks. The *Saamanhene* confessed. The *Asantehene* was furious. Because of the hostility produced by damaging rumours already linking the Golden Stool to questionable land deals in south Kumase, Osei Agyeman Prempeh II took immediate steps to suppress this latest complication. Ofori Kan Ababio was evidently told what was required of him, and on 19 July 1951 he abdicated. His stool elders were instructed to elect a replacement and to submit the name of their choice to the *Asantehene* for approval.[41]

In late July 1951 *Manwere* title to Adeɛbeba was confirmed against the claims of any and all other office holders. Stool disputes abated, but only to be replaced by conflict of another kind. In August Kwasi Manwere wrote to the Kumase Divisional Council (KDC), signing himself as spokesman for 'the common man'. His letter protested continuing chiefly arbitration of land rights in Adeɛbeba, and roundly dismissed *Manwere* and the stool holding hierarchy to which it belonged as an 'unjust', 'very much corrupt' and anachronistic legacy from a past that had no place in modern Asante. The days when 'the royal gang' could 'burn but not be burned in turn', he warned, were now at an end. This cryptic phrase bespoke defiance, for it alluded to a rallying cry then current among the opponents of established order. Its source was a title that celebrated kingly power. In tradition the *Asantehene* was lauded as being *hye wo nhye* ('he who can burn (you) but not himself be burned'). In the early 1950s critics of royalty and chiefship chanted this title and then responded with the provocative catchphrase *Nana wo gya anhye me* ('Nana, your fire does not burn me').[42]

The KDC did not reply to Kwasi Manwere's letter of August 1951 and minuted it as being from 'a well known troublemaker'. But a few weeks later Kwasi Manwere returned to the attack. He wrote informing the KDC that he intended to file writs of restraint and disclosure against the *Manwerehene* so as to halt all transactions affecting Adeɛbeba land until such time as current negotiations concerning them were made public. The *Asantehene* decided to quash this threat. In October 1951 the *Manwerehene* was summoned to attend a private meeting at the palace. The decision was taken to try to frighten Kwasi Manwere into silence, a tactic employed by Osei Agyeman Prempeh II to intimidate critical 'youngmen'. This took the standard form of calling offenders before authority so as to remind them of their status as lowly persons (*ahobrɛasefoɔ*) by browbeating, demeaning and humiliating them. Reports of this procedure mention people being stripped down to the loincloth (*danta*), slapped (*bɔ sotɔre*) about the face and legs or forced to carry out unpleasant tasks. In any event, Kwasi Manwere was brought before Osei Agyeman Prempeh II and disciplined in one way or another. But as sometimes happened in such cases, punishment only strengthened his resolve. In 1952 he tried but failed to bring destoolment charges against the *Manwerehene*. It is clear that by this time Kwasi Manwere's background, history and politics had fused together in a vendetta against Kwasi Brantuo.[43]

Matters came to a head in 1953. In March the *Manwerehene* Kwasi Brantuo visited Adeɛbeba several times to inspect survey work being carried out on his behalf. On one such trip he was confronted by Kwasi Manwere. Words were exchanged and a crowd gathered. What happened next is unclear. According to Native Authority (NA) police who were summoned by villagers to intervene, Kwasi Manwere abused and then attacked Kwasi Brantuo. The *Manwerehene* was 'struck by blows', after which he 'sat in the vehicle' that had brought him from Kumase. The upshot was that Kwasi Manwere was arrested, charged with assault and bound over to appear in court. In April the case of the *NA Police* vs. *Kwasi Manwere* was heard in the Kumase Divisional Court with the *Akyempemhene* presiding. The *Manwerehene* was not present. The charges were read and Kwasi Manwere pleaded not guilty. Police evidence was taken and then the defendant was questioned by the bench. Kwasi Manwere denied assault on Kwasi Brantuo but admitted that a quarrel had taken place. Instructed to elaborate, he said the following.

> I am speaking here for myself. The present Mawerihin [*sic*] is not the right person for the stool. When he came on I told the Elders and King Makers all of his criminal acts such as alienating Stool Lands to gain money. He is a bad lot and known so by myself and other true royals and loyalists to the stool. I investigated the situation of the Adebeeba lands he is selling with the help of certain powerful people. They want to put up building[s] to gain money. This is happening all around. He

[Kwasi Brantuo] fears me because I am telling the truth. Meeting me [at Adeεbeba] he asked what I was doing there. I told him he was alienating the lands only for himself. He became agitated and an argument came on. I did not strike him but he got the police to say so and so I am here in court now.[44]

Kwasi Manwere was convicted of felonious assault and sentenced to three months in jail. After his release he resumed his connection with opponents of the Asante establishment. He and his associates continued to agitate about developments in Adeεbeba, Ayigya and elsewhere in south Kumase. But by 1953–4 the land issue was being overtaken by and subordinated to more urgent considerations as Asante contemplated the implications of Nkrumah's policies for its own future belonging in a post-colonial Gold Coast. Throughout 1954 the Asante political landscape was reconfigured in the light of these matters. In August the Ashanti Youth Association (AYA) itself split between supporters and opponents of Nkrumah's Convention People's Party (CPP). In September the National Liberation Movement (NLM) was launched in Kumase, uniting chiefs, 'youngmen' and many others in a harmony of purpose to defend Asante interests against Nkrumah's government in Accra.[45]

Kwasi Manwere continued in allegiance to his patron Krobo Edusei and the CPP. The last known documentary reference to him is in a colonial intelligence report of 26 October 1954. By then, the struggle between the CPP and NLM in Asante was moving towards open violence. British monitoring of the situation included frequent police visits to the villages around Kumase. After one such sweep that went as far south as Ampabame, reports were filed on a number of south Kumase settlements including Adeεbeba. The British found the village supported the NLM, and it was 'calm' despite a recent visit by several CPP activists. Named as one of these was Kwasi Manwere, 'a native of the place and a known troublemaker'. What became of him after this is unclear. By the time of Ghana's independence in 1957 he was working in Accra as a trade-union official. He died there in the 1970s. Why and under what circumstances he left Asante is unknown, but presumably the decision was shaped by politics and patronage.[46]

On 24 March 1962 Nkrumah granted city status to Kumase and inaugurated a new local-government authority in an attempt to tighten his grip on the Asante capital. The Kumase City Council (1962–74) set about reorganisation on a scale not seen since 1945. It produced its Development Plan in 1964. This called for the creation of a ring road around the existing city centre. It also made financial provision for purchasing and developing land lying outside this new highway. Accordingly, the City Planning Department carried out extensive feasibility studies to a distance of five miles beyond the proposed ring road. One such investigation considered future development possibilities for land in the 'Ahinsan–Santaasi corridor' in the south. This included Adeɛbeba, and a short study was devoted to it.[47] In it the planners identified a problem that Adeɛbeba shared with every other locality investigated. This was the under-enumeration of population returned by the government census of 1960. The same deficiency was also present in the census of 1948, and in the work carried out by the ASS in 1945–6.

ASS researchers counted sixteen compound dwelling houses strung out in a 'T' shape (the street I described visiting in 1997) as 'old' Adeɛbeba village. Many of these buildings were 'old fashioned', 'traditional' or 'dilapidated'. They contained a population of 123 people. But in 1945–6 perhaps 'one half of the entire village is living away at any one time, for the most part in nearby Kumasi'. In addition, all around 'old' Adeɛbeba buildings were going up. These housed fluctuating numbers that were easier to estimate than enumerate. Hence, a census 'in the strict sense of the term' was impossible because of the dynamic fluidity of post-war south Kumase. The actual population of Adeɛbeba, the ASS concluded, might be in excess of three hundred if everyone 'belonging to the place returned all together' to be counted.[48] The government census of 1948 gave the population of Adeɛbeba as 147. But again, officialdom admitted the difficulty of enumeration, and privately acknowledged that 'a shifting situation' around south Kumase might have led to 'misleadingly low' estimates of the numbers living there.[49] The next government census in 1960 returned a figure of 434 inhabitants for Adeɛbeba.[50] But when the KCC planners finished work in the early 1960s, the Chief Survey Clerk concluded that all of the accepted population statistics for the 'Ahinsan–Santaasi corridor' were unreliably low. He communicated his worries about implementing a Development Plan based on such data, irrespective of the many other difficulties surrounding a policy for directing and rationalising land use. The KCC planning committee noted these reservations, expressed some agreement with them, and then ignored them when pressurised by the government in Accra to produce their Development Plan in 1964.[51]

The 1964 proposals included a planning map that is still used as a framework for evaluating land and sequencing development in Kumase. But from the outset it was a flexible guide to process rather than a fixed determination of policy. It was undermined and overwhelmed by numbers, by the ever rising demand for housing, by the ways in which chiefship and its many allies worked to retain historic rights of disposition over land, by local-government underfunding, and by the fluctuating fortunes of Ghana since the 1960s. Kumase local government is only one player among a number that presides over a city developed through endless negotiations rather than planning laws. Indeed, none of the historical actors considered have been able to exercise firm control and sovereign direction over land development and housing in Kumase. Post-war problems have intensified relentlessly, especially during the huge urban expansion since the 1980s. Kumase is now a city with a population estimated to be in excess of 800,000 – and still growing. In 1999 the Ghana government's Regional Minister (Ashanti) reminded the Kumase Metropolitan Assembly of the environmental impact of this galloping expansion. The town's 'enviable' reputation as 'the Garden City of West Africa', he said, was now a thing of the past; runaway growth had led to 'indiscriminate felling of the trees along most of the avenues, lanes, streets, public gardens and open spaces' in the ceaseless quest for ever more housing.[52] In 2000 the Asante regional administration launched a three-year study into the social problems arising from these developments. It was noted that the current wave of urban expansion – like all its predecessors – was being accomplished as a 'transfer of resources from the poor to the rich'. Disparities were greatest around the periphery of Kumase. There 'peri-urban villages' manifested 'increased problems of pollution, poverty, homelessness and landlessness' as they underwent incorporation and development by vested interests and speculators. This was a reprise of Adeɛbeba's experience after 1945, but exacerbated by and symptomatic of the ever accelerating growth of the Asante capital.[53]

ADEƐBEBA LIVES: PRESENCES AND ABSENCES

In the mid-1990s I put on a suit, collar and tie and went to offer my condolences to a Kumase woman friend whose brother had died in the United States. Her house was in Fankyenebra, once a village but now a congested suburb like its neighbour Adeɛbeba. I was not the only visitor. The house was full of sympathisers from the Church to which my friend belonged. This was the Assembly of Christ Redeemer, one of very many new Pentecostal denominations then active in the city.[54] I had encountered its members before in Bantama where, as I now learned, the Kumase branch of the Church held its meetings in rented rooms. These gatherings were led by the 'Very Reverend Apostle Mr Ofori' who preached the Gospel and exhorted his followers to redeem and improve their lives through faith. The person who told me this in the Fankyenebra house was a man in his mid-forties. Physical proximity in the crowded living room and a clearly shared discomfort in our stifling formal clothes coaxed both of us to conversation. Affable and talkative, he introduced himself as Ezra Amponsah. He said he came from the southern Asante town of Akrokyere in Adanse but had been called to do the Lord's work in Kumase. In turn, I told him who I was and that I had spent thirty years working on the history of Asante. This seemed to interest him. He confided that he too was a student of history and invited me to come and visit him in his Suntreso house where he would divulge the real truth about the Asante past (abakosɛm wɔ mu).

I liked the man and was intrigued to hear what he might have to say. So we fixed a date and time and I called to take tea with him. I was introduced to the members of his household and then ushered into the parlour where the curtains were drawn against the sun. Three men were already sitting there on a sofa and chairs behind a low table with teacups and a scattering of books on it. I was a little surprised, but my host moved quickly to effect introductions. Like Mr Amponsah, all of my fellow guests were members of the Assembly of Christ Redeemer. I was seated. A short prayer was said and tea was served. When the five of us were alone again Mr Amponsah called the meeting to order (quite literally) and explained its purpose to me. It transpired that we knew people in common (a university professor turned businessman, and a royal *ɔkyeame*) and that he had consulted them about me. As a result, a decision had been taken to solicit my opinions about certain historical matters that were vexing everyone now present. I nodded but kept silent. In truth my heart sank, for in recent years (and like others who work in Ghana) I had often been drawn into prolonged conversations that sought an implausible reconciliation between Asante and biblical history. None the less, my assent was taken as given and Mr Amponsah began to explain after I dutifully agreed to his suggestion that I take notes.

The source of difficulty was Mr Ofori, leader of the Assembly of Christ Redeemer (and presently away in Accra). Excellent in all respects though he was, Mr Ofori had once been a Rosicrucian and still clung to his former esotericism. He preached that the Asante were the lost part of the tribes of Israel. Thus the name Asante derived from and denoted a splitting apart and a dispersal (presumably *san* (to unfasten) + *(hwe)te* (to scatter)). But the centuries of exile were drawing to a close, for God had revealed to Mr Ofori that at the coming of the new millennium true believers would be miraculously transplanted from Asante to Israel. This was the fulfilment of the prophecy in Ezekiel 37: 21–3, the text preached most often by Mr Ofori. At this point Mr Amponsah took up the Bible from among the books on the table and read aloud the relevant passage.

> Thus saith the Lord God; Behold, I will take the children of Israel from among the heathen, whither they be gone, and will gather them on every side, and bring them into their own land: and I will make them one nation in the land upon the mountains of Israel; and one king shall be king to them all: and they shall be no more two nations, neither shall they be divided into two kingdoms any more at all: neither shall they defile themselves any more with their idols, nor with their detestable things, nor with any of their transgressions: but I will save them out of all their dwelling places, wherein they have sinned, and will cleanse them: so shall they be my people, and I will be their God.[55]

I cast about for something to say but Mr Amponsah continued without pause. He and his three friends, Christians all, were convinced that the Holy Spirit worked in Mr Ofori. But they also felt that his exegesis of Ezekiel was mistaken. The passage cited did not concern Asante. I asked how they arrived at this conclusion. All four now began talking at once. The burden of what they said was the following. There was irrefutable proof that the Asante appeared in the Bible – indeed in the Book of the Prophet Ezekiel – but not in the passage just read. The Asante were not Jews, although some of their customs and rituals were influenced by the latter when the two peoples were neighbours in antiquity.[56] How could the Asante be Jews, I was asked meaningfully, when scholarship had shown that they had a special history and a unique destiny? Indeed, Asante history antedated Jewish history. Moreover, the former and not the latter were the true chosen people, and centuries of testing by the Lord God would soon end when the Asante 'inherited the kingdom' (that was the phrase used, accompanied by cries of Amen). Mr Ofori was led into error, they concluded, by his lingering faith in mystery cults. This was a sad delusion, for there now existed 'scientific proof' of the true facts of Asante history. I responded with some generalities about historical method and then invited Mr Amponsah to present his case. I was engaged now and genuinely interested.

Once more the Bible was taken up and Mr Amponsah read out Ezekiel 23: 22–4.

> Therefore, O Aholibah, thus saith the Lord God; Behold, I will raise up thy lovers against thee, from whom thy mind is alienated, and I will bring them against thee on every side; the Babylonians, and all the Chaldeans, Pekod, and Shoa, and Koa, and all the Assyrians with them; all of them desirable young men, captains and rulers, great lords and renowned, all of them riding upon horses. And they shall come against thee with chariots, wagons, and wheels, and with an assembly of people, which shall set against thee buckler and shield and helmet round about; and I shall set judgment before them, and they shall judge thee according to their judgments.[57]

The key to this passage, he said, was the toponym Koa – 'a valley in modern day Israel'. During the fifth millennium BC people migrated there from the Sudan via Egypt. They became known as the (people of) Koa and for a time lived peacefully alongside the Jews (who were later immigrants). But Jerusalem (Aholibah) fell to the Babylonians and the Jews were sent into exile (historically 597–539 BC). So too were the Koa, treacherously enslaved by their Babylonian allies. The sufferings of both peoples ended only when the Persian king Cyrus captured Babylon. The Jews returned to Israel. But the Lord God now revealed himself to the Koa, telling them that they and not the Jews were his chosen people. He gave the Koa signs of his divine plan. First, they were told ever after to honour the name of Cyrus, the Lord God's chosen instrument of their deliverance. Second, their leader – himself renamed Cyrus – was instructed to eat a scroll of lamentation (see Ezekiel 3: 1–3) and assured that the purpose of this act would be revealed in due course. Third, they were informed that they would wander the earth until they reached a resting place. There they would undergo a time of trial, forgetting the name of the Lord God even though he would continue to watch over them. At the last, they would be recalled to the Lord God, and redeem the world in the name of his son Jesus Christ who had been rejected by the Jews.

As the Koa wandered over the earth their name transmuted first to Koana, then to Gwana, and finally to Ghana (thrice in all, a mnemonic of the Holy Trinity). The last was the name they conferred upon what they believed to be their resting place – the Western Sudanic kingdom of Ghana. But when Ghana fell under the influence of Islam (historically the eleventh century AD) the Koa left and wandered until they came to settle in Asante. This name did indeed signify a wandering or dispersal (but not in the sense adduced by Mr Ofori). Here the people received further signs from the Lord God. The appearance of the Golden Stool (*sika dwa*) was a reappearance, the manifestation in a form cleansed of the bitterness of wandering of the scroll ingested by the first Cyrus. It descended from Heaven upon the knees of Cyrus's lineal successor the first *Asantehene* Osei (i.e. Cyrus) Tutu. The ancient name of Koa was preserved in the terms *akan* and *akoa*, the first the name of the immigrant clans or families, the second the word for a virtuous person devoted to fellowship and rectitude.[58] But now the time of trial commenced. Asante flourished but it fell into idolatry. The Lord God brought it low by visiting colonialism upon it so that it might see the error of its ways and be redeemed. The instrument of this salvation was the British, for they carried the Bible into Asante. But the British were only unwitting tools of the Lord God's purpose (like the Persians centuries before). They were uncomprehending caretakers of the Scriptures now at last conferred upon the chosen people. A Golden Age had now dawned. A redeemed Koa (Asante) people were called upon to mobilise their faith so as to wrest the Christian message back from European ignorance and Jewish dismissal. This great task would be followed by an even greater, for the Lord God had charged Asante with proselytising Africa in the name of the people of Koa and in the light of their unique access to biblical truth. At the last, the Lord God would restore the true order of his creation. Black African peoples instructed and led by the Asante (Koa) would exercise benevolent dominion over Europeans, Jews and the other peoples of the earth.

I was asked for comment, the implication being that my own researches must have led me to much the same conclusions. I trod carefully around a history argued with such seriousness. I offered the truthful (but evasive) observation that the first chapter of the history authorised by the *Asantehene* Osei Agyeman Prempeh II discussed the matter of Asante connections to ancient Israel.[59] I then elaborated on some contingent points and ended by remarking truthfully (but again evasively) that nothing I knew of inclined me to agree with Mr Ofori. I put away pen and paper and thanked my host and the others. I sensed I had failed them. But smiling handshakes all around were accompanied by blessings as I took my leave.

Narrative selves are resourced from and propelled by narratable histories. That is, intersubjective accounting for oneself in relation to others similarly engaged at any given moment in time and space relies upon recounting from a personal archive of past experience. The self narrated in speech, behaviour and the rest is uniquely a product of experience available to narration. But how are such personal historical resources assembled? Clearly they are produced by memory, and it is the workings of this process that configure the presences revealed in and as Adeɛbeba lives. But what of memory itself? Although terms vary, a distinction is commonly made between episodic (autobiographical) and semantic (historical) memory. The first is the province of things experienced by oneself; the second that of things imparted to oneself by others. Both sorts of memory are stored, accessed and retrieved in shifting patterns of remembering, misremembering and forgetting. But there are problems with this distinction. Episodic memory is incorporative; it can seize upon the resources of semantic memory and recast them as things directly experienced. Semantic memory is overweening; it can annex the specifics of episodic memory and redefine them as things pedagogically imparted. The boundary between the two is permeable and has many crossing points. Take topography (a key referent in Adeɛbeba lives). Places freighted with historical memories do not yield up their only meaning via narratives stored in a linguistic form. They resonate rather than speak, and it is easier to access their semantic content by using episodic memory to weave an imaginary of self-identification; narratable histories of place rely upon willed autobiographical insertions ('what was it like then?') to retrieve the past. In truth, an episodic-semantic distinction may be useful to psychologists and linguists concerned with singular short-term memory as event; but it is much less useful to historians concerned with plural long-term memory as narrative, for in this context it is debilitated by the endless qualifications required to sustain it.[60]

It is more fruitful to shift our ground here from definitions to deployments. That is – as Halbwachs argued – narratable histories are certainly assembled from memories, but these are recalled in and rearticulated as and through communication.[61] Now this is certainly the Asante understanding of the matter. Consider the relevant Twi terms. Narrative is *asɛm*. The word has a range of situational applications; speech acts themselves (words, talking,

saying, making a speech, telling a tale or story); the referential content of
speech acts (matters for talking about; objects of discussion; events,
incidents, occurrences, concerns to be aired); the transaction of speech acts
(deliberating, negotiating, conferring, debating, and – a crucial sub-set –
pleas at law, litigation, legal judgements); and the presentation of speech
acts (deportment, demeanour, appropriate performance). History is *abasem*.
The word combines *asem* with the verb *ba* (to occur) to give the sense of 'a
recitation of happenings'. Other terms for history are *abakɔsem*, which is a
recounting of specific occurrences ('these matters but not those'); and
atetesem, which unites *asem* with the adverb *tete* (connoting antiquity). It
will be apparent that for the Asante it is communication – the quiddities of
accounting for oneself by rendering account to others in speech situations –
that constructs and grounds narratable histories that resource and propel
narrative selves. The proverb *tete ka asom* – lit. 'the past remains in the ears'
– is intended as a mnemonic of the Asante men and women who articulated
that past by speaking and listening to it. This maxim is commonly rendered
in print as 'tradition endures'. But this misses the point. It aims to objectify
the fluid process of a continuous making in speech to the fixed closure of an
established record in time. In brief, it is the literate culture's view of its oral
counterpart.

   Communicating by speaking and listening – the edifice of orality – has a
significance in the Asante structuring of reality that is so fundamental that
its implications go to the heart of cultural practice. To this day Asante
people, now long familiar with the instrumental and other advantages of
literacy, persist in the view that writing is somehow inauthentic, a form of
communication that transgresses against norms and values. Writing
(*kyerew*) is cognate with the idea of things being parcelled out until nothing
is left (cf. *gu ne nkyerew*: 'it is all used up and finished'). The self on paper is
similarly apportioned and consumed. This is antithetical to a realisation of
those narratable histories that enable the narrative self to flourish in a milieu
of talking and hearing. It is felt that writing is not really the way in which to
tend the best interests of oneself, for such necessary husbandry depends
upon face-to-face communication with others – and others too rely upon
one's own accessibility and participation in their endeavours. This is the
very bedrock of Asante cultural praxis. So it is unsurprising that Asante
attitudes towards literacy – that standard-bearer of sedulous modernity –
continue to be conditioned by a hermeneutics of suspicion. Texts can and
do engage readers, but exploring their possibilities is accomplished by
shifting the ground of interpretation from writing to speaking and listening.
A comment by Yankah is to the point here. 'The general mistrust of Euro-
mediated communication is evinced', he notes,

> by its perception and depiction by tradition in rather derogatory
> terms. Let's take a look at indigenous references to the modern media.

The Akan of Ghana refer to the telephone as, *ahomatrofo*, meaning 'liar, the tale bearing wire,' 'string or wire that conveys lies, unverified information,' not to be trusted, unreliable, dealing in falsehoods. This implies that, fast travelling news, whose veracity cannot be checked, is not trustworthy.

Similarly, 'newspaper,' called *koowaa krataa*, literally means 'loose-tongued paper,' 'tabloid,' gossip. *Koowaa* is derived from *ka no waa* as in *mekaa no waa*, 'I spoke in jest, don't take me seriously.' The general suspicion of, or dispreference for, non-indigenous modes or channels of communication may also be seen in the general word for 'foreign language': *apotɔfoɔkasa*, implying a language hurriedly improvised for ad hoc use; lacking permanence or authenticity. To speak a foreign language itself is, *potɔ*, 'mix, craft, improvise.' Thus euro-mediated language and communication cannot be substituted for pure and pristine indigenous language, devolving on the spoken word and face-to-face communication, which rely on multi-sensory experience for the encoding and decoding of meaning.[62]

It is such considerations that help make sense of the issues at stake in my account of the discussion about the Koa. The protagonists in that debate were engaged in abstracting the Bible and indigenising it to understanding and use. Now procedures of this sort are widely reported from Africa as elsewhere, but their transparency cannot and should not be presumed.[63] Commentators have tended to look at only one side of this coin – the management of understanding and use in superstructural contexts described by synergies of belief and perceptions of advantage. These are important perspectives. But they would be enhanced and enriched if attention was paid to reconstructions of understanding *for* and use *as* in infrastructural contexts grounded in the recuperated historical record of specific cultures. It is a matter for regret that issues of understanding and use (like much else) in African societies are still the subject of a presentist anthropology that pays lip service to history in depth while failing to explore it. Now I have no desire to go over ground already covered, so let me say only the following to sum up what can be deduced from situating the exemplary tale of the Koa in its Asante historical context. In the arguments deployed by my interlocutors in the Suntreso house a panoply of crucial Asante cultural readings was brought into play: the siting of the self between poles of reference and inference; the drive to define the grounds of community and identity by a shared witnessing to then and now; the quest to make a narratable history to resource and propel the narrative self; the privileging of orality as the apposite medium for reconfiguring the written word so as to create understanding *for* and use *as* in evolving temporal and personal contexts; and the investment of value in the face-to-face encounter, not only the forum of a necessary sociability but also the crucible of that endlessly recursive speaking and listening through which Asante lives are made and remade. The presences made so vividly manifest in Suntreso are kin to those others that come forward to meet us from the rich complexities of the Adeɛbeba testimonies.

The story I have told of Adeɛbeba lives is not to be summed up. The conclusions drawn from evidence analysed are interwoven with the discussion throughout the text. That said, I think it appropriate to end with some reflections upon general matters foregrounded and given salience by the approach I have adopted and the materials I have used. In the course of writing this book I have been reminded of the importance of an adequately documented historical perspective and of the problems attendant upon its absence. At one level I am simply grateful that the record concerning Asante does happen to furnish an opportunity for detailed historical investigation over an extended period of time. One simple purpose I set myself was to try to write something that did not scant the precolonial period by treating it as an ethnographic prologue to the twentieth century. Another was to attempt to recuperate the lives of ordinary Asante people in as much historical detail as the evidence would allow and sustain. I aimed for a microhistorical texture that complicated together empirical density with analytical rigour – but with the former directing and driving the latter. My account seeks to deploy theory in support of historical evidence; it tries to avoid the pitfall of using theory to fill the place of that evidence where it is lacking.

Just as the quantity and quality of historical evidence varies between societies, so too do the approaches adopted by scholars of those societies. But I think there are dangers in straying very far from a grounded history and the perspective it affords. Now, it would be a very simple matter to identify and criticise resolutely presentist analyses of African societies in which an underexplored historical dimension exists (where it exists at all) as little more than a kind of background music to the stirring orchestral thunder of contemporary relevance (I am tempted to but resist putting these last two words in inverted commas). It would be simple, but it would also be facile; like the poor proverbially, the *bien pensant* is always with us. Instead, I want to look at work that attempts with serious intent to address the difficulties raised by a paucity of historical evidence.

In a recent paper that is at once deeply informed and extremely subtle, Jane Guyer has suggested that in Equatorial Africa

> in the centuries before its conquest social and cultural life was far more inventive from day to day than we can now easily imagine, steeped as old intellectual frameworks are in the equation between non-literacy and a repetitive 'tradition,' and framed as our own social life has been by the organized repositories, routinized access and incremental growth patterns that ensure order and longevity to our own legacies of

knowledge. Alongside the kinship, kingship and cult of classic social organization analysis, attentive reading of African sources suggests another and different social project: the creation of variety amongst people in their skills and intellectual reach, not only reproducing a finite set of known roles and functions with respect to 'a system of thought' but also endorsing a constant and volatile engagement on its boundless frontiers. People's idiosyncratic capacities for living on one or another of those frontiers were not conceptualized or selectively cultivated as if they were simply human raw material to be shaped in the cultural image and slotted into corresponding social roles, nor as a natural source of skills in the interested pursuit of purpose, or agency ... Rather, the human potentiality for originality and difference with respect to particular skills and domains of knowledge – those qualities consigned in western thought to the natural categories of tempera-ment and talent – were created, fostered, accessed and mobilized by social and cultural processes that escape our current modernist analytical categories for a division of labour in society or a sociology of knowledge. These were, in their own way, information societies.[64]

I have quoted this at some length because it forms the preamble to a *tour de force* of sustained argument and deliberation. In what follows Guyer has interesting and complex things to say about people and knowledge, and about the possibilities and problems of four disciplinary perspectives – demography, art history, anthropology and philosophy. However, a close reading suggests that throughout the paper the author is performing a balancing act with great skill and ingenuity. The argument is a tightrope stretched across a chasm – the scarcity of detailed historical evidence of a directly empirical kind concerning the societies discussed. To which comment it might be legitimately retorted: what then is to be done when historical processes can be deduced but not so readily documented? I have no answer to this question, but I do have a caution concerning it. I have selected Guyer as exemplar here quite deliberately (although there are other possible candidates), because work like hers is genuinely innovative and thought provoking in its attempt to bring a plurality of approaches to bear upon deficits in the historical evidence. This is a fine and fertile scholarship. But it resurrects now venerable questions about articulations between ethnography and history, and the extent to which the former can supply the place of the latter.[65]

Such questions become most urgent in those determinedly presentist writings that can be read as contributions to an emerging 'moral historio-graphy' of Africa.[66] This project is different from the one customarily associated with historians. In this 'moral historiography' of Africa the vision of practitioners is fixed, not on how specific presents were shaped by particular pasts, but rather upon the problems of the anxious present itself.

From this perspective history is summoned up in bits and pieces, and only inasmuch as it can be used to endorse clamant arguments about contemporary crises in Africa or current disputations in writing about Africa. This can sometimes descend into the bathos of autobiographical confession, but more prevalent is the yearning attempt to manufacture a 'moral historiography' in which solace for the various pessimisms surrounding Africa's present is sought in interestedly partial readings of its past. Forty years ago the infant historiography of Africa struggled to make headway against the intransigencies of colonial and racial prejudice. Such attitudes persist and still have to be fought, but today and in addition the 'moral historiography' of Africa sometimes seems in danger of burdening the continent's past (or at least some selected understandings of it) with the insupportable task of redeeming the present and promising the future. African historiography was and is about the wish to explore and explain the past in all of its exhilarating but also sometimes sobering detail. African 'moral historiography' appears to see in that same wish only the possibility of wish-fulfilment. These two agendas are distinct in principle and should remain so in practice.

At the very last then, what absences still elude the historian's research? The most significant is something that perhaps must always lie just beyond the grasp of the most scrupulous *microstoria* or the most nuanced *Alltagsgeschichte*. Simply, it is very difficult indeed to access historical lives – Adeɛbeba lives – at any level of contemplative inwardness (*Innerlichkeit*). The effort to gain a purchase on this constituent of the human defeated even Benjamin, who ended by mystifying it as unrecoverable 'magical experience'.[67] Thus, we have no way to assess how any Adeɛbeba person felt about the implications of living one particular life rather than another. Neither can we read the ledgers in which Adeɛbeba people submitted the content of their lives to their own inner judgement. In this regard we can do no more than bear in mind the emotional quiddity of each and every Adeɛbeba life, while at the same time acknowledging – with Benjamin – that recuperating this is beyond historical reach.

ABBREVIATIONS

ARA	Algemeen Rijksarchief (The Hague, Netherlands)
ASSB	Ashanti Social Survey Papers (Birmingham University, UK)
ASSB/1	Ashanti Social Survey Papers (Birmingham University, UK) 'Adeɛbeba Household Survey'
ASSB/2	Ashanti Social Survey Papers (Birmingham University, UK) 'Interviews and Conversations about the Adeɛbeba Household Survey'
ASSC	Ashanti Social Survey Papers (Cambridge University, UK)
BMA	Basel Mission Archives (Basel, Switzerland)
GNAA	Ghana National Archives (Accra, Ghana)
GNAK	Ghana National Archives (Kumase, Ghana)
IKAP	I. K. Agyeman Papers (Kumase, Ghana)
KCC	Kumase City Council Papers (Kumase, Ghana)
KITLV	Koninklijk Instituut voor Taal-, Land-, en Volkenkunde (Leiden, Netherlands)
KMA	Kumase Metropolitan Assembly (Kumase, Ghana)
KTC	Kumase Town Council Papers (Kumase, Ghana)
MRO	Manhyia Record Office (Kumase, Ghana)
MRO/HA	Manhyia Record Office (Kumase, Ghana). 'The History of Ashanti', ms (with letters and accompanying notes) prepared by a Committee of Traditional Authorities under the Chairmanship of *Asantehene* Osei Agyeman Prempeh II, n.d. (but in the 1940s)
MSP	Manwere Stool Papers (Kumase, Ghana)
OMP	Old Manhyia Palace (Kumase, Ghana: now the Manhyia Palace Museum)
OMP/AP	Old Manhyia Palace (Kumase, Ghana). Papers of the *Asantehene* Agyeman Prempe (1888–1931)
OMP/OAPII	Old Manhyia Palace (Kumase, Ghana). Papers of the *Asantehene* Osei Agyeman Prempeh II (1931–70)
OMP/Fry and Drew (1945)	Old Manhyia Palace (Kumase, Ghana). E. Maxwell Fry (FRIBA) and Jane B. Drew (FRIBA), 'Draft Town Planning Scheme for Kumasi: Report', submitted to the Office of the Town Planning Adviser to the Resident Minister, West Africa (August 1945), with notes and comments by the *Asantehene* Osei Agyeman Prempeh II
PRO	Public Record Office (London, UK)
RH, CRP	Rhodes House, Colonial Records Project Papers (Oxford University, UK)
RSRP	Robert Sutherland Rattray Papers (Royal Anthropological Institute, London)
RU	Rhodes University, Cory mss (Grahamstown, South Africa)
USTK	University of Science and Technology (Kumase, Ghana)
WMMS	Wesleyan-Methodist Missionary Society Archives (SOAS, London University, UK)

NOTES

CHAPTER 1 INTRODUCTION

1. Fortes, Steel and Ady (1947).
2. See Rathbone (1992), I, xxxi–lxxviii for British policy.
3. Consult Meyerowitz, Amu, Fortes, Clarke and Mumford (1937) for the original scheme and Fortes (1974 and 1974a) for a retrospect. Kuklick (1991) and Goody (1995) give different interpretations of the anthropological project.
4. ASSB, CCA to Fortes, dd. Kumase, 6 March 1945.
5. Fortes, Steel and Ady (1947). Compare ASSB, Fortes to Saunders, dd. Kumase, 15 July 1945.
6. Fortes, Steel and Ady (1947); ASSB, 'Register of African Field Staff', 30 January 1946; R. Steel, Personal Communications, 22 December 1988 and 20 March 1991.
7. ASSB, Steel to Frimpong, dd. Oxford, 3 March and 7 August 1949. Compare Kyei (1992), 1–6.
8. R. Steel, Personal Communication, 13 December 1990.
9. Ibid.
10. Ibid., 20 March 1991. See too ASSB, Port Traffic Manager to West African Institute, dd. Takoradi, 11 August 1947 and Gold Coast Department of Agriculture to Steel, dd. Aburi, 2 February 1948.
11. Fortes (1948; 1954).
12. See for instance Steel (1952) and Fortes (1969; 1970; 1977; 1978). Barnes (1971) has acute comment.
13. R. Steel, Personal Communication, 2 April 1992.
14. Ibid., 22 December 1988; M. Fortes, Personal Communication, 11 April 1980.
15. I thank my friend and colleague Nana Arhin Brempong (Professor Kwame Arhin) for conversation about the changing face of Kumase.
16. The dynamics involved are variously discussed in Arhin (1983; 1999); McCaskie (1980; 1995); Wilks (1975 [1989]; 1977, 1993).
17. BMA, D–31.1,25, 'Asante' by A. Ph. Bauer, dd. Kumase, 10 May 1907. Compare this with Gold Coast 1:125,000, Sheet 72.K.1 Coomassie (Kumase), prepared by the Director of Surveys, 30 August 1907.
18. ASSB, Testimony of Kwadwo Toase, December 1945.
19. For the 1945 figure see OMP/Fry and Drew (1945).
20. KMA, KTC Papers (1943–54), 'Housing in Kumasi: B. Registration', October 1945. For housing since 1945 consult Tipple (1987); Tipple and Willis (1991); Tipple and Owusu (1994); Tipple, Korboe and Garrod (1997).
21. ASSC, 3.2 'Houses at Kumasi'; ASSB, 'A Conversation with Mr Gyima of Asokore', 1946. For context see McCaskie (1986).
22. ASSB, 'Mr Nyantakyi's House at Kumasi', 1945.

23. Amakom affairs are reconstructed from MRO, AK3, 'Kumasi Villages: Correspondence (Amakom, Bomso, Dichemso) 1930–40'; GNAK, ARG 3/3/ 17/9, 'Kumasi Town Layout 1924–32'; OMP/OAPII, *Asantehene* Osei Agyeman Prempeh II to *Amakomhene* Kwaku Ata, 11 June and 7 August 1936.
24. See RH, CRP, Mss. Brit. Emp. s.344 (Papers of Sir Charles Henry Harper), 'Some Notes on Coomassie Stools and on the Coomassie Council: A Memorandum by CCA Harper', dd. Kumase, 24 April 1923; GNAA, ADM 11/1/1902, 'Chief Commissioner (Ashanti): Diary 1919–22.' Consult Tordoff (1965) for the administrative context and Wilks (2000) for a suggestive discussion.
25. Gold Coast and Ashanti, Kumasi Lands Ordinance, Cap. 145 (1943), Section 3.
26. KMA, 'Interim Plan (to 2005): Kumasi Housing', dd. 1990. For a very recent discussion see Sinai (1998).
27. Sɔkɔban used to be famous for its palm oil.
28. Government of Ghana, *The Report of the Commission of Enquiry into the Affairs of the Kumasi City Council* (1968), Part VIII, 111–12.
29. See McCaskie (1976a; 1980a).
30. Fortes (1978a); Social Science Research Council (UK), 'Kinship Organization in Cocoa Production among the Ashanti, 1945 to the Present', by M. Fortes and V. Ebin (Final Report 667:390, January 1980).
31. R. Steel, Personal Communications, 11 November 1987; 3 March 1988.
32. Ibid., 13 June and 22 December 1988.
33. Revel (1995), 46.
34. Levi (1988), xvi. See further Muir and Ruggiero (1992). For Africa compare Viti (1998). I thank Pierluigi Valsecchi and Fabio Viti for discussion and insights.
35. Consult the journal *Quaderni storici*. I thank Chris Wickham for help with queries about Italian historiography.
36. Lepetit (1993; 1995); Revel (1996).
37. Clear influences here are F. Barth, M. de Certeau and P. Ricoeur.
38. Lepetit's phrase echoes Marc Bloch. Compare here the perspective of Chartier (1998), 213–33.
39. Joas (1985); Schutz (1964; 1970; 1973).
40. Lüdtke (1995), 3–40.
41. Medick (1995), 41–70.
42. Ginzburg and Poni (1985); Ginzburg (1993); Schulze (1994). I thank Martin Schaffner for drawing my attention to Ginzburg's essay.
43. Medick and Sabean (1984); Sabean (1998).
44. Exceptions here include the markedly different approaches of Cohen (1985); Cohen and Atieno Odhiambo (1989; 1992); White (1987); Van Onselen (1996).
45. A rhetorical question, for I am not alone. See Peel (1994; 1995).
46. Symptomatic essays are collected together in Comaroff and Comaroff (1993; 1999).
47. Radcliffe-Brown (1952), 192.
48. Rosaldo (1986), 93.
49. Brodsky (1995), 275.

CHAPTER 2 ADEƐBEBA LIVES: THE NINETEENTH CENTURY

1. MRO/HA, 10.7.
2. Ricketts (1831), 120. See too PRO, CO 267/74, Purdon to Bathurst, dd. Accra, 10 August 1826.
3. GNAK, D.538, 'Traditional History of the Divisions: History of Ahuren narrated by Ohene Ata Gyamfi and Others', n.d.

4. For orientation see Wilks and McCaskie (1977).
5. See McCaskie (1995; 1995a) and also OMP/OAPII, H. Owusu Ansa to *Asantehene* Osei Agyeman Prempeh II, 11 and 17 October 1940.
6. MRO/HA, 10.7.
7. MRO, Asantehene's Divisional Court 'B', Court Record Book 52, 26 June–31 October 1950, *Manwerehene Kwasi Brantuo* vs. *Kyei Tra*, commenced 6 September 1950, evidence of Kwasi Brantuo.
8. *The West African Herald* (Accra), 2nd series, 4/7, 13 June 1871. For context and discussion see McCaskie (1995a; 1998).
9. MRO/HA, 11.6. See Wilks, Levtzion and Haight (1986) for the Gonja perspective.
10. RU, Cory Ms. 15,104, 'Journal of the Rev. George Chapman, 1843–1857', entry dd. Kumase, 3 June 1844.
11. Ibid., entry dd. Kumase, 15 July 1844.
12. GNAA, ADM 11/1/1338, Case EP 200/1924, 'Report of an Enquiry into the Tribal Organization of the Adonten Abrempon of Kumasi', 1925, 68–9, evidence of Kumase *Akyeamehene/Domakwaehene* Kwasi Apea Nuama. I reproduce the full text of the original but have broken it down into discrete episodes to ease comprehension.
13. The quoted material concerning the hunt is from WMMS, W. West to General Secretaries, dd. Cape Coast, 9 June 1862 (with an account of his residence in Kumase, 17 March to 22 April 1862). West's description of 'hunting the elephant' on 30 March 1862 is the only extant eyewitness account from the nineteenth century. But he did not name the 'old chief' who was the aspirant *ɔbirɛmpɔn* on this occasion.
14. Apart from diverse oral materials my reconstruction of the matter of the Adeɛbeba/Adeɛmmra lands draws chiefly upon the following: MRO, Kumasihene's Tribunal, Civil Record Book 6, 22 January–8 May 1928 and Civil Record Book 7, 8 May–13 September 1929, *Atasomaaso odekuro Kwaku Adae* vs. *Adeɛmmra odekuro Kofi Adu*, commenced 13 February 1929; ibid., Civil Record Book 10, 5 June–1 October 1930, *Ankobiahene Kwame Kusi* vs. *Kwasi Kobi of Santaase*, commenced 23 June 1930; ibid., Akwamu Tribunal, File 12, *Aboabo odekuro Kwame Tawia* vs. *Yaw Tia*, commenced 25 June 1938; ibid., File A.113, 'Correspondence concerning the Adiebeba lands belonging to the Manweri Stool', 1937–43; OMP/AP, No. 20, 9/29, E. Prempeh to DC (Kumase), 26 March 1929; ibid., No. 27, 4/30, E. Prempeh to DC (Kumase), 4 April 1930.
15. BMA, D-20.4,5, N.V. Asare, 'Asante Abasɛm (Twi Kasamu)', 1915.
16. My understanding here has benefited from talks over the years with *Manwerehene* Nana Kwabena Boaten; *Asabihene* Asabi Boakye II; *Ɔkyeame* Boakye Tenten (Kofi Apea Agyei); I. K. Agyeman; Anthony Kwadwo; Osei Bekere; Yaw Twimasi; the Amoateng family, and particularly John, Nana Yaw and Louisa; and C. Osei Bonsu, who responded to a number of written queries. I am grateful to them all and most especially to the late *Asantehene* Opoku Ware II, who made it possible for me to raise the matter of Adeɛbeba with members of the Ashanti Regional House of Chiefs. Crucial information and key contacts came from these encounters.
17. ASSB/1 and ASSB/2. Both these files contain a miscellany of data. I cite individual documents contained within each of them by title and date where these were provided by ASS researchers. Where there is no title I assign the document to the name of the person giving the testimony; where there is no date I record the document as 1945–6. I have followed the same procedure with regard to ASSB materials not filed in ASSB/1 or ASSB/2. See further in this

present context MRO, K/33, 'Kumasi Village Affairs: Letters, Documents etc. on the Affairs of Adiebeba', 11/31, Testimony (sworn and notarised) of Yaw Antwi Abayie, 11 March 1951.

18. ASSB/2, Testimony of Kwadwo Konkoma, 22 January 1946; see McCaskie (1980a; 1995a) for context and discussion.

19. See McCaskie (1994) for the Kwaso Deduaku twins.

20. ASSB, 'What Yow Ankama Says About His Life', 1945–6.

21. Nora (1984) has discussion relevant to these matters.

22. ASSB, Testimony of Akosua Ababio, 1945–6; for Atasomaaso see GNAK, D.1171, CCA F.C. Fuller to *Adumhene* Asamoa Toto, dd. Kumase, 13 March 1906.

23. ASSB, 'How the Village of A[deɛbeba] Grew', 1945–6.

24. 'K.B.' may be Kwabena (Asare?) Boakye, a Public Works Department carpenter who supplied information in other contexts.

25. ASSB, 'How the Village of A[deɛbeba] Grew', 1945–6; ASSB/1, 'The Farming Year as Told by Mr. Ed. Otcheri and Benjamin Kwansa', 9 November 1945.

26. ASSB/2, Testimonies of Kwabena Donko, 9 and 22 January 1946.

27. MRO, File C/1003, 'Miscellaneous Letters (Stool Lands in the Kumasi Division)', *Manwerehene* Kwasi Brantuo to *Asantehene* Osei Agyeman Prempeh II, dd. Kumase, 3 June 1951, enclosing the (sworn and notarised) Testimonies of Kwabena Donko, Afua Ntim and Afua Amoakwaa.

28. Some accounts say that Sakyiamaa took leave of her senses and only recovered them when Kwabena Domfe killed the crocodile.

29. MRO, Ankobia Clan Tribunal, Case 7/33, *Kwadwo Buaben per Abena Akruwaa* vs. *Kwasi Heman*, commenced 8 August 1932 (continuation and judgment not found). Kwadwo Buaben was later an ɔkyeame to the *Manwere* stool.

30. ASSB, 'Kweku Adadie Speaks Forth His Mind', 1945–6; ASSB/2, 'What Mr. A[dade] Knows About Life in the Village', 1945–6.

31. ASSB/2, 'Talking With Miss Adelaide Oppong', 1945–6.

32. ASSB, 'The Story of an Unsuitable Marriage', January 1946. Afua Tweneduaase's mother Yaa Akumaa was a cloth trader. After her Santaase husband died about 1935 she married Abraham Dickson, a Fante who owned a transport business and who built the Wesleyan-Methodist chapel at Boko west of Kumase. 'Reverend' Dickson was well known in Kumase as a musician, choirmaster and bandleader. He died on 6 March 1957, the day that Ghana became independent. For the royal *nhenkwaa* at Santaase see OMP/AP, No. 17, 4/27, E. Prempeh to DC (Kumase), 11 July 1927.

33. See Kyei (1992) on marriage as an institution.

34. ASSB/2, Testimony of Yaa Afeni, 20 December 1945; MRO, KU/89, 'Letters, mainly concerning Kumawu Affairs', Yaa Fena to Nana Brentuo Kyiriapim, dd. Odumase and Kumase, 10 October and 22 November 1934.

35. ASSB/2, 'Kofi Kwaakye', 4 September 1945; ibid., Testimonies of Kofi Manu and Amma Tiriwaa, 1945–6.

36. ASSB, 'Talking About Childhood: Reminiscences Recorded by I[saac] Amankwah', 1945–6.

37. Ibid.

38. Ibid., 'Life and Times of Mr. [Kwaku] Agyemang', December 1945.

39. MRO, File C/1003, 'Miscellaneous Letters (Stool Lands in the Kumasi Division)', *Manwerehene* Kwasi Brantuo to *Asantehene* Osei Agyeman Prempeh II, dd. Kumase, 3 June 1951. See McCaskie (1998a) for a discussion of legal process.

40. This episode gave rise to a song. J. C. Frimpong heard it performed but did not record the words. See ASSB, JCF[rimpong] 'Fieldwork Notebook', 1945–6.

41. ARA, NBKG 721, De Heer to Elias, dd. Kumase, 17 December 1865; KITLV, Ms. H.509, 'Aanhangsel: Extract uit het journaal gehouden te Comassie door eenen tapoeier [P. de Heer]', entry dd. Kumase, 7 September 1866; MRO, No. 71, 'Affairs of Adiebeba', Yaw Tia, Kofi Pon, Kwaku Kankama et al. to *Asantehene*, 3 February 1950; MSP, 'A Great Day in [the] History of Manwere', prepared by Silas Boateng, n.d. (but 1941–3), enclosing 'An Account of Stool Histories and Regalia by KA [*Asramponhene ɔheneba* Kwadwo Afodwo].'

42. The *Manwerehene* Nana Bafuo Kwabena Boaten who told me this in 1976 had personalised stationery in which he was named 'Manwere Brentuo' beneath a crest showing a stool surmounted by a bunch of (treasury) keys with the motto 'Yeda Onyame Ase' (*yɛda nyame ase*: 'we thank God') inscribed below.

43. KITLV, Ms. H.509, 'Aanhangsel: Extract uit het journaal gehouden te Comassie door eenen tapoeier [P. de Heer]', entry dd. Kumase, 28 May 1867.

44. See McCaskie (1989; 2000) for discussion.

45. MRO/HA, 12.3–4.

46. MSP, 'History of Manwere Stool from the Beginning to the Present Day prepared by Y[aw] K[umaa] [the *Manwerehene* Kwasi Brantuo IV] and His Elders', n.d. (but 1942–6).

47. C.938, *Correspondence Relating to Ashanti 1901* (1902), Nathan to Chamberlain, dd. Kumase, 19 March 1901, enclosing No. 3, List 'Y' (Revision of Resident's List 'B', Leaders of Rising in Ashanti), No. 26, Kwoku Krah.

48. OMP, 'Kumasi Stool Affairs: Evidence on the Establishment of Clan Tribunals, Ankobia, 1927–8', Testimonies submitted by *Manwerehene* Kwasi Kyerapem, *Kumawuhene* Kwame Affram, Kyirapatre *odekuro/Ankobia Mmagyegyefoɔhene* Yaw Tuo, dd. Kumase, 3–6 April 1927; ibid., 'Position of the Kumasi Stools', a sworn deposition made by *Akyeamehene/Domakwaehene* Kwasi Apea Nuama, dd. Kumase, 3 May 1927. See McCaskie (1984) for context.

49. ASSB, 'The God Atweri: A Talk with Benjamin Osei Addai', 1945–6; ibid., 'What Mr A[dade] Knows About Village Life', 1945–6. Wilks (1975 [1989]), 492–665 is a *tour de force* of narrative writing and an indispensable guide to the period 1873–1901. Another perspective is provided by Lewin (1978).

50. ASSB/2, Testimonies of Amma Sewaa, Kwadwo Konkoma and Yaa Sakyiwaa, 1945–6.

51. Ibid., Testimony of Kwabena Donko, 22 January 1946.

52. This geographical reconstruction is based on a wide range of sources. Fundamental is MRO/HA, 15.1 ff. and enclosure, 'The History of Edweso'.

53. ASSB, 'A Talk with Kofi Kwaakye', 1945–6; ibid., 'Notes Taken on a Tour: Pramiso, Amansie Jachie, Sawia, Chirapatre, etc., etc. by B. Otchere', October 1945; OMP/AP, No. 71, 57/29, 'Gyasi Stool', E. Prempeh to DC (Kumase), 13–27 July 1929 ; MRO, Kyidomhene's Tribunal, Letter and Document Book 4, *Ampabamehene* Kwadwo Mensah to *Asantehene* Osei Agyeman Prempeh II and *Akyempemhene ɔheneba* Owusu Afriyie, 27 July and 7 August 1937.

54. MSP, 'A Great Day in [the] History of Manwere', prepared by Silas Boateng, n.d. (but 1941–3), enclosing 'An Account of Stool Histories and Regalia by KA [*Asramponhene ɔheneba* Kwadwo Afodwo]'; for some account of the later history of Akyampon Panin's remains see BMA, D–1.88,76, N.V. Asare, Annual Report of the Basel Mission in Kumase (1907), dd. Kumase, 29 February 1908.

55. OMP/AP, No. 17, 19/28, E. Prempeh to *Anamenakohene* Kwabena Dwoben, 11 November 1928.

56. ASSB, Testimonies of Adolphus Kwaku Boateng, Afua Agyampomaa and Yaw Daanani, 1945–6; for the evidence of Abena Akwaduo see ibid., 'Talking About Childhood: Reminiscences Recorded by I[saac] Amankwah', 1945–6.

57. Ibid., 'Life and Times of An Ashanti Gentleman: Sam. K. Baako', 1945–6.
58. OMP/AP, No. 33, 30/29, E. Prempeh to DC (Kumase), 12 August 1929, enclosing Abena Wono to *Kumasihene*, n.d. (but June 1929); MRO, Ankobia Clan Tribunal, A.19, 'Summaries of Matters Arising (Summonses, Correspondence etc. concerning Cases of Theft, Debt, Assault etc.), 1935–38', *Kwasi Pepra* vs. *Samuel Badu*, September–October 1938; ASSB/1, 'A Talk with Esther Abakwaah', 1946 (Esther Abakwaah was Kwasi Pepra's sister).
59. ASSB/1, Testimonies of Yaw Dabo, 11 and 13 October 1945. Apart from his Adeɛbeba food farm, Yaw Dabo also grew cocoa on land north of the Ofin river near Beposo west of Kumase.
60. ASSC, 9.66. The detailed autobiography recounted in this text is anonymous. But collateral evidence in ASSB/2 confirms the identity of the speaker as Yaw Firempon. His mother Yaa Gyebuaa of Nyeɛso was a daughter of Kwadwo Antwi of Adeɛbeba, who served as *ahenkwaa* to the *Asantehene* Kofi Kakari. Yaa Gyebuaa's full sister Amma Afrakumaa herself married in Adeɛbeba. In 1946 her aged daughter Yaa Amanfro described Yaw Firempon as 'my mother's sister's son, the only one'. In the text cited the speaker identified here as Yaw Firempon stated 'I was the only son of my mother.'
61. ASSB, Testimonies of J. K. Obeng, 1945–6. Compare Wilks (1993a), 262.
62. ASSB, Testimonies of Opoku Adade, 2, 3 and 7 January 1946. For Kofi Manwere see GNAK, ARG 6/2/50, 'Manwere Native Affairs 1943–5', Adeɛbeba *obaapanin* Amma Agyeman to *Asantehene*, 28 February 1944, enclosing 'Genealogy of Manwere Stool Families'.
63. For one account of Pataku's moneylending see MRO, Z/AC.1177, 'Kumasi Zongo 1928–36', Mallam Sulley Lagos to *Kumasihene*, 12 January 1934.
64. ASSB/2, Testimonies of Kwadwo Konkori and 'A.M.', 1945–6. 'A.M.' was a seamstress but her identity is unclear. The fullest listing of Asante barricades is in IKAP, 'The Golden Stool in Our Modern Age', a ms prepared by I. K. Agyeman on behalf of the Ashanti Kotoko Union Society on the 50th Anniversary of the Yaa Asantewaa War, n.d. (but 1950–1).
65. ASSB/1, Testimony of Afua Tweneboaa, 1945–6. Abena Akyiaa may have returned to Adeɛbeba at some later date. She is perhaps to be identified with the woman of the same name who tried to introduce the *ntoa* witch-finding shrine into Adeɛbeba in the 1920s and who went about challenging village women to confess using the *ntoa* formula, *ɔkwa yɛ dɛ aberewa wate* ('listen old woman, isn't life worth having?'). On *mmobomme* generally see Jones (1993).
66. ASSB, Testimony of Kwabena Dwumo, 7 October 1945. Kwabena Dwumo was over eighty when he supplied his recollections. He was then a widower who lived in Adeɛbeba but had a house at Ahensan. He was in business at one time with Kwabena Addai and in the 1910s–1920s he made money working as a goldsmith in Akuapem.
67. Ibid., 'What Mr E. Osei (Court Registrar) Has To Say about The Past and Present Times, written down by Seth Adjaye', 1945–6.
68. MSP, 'History of Manwere Stool from the Beginning to the Present Day prepared by Y[aw] K[umaa] [the *Manwerehene* Kwasi Brantuo IV] and His Elders', n.d. (but 1942–6); GNAK, D.2299, 'Jasiwa Stool Vacancy, 1937–9', J. Y. Kumah [the future *Manwerehene* Kwasi Brantuo IV] to *Asantehene*, dd. Medical Services Dept., Tamale, 17 January 1938. For the destoolment of Kwame Tua see ibid., ARG 1/2/1/3, 'Deposition of Chief Kwami Tua (from Gaasiwa Stool) by his Subjects' and for context see McCaskie (1992).
69. GNAK, ARG 1/2/1/50, 'Chief Kofi Nti: Subjects at Drobonsu 1907–17' should be added to the materials referenced in McCaskie (1976a). For Kumawu see Berry (1998).

70. ASSB, C. E. Osei to Fortes, dd. Kumase, 12 February 1946.
71. OMP/AP, No. 9, 4/26, Kwasi Kyerapem to E. Prempeh, 18 March 1925, enclosing 'A Petition of [*sic*] Relief from Your Humble Servant'. A more circumspect account is in MSP, 'History of Manwere Stool from the Beginning to the Present Day prepared by Y[aw] K[umaa] [the *Manwerehene* Kwasi Brantuo IV] and His Elders', n.d. (but 1942–6).
72. ASSB, 'A Talk with the Bosom Linguist Kwasi Fi (by J. C. Frimpong)', 5 September 1945.
73. Ibid., 'History of the descent of a Fetish. Kwabena of Adeebeba', 1945–6. See McCaskie (1995), 109–10 and 117.
74. Compare ASSB, 'A Tale by Mr. Afriyie', 1945–6, which reports that one Akwasi Afrifa was 'burned all over the body by his rejection by Dwemo', i.e. the *ɔbosom taa dwum* at Saawua. So severe were his injuries that he was brought to Kumase to be inspected by the *Asantehene* Osei Yaw (1823–34). But treatment failed and he died insane.
75. Ibid., 'A Talk with Kwasi Fi of Adeebeba', 1945–6; 'Kwasi Fi', August 1945; 'K[wasi] F[i] Talks of the A[deebeba] Fetish', August 1945; 'A Memory of Old Ashanti Days', 1945–6. Kwasi Fi was a crucial ASS informant. Naturally loquacious, he cast himself as the historian of his community and as an informed witness to the Asante past.
76. Ibid., 'A History of the Adiebeba Fetish by Kwasi Fi and Others', 18 October 1945; OMP, 'Otumfuo. The Potential of Ashanti Nation (with Notes on Royalty) by Bema Owusu Ansah', 1937 is an authoritative account of *tumi*; see too Akyeampong and Obeng (1995).
77. ASSB, 'History of the descent of a Fetish. Kwabena of Adeebeba', 1945–6.
78. Ibid., 'A Talk with Kwasi Fi of Adeebeba', 1945–6.
79. Ibid.
80. Amma Kyirimaa's second husband Mensa Kwakwa was also married to the *Kwasohemaa* Afua Tiaa Birago. See MRO, 'Mponoa Village Affairs 1939–44', *Kwasohene* Kwabena Asare Gyebi to Kumase Divisional Council, 11 December 1940.
81. ASSB, 'Kwasi Fi', August 1945.
82. Thus and tellingly, in ibid., 'A Talk with the Bosom Linguist Kwasi Fi (by J. C. Frimpong)', 5 September 1945, Amma Kyirimaa's brother stated that she was 'by the Fetish enabled to be often in two places at the same moment'.
83. On the importance of constructing a shrine to the specifications of its resident *ɔbosom* see ibid., 'Kwame Amoah, Priest of Dinkyini Kokobin Speaks of His Craft and Practices', 1945–6.
84. Thus, as Fortes once remarked to me, the Asante saw their 'gods' as being above but not beyond human social norms.
85. ASSB, 'A Talk with Kwasi Fi of Adeebeba', 1945–6.
86. Ibid., 'What an Ashanti Man (Yaw Oppong) Has To Say About the Fact of Witches in Village Life', 1945–6.
87. See McCaskie (1981) and in another context (1995), 123.
88. ASSB/2, Testimony of J. Agyeman Asare, 28 December 1945. This witness stated that when he was a child in Adeebeba his mother lodged a man and his wife from distant Atwidie near Bompata in Asante Akyem who had come to consult *taa kwabena bena* about their 'sad absence of children'. The couple had already visited a succession of shrines to no avail, most recently that of *ansa kobi* at Atonso.
89. ASSB, 'A History of the Adiebeba Fetish by Kwasi Fi and Others', 18 October 1945.

CHAPTER 3 ADEƐBEBA LIVES: CONTEXTUALISING COMMUNITY AND IDENTITY

1. The euphemism for this episode in Kumase royal tradition is *biribi* (lit. 'something (or other, of no importance)'). McCaskie (1995a) has a discussion of the use of such avoidance terms [*kwatisεm*]. See also Akyeampong (1999), 286–7.

2. ASSC, 8.23, 'Funeral Customs among the Akans', 1945–6. See too the explanatory account of 'carrying the corpse' (of the *ahenkwaa* Kwaku Nkansa of Asokwa) in OMP/AP, No. 38, 46/28, E. Prempeh to DC (Kumase), 12 May 1928.

3. ASSB, 'A History of the Adiebeba Fetish by Kwasi Fi and Others', 18 October 1945.

4. Ibid. and ASSB, 'The Shoemaker Kwabena Mensah', 2 May 1945. Kwabena Mensa was a son of Kofi Asare Bediako's mother's younger sister Abena Asianowaa.

5. The officer was presumably the Kumase cantonment magistrate Capt. H. A. Kortright who appears elsewhere in the Adeεbeba testimonies as 'Cartright' [*sic*]. MRO, Criminal Record Books Kumase, 1/2, Index 1902–10 contains a docket (No. 17 of 3 September 1908, initialled by Kortright) that records the discovery and identification of Kofi Asare Bediako's body. Ibid., Palaver Book Correspondence 1905–13, Hobart to Kortright, 19 September 1908, sanctions a continuation of the police investigation of the death. But ibid., Minute by C. H. Hobart DC (Kumase), 20 October 1908, closes the matter of 'Bedakoo' for lack of evidence and orders the transfer of all documents concerning it to the office of the cantonment magistrate. Unfortunately the relevant files have been misplaced since the 1950s; see GNAK, B3296, 'Transfer of Regional Office Records', Report by M. D. Gass (Asst. Regional Officer, Kumase), 27 April 1956. The reconstruction offered here would not have been possible without clues unearthed by the combined efforts of Thomas Aning, Gina and Greg Spencer, and Euphemia Wiredu. I am grateful to them all.

6. ASSB, 'A History of the Adiebeba Fetish by Kwasi Fi and Others', 18 October 1945.

7. Consult McCaskie (1986; 1986a; 1992a; 1995; 1998a).

8. See now Peel (2000).

9. Compare Goodman (1978).

10. Deleuze (1990); Deleuze and Guattari (1984; 1987).

11. Taylor (1995), 173–4. Consult too Taylor (1985; 1985a).

12. Brandom (1994), 636.

13. Ibid., 643.

14. ASSB, 'Abina Gyebi Confesses "Meye Obayifo" ("I am a Witch")', 7 December 1945; ibid., 'A Talk with the Bosom Linguist Kwasi Fi (by J. C. Frimpong), 5 September 1945. Kwasi Fi introduced the ASS researchers to Abena Gyebi who 'spoke openly of her bad deeds'.

15. Appiah (1990).

16. Ibid., 24.

17. GNAK, ARG 1/2/25/10, 'Conspiracy against Otumfuo Osei Agyeman Prempeh II, 1935–6' details consternation arising from the false allegation that the *Asantehene* was circumcised. See Tordoff (1965) and McCaskie (1998b) for context.

18. ASSB, W. Boateng to Fortes, 6 November 1945.

19. Ibid., 'Notes (taken by Steel) from the Records of the Chief Medical Officer, Kumasi.' By the 1940s the fashion for male circumcision had waned. See ibid., Saunders to Fortes, 11 March 1946 and ASSC, 8.62. For an excellent discussion of youth, fashion and rebellion see Akyeampong (1996), 47–69.

20. ASSB, 'What Mr. A[dade] Knows About Village Life', 1945–6.
21. ASSB/2, Testimonies of J. K. Obeng, 1945–6.
22. ASSB, 'What Yow Ankama Says About His Life', 1945–6.
23. Ibid., 'A Talk with the Bosom Linguist Kwasi Fi (by J. C. Frimpong)',
    5 September 1945.
24. Ibid.; ASSB/2, Testimonies of J. K. Obeng, 1945–6.
25. Brandom (1994). Compare Habermas (1984; 1987); Luhmann (1998); and
    Taylor (1989).
26. Wiredu (1996), 141.
27. Ibid., 139–40 and for the consistency of Wiredu's approach compare Wiredu
    (1980).
28. Gyekye (1997), 51–2. See further Gyekye (1987; 1988; 1996).
29. Compare the comment in McCaskie (1995), 102–3.
30. ASSB/1, Testimony of Kwaku Atuahene, 1945–6; ibid., 'A[dwowaa] Y[amoaa]
    and Others on Sex and Marriage', 1945–6.
31. ASSB, 'Homesickness for Village Life (in Ashanti of Today) (by Amos
    Mensah)', 1945–6.
32. Fortes (1974a), 32.
33. Horton (1983), 67 and 70.
34. ASSB, 'Talking About Childhood: Reminiscences Recorded by I[saac]
    Amankwah', 1945–6.
35. Gyekye (1987), 161.
36. ASSB/1, 'Ketewah Household' (with App. A, 'List of Members with Ages,
    Family Relations, Occupations, Incomes etc.'; App. B, 'The Life of Mr
    Ketewah'; App. C, 'Life in the Kumasi Household'; and 'Notes and Summary
    by RS[teel]'), 1946. The *Manwerehene* Kwasi Brantuo IV was called Yaw
    Kumaa prior to his installation and worked as a First Division Nurse in
    Government Hospitals at Tamale and Agogo. His education was paid for by
    sponsors who responded to appeals by his mother Amma Atakoraa. Kwaku
    Ketewa was one such sponsor. See MSP, 'History of Manwere Stool from the
    Beginning to the Present Day prepared by Y[aw] K[umaa] [the *Manwerehene*
    Kwasi Brantuo IV] and His Elders', n.d. (but 1942–6).
37. ASSB/1, 'Ketewah Household', App. B, 'The Life of Mr Ketewah.'
38. For different approaches to writing historical modernities see for example
    Appadurai (1996), Gumbrecht (1997) and Lukacs (1998). Two studies of
    contemporary witchcraft that are full of insights but that leave the reader
    wanting more historical depth are Geschiere (1997) and Meyer (1999).
39. Berman (1982).
40. See Habermas (1987a) and Passerin d'Entrèves and Benhabib (1996).
41. I owe the medical metaphor to Deleuze and Guattari (1987). Compare here the
    remark by Foucault in his inaugural *leçon* at the Collège de France (1970). The
    outlines of historically 'massive phenomena', he urged, could only be revealed
    by 'pushing to its extreme the fine grain of the event'. A surprising statement
    perhaps, and surprising too in a different way for Braudel, who was in the
    audience. See Foucault (1981), 68 and Eribon (1991), 213.
42. See Deleuze (1990) for axes and rhizomatic connectivities.
43. See Richards (1993) for the larger general context.
44. ASSB/2, Testimony of Kwadwo Asaaman, 30 November 1945.
45. See McCaskie (1976).
46. ASSB, 'The Midwife A[bena] A[santewaa]', 1945–6.
47. Cohn (1996) is exemplary in pursuit of such inscriptions.
48. See representatively Benjamin (1999); Bachelard (1936); Lefebvre (1981);

Bakhtin (1984); de Certeau (1997); Foucault (1980); Pred (1990; 1990a).
49. Gyekye (1997), 281.
50. For an instance of the historical effects of 'recursive modernities' consult Dayan (1995), Trouillot (1995) and Wilentz (1989).
51. Arhin (1983a; 1986); McCaskie (1992; 2000a).

CHAPTER 4 ADEƐBEBA LIVES: THE TWENTIETH CENTURY

1. On the railway see Colonial Reports (Annual), *Report on the Blue Book of the Gold Coast, Ashanti and the Northern Territories* (1903), 42–6; and consult Dickson (1969), 229–34.
2. ASSB/2, Testimonies of Afua Nsoro and Afua Dinkyim, 11 and 15 October 1945; ASSB, 'Christians [*sic*] Community (by E. Aboagye)', 1945–6.
3. ASSB, 'A Talk with Kwasi Fi of Adeɛbeba', 1945–6.
4. Ibid., 'A Tale by Mr. Afriyie', 1945–6; ASSB/2, Testimonies of Afua Nsoro, 11 and 15 October 1945; Fuller (1921), 224. For Yaw Kusi see MRO/HA, 15.58. It is widely recalled that he was driven mad because he presumed to wear the war coat of the mid-nineteenth-century *Nsumankwaahene* Domfe Ketewa.
5. Kay (1972), 135–8 and 176–93 is a useful summary.
6. In male folklore Mampon women were celebrated for their beauty and sexuality. They were impolitely if admiringly nicknamed *kwaadweaa* (after a decoction used to restore vaginal elasticity after frequent intercourse). Both Fortes and myself were assured that they 'drew up the knees' (that is were notably active sexual partners).
7. ASSB, 'His Marital History Recounted by Kweku Anti (taken down by J. C. F[rimpong])', 11 February 1946; compare ASSC, 9.63.
8. ASSB, 'Life of a Wanderer. Kwadjo Abanie Retells His Experiences of What Life Has Taught Him', January–February 1946.
9. See Arhin (1976–7; 1995) on 'the pressure of cash'.
10. ASSB, 'A Foodseller Y[aa] B[uoho]', 1945–6.
11. Austin (2001: in press). I thank Gareth Austin for sharing with me his unrivalled knowledge of the history of cocoa in Asante.
12. ASSB, 'Agriculture. Cocoa at Konongo: The 'Chief Farmer' Kwabina Bruku', 1945–6; ibid., 'Asafo Adjaye Ko', compiled from interviews with 'elders of Juabin, Konongo, Asokore, etc.' by M. Fortes, 1946. See Addo-Fening (1973; 1973a) for background.
13. ASSB, 'Coming of Cocoa Crop Into The Village (Notes by Ed. Okai)', January 1946. Edward Okai worked for the Forestry Department. He acted as guide/interpreter when Steel visited remote Asamama in the Obuase range south of lake Bosomtwe. See ibid., R. Steel, 'Notebook of a Tour (Kumasi–Bogyesango)', October 1945.
14. Ibid., 'Talking About Cocoa Farming', Testimony of K(ofi) N(yame), February 1946.
15. Ibid., Testimonies of B[enson] A[nane], February 1946.
16. Ibid. Compare ASSB, 'Mr Nyantakyi. His Views – "Money Lacking in Life Today"', n.d. (but recorded in Kumase, 1946).
17. For the larger picture consult Austin (1988; 1996; 1998) and Arhin (1978).
18. Beckett (1944), 71; compare Irvine (1969), 9.
19. ASSB, 'Talking About Cocoa Farming', Testimonies of K(wame) A(boagye), December 1945 and January 1946.
20. Ibid., 'Reasons For Indebtedness (Cocoa Farms)', 1945–6.
21. See McCaskie (1998c).

22. McCaskie (1986).
23. MRO, 166/32/V2, 'Correspondence relating to the Destoolment of Kwaku Dua
    Mampong, 1931–5', enclosing 'An Enquiry into Financial Affairs of the
    Mampong Stool (with a List of Stool Debts).' For context see McCaskie (1985).
24. ASSB, 'Reasons For Indebtedness (Cocoa Farms)', 1945–6.
25. ASSB/1, Testimony of Abena Afre, 30 September 1945.
26. For Kumase attitudes towards the remainder of Asante see McCaskie (1995),
    84–5; see too the discussion in Akyeampong (1996), 52.
27. ASSB, 'House D.117: Residential Survey (Notes on People Living There)',
    1945–6. For Adu Abankro see OMP/AP, No. 117, 81/28, E. Prempeh to
    Saawua odekuro Kwaku Agyeman, 21 March 1928.
28. ASSB, 'Living At Kumasi. Mr Antwi's Story of His Experiences', 9 January
    1946.
29. Brown (1972) and Donkoh (1994) discuss change in this period.
30. The name Kwaku Dwumo suggests that the famous manifestation of the dwumo
    ɔbosom at Kokofu played a role in the conception or birth of Kwabena Bonsu's
    father.
31. See McCaskie (1985) for Kwaku Dua Agyeman. ASSC, 3.1, 'Capture of
    Prempeh and Yaa Asantewaa War by ex-Mamponhene Kwaku Dua' and ASSC,
    'The Biography of Mansa [sic] Bonsu', both 1945–6, are autobiographical
    testimonies by him.
32. Kwabena Bonsu gave several accounts of his life. This quotation is from ASSC,
    9.66. More detailed versions are ASSB/2, Testimonies of Kwabena Bonsu, 19
    December 1945 and 3 February 1946; ASSB/1, 'Household Composition,
    Selected (With Biographical Returns)', No. 4 (Kwabena Bonsu), 1945–6;
    ASSB/2, 'Further Chat with K[wabena] B[onsu]', 1946.
33. Consult Patterson (1981).
34. For an example of the resurrection of rural claims to a more active participation
    in modern Asante life see Nana Akwasi Abayie Boaten I (1990).
35. ASSB, 'Opinion of a Contrasting Life in Town and Village', 1945–6. See too
    ASSB/2, Testimonies of Yaw Aprutwum, November 1945; ASSB/1, 'House-
    hold Organisation and Expenditure', No. 17 (Abina Murosah), 1945–6.
36. Compare Prendergast (1992).
37. BMA, D-20.4,5, N.V. Asare, 'Asante Abasɛm (Twi Kasamu)', 1915.
38. ASSB, 'The Kumasi Market (Survey Report) by Caroline A. Awua', 1945; ibid.,
    'A Notebook on Produce Sellers and Prices in Kumasi and Mamponten Markets
    by Caroline A. Awua', 1945; ibid., 'Notes on Markets (Kumasi) by F. V. Gyan
    Mante', 1946. For context see Clark (1994).
39. ASSB, 'Report on the Survey of Kumasi Market by Emily A. Selanor', 1946.
40. Ibid., 'Yaa Denteh the Kumasi Trader by E. Antwi-Barimah', 1945. OMP/AP,
    No. 91, 67/28, E. Prempeh to CCA, 21 December 1928 records Agyeman
    Prempe's own attempt to open a 'firm store'.
41. ASSB, 'Notebook of Statements Made by Village Dwellers (Adults and
    Schoolchildren) About the Kumasi Markets Situation, taken down (in English
    and Twi) by E. Selanor', November–December 1945.
42. Ibid., 'Yaa Denteh the Kumasi Trader by E. Antwi-Barimah', 1945.
43. Ibid., 'Onion Farming Family in A[deɛbeba]', No. 2 (Abina Asisiwah),
    15 November 1945.
44. Ibid., No. 6 (Fua (sic) Akroma), 19 November 1945 and No. 4 (Kojo Assamang),
    3 December 1945.
45. Ibid., 'Kwabena Mensah. A Gentlemen [sic] of Leisure', 1946.
46. ASSB/1, Testimony of Owusu Gyebi, October 1945.

47. ASSB, 'Notebook of Statements Made by Village Dwellers (Adults and Schoolchildren) About the Kumasi Markets Situation, taken down (in English and Twi) by E. Selanor', November–December 1945.
48. See the encounter with Kumase during the First World War of a child from remote Agogo as recounted in Kyei (n.d.), II, 27–36.
49. Consult Arhin (1983); compare Akyeampong (1996), 52.
50. Kyei (n.d.), II, 33. Consult Schivelbusch (1995) for discussion of the cultural impact of gas and electric lighting.
51. ASSB/2, Testimonies of Afua Nsoro, 11 and 15 October 1945; ASSB, 'Kwasi Fi', August 1945.
52. Appiah (1995), 33.
53. See Arhin (1974) for this text and a discussion of it.
54. ASSB, 'Notebook of Statements Made by Village Dwellers (Adults and Schoolchildren) About the Kumasi Markets Situation, taken down (in English and Twi) by E. Selanor', November–December 1945.
55. RSRP, Ms. Bundle 107, Notebook 3, 1809–10.
56. ASSB, 'Making The Farm. The Man and Woman's Part (Kwabina Buo)', 1946.
57. Ibid., 'Kwasi Fi', August 1945.
58. Ibid., 'The Matrimonial State (Talking It Over)', No. 11 (Yaw Tintin), 20 January 1946.
59. Ibid.
60. Indispensable work is now set out at length in Allman and Tashjian (2000).
61. See McCaskie (1981a); Allman (1996).
62. We have already encountered Afua Nimaako, originally from Heman and one of the founding pioneers of Adeɛbeba. Adu Asabi was a son of Afua Nimaako's daughter Amma Donko.
63. ASSB/1, 'Location, Size, Ownership of Cocoa Farms Surveyed', (copy of) Akosua Gyankumaa to Registrar, Asantehene's Native Court, 12 December 1937 (marked 'Particular of Claim').
64. Ibid., (copy of) Osei Agyekum et al. to Registrar, Asantehene's Native Court, 16 December 1937.
65. ASSB, 'The Matrimonial State (Talking It Over)', No. 14 (Yaa Prabon), 1945; No. 16 (Yaa Ankyewaa), 1946; No. 20 (Afua Dinkyim), 1946. In ASSB, 'Notes Taken on a Tour: Pramiso, Amansie Jachie, Sawia, Chirapatre, etc., etc. by B. Otchere', October 1945, a woman named Akua Sapon, encountered at Kyirapatre, claimed that she had been forced to leave Adeɛbeba after the death of her husband because she could no longer subsist there. See further Tashjian (1996).
66. ASSB/2, 'Women at A[deɛbeba] Talk Over Marriage and Sex Matter [sic] by C[aroline] A[wua] and G[race] A[champong]', 1945–6.
67. ASSC, 9.63.
68. See Akyeampong (2000); Akyeampong and Obeng (1995).
69. See Bataille (1991), II, for the relationship between sexual energy and consumption; and compare Dodd (1994), 154, on accumulation as an 'ideal of unfettered empowerment, of complete freedom to act and assimilate at will'. I thank Achille Mbembe for sending me back to Bataille, and Karin Barber for countless conversations about wealth, consumption and personhood.
70. ASSB, 'Witchcraft in This Present Day', 1945–6, and ASSC, 7.11 and 9.63.
71. ASSB, 'The Matrimonial State (Talking It Over)', No. 7 (Kwaku Frimpon Mensa), 1945; see ibid., C. Frimpon Mensa to Fortes, 27 January 1946 for this man's testimony on middle-class consumption.
72. ASSB, 'Talk with Wm. Otchere the Bridegroom and His Friends about Sex and Marriage (by M. Fortes)', 3 September 1945.

73. ASSC, 9.63; ASSB, 'Witchcraft in This Present Day', 1945–6; ibid., 'A Tale by Mr. Afriyie', 1945–6.
74. See Allman (1996a; 1997).
75. Consult Honneth (1995) and Honneth and Joas (1988); compare Habermas (1992), Taylor (1992) and Tugendhat (1986).
76. Consult McCaskie (1995a; 2000a).
77. McCaskie (1995), 88–95 and 247–50.
78. ASSC, 9.66.
79. For the *flâneur* see Benjamin (1999) on Baudelaire.
80. Kwabena Bonsu stated that the compensation demanded of him was variously £37, 'about' £40, or 'a big sum of money'.
81. ASSC, 9.66; see further the items listed at note 32 above.
82. This section is based on ASSB/2, '"Trials of Modern Life": Yaa Agyapong and Daughters Speak Of Their Difficulties' by E. S(elanor), 1945–6; ibid., Testimonies of Yaa Agyapon, Kwabena Amponsa and Abena Nsiah, 1945–6; ibid., 'Steps Taken To Groom Ashanti Girls To Accomplishing [*sic*] (The Education of Morality and Etiquette For The Female Of Modern Day)' by R(uth) O(wusu)-M(ensah), 1945–6.
83. Compare ASSC, 9.63 in which A.K. of K. informed J. C. Frimpong about the physical inspection and consequent approval or disapproval of girls undergoing *bragorɔ*.
84. The Fante rite was fashionable in colonial Kumase. It followed Asante fundamentals but curtailed ceremony, display and expenditure. But the customary nubility rites were still performed in Adeɛbeba after the events described here; see ibid. for Afua Pomaa's account of her 1945 celebration. Kyei (1992), 120–31, is a detailed account of what was involved.
85. This was a calculated insult, for *eye twa* can signify that something (e.g. a face) bears a scar, but it can also be inflected to mean that something is indeed the case. Afua Ntim was using the flexibilities of utterance to say that Akua Timpomaa was marked like a slave *and* that this assertion was unquestionably true.
86. See the maxim *atantanɛɛ nti na yɛ to ɔdɔnkɔ* ('we buy a slave for filthy work').
87. ASSB, 'History of the descent of a Fetish. Kwabena of Adeebeba', 1945–6; ibid., 'A Talk with the Bosom Linguist Kwasi Fi (by J. C. Frimpong)', 5 September 1945; ibid., 'Kwasi Fi', August 1945; ibid., 'K[wasi] F[i] Talks of the A[deɛbeba] Fetish', August 1945.
88. Ibid., 'A Talk with the Bosom Linguist Kwasi Fi (by J. C. Frimpong)', 5 September 1945.
89. See Sarpong (1977), 47–55, for *kyiribra*.
90. See OMP/OAPII, 'Gyasi In The History Of Ashanti Constitution', 1941, for some account of Kwabena Kokofu's influence.
91. ASSB, 'What An Ashanti Man K[ofi] M[anwere] Has To Tell About His Life And Times', 1945–6. For Kofi Manwere's other testimonies see ASSB/2, 'K[ofi] M[anwere]', 1946; ibid., 'The Troubled Soul of K[ofi] M[anwere] Come To His Peace At Last', 1946; ibid. 'Thought and Opinions of K[ofi] M[anwere] Told By Himself (An Ashanti Man Tells Out His Secret Thoughts)' 1946; ASSC, 9.66. See ASSB, 'Ayete Marriages', 1945–6; MRO, Court Record Books (Unaccessioned), *obaapanin Abena Afrah* vs. *Kwame Antohene*, 1958–9 is a detailed historical account of its workings. I am grateful to Amy Settergren, who located this file and supplied me with a copy of it.
92. ASSB, 'What An Ashanti Man K[ofi] M[anwere] Has To Tell About His Life And Times', 1945–6; ibid., 'The Troubled Soul of K[ofi] M[anwere] Come To His Peace At Last', 1946.

93. Ibid., 'A Talk with Kwasi Fi of Adeɛbeba', 1945–6, states that one of the wives of Yaw Firempon's father the Kumase *Mpaboahene* Kwame Gyabo was from Adeɛbeba. The woman is not identified, but she was a neighbour and perhaps a kinswoman of Amma Kyirimaa.

94. In the subsistence economy of precolonial rural Asante the phrase connoted 'food' in the literal sense. But in the monetised economy of colonial Asante *akɔnhama* became *akɔnhama sik*a ('subsistence money') or *adidi sik*a ('money with which to eat', commonly rendered as 'chop money').

95. The names Manwere and Abanase suggest a link with government. Manwere needs no explanation. For Abanase consult Wilks (1975 [1989]), 200–1 and 426–7; see also the summary account of Perrot (1999).

96. For *aberewa* see McCaskie (1981) and Gray (1994).

97. ASSB, 'A[kosua] P[okuaa] of A[deɛbeba] Gives Account of What She Saw And Did in Those Days When Kwabena Benna was Potential', 1945–6; ibid., 'A Sorrowful Matter (Trials and Tribulations)', 1945–6; ASSC, 9.66. Consult Copenhaver (1992) for Tat (the son of Hermes Trismegistus); and see Braffi (1984) and Agyemang (n.d.) for the hermetic tradition in Asante.

98. For *bra kunde* see GNAA, ADM 11/1679, 'Native Customs and Fetish 1908–1948', enclosing 'A Memorandum on Fetish Kundi', 1939–40.

99. See the items listed at note 91 above. My reconstruction is based on all of these sources. Kofi Manwere is also mentioned in testimonies given by his Adeɛbeba neighbours.

100. The sources do not name Yaw Firempon's associates in this context, but it is known that he was familiar with the wealthy and powerful Kumase *Adontenhene* Kwame Frimpon.

101. Consult Agyemang (n.d.) for Asante readings of the Books of Judah, Moses and Zebulon in the *Pseudepigrapha*.

102. ASSB, 'Charlatanry and our school children', 1945–6.

103. Kofi Manwere's instructing priest was Fr Peter of the Anglican Order of St Benedict (founded 1914). For Fr Peter's Anglo-Catholicism see GNAK, ADM 223, Kumasi District Record Book, 1924–5, Draft of a letter by H. Webster, dd. Kumase, 12 December 1924 (copy; original intended for newspaper publication but never sent). Consult Jenkins (1974) for the background to Anglo-Catholicism within the Anglican Communion in Kumase.

104. See GNAK, D.87, 'Fetishes (Miscellaneous)', enclosing 'Report on the Senyakopo Fetish at Twenedurase, Kwahu District', 6 June 1926.

105. ASSB, 'Witchcraft in This Present Day', 1945–6.

106. J. C. Frimpong was an acutely sensitive fieldworker. He also had an engaging sense of humour. See ibid., J. C. Frimpong to Steel, 11 November 1945 and to Fortes, 26 January 1946. The second letter is a detailed account of the Bekwai *akwasidae* that was celebrated on 20 January 1946. But it is written on personalised stationery with the motto 'Graduate: University of hard knocks' printed in 'academic Gothic' beneath the author's name.

107. Ibid., 'Sitting on the Fence' (all capitalised in original), 1945–6.

108. Ibid., 'A Talk with Kwasi Fi of A[deɛbeba]', 1945–6.

CHAPTER 5 CONCLUSION

1. I thank all those who agreed to talk about the matters discussed in this chapter on the condition of strict anonymity. I am also grateful for the opportunity to consult two private collections of papers that detail the history of land development in south Kumase; again, access did not include leave to cite the

materials I was permitted to read. It should be understood that this chapter bears upon still current issues of property ownership and revenue.

2. ASSB, 'The Planning Exhibition by R. S[teel]', 22 October 1945.
3. *Programme: Town Planning Exhibition, Kumasi (Tuesday 16 October to Friday 19 October 1945)* (1945). The copy in OMP was presented to the *Asantehene* Osei Agyeman Prempeh II and is annotated by him.
4. OMP/Fry and Drew (1945). Again, this is a presentation copy that is annotated by the recipient Osei Agyeman Prempeh II.
5. Ibid., 'Diagram 15: Proposed New Housing Areas.'
6. Consult Rathbone (1992), I, xxxix–xli. See further Burns (1949), 189–215, and GNAK, ADM 51/5, Adjunct 3 (Regional Office), 'Ashanti Affairs: A Memorandum by the CCA (E. G. Hawkesworth)', n.d. (but 1943).
7. A full set of these planning schemes is deposited in USTK, Faculty of Architecture, Department of Planning and Housing Research.
8. OMP/Fry and Drew (1945). See also Fry (1946).
9. See Fry, Ford and Drew (1947); Fry and Drew (1956; 1976). I thank the late Jane Drew for her recollections of working on the formulation of the KDTPS.
10. See Frampton (1992) for context.
11. Consult Sarin (1982); for a comprehensive listing of commissions by Fry and Drew see Emanuel (1994), 260–1 and 326–8; for the later career of Fry and Drew in Britain see Hitchins (1978).
12. The words quoted are from Fry's testament concerning his life's work in Emanuel (1994), 327.
13. OMP/Fry and Drew (1945), 58.
14. Drew recalled that she and Fry were daunted by the intricacies of land ownership and cautioned against offending vested interests in Kumase. In hindsight she regretted the absence of direct Asante input in their work.
15. OMP/Fry and Drew (1945), 2.
16. Ibid., 3, 14–15, 39, 44 and 55.
17. Fry (1946), 625. Once again I thank Jane Drew. I am also grateful to Graham Tipple for help with the history of housing in Kumase. For an overview see Korboe and Tipple (1995), in addition to the items listed at Chapter 1, note 20 above.
18. OMP/Fry and Drew (1945), 48.
19. Jane Drew, Personal Communication, 1 May 1990.
20. I am grateful to the late *Asantehene* Opoku Ware II for permitting me to read his predecessor's notes on the KDTPS.
21. OMP/Fry and Drew (1945), enclosing Notes and Marginalia written by the *Asantehene* Osei Agyeman Prempeh II, with additional notes by H. Owusu Ansa, J. W. K. Appiah, I. K. Agyeman and J. S. Kankam.
22. Unless otherwise indicated the main sources used to reconstruct the history of Ayigya are: MRO, Civil Record Files, Divisional Court 'B', No. 110, *Kwame Badu* vs. *M. Sapong* (for *Gyenyaasehene*), *M. Salim and B. K. Owusu*, commenced 12 November 1952; ibid., No. 172, in re 'Kantinkronu Subjects at Ayija', *Akyempemhene ɔheneba* Boakye Dankwa to *Asantehene* Osei Agyeman Prempeh II, 2, 14 and 21 December 1952; ASSB, 'The Daily Round in the Ayija and Adjinasi Villages', by Peter Darkwah, 1945–6; ibid., 'The Fetish Priest Adu Anwona of Eduadin at Sipe', 1945–6; USTK, Faculty of Architecture, Department of Planning and Housing Research, J. Stanley, *The Legality of Ayija: A Case Study of Development Procedures in a Suburb of Kumasi* (1974). I thank Panin Kwame Bom, Frederick A. Akyampong and the late B. D. Addai for help and discussion.

23. See McCaskie (2000b: in press) for Kofi Sraha.
24. The main Kumase–Accra road was rerouted south of Ayigya in 1951.
25. USTK, Faculty of Architecture, Department of Planning and Housing Research, 'Survey of Anloga and Ayija (with a Statistical Appendix on Plot Sizes and Building Types)', carried out by the Survey Office, Kumasi Municipal Council, July 1959. GNAK, Census Survey Box 7, 'Interim Data Returns' collated by the Methods and Standards Unit, Census Office, 1961, includes a map of Ayigya marked with large numbers of reserved plots and uncompleted buildings.
26. West Ayigya was also built to relieve the pressure on middle-class housing in neighbouring Bomso. This had arisen because of plans to develop USTK on a site immediately to the south of a line running from west to east through Bomso, Sisaaso, Ayigya, Kantinkronu and Dom. Bomso was greatly affected, for it abutted on the north-west corner of the proposed university campus.
27. Republic of Ghana, *Report of the Jiagge Commission: Assets of Specified Persons*, V (1969), Krobo Edusei, 95.
28. OMP/AP, No. 13, 20/26, E. Prempeh to Yaw Brantuo, Kwaku Buo, Amma Takyiwaa et al., 4 December 1926.
29. ASSB, 'K[wasi] F[i] Talks of the A[deɛbeba] Fetish', August 1945.
30. See McCaskie (1998b) for E. C. Bobie Ansa.
31. OMP/OAPII, *Asantehene* Osei Agyeman Prempeh II to DC (Kumase), 22 January 1938.
32. People like 'the auctioneers' knew the risks they were running by confronting chiefship. But their watchwords, I am told, were 'dare all' and 'nothing ventured, nothing gained'.
33. OMP, 'Proceedings of Meetings of the Committee of Privileges', 17–18 December 1935 and 3 February 1936 in re 'Kumawu's Claim to Drobonso'.
34. Ibid.
35. MSP, 'A Great Day in [the] History of Manwere', prepared by Silas Boateng, n.d. (but 1941–3), 3.
36. See OMP, 'Proceedings of Meetings of the Committee of Privileges', 27 June 1935 for the *Asantehene* Osei Agyeman Prempeh II on the meaning of *nkabɔm(u)*. See Wilks (1998) for discussion.
37. MRO, K/33, 'Kumasi Village Affairs: Letters, Documents etc. on the Affairs of Adiebeba', *Manwerehene* Kwasi Brantuo IV to *Asantehene* Osei Agyeman Prempeh II, 19 and 26 February, 11 March and 17 April 1951; ibid., 11–12/17/19–20/31, Testimonies of Yaw Gyamera, Abena Ofim, Amma Bosua, Yaw Ankama, Yaw Antwi Abayie (sworn and notarised by I. Twenebuah in the presence of Kwasi Brantuo IV), January–March 1951. See further ibid., File C/1003, 'Miscellaneous Letters (Stool Lands in the Kumasi Division)', *Manwerehene* Kwasi Brantuo IV to *Asantehene* Osei Agyeman Prempeh II, 3 June 1951, enclosing the sworn and notarised testimonies of Kwabena Donko, Afua Ntim and Afua Amoakwaa. Once again I must thank Nana Arhin Brempong (Kwame Arhin), this time for mobilising searches by the MRO staff in 1994–7 for unclassified files I had first skimmed in the 1970s; not only were these located, but so too were other materials that greatly enriched my understanding of Adeɛbeba affairs.
38. Ibid., K/33, 'Kumasi Village Affairs: Letters, Documents etc. on the Affairs of Adiebeba', *Manwerehene* Kwasi Brantuo IV to *Asantehene* Osei Agyeman Prempeh II, 19 and 26 February, 11 March and 17 April 1951.
39. Ibid., File C/1003, 'Miscellaneous Letters (Stool Lands in the Kumasi Division)', *Asantehene* Osei Agyeman Prempeh II to *Manwerehene* Kwasi Brantuo IV, 15 May 1951.

40. I wish to reiterate my gratitude to those who agreed to discuss this matter. The single public reference to it known to me is in Kurankyi-Taylor (1951), II, 338–9. For some account of the climate in which it occurred see Busia (1951), 189–90. The gunman was removed to Nsawam in the Gold Coast Colony by the British.

41. Some confirmation of this account can be found in other than oral sources. See MRO, K/33, 'Kumasi Village Affairs: Letters, Documents etc. on the Affairs of Adiebeba', Testimonies of Yaw Gyamera, Abena Ofim, Amma Bosua, January 1951. Ibid., GSA/5, 'Gyasi Clan Affairs: Correspondence concerning the Abdication of Samanghene Ofori Kain II (18 July 1951)' contains documents preferring charges of various kinds against the *Saamanhene*; thus Saawua *Krontihene* Kwasi Pon et al. to *Asantehene* Osei Agyeman Prempeh II, 4 July 1951 alleges that Ofori Kan Ababio was employing an agent (Kwasi Boakye?) to deal in stool lands around Toase.

42. Ibid., K/33, 'Kumasi Village Affairs: Letters, Documents etc. on the Affairs of Adiebeba', Kwasi Manwere to Kumasi Divisional Council, 19 August 1951.

43. Ibid., Kwasi Manwere (on behalf of 'Patriotic Youngmen') to Kumasi Divisional Council, 16 January 1952. Ibid., Minutes of the Ashanti Confederacy Council, 3rd Session 1950, entry dd. 22 June 1950 has an account of the browbeating of three critical 'youngmen' – J. K. Donkoh (later CPP Ashanti Regional Chairman), Atta Mensah (later CPP MP for Mampon) and Kwame Adjaye – by the *Asantehene*. What this official account does not reveal is that all three were beaten, stripped and made 'to wash off the stones and gravel' in front of the palace before a jeering crowd. Eyewitness and other reports of this are widespread.

44. Ibid., K/33, 'Kumasi Village Affairs: Letters, Documents etc. on the Affairs of Adiebeba', enclosing 'Copy of Proceedings: in the Kumasi Divisional Native Court (Case 9, Folio 34) in re *KDNC* vs. *Kwasi Manwere*', [April] 1953.

45. See Austin (1964); Rathbone and Allman (1991); Allman (1993); Rathbone (2000) for general context and discussion.

46. MRO, Intelligence Reports (Ashanti), Local KD/7 (Secret), 'Political Activities, Kumasi District (South)', 26 October 1954. This file is countersigned 'no action' above the initials of the Superintendent of Police (Ashanti).

47. KMA, KCC Papers (1962–74), City Planning Department, Office of the Chief Survey Clerk, 'Report on the Ahinsan–Santaasi Corridor', 1963, enclosing App. 1, Villages, No. 7, Adiebeba.

48. ASSB/1, 'Population File', 1945–6.

49. GNAK, Census Survey Box 2, File 00/AC2, '1948 Population Census: A Memorandum concerning Kumasi', March 1960.

50. Government of Ghana, *1960 Population Census of Ghana. Volume I. The Gazetteer. Alphabetical List of Localitie*s (1962), 15.

51. KMA, KCC Papers (1962–74), City Planning Department, Minute by the KCC Chairman (J. Owusu), circulated to City Engineer and Chief Survey Clerk, 2 December 1963.

52. See 'Address by Hon. Kojo Yankah, Regional Minister, Ashanti, at the Emergency Meeting of the Kumasi Metropolitan Assembly on Wednesday, 13 January 1999', in Korboe, Diaw and Devas (2000), 215–27.

53. See *Daily Graphic* (Accra), 19 February 2000, 17.

54. See Gifford (1998), 57–111 for general context.

55. *The Bible*, Authorized Version, ed. J. Stirling for The British and Foreign Bible Society, London (1954), 682. For a helpful discussion of Ezekiel see Rosenberg (1987).

56. Compare here Bowdich (1821) on the connections between Asante, Egypt and

Abyssinia.
57. *The Bible* (1954), 667–8.
58. Indeed, the term *akoa* carries these meanings as well as that of being a subject.
59. MRO/HA, 1.
60. For some useful discussion consult Bloch (1998).
61. See especially Halbwachs (1925; 1950).
62. Yankah (1998), 5.
63. See here Spence (1996).
64. Guyer (1996), 1–2.
65. These issues come to mind when reading – for example – Clark (1999; 1999a) on Asante.
66. For the approach I have in mind consult Hountondji (1997) and Zeleza (1997).
67. See Honneth (1998) for discussion.

BIBLIOGRAPHY

ARCHIVES, FIELD MATERIALS, ETC.

All items under this rubric have been fully described in the Notes. Readers should consult the alphabetical list of Abbreviations used in the Notes to identify the name and location of the major classes of materials consulted.

BOOKS, BOOK PARTS, ARTICLES, THESES,
DRAFT PAPERS, ETC.

Addo-Fening, R. 1973. 'Asante refugees in Akyem Abuakwa, 1875–1912', *Transactions of the Historical Society of Ghana* 14 (1), 39–64.

Addo-Fening, R. 1973a. 'The background to the deportation of King Asafo Agyei and the foundation of New Juaben', *Transactions of the Historical Society of Ghana* 14 (2), 213–28.

Agyemang, I. T. n.d. *What the Occult Masters say about the Golden Stool and Asante Kingdom.* Kumase: Golden Key Publishing.

Akyeampong, E. A. 1996. *Drink, Power, and Cultural Change: a social history of alcohol in Ghana, c. 1800 to recent times.* Portsmouth, NH: Heinemann; Oxford: James Currey.

Akyeampong, E. A. 1999. 'Christianity, modernity and the weight of tradition in the life of *Asantehene* Agyeman Prempeh I, c. 1888–1931', *Africa* 69 (2), 279–311.

Akyeampong, E. A. 2000. '*Wo pe tam won pe ba* ("You like cloth but you don't want children"): urbanization, individualism and gender relations in Colonial Ghana, c. 1900–1939' in D. Anderson and R. Rathbone (eds), *Africa's Urban Past*, pp. 222–35. Oxford: James Currey.

Akyeampong, E. A. and P. Obeng. 1995. 'Spirituality, gender, and power in Asante history', *International Journal of African Historical Studies* 28 (3), 481–508.

Allman, J. M. 1993. *The Quills of the Porcupine: Asante nationalism in an emergent Ghana.* Madison, WI: University of Wisconsin Press.

Allman, J. M. 1996. 'Adultery and the state in Asante: reflections on gender, class, and power from 1800 to 1950' in J. Hunwick and N. Lawler (eds), *The Cloth of Many Colored Silks: papers on history and society Ghanaian and Islamic in honor of Ivor Wilks*, pp. 27–65. Evanston, IL: Northwestern University Press.

Allman, J. M. 1996a. 'Rounding up spinsters: unmarried women and gender chaos in colonial Asante', *Journal of African History* 37 (2), 195–214.

Allman, J. M. 1997. 'Fathering, mothering and making sense of *Ntamoba*: reflections on the economy of child-rearing in colonial Asante', *Africa* 67 (2), 296–321.

Allman, J. M. and V. Tashjian. 2000. '*I will not eat stone*': a women's history of colonial Asante.* Portsmouth, NH: Heinemann; Oxford: James Currey.

Appadurai, A. 1996. *Modernity at Large: cultural dimensions of globalization.* Minneapolis and London: University of Minnesota Press.

Appiah, J. 1990. *Joe Appiah: the autobiography of an African patriot.* New York, Westport CT and London: Praeger.

Appiah, K. Anthony. 1995. 'How to succeed in business by really trying', *The New York Review of Books* 42 (1), 33–6.

Arhin, K. 1974. 'Some Asante views of colonial rule: as seen in the controversy relating to death duties', *Transactions of the Historical Society of Ghana* 15 (1), 63–84.

Arhin, K. 1976–7. 'The pressure of cash and its political consequences in Asante in the colonial period', *Journal of African Studies* Winter Issue, 453–68.

Arhin, K. (ed.). 1978. *The Minutes of the Ashanti Farmers Association Limited 1934–36.* Legon: Institute of African Studies.

Arhin, K. 1983. 'Peasants in nineteenth century Asante', *Current Anthropology* 24 (4), 471–80.

Arhin, K. 1983a. 'Rank and class among the Asante and Fante in the nineteenth century', *Africa* 53 (1), 2–22.

Arhin, K. 1986. 'A note on the Asante *Akonkofo*: a non-literate sub-elite, 1900–1930', *Africa* 56 (1), 25–31.

Arhin, K. 1995. 'Monetization and the Asante state' in J. I. Guyer (ed.), *Money Matters: instability, values and social payments in the modern history of West African communities,* pp. 97–110. Portsmouth, NH: Heinemann; London: James Currey.

Arhin, K. 1999. 'The nature of Akan government' in P. Valsecchi and F. Viti (eds), *Mondes Akan/Akan Worlds: Identité et pouvoir en Afrique occidentale/identity and power in West Africa,* pp. 69–80. Paris: L'Harmattan.

Austin, D. 1964. *Politics in Ghana 1946–1960.* London: Oxford University Press for the Royal Institute of International Affairs.

Austin, G. M. 1988. 'Capitalists and chiefs in the cocoa hold-ups in south Asante, 1927–1938', *International Journal of African Historical Studies* 21 (1), 63–95.

Austin, G. M. 1996. 'Mode of production or mode of cultivation: explaining the failure of European cocoa planters in competition with African farmers in colonial Ghana' in W. G. Clarence-Smith (ed.), *Cocoa Pioneer Fronts since 1800: the role of smallholders, planters and merchants,* pp. 154–75. Basingstoke: Macmillan; New York: St Martin's Press.

Austin, G. M. 1998. 'The advance system in Ghanaian cocoa buying, 1915–1938: competition, conflict and the question of rent' [draft paper].

Austin, G. M. 2001 [in press]. *From Slavery to Free Labour in Rural Ghana: labour, land and capital in Asante, 1807–1956.* Oxford: James Currey.

Bachelard, G. 1936. *La Dialectique de la durée.* Paris: Boivin.

Bakhtin, M. 1984. *Rabelais and His World.* Bloomington and Indianapolis: Indiana University Press.

Barnes, J.A. 1971. *Three Styles in the Study of Kinship.* London: Tavistock Publications.

Bataille, G. 1991. *The Accursed Share: an essay on general economy. I. Consumption. II. The History of Eroticism. III. Sovereignty* [in two volumes]. New York: Zone Books.

Beckett, W. H. 1944. *Akokoaso: a survey of a Gold Coast village.* London: Percy Lund Humphries for the London School of Economics.

Benjamin, W. 1999. *The Arcades Project.* Cambridge, MA and London: The Belknap Press of Harvard University Press.

Berman, M. 1982. *All That is Solid Melts into Air: the experience of modernity.* New York: Simon and Schuster.

262   ASANTE IDENTITIES

Berry, S. 1997. 'Tomatoes, land and hearsay: property and history in Asante in the time of structural adjustment', *World Development* 25 (8), 1225–41.
Berry, S. 1998. 'Unsettled accounts: stool debts, chieftaincy disputes and the question of Asante constitutionalism', *Journal of African History* 39 (1), 39–62.
Bloch, M. E. F. 1998. *How We Think They Think: anthropological approaches to cognition, memory, and literacy.* Boulder, CO: Westview Press.
Boaten I, Nana Akwasi Abayie 1990. *Economic Survey of Kwabre District: a study in rural development.* Legon: Institute of African Studies.
Bowdich, T.E. 1821. *An Essay on the Superstitions, Customs, and Arts, common to the Ancient Egyptians, Abyssinians, and Ashantees.* Paris: J. Smith.
Braffi, E.K. 1984. *The Esoteric Significance of the Ashanti Nation.* Kumase: published by the author.
Brandom, R. B. 1994. *Making it Explicit: reasoning, representing and discursive commitment.* Cambridge, MA and London: Harvard University Press.
Brodsky, J. 1995. 'Homage to Marcus Aurelius' in *On Grief and Reason: essays*, pp. 267–98. London: Hamish Hamilton.
Brown, J. W. 1972. 'Kumasi, 1896–1923: urban Africa during the early colonial period', Ph.D. Dissertation. University of Wisconsin-Madison.
Burns, Sir Alan. 1949. *Colonial Civil Servant.* London: George Allen and Unwin.
Busia, K. A. 1951. *The Position of the Chief in the Modern Political System of Ashanti: a study of the influence of contemporary social changes on Ashanti political institutions.* Oxford: Oxford University Press for the International African Institute.
Chartier, R. 1998. '*L'histoire entre géographie et sociologie*' in *Au bord de la falaise: l'histoire entre certitude et inquiétude*, pp. 213–33. Paris: Albin Michel.
Clark, G. 1994. *Onions are my Husband: survival and accumulation by West African market women.* Chicago and London: Chicago University Press.
Clark, G. 1999. 'Negotiating Asante family survival in Kumasi, Ghana', *Africa* 69 (1), 66–85.
Clark, G. 1999a. 'Mothering, work, and gender in urban Asante ideology and practice', *American Anthropologist* 101 (4), 717–29.
Cohen, D.W. 1985. 'Doing social history from Pim's doorway' in O. Zunz (ed.) *Reliving the Past: the worlds of social history*, pp. 191–232. Chapel Hill: University of North Carolina Press.
Cohen, D. W. and E. S. Atieno Odhiambo. 1989. *Siaya: the historical anthropology of an African landscape.* London: James Currey; Nairobi: Heinemann Kenya; Athens, OH: Ohio University Press.
Cohen, D. W. and E. S. Atieno Odhiambo. 1992. *Burying S.M.: the politics of knowledge and the sociology of power in Kenya.* Portsmouth, NH: Heinemann; London: James Currey.
Cohn, B.S. 1996. *Colonialism and Its Forms of Knowledge: the British in India.* Princeton: Princeton University Press.
Comaroff, J. and J. L. (eds). 1993. *Modernity and Its Malcontents: ritual and power in postcolonial Africa.* Chicago and London: University of Chicago Press.
Comaroff, J. and J. L. (eds). 1999. *Civil Society and the Political Imagination in Africa: critical perspectives.* Chicago and London: University of Chicago Press.
Copenhaver, B. P. (ed). 1992. *Hermetica: The Greek Corpus Hermeticum and the Latin Asclepius in a New English Translation, with Notes and Introduction.* Cambridge: Cambridge University Press.
Dayan, J. 1995. *Haiti, History and the Gods.* Berkeley, Los Angeles and London: University of California Press.
de Certeau, M. 1997. *Culture in the Plural.* Minneapolis and London: University of Minnesota Press.

Deleuze, G. 1990. *Pourparlers 1972–1990*. Paris: Les Éditions de Minuit.

Deleuze, G. and F. Guattari. 1984. *Capitalism and Schizophrenia. I. Anti-Oedipus*. London: Athlone Press.

Deleuze, G. and F. Guattari. 1987. *Capitalism and Schizophrenia. II. A Thousand Plateaus*. Minneapolis and London: University of Minnesota Press.

Dickson, K. B. 1969. *A Historical Geography of Ghana*. Cambridge: Cambridge University Press.

Dodd, N. 1994. *The Sociology of Money: economics, reason and contemporary society*. Cambridge: Polity.

Donkoh, W. J. 1994. 'Colonialism and cultural change: some aspects of the impact of modernity upon Asante'. Ph.D. Dissertation. University of Birmingham.

Emanuel, M. (ed.). 1994. *Contemporary Architects*. London: Macmillan.

Eribon, D. 1991. *Michel Foucault*. Cambridge, MA: Harvard University Press.

Fortes, M. 1948. 'The Ashanti social survey: a preliminary report', *Rhodes-Livingstone Journal* 6, 1–36.

Fortes, M. 1954. 'A demographic field study in Ashanti' in F. Lorimer (ed.) *Culture and Human Fertility*, pp. 253–339. Paris: UNESCO.

Fortes, M. 1969. *Kinship and the Social Order: The Legacy of Lewis Henry Morgan*. Chicago: Aldine Publishing.

Fortes, M. 1970. *Time and Social Structure and Other Essays*. London: Athlone Press.

Fortes, M. 1974. 'Prologue: family studies in Ghana 1920–1970' in C. Oppong (ed.), *Domestic Rights and Duties in Southern Ghana: Legon family research papers no. 1*, pp. 1–27. Legon: Institute of African Studies.

Fortes, M. 1974a. 'Introduction: the Akan family system today' in C. Oppong (ed.), *Domestic Rights and Duties in Southern Ghana: Legon family research papers no. 1*, pp. 28–34. Legon: Institute of African Studies.

Fortes, M. 1977. 'Custom and conscience in anthropological perspective (The Ernest Jones Memorial Lecture of the British Psychoanalytical Society, London, 1973)', *International Review of Psychoanalysis* 1977 (4), 127–54.

Fortes, M. 1978. 'An anthropologist's apprenticeship', *Annual Review of Anthropology* 7, 1–30.

Fortes, M. 1978a. 'Akan studies: an address', delivered at the Workshop on the Akan (Northwestern University, 20–3 April).

Fortes, M., R. W. Steel and P. Ady. 1947. 'Ashanti survey, 1945–46: an experiment in social research', *The Geographical Journal* 110 (4–6), 149–79.

Foucault, M. 1980. *Power/Knowledge: selected interviews and other writings, 1972–1977*. Brighton: Harvester Press.

Foucault, M. 1981. 'The Order of Discourse' in R. Young (ed.), *Untying the Text: a poststructuralist reader*, pp. 27–54. London: Routledge.

Frampton, K. 1992. *Modern Architecture: a critical history*. London: Thames and Hudson.

Fry, E. Maxwell. 1946. 'Developing in "the most beautiful town in West Africa" – Kumasi', *West African Review* 57, 625–7.

Fry, E. Maxwell and Jane B. Drew. 1956. *Tropical Architecture in the Humid Zone*. London: Batsford.

Fry, E. Maxwell and Jane B. Drew. 1976. *Architecture and the Environment*. London: Allen and Unwin.

Fry, E. Maxwell, H. L. Ford and Jane B. Drew. 1947. *Village Housing in the Tropics*. London: Lund Humphries.

Fuller, Sir Francis. 1921. *Ashanti: a vanished dynasty*. London: John Murray.

Geschiere, P. 1997. *The Modernity of Witchcraft: politics and the occult in postcolonial Africa*. Charlottesville and London: University Press of Virginia.

Gifford, P. 1998. *African Christianity: its public roles*. Bloomington and Indianapolis: Indiana University Press.

Ginzburg, C. 1993. 'Mikro-Historie. Zwei oder drei Dinge, die ich von ihr weiss', *Historische Anthropologie* 1 (2), 169–92.

Ginzburg, C. and C. Poni. 1985. 'Was ist Mikrogeschichte?', *Geschichtswerkstatt* (6), 37–60.

Goodman, N. 1978. *Ways of Worldmaking*. Indianapolis: Hackett.

Goody, J. 1995. *The Expansionist Moment: the rise of social anthropology in Britain and Africa 1918–1970*. Cambridge: Cambridge University Press.

Gray, N. 1994. 'Aberewa: utopianism and opportunity in a new religious movement'. M.A. Thesis. Columbia University.

Gumbrecht, H. U. 1997. *In 1926: living at the edge of time*. Cambridge, MA and London: Harvard University Press.

Guyer, J. I. 1996. 'Traditions of invention in equatorial Africa', *African Studies Review* 39 (3), 1–28.

Gyekye, K. 1987. *An Essay on African Philosophical Thought: the Akan conceptual scheme*. Cambridge: Cambridge University Press.

Gyekye, K. 1988. *The Unexamined Life: philosophy and the African experience*. Accra: Ghana Universities Press.

Gyekye, K. 1996. *African Cultural Values: an introduction*. Accra: Sankofa Publishing.

Gyekye, K. 1997. *Tradition and Modernity: philosophical reflections on the African experience*. New York: Oxford University Press.

Habermas, J. 1984. *The Theory of Communicative Action. I. Reason and the Rationalisation of Society*. London: Heinemann.

Habermas, J. 1987. *The Theory of Communicative Action. II. System and Lifeworld*. Cambridge: Polity.

Habermas, J. 1987a. *The Philosophical Discourse of Modernity: Twelve Lectures*. Cambridge: Polity.

Habermas, J. 1992. *Moral Consciousness and Communicative Action*. Cambridge: Polity.

Halbwachs, M. 1925. *Les Cadres Sociaux de la Mémoire*. Paris: Presse Universitaire de France.

Halbwachs, M. 1950. *La Mémoire Collective*. Paris: Presse Universitaire de France.

Heller, A. 1984. *Everyday Life*. London and New York: Routledge and Kegan Paul.

Hitchins, S. 1978. *Fry, Drew, Knight, Creamer: Architecture*. London: Lund Humphries.

Honneth, A. 1995. *The Struggle for Recognition: the moral grammar of social conflicts*. Cambridge: Polity.

Honneth, A. 1998. 'A communicative disclosure of the past: on the relation between anthropology and philosophy of history in Walter Benjamin' in L. Marcus and L. Nead (eds), *The Actuality of Walter Benjamin*, pp. 118–34. London: Lawrence and Wishart.

Honneth, A. and H. Joas. 1988. *Social Action and Human Nature*. Cambridge: Cambridge University Press.

Horton, R. 1983. 'Social psychologies: African and Western' in M. Fortes, *Oedipus and Job in West African Religion*, pp. 41–82. Cambridge: Cambridge University Press.

Hountondji, P. (ed.). 1997. *Endogenous knowledge: research trails*. Dakar and London: CODESRIA and ABC.

Irvine, F. R. 1969. *West African Crops*. Oxford: Oxford University Press.

Jenkins, P. 1974. 'The Anglican Church in Ghana, 1905–1924. I and II',

Transactions of the Historical Society of Ghana 15 (1), 23–39 and 15 (2), 177–200.

Joas, H. 1985. *G. H. Mead: a contemporary re-examination of his thought.* Cambridge: Polity.

Jones, A. 1993. '"My arse for Akou": a wartime ritual of women on the nineteenth-century Gold Coast', *Cahiers d'Études africaines* 132 (xxxiii–4), 545–66.

Kay, G. B. (ed.). 1972. *The Political Economy of Colonialism in Ghana: a collection of documents and statistics 1900–1960.* Cambridge: Cambridge University Press.

Korboe, D., K. Diaw and N. Devas. 2000. *Urban Governance, Partnership and Poverty: Kumasi.* Birmingham: School of Public Policy (Working Paper 10).

Korboe, D. and G. Tipple. 1995. 'City profile – Kumasi', *Cities* 12 (4), 267–74.

Kuklick, H. 1991. *The Savage Within: the social history of British anthropology 1885–1945.* Cambridge: Cambridge University Press.

Kurankyi-Taylor, E. E. 1951. 'Ashanti Indigenous Legal Institutions and Their Present Role'. Ph.D. Dissertation, 2 vols. Cambridge University.

Kyei, T.E. 1992. *Marriage and Divorce among the Asante: a study undertaken in the course of the Ashanti Social Survey (1945).* Cambridge: African Studies Centre (Monograph Series, 14).

Kyei, T. E. n.d. 'My memoir', 6 vols (typescript): Agogo and Kumase [to appear in abbreviated form as J. M. Allman (ed.) *Our Days Dwindle: the autobiography of 'Teacher' Kyei.* Portsmouth, NH: Heinemann].

Lefebvre, H. 1981. *Critique de la vie quotidienne.* Paris: L'Arche Éditeur.

Lepetit, B. 1993. 'Architecture, géographie, histoire: usages de l'échelle', *Genèses* 13, 118–38.

Lepetit, B. (ed.) 1995. *Les formes de l'expérience: une autre histoire sociale.* Paris: Albin Michel.

Levi, G. 1988. *Inheriting Power: the story of an exorcist.* Chicago and London: University of Chicago Press.

Lewin, T. J. 1978. *Asante before the British: the Prempean years, 1875–1900.* Lawrence, KS: The Regents Press of Kansas.

Lüdtke, A. (ed.) 1995. 'Introduction: what is the history of everyday life and who are its practitioners' in *The History of Everyday Life: reconstructing historical experiences and ways of life,* pp. 3–40. Princeton: Princeton University Press.

Luhmann, N. 1998. *Observations on Modernity.* Stanford: Stanford University Press.

Lukacs, J. 1998. *A Thread of Years.* New Haven and London: Yale University Press.

McCaskie, T. C. 1976. 'Social rebellion and the inchoate rejection of history: some reflections on the career of Opon Asibe Tutu', *Asante Seminar: The Asante Collective Biography Bulletin* 4, 34–8.

McCaskie, T. C. 1976a. 'The history of the Manwere *nkoa* at Drobonso', *Asante Seminar: The Asante Collective Biography Bulletin* 6, 33–8.

McCaskie, T. C. 1980. 'Time and the calendar in nineteenth-century Asante: an exploratory essay', *History in Africa* 7, 179–200.

McCaskie, T. C. 1980a. 'Office, land and subjects in the history of the Manwere *Fekuo* of Kumase: an essay in the political economy of the Asante state', *Journal of African History* 21 (2), 189–208.

McCaskie, T. C. 1981. 'Anti-witchcraft cults in Asante: an essay in the social history of an African people', *History in Africa* 8, 125–54.

McCaskie, T. C. 1981a. 'State and society, marriage and adultery: some considerations towards a social history of precolonial Asante', *Journal of African History* 22 (4), 477–94.

McCaskie, T. C. 1984. '*Ahyiamu* – "A place of meeting": an essay on process and event in the history of the Asante state', *Journal of African History* 25 (2), 169–88.

McCaskie, T. C. 1985. 'Power and dynastic conflict in Mampon', *History in Africa* 12, 167–85.

McCaskie, T. C. 1986. 'Accumulation, wealth and belief in Asante history. II. the twentieth century', *Africa* 56 (1), 3–23.

McCaskie, T. C. 1986a. 'Komfo Anokye of Asante: meaning, history and philosophy in an African society', *Journal of African History* 27 (2), 315–39.

McCaskie, T. C. 1989. 'Death and the *Asantehene*: a historical meditation', *Journal of African History* 30 (3), 417–44.

McCaskie, T. C. 1992. 'You must Dis/miss/mis/re/member This: Kwame Tua in time and other passages from Asante history' [draft paper presented at the Red Lion Seminar, Northwestern University/University of Chicago].

McCaskie, T. C. 1992a. 'People and animals: constru(ct)ing the Asante experience', *Africa* 62 (2), 221–47.

McCaskie, T. C. 1994. 'Claim and Redemption: relations between system and subject in the accumulation of wealth in nineteenth-century Asante' [draft paper presented at the ASAUSA Annual Conference, Toronto].

McCaskie, T. C. 1995. *State and Society in Pre-colonial Asante*. Cambridge: Cambridge University Press.

McCaskie, T. C. 1995a. '*Konnurokusɛm*: kinship and family in the history of the *Oyoko Kɔkɔɔ* dynasty of Kumase', *Journal of African History* 36 (3), 357–89.

McCaskie, T. C. 1998. 'Asante and Ga: the history of a relationship' in P. Jenkins (ed.), *The Recovery of the West African Past: African pastors and African history in the nineteenth century. C.C. Reindorf and Samuel Johnson*, pp. 135–53. Basel: Basler Afrika Bibliographien.

McCaskie, T. C. 1998a. 'Custom, tradition and law in precolonial Asante' in E. Adriaan B. van Rouveroy van Nieuwaal and W. Zips (eds), *Sovereignty, Legitimacy and Power in West African Societies: perspectives from legal anthropology*, pp. 25–47. Hamburg: Lit Verlag.

McCaskie, T. C. 1998b. '*Akwankwaa*: Owusu Sekyere Agyeman in his life and times', *Ghana Studies* 1, 91–122.

McCaskie, T. C. 1998c. 'Usury: tales from the life of money in colonial Asante' [draft paper presented at the University of Ghent].

McCaskie, T. C. 2000. 'Trees and the domestication of power in Asante thought', in R. Cline-Cole and C. Madge (eds), *Contesting Forestry in West Africa*, pp. 104–123. Aldershot: Ashgate.

McCaskie, T. C. 2000a. 'The consuming passions of Kwame Boakye: an essay on agency and identity in Asante history', *Journal of African Cultural Studies* 13 (1), 43–62 [special issue in honour of Terence Ranger ed. by J. Lonsdale].

McCaskie, T. C. 2000b. 'The last will and testament of Kofi Sraha: a note on accumulation and inheritance in colonial Asante', *Ghana Studies* 2.

Medick, H. 1995. '"Missionaries in the Rowboat?" Ethnological Ways of Knowing as a Challenge to Social History', in A. Lüdtke (ed.) *The History of Everyday Life: reconstructing historical experiences and ways of life*, 41–70. Princeton: Princeton University Press.

Medick, H. and D. Sabean (eds). 1984. *Interest and Emotion: essays on the study of family and kinship*. Cambridge: Cambridge University Press.

Meyer, B. 1999. *Translating the Devil: religion and modernity among the Ewe in Ghana*. London: Edinburgh University Press for the International African Institute.

Meyerowitz, H. V., E. Amu, M. Fortes, F. Clarke and W. B. Mumford. 1937. *Memorandum on a Proposed Institute of West African Culture at Achimota*. Achimota College, Accra: Colonial Office Advisory Committee on Education.

Muir, E. and G. Ruggiero (eds). 1992. *Microhistory and the Lost Peoples of Europe.* Baltimore: The Johns Hopkins University Press.

Nora, P. (ed.). 1984. 'Entre mémoire et histoire' in *Les Lieux de mémoire. I. La République*, pp. xvii–xlii. Paris: Gallimard.

Passerin d'Entrèves, M. and S. Benhabib (eds). 1996. *Habermas and the Unfinished Project of Modernity.* Cambridge: Polity.

Patterson, K. David 1981. *Health in Colonial Ghana: disease, medicine and socio-economic change, 1900–1955.* Waltham, MA: Crossroads Press.

Peel, J. D. Y. 1994. 'Review article: historicity and pluralism in some recent studies of Yoruba religion', *Africa* 64 (1), 150–66.

Peel, J. D. Y. 1995. 'For who hath despised the day of small things? Missionary narratives and historical anthropology', *Comparative Studies in Society and History*, 37 (3), 581–607.

Peel, J. D. Y. 2000. *Religious Encounter and the Making of the Yoruba.* Bloomington and Indianapolis: Indiana University Press.

Perrot, C-H. 1999. 'Un musée royal au début due XIXe siècle en Ashanti: L'Aban', *Cahiers d'Études africaines* 155–6 (xxxix–3/4), 875–84.

Pred, A. 1990. *Making Histories and Constructing Human Geographies.* Boulder, CO: Westview Press.

Pred, A. 1990a. *Lost Words and Lost Worlds: modernity and the language of everyday life in late nineteenth-century Stockholm.* Cambridge: Cambridge University Press.

Prendergast, C. 1992. *Paris and the Nineteenth Century.* Oxford and Cambridge: Blackwell.

Radcliffe-Brown, A.R. 1952. *Structure and Function in Primitive Society.* London: Cohen and West.

Rathbone, R. (ed.). 1992. *Ghana. I. 1941–1952* and *II. 1952–1957* (British Documents on the End of Empire. Series B, 1). London: HMSO for the Institute of Commonwealth Studies.

Rathbone, R. 2000. *Nkrumah and the Chiefs: the politics of chieftaincy in Ghana 1951–60.* Oxford: James Currey; Accra: F. Reimmer; Athens, OH: Ohio University Press.

Rathbone, R. and J. M. Allman. 1991. 'Discussion: "the youngmen and the porcupine"', *Journal of African History* 32 (2), 333–8.

Revel, J. 1995. 'Introduction' in J. Revel and L. Hunt (eds), *Histories: French constructions of the past*, pp. 1–63. New York: The New Press.

Revel, J. (ed.). 1996. *Jeux d'Echelles: La Micro-analyse à l'Expérience.* Paris: Gallimard le Seuil.

Richards, T. 1993. *The Imperial Archive: knowledge and the fantasy of empire.* London and New York: Verso.

Ricketts, H. J. 1831. *Narrative of the Ashantee War.* London: Simpkin and Marshall.

Rosaldo, R. 1986. 'From the door of his tent: the fieldworker and the inquisitor' in J. Clifford and G. E. Marcus (eds), *Writing Culture: the poetics and politics of ethnography*, pp. 77–97. Berkeley: University of California Press.

Rosenberg, J. 1987. 'Jeremiah and Ezekiel', in R. Alter and F. Kermode (eds), *The Literary Guide to the Bible*, pp. 184–206. London: William Collins.

Sabean, D. W. 1998. *Kinship in Neckarhausen, 1700–1870.* Cambridge: Cambridge University Press.

Sarin, M. 1982. *Urban Planning in the Third World: the Chandigarh experience.* London: Mansell.

Sarpong, P. K. 1977. *Girls' Nubility Rites in Ashanti.* Accra and Tema: Ghana Publishing Corporation.

Schivelbusch, W. 1995. *Disenchanted Night: the industrialization of light in the nineteenth century.* Berkeley, Los Angeles and London: University of California Press.

Schulze, W. (ed.). 1994. *Sozialgeschichte, Alltagsgeschichte, Mikro-Historie: eine Diskussion*. Göttingen: Vandenhoeck and Ruprecht.

Schutz, A. 1964. *Collected Papers. I. The Problem of Social Reality*. The Hague: Martinus Nijhoff.

Schutz, A. 1970. *Collected Papers. II. Studies in Social Theory*. The Hague: Martinus Nijhoff.

Schutz, A. 1973. *Collected Papers. III. Studies in Phenomenological Philosophy*. The Hague: Martinus Nijhoff.

Sinai, I. 1998. 'Housing uses and housing choices in Kumasi, Ghana', Ph.D. Dissertation. University of North Carolina-Chapel Hill.

Spence, J. 1996. *God's Chinese Son: the Chinese heavenly kingdom of Hong Xiuquan*. New York: W. W. Norton.

Steel, R. W. 1952. 'The towns of Ashanti: a geographical study' in *Compte Rendu du XVIe Congrès International de Géographie, Lisbonne, 1949*, pp. 81–93. Lisbon: Centro Tip. Colonial.

Tashjian, V. B. 1996. '"It's mine" and "it's ours" are not the same thing: changing economic relations between spouses in Asante', in J. Hunwick and N. Lawler (eds), *The Cloth of Many Colored Silks: papers on history and society Ghanaian and Islamic in honor of Ivor Wilks*, pp. 205–22. Evanston, IL: Northwestern University Press.

Taylor, C. 1985. 'What is human agency?' in *Philosophical Papers. I. Human Agency and Language*, pp. 15–44. Cambridge: Cambridge University Press.

Taylor, C. 1985a. 'Understanding and ethnocentricity', in *Philosophical Papers. II. Philosophy and the Human Sciences*, pp. 117–33. Cambridge: Cambridge University Press.

Taylor, C. 1989. *Sources of the Self: the making of the modern identity*. Cambridge: Cambridge University Press.

Taylor, C. 1992. *The Ethics of Authenticity*. Cambridge, MA: Harvard University Press.

Taylor, C. 1995. 'To follow a rule', in *Philosophical Arguments*, pp. 165–80. Cambridge, MA: Harvard University Press.

Tipple, A. G. 1987. *The Development of Housing Policy in Kumasi, Ghana, 1901 to 1981: with an analysis of the current housing stock*. Newcastle: CARDO, University of Newcastle-upon-Tyne.

Tipple, A. G., D. T. Korboe and G. D. Garrod. 1997. 'A comparison of original owners and inheritors in housing supply and extension in Kumasi, Ghana', *Environment and Planning B. Planning and Design* 24, 889–902.

Tipple, A. G. and S. E. Owusu. 1994. *Transformations in Kumasi, Ghana, as a Housing Supply Mechanism: a preliminary study*. Newcastle: CARDO, University of Newcastle-upon-Tyne.

Tipple, A. G. and K. G. Willis. 1991. 'Tenure choice in a West African city: Kumasi, Ghana', *Third World Planning Review* 13 (1), 27–45.

Tipple, A. G. and K. G. Willis. 1992. 'Why should Ghanaians build houses in urban areas? An introduction to private sector housing supply in Ghana', *Cities* Feb., 60–74.

Tordoff, W. 1965. *Ashanti under the Prempehs 1888–1935*. Oxford: Oxford University Press.

Trouillot, M-R. 1995. *Silencing the Past: power and the production of history*. Boston: Beacon Press.

Tugendhat, E. 1986. *Self-Consciousness and Self-Determination*. Cambridge, MA: MIT Press.

Van Onselen, C. 1996. *The Seed is Mine: the life of Kas Maine, a South African sharecropper, 1894–1985*. New York: Hill and Wang.

Viti, F. 1998. *Il potere debole: antropologia politica dell'Aitu* nvle (*Baule, Costa d'Avorio*). Milan: Franco Angeli.

White, L. 1987. *Magomero: portrait of an African Village.* Cambridge: Cambridge University Press.

Wilentz, A. 1989. *The Rainy Season: Haiti since Duvalier.* London: Jonathan Cape.

Wilks, I. 1975 [1989]. *Asante in the Nineteenth Century: the structure and evolution of a political order* (reprinted with a new *Preamble*): Cambridge: Cambridge University Press.

Wilks, I. 1977. 'Land, Labour, Capital and the Forest Kingdom of Asante: A Model of Early Change' in J. Friedman and M.J. Rowlands (eds), *The Evolution of Social Systems,* pp. 487–534. London: Duckworth.

Wilks, I. 1993. 'Land, labor, gold, and the forest kingdom of Asante: a model of early change' in *Forests of Gold: essays on the Akan and the kingdom of Asante,* pp. 41–90. Athens, OH: Ohio University Press.

Wilks, I. 1993a. 'What manner of persons were these? Generals of the Konti of Kumase' in *Forests of Gold: essays on the Akan and the kingdom of Asante,* pp. 241–92. Athens, OH: Ohio University Press.

Wilks, I. 1998. '"Unity and progress": Asante politics revisited', *Ghana Studies* 1, 151–79.

Wilks, I. 2000. 'Asante nationhood and colonial administrators, 1896–1935' in C. Lentz and P. Nugent (eds), *Ethnicity in Ghana: the limits of invention,* pp. 68–96. London: Macmillan and New York: St Martin's Press.

Wilks, I., N. Levtzion and B. M. Haight. 1986. *Chronicles from Gonja: a tradition of West African Muslim historiography.* Cambridge: Cambridge University Press.

Wilks, I. and T. C. McCaskie. 1977. 'ACBP/pcs/51: Kwasi Brantuo', *Asantesεm: The Asante Collective Biography Bulletin* 7, 14–7.

Wiredu, K. 1980. *Philosophy and an African Culture.* Cambridge: Cambridge University Press.

Wiredu, K. 1996. 'The need for conceptual decolonization in African philosophy' in *Cultural Universals and Particulars: an African perspective,* pp. 136–44. Bloomington and Indianapolis: Indiana University Press.

Yankah, K. 1998. *Free Speech in Traditional Society: the cultural foundations of communication in contemporary Ghana.* Accra: Ghana Universities Press.

Zeleza, P. T. 1997. *Manufacturing African Studies and Crises.* Dakar: CODESRIA Book Series.

INDEX